THE
ARCHITECTURE
OF WALES
SERIES

THE
ARCHITECTURE
OF WALES
SERIES

RSAW

Architecture.com/wales

Published in cooperation with
The Royal Society of Architects in Wales -
Cymdeithas Frenhinol Penseiri yng Nghymru

Percy Thomas

Modern Architecture as a National Service

Robert Proctor

University of Wales Press

www.uwp.co.uk

British Library CIP Data
A catalogue record for this book is available from the British Library

ISBN 978-1-83772-210-5
eISBN 978-1-83772-211-2

For GPSR enquiries please contact:
Easy Access System Europe Oü, 16879218
Mustamäe tee 50, 10621, Tallinn, Estonia. *gpsr.requests@easproject.com*

RSAW
Architecture.com/wales

MIX
Paper | Supporting responsible forestry
FSC® C013604

Printed and bound by CPI Group (UK) Ltd, Croydon, CR0 4YY

Contents

General Editor's Preface

Given the conventional image of Wales as a land of song and poetry, architecture and the visual arts can be easily overlooked, a neglected poor relation to the country's seductive musical and literary traditions. Relatively little has been published about the architectural heritage of our nation, despite the fact that buildings and places have been created in Wales that bear comparison with contemporaneous examples elsewhere, produced by architects engaged in the same wider cultural currents and discourse. There are many reasons for this: Wales has so often been judged as being too small, too homely, or simply not distinctive or fashionable enough to attract the sustained attention of architectural critics and historians. Add to this a lack of consistent patronage and a deeply ingrained Nonconformist tradition that discourages any form of showing off, and it is not surprising perhaps that we lack a more complete record of the architectural achievements of past generations.

Of course, the truth is that Wales has a rich built heritage, from the medieval to the modern. Its architectural character is very different from that of the other nations of the British Isles, and it is this very distinctiveness that deserves to be celebrated. The Royal Society of Architects in Wales is delighted to present, with the University of Wales Press, a series of books exploring the architecture of Wales, adding new chapters to the evolving story of the buildings, places and spaces of our 'damp, demanding and obsessively interesting country'.[1]

Mary Wrenn
The Royal Society of Architects in Wales (RSAW)
represents and supports Chartered Members of
the Royal Institute of British Architects (RIBA) in Wales

1 Jan Morris, *Wales: Epic Views of a Small Country*.

Acknowledgements

Thanks, first of all, to Jonathan Vining of the Royal Commission on the Ancient and Historic Monuments of Wales, and Mary Wrenn of the Royal Society of Architects in Wales for setting me off on this project, as well as to Sarah Lewis at the University of Wales Press for embracing it and patiently waiting for my manuscript after a certain virus threw everything into disarray.

Much of my research for this project benefited from grant funding: the Paul Mellon Centre for Studies in British Art gave a Research Support Grant in 2018 for research travel and a Mid-Career Fellowship in 2021, which enabled me to complete the research and draft substantial parts of the manuscript; a British Academy/Leverhulme Small Research Grant awarded in 2019 funded most of the rest of the research; the Society of Architectural Historians of Great Britain contributed to the costs of image reproductions; and the Royal Society of Architects in Wales has funded publication costs. I am grateful to them, and to my colleagues at the University of Bath, particularly Fiona Pettengale, Jack Robson, Sarah Jones, Stephen Emmitt and Alex Wright for supporting the project.

For their continuous kind advice and particularly for reading drafts, I owe much gratitude to Elaine Davey and Alistair Fair. For other significant academic exchange and opportunities, accepting conference papers and inviting talks, editing articles, supporting grant applications, and as interlocutors in conversations on the work, I would like to thank Elizabeth Darling, Neal Shasore, Jessica Kelly, Ed DeVane, Vaughan Hart, Ewan Harrison, Judi Loach, Mike O'Mahony, Claire O'Mahony, Julian Holder, Alan Powers, Elain Harwood, Mariadele Boccardi, Emma West, Susan Fielding and Otto Saumarez Smith.

There were many others who assisted my research by revealing new sources, sending me important information and even work of their own, sometimes unpublished, or by enabling access to sources, buildings, photographs and people. For such generosity I particularly thank David Lermon, Ian Pepperell, Julian Owen, Jonathan Adams, Sophie Weeks, Craig Owen, Mari Lowe, Edward Holland, Nicholas Adams, Philip Thornborow, Alan Legg, Andy Foster, Liz Jennings, Alan Lynes, Tracy Ellicott, Christine Howard, Robin Moore, Howard Williams, the Reverend Jill-Hailey Harries, Kevin Sutton, Ali Ashraf, Lionel East, Nick Loveland and Cheung Lintak. In addition, I am grateful to the many archivists and librarians who helped at various stages of the project – above all, the tireless David Stacey and colleagues at the University of Bath, and also Ian Beavis, Lowri Jenkins, Lisa Tallis, Julie Archer, Edith Hughes, Lynne Moore, Emily Hewitt, John Simpson, Ed Bartholomew, Alan Randall, Penny Icke, Hannah Price and Richard Wiltshire, as well as the wonderful staff at the Glamorgan Archives and West Glamorgan Archive Service.

Many architects who formerly worked in the practice, and some others involved in their buildings, kindly and willingly gave their time to be interviewed (and may be found acknowledged in the references), often also giving me original documentation – I thank them for their contributions to the research, offering apologies to all those I did not get around to meeting. Others also granted me privileged access to family members, friends, memories and research sources, and permission to reproduce material, and I thank them sincerely, though for their privacy I will not name them individually here. No special association with or authorisation of this book should be assumed by any of these acknowledgements.

I am painfully aware of all the information and advice that I received gratefully but have not been able to employ, as time, word counts and the limited capacity of my brain were exhausted; and I am sure, too, that mistakes will have crept into the text – errors and omissions for which I accept responsibility with hopes for future opportunities to correct and extend the record. In particular, it is often impossible to attribute design work to the right architects with complete confidence, and word limits have prevented detailed accounts of design responsibilities. I offer apologies to anyone I have neglected and will always welcome further information.

List of Illustrations

For clarity, acknowledgements for illustrations are provided in captions throughout the book. In general, any material for which copyright belongs to Sir Percy Thomas is reproduced by permission of his estate and any material in copyright of Sir Percy Thomas & Son and the Percy Thomas Partnership is reproduced by permission of WSP UK Ltd, and where relevant with the permission of specific architects or their estates. Every effort has been made to obtain permission to publish from copyright holders and to include correct acknowledgements alongside illustrations, but if any have been inadvertently overlooked, the publishers will be pleased to make the necessary arrangement at the first opportunity. Dates of buildings comprise the year when the design was first made (or a competition date), if known, and the date of completion or official opening.

Colour Plates

Figures

Abbreviations

AUA	Aberystwyth University Archives, Aberystwyth
BA	Bristol Archives
BBCC	BBC Wales Archive, Cardiff
BBCR	BBC Written Archives, Reading
BCL	Birmingham Central Library
BUASC	Bangor University Archives and Special Collections, Bangor
CAS	Conwy Archives Service, Conwy
CAHGA	Carmarthenshire Archives Holdings, held at Glamorgan Archives, Cardiff
CALS	Cheshire Archives and Local Studies, Chester
CDA	Clifton Roman Catholic Diocesan Archives, Bristol
CHLA	Community History Library, Accrington
CMA	Calvinistic Methodist Archives at NLWA
CUSCA	Cardiff University Special Collections and Archives
DHC	Dorset History Centre, Dorchester
GAC	Glamorgan Archives, Cardiff
GCA	Gwent Crematorium Archives, Croesyceiliog
LHLW	Local History Library, Museum of Wigan Life, Wigan
MDA	Menevia Roman Catholic Diocesan Archives, Swansea
NLWA	National Library of Wales Archives, Aberystwyth
PALS	Plymouth Archives and Local Studies, Plymouth
PTA	Percy Thomas Archive at RCAHMW
RBAS	Richard Burton Archives, Swansea University, Swansea
RCAHMW	Archives of the Royal Commission on the Ancient and Historical Monuments of Wales, Aberystwyth
RIBAL	Royal Institute of British Architects Library, London
SAS	Southampton Archives, Southampton
SFNMHA	St Fagans National Museum of History Archives
SLHL	Salford Local History Library
SLS	Southampton Local Studies and Maritime Library, Southampton
THA	Tower Hamlets Local History Library and Archives, London

THBC	Tower Hamlets Borough Council
TNA	The National Archives, London
TWBA	Tunbridge Wells Borough Archives
UMSC	University of Manchester Library Special Collections, Manchester
WAAS	Worcester Archive and Archaeology Service
WCARB	Wolfson Centre for Archival Research, Birmingham
WGAS	West Glamorgan Archive Service, Swansea
WNMAR	Welsh National Memorial Association Records at NLWA

The Royal Commission on the Ancient and Historical Monuments of Wales and its Archives

The Royal Commission on the Ancient and Historical Monuments of Wales, established in 1908, is the investigation body and national archive for the historic environment of Wales. It has the lead role in ensuring that Wales's archaeological, built and maritime heritage is authoritatively recorded and seeks to promote the appreciation of this heritage nationally and internationally. It curates the National Monuments Record of Wales (NMRW), which holds the archive for the built heritage of Wales consisting of surveys, photographs, aerial photographs, plans, maps, reports, books and periodicals on archaeology, architecture, industrial archaeology and maritime history. Within the NMRW you can find the archives of the Percy Thomas Partnership and the work of the practice when it was known as Sir Percy Thomas & Son. This contains a wealth of material including photograph albums, slides and promotional items dating from the 1930s to the end of the twentieth century. As with all the archives held by the Royal Commission, it is freely accessible through Coflein, our online site database and catalogue, *www.coflein.gov.uk*, or through our enquiry service. Visitors are welcome to use the specialist library and search room, which is open Monday to Thursday 9.30 a.m. to 4 p.m., and Wednesday 10.30 a.m. to 4.30 p.m. Please see our website at *www.rcahmw.gov.uk*, or contact us at *nmr.wales@rcahmw.gov.uk* for further information.

CBHC RCAHMW

RCAHMW

Ffordd Penglais, Aberystwyth, Ceredigion SY23 3BU

Tel. 01970 621 200

1

Introduction

On the evening of Monday 4 November 1935, Percy Thomas of Cardiff gave his first annual inaugural address to the Royal Institute of British Architects as its new president (see Figure 1.1). Aged fifty-two, he was the youngest yet elected. He was speaking in the lecture theatre of the Institute's recently completed headquarters building in London. His theme was a question that the Institute had debated for some time: how to increase the range of building work under the control of professionally trained architects, to banish a prevailing 'ugliness and disorder' through good design and planning. Whereas in the past, Thomas said, the architect's patron had most often been the Church or the aristocracy, the rise of democracy in the twentieth century meant that architects now worked principally in the service of 'the whole community', represented especially by local and national government. Thomas urged architects, therefore, to prove their worth to society. They should, he said, welcome opportunities to improve even mundane elements of the built environment - the 'bus shelter, the lamp standard, the little transformer station'. Furthermore, they needed to demonstrate professionalism and skill, accepting their clients' needs and budgets while creating 'beautiful buildings'.[1] At another lecture for the RIBA the following year, Thomas described this wider, social mission of the architect, and the RIBA as the profession's representative body, as a 'National Service'. 'We exist solely to serve the community', he declared, 'and we must bend our utmost powers to that end'.[2] Taking my cue from these striking phrases, I

1.1 Portrait photograph of Percy Thomas as RIBA President, 1935 (unknown photographer; from *Journal of the Royal Institute of British Architects*, 9 November 1935).

argue that Percy Thomas and the subsequent practice bearing his name sought to implement this distinctively modern ideal of architecture in the service of a democratic citizenship. Modern architecture as a service to the nation was, simply put, the ethos of the Percy Thomas practice. Yet this deceptively simple concept involves many contradictions.

This book is not the biography of an architect, but an architectural history of a practice, examining the 'work' rather than the 'life', considering architecture less as the result of individual artistic genius than as the product of professional people in different disciplines and bodies seeking to resolve the needs of their time.[3] It therefore observes the clients and patrons of buildings as well as the architects. This follows a long-standing approach in architectural history considering the production of buildings from perspectives beyond the drawing board, looking at buildings as evidence informing our understanding of the wider social and political forces behind them, considering the meanings and activities that they were designed to promote. The range of the practice's work was immense, from suburban houses to gigantic steelworks, from chapels to hospitals, from town halls to power stations, and Percy Thomas's practice undertook work across Britain almost from its foundation, later opening offices in English cities and overseas. This book is therefore in some ways also an architectural history of twentieth-century Britain. Yet the firm's origin and controlling office remained in Cardiff, rooting it firmly in Wales. It was the most productive Welsh architectural practice, and made vital contributions to this country's built environment.

The Welshness of Percy Thomas is an important theme, therefore, and so is what the architecture suggests about the Britishness of Wales, a continually contested relationship throughout the twentieth century. Elaine Davey argues that the practice engaged in a 'nation-building project', and much evidence supports her view of a Welsh architectural firm designing the identity of a new, modern Wales.[4] Yet Davey acknowledges competing visions of Wales; and there is evidence that identities and sources of power between Wales and Britain were multiple, often in tension with each other.[5] Moments of tension and conflict are evident in some of the practice's work, suggesting that the idea of the 'nation' was continually being negotiated.

The argument for 'nation-building' in both Welsh and British senses arises because so much of the practice's work related directly or indirectly to government. Local authorities built town halls in the 1930s and concert halls in the 1980s; regional hospital boards commissioned hospitals for the National Health Service after the Second World War; universities invited plans for campuses and their buildings, funded largely by national government; the British Electricity Authority sought Thomas's advice on power stations and the Ministry of Transport on bridges and roads; late twentieth-century buildings included the Board of Trade's Business Statistics Office in Newport and the National Physical Laboratory in Teddington. The organisation of 'government' or 'the state' was fragmented administratively and geographically. Moreover, even when private or commercial patrons such as the Grosvenor Estate or the British Nylon Spinners company commissioned the practice, the state often stimulated, enabled and controlled their projects. Government policies changed dramatically during the century, particularly between the ideologically driven administrations of Clement Attlee and Margaret Thatcher, and much political debate concerned the nature of the state: how extensive it should be; how far it should intervene in people's lives; how much power it should wield over the nation's economy and geography – debates often articulated around buildings.[6] Buildings visually demonstrated the nature of the state, and their spaces housed and organised its functions, while the state's regulatory and economic regimes influenced architectural forms.[7]

A conventional understanding of twentieth-century British politics has assumed that Labour and centrist Conservative governments of the 1940s to the 1960s expanded state control with the institution of a 'welfare state' and the nationalisation of healthcare, transport and many industries, while ideologically driven 'neoliberal' governments subsequently dismantled the state from the 1980s. This rise-and-fall narrative has been increasingly questioned from many directions. Earlier pre-war elements of state-directed or state-supported welfare and control have been revalued.[8] Some have conceptualised a post-war 'developmental state' in cooperation with business.[9] Work on the 1980s has questioned the extent to which ideology and practice were aligned, and demonstrated continuities with the past in government strategies in that period, contradicting political rhetoric.[10] Much of Percy Thomas's work expressed and embodied such political processes seeking to order and shape the role of the state within Wales and Britain in different ways across the century, and the firm's buildings were sometimes themselves debated using arguments about the purpose of the state, shaping public conceptions of its nature.

Thomas's contention that architects had a duty of 'service' to the community beyond their immediate clients related to the continuing professionalisation of architecture, fostered by the RIBA in its reforms to architectural education and its lobbying for legislation. At a period when architects were seeking protection for their title and debating the architect's independence against the backdrop of increasing employment of architects by government and business, claiming professional advantages meant also accepting an ethical responsibility.[11] Thomas's contemporary Charles Holden expressed this attitude when he wrote that 'service, service and again service is the beginning, the middle and the end of architecture', and aesthetics merely 'the outcome of the architect's pleasure' in duty, a stance he reiterated when Thomas presented him with the Royal Gold Medal for architecture in 1936.[12] This attitude flourished after the Second World War, motivating many idealistic young architects to join government or local authority architects' departments in a commitment to the public good, but it also influenced private architects, and is evident in much of the Percy Thomas practice's work.

This concept of the wider social client emerged alongside a distinctively twentieth-century concept of democratic citizenship. This was the century in which the vote first became universal, extended in stages to all men over twenty-one from 1918, and to all women after another decade. This extension of the franchise was often viewed as a consequence of the First World War, when people of all backgrounds were thrown together in the national cause.[13] Percy Thomas was among them. His autobiography vividly describes his experiences building trenches and defences on the Western Front. He enlisted at the end of 1915, reluctantly leaving his young family and his new architectural practice in Cardiff. After joining the Artists' Rifles with many other artists and architects, he transferred to the Royal Engineers, reaching the rank of captain in summer 1918. Twice mentioned in dispatches, he received the OBE for his record.[14] Thomas wrote that the 'experience of administration and of dealing with all kinds of men' during the war subsequently benefited his career as an architect.[15] His contemporary Charles Reilly praised Thomas's earnest engagement with building users, not just clients: for the Bristol Police and Fire Station competition in Bristol, 'he interviewed everyone he could think of who could tell him anything about the use of such buildings, from magistrates to firemen and policemen'.[16] Thomas told students that the architect needed 'a thorough knowledge of the habits and customs of the people who are going to occupy the building'.[17] This social concern for ordinary people remained significant in the practice's later architecture. The building could dignify its occupants, and in organising their relationships to each other could promote their participation in a democratic society. Large communal spaces - whether the assembly hall of a civic centre or the glazed atrium of an office - assembled and organised corporate bodies of people to effect their shared identity as citizens.[18] Generous civic spaces form the heart of many of the practice's buildings.

Debates over democratic citizenship and the power of the state were therefore linked in the twentieth century. With increased democratic participation came pressure on government to ensure higher standards of living for all, and consequently waves of growth in state-provided welfare throughout the twentieth century, the post-1945 welfare state and a more coherent programme extending many earlier developments. Universal free education and eventually higher education, good housing and expanded utilities, affordable and ultimately free healthcare for all, high employment in thriving industries, all required enormous state investment in buildings and infrastructure, and places for their administration. The majority of the Percy Thomas practice's work contributed to such social developments, revealing their changing nature over the century. Its body of architecture demonstrates in these different ways the ethos of 'national service' that Thomas advocated as architecture's driving purpose in the twentieth century.

The phrase 'modern architecture' also requires consideration, since much of Thomas's practice cannot be straightforwardly categorised as belonging to the 'modern movement'. European modernism was widely understood in Britain by the early 1930s as young architects adopted it for adventurous clients, but Thomas belonged to an older generation, and spurned avant-garde modernism: most of his work adopted symmetrical planning and classical styles, though increasingly shorn of ornamental detail. His work sits within an alternative twentieth-century British tradition alongside such contemporary architects as Edwin Lutyens, Giles Gilbert Scott and Holden. This approach developed distinctive new tendencies - simplified volumes; expressive massing; a creative handling of historical details against plain surfaces. It was 'modern' without being 'modernist', and explicitly understood in these terms. Reilly admired Thomas's Guildhall at Swansea, for example, as 'the nearest yet that we have got to a modern town hall in this country', while describing his design as 'a classical approach to modernism'.[19]

In considering the Percy Thomas practice's relationship to architectural movements, architecture can be thought of as a discourse, in which buildings represent different positions exploring shared questions in dialogue with each other.[20] This book is less concerned with assessing the aesthetic quality of buildings than with explaining the reasons for their design. Comparisons with work by other architects are therefore less a matter of ranking or judgement or even of tracing artistic influences than they are intended to locate the practice within a spectrum of contemporary possibilities, helping to understand architectural intention and meaning. After the Second World War, the firm's work ventured towards modernism, but remained deliberately apart from the more experimental modernism of the period, seeking to develop rather than abandon the social and civic forms of the past. From the 1960s onwards, the practice more earnestly embraced contemporary modernism, including brutalism, attracted to its social ethos and its emerging capacity for civic expression. From the 1970s new attitudes in architecture and wider culture brought an increasing fragmentation and diversity of approaches to the practice, even sometimes a total repudiation of modernism, equally articulated as social concerns. The practice's positions in relation to these different mainstream movements, rather than its identification with a single stylistic or ideological approach, makes it an unusually clear lens through which to understand twentieth century architecture more generally.

The word 'modern', however, implies wider senses in which Percy Thomas's architecture related to its time beyond architectural approaches. It was modern also in its engagement with crucial problems and transformations of the twentieth century. Percy Thomas designed Swansea Guildhall, for example, as a 'civic centre', a new concept of a multi-functional public complex, then an important concern for politicians as well as architects, incorporating an assembly hall, law courts and administrative offices: it was modern in its new conceptions of what the town hall represented and the purposes it had to fulfil.[21] When Thomas later engaged with industry, his practice explored new technologies and ideas about business practices in an economic framework rapidly being reinvented by the state. The International Convention Centre in Birmingham, completed in 1991, is difficult to place in any obvious architectural movement; it is modern, however, in its new gigantic scale, its engagement with a new corporate culture, the technical advances of its engineering, and in its optimistic faith that thousands of tonnes of concrete, steel and glass could transform the social and economic fortunes of a city. Percy Thomas's architecture was 'modern' therefore in this much wider cultural sense. Often across its history the firm's assimilation of modernity is manifested in American influences, and this theme of Americanisation as modernisation will be highlighted throughout.[22] Louise Miskell argues that glances from Wales across the Atlantic also enabled a degree of freedom and autonomy from British cultural hegemony in developing its own modernity.[23]

Modernity may become visibly heightened through buildings: in modern construction technology, such as the precast concrete cladding of a university building; or in completely new building types, such as the power station. Such highly visible developments had important symbolic and political impacts in Wales, suggesting a new national identity, contrasting with older traditions of industry and agriculture. But modernity has been more critically assessed, linked to a destructively unstable capitalism striving for expansion, erasing tradition, place and community, enabled by the state.[24] Such themes are also evident in the architectural history of Percy Thomas's practice. Some buildings literally housed contemporary capitalism, shaping its expansion; others contributed to a state framework for its needs; many big developments in which Percy Thomas took part - roads, steelworks, hospitals - promised modernity and prosperity, but involved social, cultural and ecological upheaval.

While modernity is often associated with globalising tendencies, however, and modern spaces criticised as banal and lacking a sense of place, it is important to consider the ways in which modernity was enshrined in and through specific places. When architects imbued with an ethos of service engaged with the processes and institutions of modernity, they often sought to reconcile them to the culture of a specific place.[25] Architecture could help create new forms of community and consensus around modern development.

Outline of the Book

These themes weave through this narrative of the Percy Thomas practice, while the sequence is broadly chronological, charting the historical changes within which those debates played out. Each section focuses on specific areas of activity and concentrated aspects of the larger argument, moving forward not in a single arc but in a series of overlapping loops. I begin by considering Percy Thomas's interwar civic architecture in relation to emerging conceptions of democratic citizenship. The next chapter examines private and commercial buildings and non-governmental buildings such as churches within this framework, progressing to the post-war period. The following chapter considers the practice's work for the industry and infrastructure of the welfare state, including hospitals and universities. Then I examine ideas of place and context in post-war and late twentieth-century buildings, from modernist cultural buildings in Wales to the modification and, ultimately, rejection of modernism by branches of the practice. Finally, I address the later period under the supposed 'neoliberalism' of Conservative and New Labour governments, when new forms of capitalist economy brought new spatial and architectural types, while many continuities remained in conceptions of the welfare state. Percy Thomas's work, I argue, sought to sustain twentieth-century values of citizenship and community even in that new political atmosphere.

The scale of Percy Thomas's output precludes a total survey. The practice produced some 600 buildings and projects between 1909 and 2004, many more of significance than it is possible to explore in this volume. The book is perhaps biased towards the early and middle periods, and the last two decades are covered in more selective and concentrated form despite a greater output. This partly reflects my personal interests as a historian intrigued by the past beyond living memory, as recent decades are harder to assess with detachment.

Another problem for the historian is the absence of any comprehensive Percy Thomas archive. Even before an office clearance in the early years of this century, flooding had destroyed much material in the Cardiff office's basement. Research required assembling material from many sources, including institutions that commissioned the firm. Since central government was an important client, the National Archives have been productive; local government and university records are reasonably comprehensive; coverage from other bodies is patchy or inaccessible. Archival research focused on the period up to 1975; the later period draws more on published sources, especially newspapers and architectural journals. Newspapers contain a wealth of commentary and documentation because the practice's work impinged so much on public and political spheres. Many practice architects also generously gave time to discuss their work. There are undoubtedly rich discoveries yet to be made for those interested in bridging the many holes in this research. This book is a particular and personal view of the firm's architecture; and while aiming to be reasonably definitive, completeness has never been the intention.

Several important published sources gave a foundation for this book. The first outline of the practice was Percy Thomas's autobiography, frustratingly incomplete, sometimes inaccurate and surprisingly impersonal.[26] Most important is the work of Elaine Davey, particularly her PhD thesis, which, while concentrating on the Welsh Folk Museum, includes much valuable wider information.[27] Davey's work followed that of librarian Philip Thornborow, whose bibliography of publications on Thomas remains useful.[28] Otherwise, existing secondary research is limited to specific buildings and places. John Hilling, most notably, who briefly worked for the practice, has written about Cardiff Civic Centre and discusses other buildings in his survey of the architecture of Wales.[29] There is an excellent book of essays on Swansea Guildhall; valuable new work by Miskell and Leon Gooberman on Welsh industry; and significant work exists on other buildings, particularly the International Convention Centre in Birmingham.[30] Throughout I have sought to engage with wider work on political, economic, cultural and architectural history, to see where the buildings amplify, modify or even refute prevailing narratives.

Biography of a Practice

While the practice sustained a principle of service following from Thomas's early success in public buildings, the expression of that ethos varied over the century, not only with changing historical circumstances and political movements, but also as younger architects with new design philosophies arrived, and as the practice became larger and more dispersed. An initial overview of the practice's history will introduce key characters and scenes in its life.

Thomas dated the founding of his practice in his home town of Cardiff to 1912, after he and his friend Ivor Jones won the prestigious competition for the town's municipal Technical College the year before and set up an office at St John's Square in the commercial centre to work on that project. By then Thomas already had experience in a range of practices. He began as an apprentice to E. H. Bruton of Cardiff, an architect of churches, chapels and schools, and claimed to have designed his 1904 competition entry for a Cardiff secondary school, awarded third place.[31] That year he left for Lancashire, joining the firm of J. C. Prestwich & Son at Leigh, a substantial practice, designers of commercial and municipal buildings including schools and hospitals. There Thomas befriended the architect Ernest Prestwich, with whom he would later collaborate on several important projects. He also worked briefly for Stott & Sons of Manchester, architects and textile-mill owners, though his employment there coincided with a depression in the Lancashire cotton industry and little building work.[32] In between he travelled south to spend two years with R. E. Brinkworth in Bath, for whom he claimed to have designed a school, almost certainly the handsome St Peter's Church of England Secondary School in Devizes, a free classical building with an Art Nouveau feel of 1906, with a simple, well-organised symmetrical plan around a central top-lit assembly hall (see Figure 1.2).[33] In 1909 Thomas and Jones won a competition for a Young Men's Christian Association (YMCA) building in Merthyr Tydfil. Thus, Thomas's early experiences of architecture encompassed buildings of an educational and civic character and to a lesser extent those of a utilitarian, industrial purpose, two fields that would become key planks of the future practice.

Competitions were a recurrent feature of the practice's work, long typical for civic buildings, and something for which Thomas cultivated a facility during his apprenticeship by participating from 1901 to 1904 in the Designing Club of the *Building News*, run by its editor Maurice Bingham Adams. This was a correspondence course for architectural apprentices, who sent drawings responding to briefs and read Adams's criticisms of their entries. Adams ranked designs and published the best, awarding annual prizes. Thomas found this a formative experience, as Holden had done a decade before him.[34] He entered irregularly under the pseudonym 'Viking', achieving first place and praise from Adams for designs for a 'Boating Clubhouse' and a secondary school, the latter perhaps adapted for Bruton, though quite rustic in style for a rural location.[35] Adams often discussed style, but prioritised planning, examining designs for their organisational solutions to the brief. It was excellent preparation for architects hoping to make their fortunes in competitions. Meanwhile, in further anticipation of future success, Thomas won a competition for a 'Semi-Detached Villa' for the art exhibition of the National Eisteddfod at Llanelli in 1903.[36]

1.2 St Peter's Church of England Secondary School, Devizes, 1906 (photo: author).

In establishing his practice, Thomas joined forces with the older Ivor Jones, who had taken over his father's practice of J. P. Jones, Richards & Budgen in Cardiff. According to Reilly, Jones looked after the administration and left design to Thomas, a claim supported by other evidence: even when magazines published relatively modest buildings under the practice name of Ivor Jones and Percy Thomas, they often specifically credited Thomas as architect, especially from around 1930.[37] Jones taught at the Welsh School of Architecture and was prominent in the South Wales Institute of Architects, but when buildings were under way Thomas signed letters, went to meetings and attended opening ceremonies.[38] It seems reasonable therefore to attribute the design work predominantly to Thomas while acknowledging their partnership. In 1935 they moved from St John's Square to a Victorian villa on Cathedral Road, and the following year they parted company.[39] Thomas then stayed at Cathedral Road, which remained his practice's largest office until the twenty-first century.

Ernest Prestwich occasionally participated in projects, first joining Jones and Thomas for an unsuccessful entry for the Board of Trade competition in 1914. In the early 1930s Prestwich and Thomas entered several competitions without Jones, briefly forming a loose partnership in the late 1930s,[40] and appear again in association with each other in the 1950s for a proposed civic centre in Wigan, ultimately designed by Thomas's firm.[41] There is a stylistic consistency in the interwar work shared with Prestwich, a severe neo-Georgian style, often in brick.

Throughout this interwar period, Percy Thomas specialised in substantial civic buildings, many won in competitions. The Cardiff Technical College was the first of three buildings that he designed in the Civic Centre before the Second World War, and his other civic work included fire and police stations, civic centres in Tunbridge Wells and Swinton and Pendlebury, and Carmarthenshire County Hall. The masterpiece of his career was Swansea Guildhall, a substantial civic complex in a consistent monumental, stripped back classical style. By the mid-1930s, following the prestige endowed by his presidency of the RIBA, Thomas was in demand as a consultant for councils, universities including the University College of Wales at Aberystwyth, and other significant institutions. Nevertheless, he accepted a constant stream of more modest commercial and domestic commissions, from pubs to department stores and suburban houses, giving a steady income between larger jobs. Despite copious work, Thomas enjoyed sitting on committees, his RIBA presidency of 1935 to 1937 following several years within its administration and followed by an unusual second term as president from 1943 to 1946. The Institute awarded him its annual Royal Gold Medal in 1939, and thus his name is inscribed three times in the foyer of its Portland Place headquarters in London.[42] He was knighted in 1946.

The Second World War marked a distinct break in the practice, after which Thomas's son Norman Percy Thomas joined the office, increasingly taking control. Norman Thomas studied at the Welsh School of Architecture before the war, winning the RIBA's Archibald Dawnay prize for a construction study in 1935.[43] After a period working for T. Cecil Howitt in Nottingham, one of his father's main competitors for civic buildings, he left for New York, where he worked at the fledgling firm of Skidmore & Owings alongside a youthful Gordon Bunshaft in the late 1930s.[44] He would most likely have worked on their buildings for the New York World's Fair of 1939, influenced by Le Corbusier and, to some extent, Scandinavian modernism.[45] After returning to Europe to serve in the Second World War, including the Normandy landings, for which he too was mentioned in dispatches and awarded an MBE, he joined the Cardiff office in 1946, and by the following year the practice was renamed Sir Percy Thomas & Son.[46] The firm expanded from its base in Cardiff to establish offices in Swansea, Bristol and Shrewsbury under Norman Thomas's regimental style of leadership, employing seventy architects by 1963.[47] Sir Percy Thomas became an increasingly symbolic presence in the office before and after retiring in 1960, but undertook personal consultancy projects through the practice, particularly working with R. F. (Frank) Buckley, a talented architect and perspectivist accorded a room in the Cathedral Road basement.[48]

This period saw a step change in the number of commissions, thanks largely to the post-war government's policies of recovery through economic stimulus and the rise of the welfare state. Norman Thomas, assisted by administrator and later practice partner Peter Newton, sagely decided to specialise in education and healthcare, and work for the colleges of the University of Wales and for hospitals flourished. So, too, did work for industry, including the new Steel Company of Wales. These three fields remained central to the firm's work even in the twenty-first century.

Architecturally, this second period is more complicated than the first: while aspects of modernism were accepted, classical elements persisted in such motifs as simplified porticos. But younger architects joining the practice in the 1950s and 1960s transformed its approach under Norman Thomas's oversight.[49] William Marsden was particularly important. He had studied at the Manchester School of Architecture, trained with architects in Lancashire, and worked for the Borough Architect of Torquay in the 1930s before joining Percy Thomas around 1935.[50] He led the Shrewsbury office from 1960, and designed significant modern buildings in Aberystwyth and Bangor for the University of Wales. Frederick Jennett and John Vergette were also important. The former led the Bristol office from 1963, later succeeding Norman Thomas as chairman.[51] Vergette, trained at the Welsh School of Architecture, had a significant hand in many of the practice's buildings in Wales after arriving in 1955, especially from the Swansea office, where he became a partner in 1965.[52] Wallace Sweet joined in 1957 and worked in the Swansea office before moving back to Cardiff, where he was involved in major buildings. Keith Mainstone, meanwhile, a graduate of the Bristol School of Architecture, joined in 1958, became a partner in 1965 and led the firm's work for industry.[53] Women architects were present in the practice from the 1950s, though are rarely named.[54] Two graduates of the Welsh School of Architecture were especially significant: Maureen Kelly (later Kelly Owen) left early to raise a family, but designed a hall of residence in Cardiff in the early 1960s; and Patricia Townsend joined the Bristol office in 1964, designing hospitals and housing after some notable experience in England working on Hertfordshire schools and a London hospital for Ralph Tubbs.[55] For architects of this generation, the modern movement was no longer contentious, but an accepted norm.

Ivan Dale Owen had the most rigorous modernist training of any of Percy Thomas's architects of this period. After graduating from the Welsh School of Architecture in 1949, he took a diploma at the School of Planning and Research for Regional Development, an offshoot of the Architectural Association, led by its former principal E. A. A. Rowse. After a period back in Wales at Cwmbran New Town, he received a Fulbright Scholarship to study for a Master of Architecture course run jointly by the Massachusetts Institute of Technology (MIT) and Harvard University, attending from 1954 to 1955. At MIT, lecturers included Pietro Belluschi and Kevin Lynch, and Walter Gropius's influence persisted. Owen then worked for Gropius's practice The Architects' Collaborative before returning to London, to Minoprio, Spenceley & Macfarlane and Sir William Holford & Partners. He joined Percy Thomas's Cardiff office in 1958.[56] Owen was thus imbued with new American architectural methods and ideas and committed to modernism as an all-encompassing approach. Moreover, he was a principled and charismatic architect who wrote copiously in elegant and persuasive prose, convincing others, including clients and colleagues, of the ethical values of modern architecture. His own design work focused on planning, and he encouraged younger colleagues to develop projects to his initial concepts.[57]

The third phase began in 1971 with a reorganisation and name change to the Percy Thomas Partnership (PTP), as Norman Thomas partially retired. By now there were more than 100 staff, and the firm's complexity required a different structure.[58] A new group of practice partners included Owen and Mainstone, led by Jennett as chairman.[59] Jennett pursued a dynamic expansion, opening a London office later that year, followed by offices in Manchester, Birmingham and Nottingham. Edinburgh followed through merger with Kneale & Russell in 1991.[60] Other changes in the firm's structure took place in the 1980s when specialist groups became separate companies – PTP Landscape and Urban Design, involving Sue Radley, Jane Findlay, David Daniell and others; PTP Seward, an interior design company run by Julian Seward; PTP Graphics, run by Vivyan Davies, and PTP Design Group. These sat mainly in practice offices and would join architectural projects as needed, alongside independent work where architects were not required.

Jennett also extended the practice overseas, using two techniques. One was to market the practice's expertise in hospitals with the backing of the British government, gaining substantial work in the Middle East, north Africa and Malaysia in the 1970s and 1980s. The other was to enter international competitions, with notable successes in Hong Kong. Gerhard Hattingh, trained at Cape Town, established the Hong Kong office in collaboration with a local practice and worked there in the 1980s and 1990s.[61] Yet despite PTP's internationalisation, the Cathedral Road villa in Cardiff, extended to the rear, remained important as its administrative headquarters.

The second generation passed on its values to younger architects. Ian Pepperell joined in Cardiff for a project with Mainstone in 1968, becoming a partner in 1983, and designed significant buildings in Wales and beyond, particularly for industry.[62] Neil Graham, John Rudge and Pepperell joined Vergette in the huge team designing the Birmingham International Convention Centre in the 1980s. Vergette was chairman from 1990 and chief executive from 1993, until Rudge took the latter post in 1996. Ronald Weeks was one of the outstanding younger architects, a talented designer who had studied at the Bartlett, won the RIBA's Soane Medallion, and spent a year on a scholarship at the École des Beaux-Arts in Paris. Jennett appointed him at the Bristol office in the late 1960s where he designed Clifton Roman Catholic Cathedral with a rigorous modern movement approach.[63] Before its completion he moved to the new London office, and went on to design some of the firm's most important buildings.

The firm was big by contemporary standards, claiming to be the fourth largest in Britain in 1988, peaking around 1990 with about 300 architects, and always the largest architectural practice in Wales.[64] Its size and reputation for competence attracted projects of great scale and technical complexity. Architects could move freely between offices, project teams and building types, including overseas. Yet, unlike some practices, PTP refrained from imposing any house style, advertising a 'design service which responds to the circumstances of each commission'.[65] This period is defined by increasing design diversity, reflecting a wider confusion in architecture outside the practice, but also characteristic of what Nicholas Adams calls a 'partnership practice', as partners had equal status and autonomy, allowing 'dissent'.[66] While the London and Cardiff offices adopted high-tech approaches for factories, offices and even schools, Peterjohn Smyth at the Bristol office cultivated classical and vernacular design, attracting the patronage of the Prince of Wales for major work at Poundbury, the traditionalist town planned by Léon Krier. Meanwhile, the technically demanding work of hospital architecture remained important, each new advance in thinking closely monitored, with healthcare specialists in most offices. These included Mike Nightingale, who had previously worked for the most important modern hospital architects of the twentieth century, Llewellyn-Davies & Weeks.[67] Architects Julian Cockayne in London, who had developed hospital expertise working at practices in New York, John Pickup in Manchester and Roger Cockle and Allan Clark in the midlands also specialised in the type.

Underlying the loose, flexible approach to staffing and design, Jennett established a fixed element in the 1970s that benefited the practice's operation, converting the Shrewsbury office into a 'Central Technical Services' department under Keith Cluderay, housing an enormous mainframe computer nicknamed 'Percy' churning out drawings to support the more demanding projects, running one of the first computer-aided design systems in Britain.[68] This facility reduced the drudgery of technical drawing and allowed architects more time for design, helping PTP to sustain a high design standard alongside its professionalism.

The Percy Thomas Partnership ended in 2004 after a decade of financial problems mainly caused by interruptions in large, risky projects. Capita, a multi-pronged services company, acquired PTP at a vulnerable moment to obtain its expertise, especially in healthcare. This study ends at that point, though some continuities remained within and beyond the practice.

Despite the later practice's diversity, certain themes persisted in its work from Thomas's early twentieth-century interests into the new millennium. Specific building types predominate throughout: big urban civic buildings with multiple functions, from interwar town halls to the Wales Millennium Centre; educational buildings with civic purposes, whether schools or universities; hospitals, a highly specialised building type; and buildings for industry and corporate administration. Even private commissions were often closely linked to British and Welsh government bodies; and even commercial clients valued the practice's principle of embodying civic, democratic attitudes - serving the 'whole community', in Thomas's words - in architectural, spatial form. Stylistically, the practice followed prevailing twentieth-century trends, but used architectural form to express wider conceptions of society and the nation, and to value the civic context. Percy Thomas's buildings are particularly direct expressions of the workings and desires of the institutions that they housed, and therefore also of the state, throughout the twentieth century. ■

01
Introduction
References

1. Percy E. Thomas, 'The RIBA Inaugural Address', *Architect & Building News*, 8 November 1935, pp. 161–4; Percy Thomas, 'The Inaugural Address', *Journal of the Royal Institute of British Architects*, 9 November 1935, pp. 5–13; 'The Nation Needs the Skilled Planner', *Architect & Building News*, 8 November 1935, pp. 145–6.

2. Percy Thomas, 'RIBA: Inaugural Address', *Architects' Journal*, 6 November 1936, pp. 624–6; 'The Inaugural Address by the President, Mr. Percy Thomas, OBE, FRIBA', *Journal of the Royal Institute of British Architects*, 7 November 1936, pp. 5–10.

3. For a similar argument see, for example, Alistair Fair, *Peter Moro and Partners* (Swindon: Historic England and Liverpool University Press, 2021), p. 12.

4. Elaine Davey, 'A National Architect? The Percy Thomas Practice and Welsh National Identity' (unpublished PhD thesis, Cardiff University, 2013), p. 114; Elaine Davey and Huw Thomas, '"Chief Creator of Modern Wales": The Neglected Legacy of Percy Thomas', *North American Journal of Welsh Studies*, 9 (2014), 54–70; Davey's sources include Kenneth O. Morgan, *Rebirth of a Nation: Wales, 1880–1980* (Oxford: Clarendon Press, 1981); John Davies, *A History of Wales* (London: Penguin, 1994); Graham Day, *Making Sense of Wales: A Sociological Perspective* (Cardiff: University of Wales Press, 2002).

5. Davey, 'A National Architect?', pp. 95–101; Ralph Fevre and Andrew Thompson (eds), *Nation, Identity and Social Theory: Perspectives from Wales* (Cardiff: University of Wales Press, 1999); Richard Weight and Abigail Beach (eds), *The Right to Belong: Citizenship and National Identity in Britain, 1930–1960* (London: I.B. Tauris, 1998); Helen Brocklehurst and Robert Phillips (eds), *History, Nationhood and the Question of Britain* (Basingstoke: Palgrave Macmillan, 2004); Duncan Tanner, Chris Williams, Wil Griffith and Andrew Edwards (eds), *Debating Nationhood and Governance in Britain, 1885–1945: Perspectives from the 'Four Nations'* (Manchester: Manchester University Press, 2006).

6. For example, James E. Cronin, *The Politics of State Expansion: War, State and Society in Twentieth-Century Britain* (London: Routledge, 1991).

7. Henri Lefebvre, *The Production of Space* (Oxford: Basil Blackwell, 1991); see also, for example, Greg Hise, 'Architecture as State Building: A Challenge to the Field', *Journal of the Society of Architectural Historians*, 67/2 (2008), 173–7; Jean-Louis Cohen, 'Scholarship or Politics? Architectural History and the Risks of Autonomy', *Journal of the Society of Architectural Historians*, 67/3 (2008), 325–9.

8. For example, Noel Whiteside, 'Private Provision and Public Welfare: Health Insurance Between the Wars', and Jose Harris, 'Political Thought and the Welfare State 1870–1940: An Intellectual Framework for British Social Policy', in David Gladstone (ed.), *Before Beveridge: Welfare Before the Welfare State*

(London: Institute of Economic Affairs, 1999), pp. 26–63; Bernard Harris, *The Origins of the British Welfare State: Society, State and Social Welfare* (Basingstoke: Palgrave Macmillan, 2004); for applications to architecture, Elizabeth Darling, *Re-Forming Britain: Narratives of Modernity Before Reconstruction* (London: Routledge, 2007); David Brady, 'Public or Private? London Medical Buildings of the Interwar Years', *Twentieth Century Architecture*, 13, 'The Architecture of Public Service' (2018), 63–79.

9. David Edgerton, *The Rise and Fall of the British Nation: A Twentieth-Century History* (London: Penguin, 2019); see also Sam Wetherell, *Foundations: How the Built Environment Made Twentieth-Century Britain* (Princeton NJ: Princeton University Press, 2020), for example, pp. 7–8.

10. For example, Otto Saumarez Smith, 'Action for Cities: The Thatcher Government and Inner-City Policy', *Urban History*, 47/2 (2020), 274–91; Guy Ortolano, *Thatcher's Progress: From Social Democracy to Market Liberalism through an English New Town* (Cambridge: Cambridge University Press, 2019).

11. Mark Crinson and Jules Lubbock, *Architecture: Art or Profession? Three Hundred Years of Architectural Education in Britain* (Manchester: Manchester University Press, 1994); on ethics, Harold Perkin, *The Rise of Professional Society: England since 1880* (London: Routledge, 1989), pp. 116–23.

12. Eitan Karol, *Charles Holden, Architect* (Donington: Shaun Tyas, 2007), pp. 6–7, citing Charles Holden, 'Thoughts on Architecture', *Journal of the Royal Institute of British Architects*, June 1942, p. 130.

13. Arthur Marwick, *The Deluge: British Society and the First World War* (London: Macmillan, 1973), pp. 87–111, 261–2, 293, 299.

14. The National Archives, London (TNA), WO339/73900, War Service Record for Percy Thomas; 'The News of the Week', *Architect & Building News*, 3 May 1935, pp. 110–12 (110).

15. Percy Edward Thomas, *Pupil to President: Memoirs of an Architect* (Leigh-on-Sea: F. Lewis, 1963), p. 28.

16. Charles Reilly, 'Some Younger Architects of Today: Percy Thomas', *Building*, February 1931, pp. 60–5 (62).

17. Percy Thomas, 'RIBA: President's Address to Students', *Architects' Journal*, 30 January 1936, pp. 189–90 (190).

18. For example, see Tom Hulme, *After the Shock City: Urban Culture and the Making of Modern Citizenship* (Woodbridge: Royal Historical Society and The Boydell Press, 2019), p. 9; N. E. Shasore, 'Southampton Civic Centre: Patronage and Place in the Interwar Architecture of Public Service', *Twentieth Century Architecture*, 13 'The Architecture of Public Service' (2018), 41–61 (47).

19. C. H. Reilly, 'Criticism 1: The Town Hall Problem', *Architectural Review*, March 1935, pp. 113–15 (115); Reilly, 'Percy Thomas', p. 65.

20. Sarah Williams Goldhagen, 'Something to Talk About: Modernism, Discourse, Style', *Journal of the Society of Architectural Historians*, 64/2 (2005), 144–67 (although I broaden my interpretation beyond the modern movement).

21. On modernism versus modernity, James Greenhalgh, *Reconstructing Modernity: Space, Power and Governance in Mid-Twentieth Century British Cities* (Manchester: Manchester University Press, 2017), for example, pp. 13–14, 60.

22. Murray Fraser with Joe Kerr, *Architecture and the 'Special Relationship': The American Influence on Post-War British Architecture* (Abingdon: Routledge, 2007), for example, pp. 10–12.

23. Louise Miskell, 'Doing It for Themselves: The Steel Company of Wales and the Study of American Industrial Productivity, 1945–1955', *Enterprise & Society*, 18/1 (2017), 184–213.

24. Anthony Giddens, *The Consequences of Modernity* (Cambridge: Polity Press, 1990).

25. On placelessness and modernity, Marc Augé, *Non-Places: An Introduction to Supermodernity* (London: Verso, 2009); on British modernity, Brian Short, David Gilbert and David Matless, 'Historical Geographies of British Modernity', in David Gilbert, David Matless and Brian Short (eds), *Geographies of British Modernity: Space and Society in the Twentieth Century* (Malden: Blackwell, 2003), pp. 1–27.

26. Thomas, *Pupil to President*.

27. Davey, 'A National Architect?'; Davey and Thomas, '"Chief Creator of Modern Wales"'.

28. P. Thornborow, *Sir Percy Thomas: A Bibliography and Partial Catalogue of Works* (Cardiff: UWIST Library, 1984).

29. John B. Hilling, *The History and Architecture of Cardiff Civic Centre: Black Gold, White City* (Cardiff: University of Wales Press, 2016); John B. Hilling, *The Architecture of Wales: From the First to the Twenty-First Century* (Cardiff: University of Wales Press, 2018).

30. J. R. Alban (ed.), *The Guildhall, Swansea: Essays to Commemorate the Fiftieth Anniversary of Its Opening* (Swansea: Swansea City Council, 1984); Miskell, 'Doing It for Themselves'; Leon Gooberman, *From Depression to Devolution: Economy and Government in Wales, 1934–2006* (Cardiff: University of Wales Press, 2017); Louise Miskell (ed.), *New Perspectives on Welsh Industrial History* (Cardiff: University of Wales Press, 2020); Terry Grimley, *Symphony Hall: A Dream Realised* (Birmingham: Boydell and Brewer, 2014); Timothy Ross Hall, 'Urban Regeneration and Cultural Geography: The International Convention Centre, Birmingham' (unpublished PhD thesis, University of Birmingham, 1994).

31. Thomas, *Pupil to President*, p. 17 (he incorrectly states it was placed second); 'Cardiff School Board', *Western Mail*, 5 February 1904, p. 5.

32. Thomas, *Pupil to President*, p. 19; Roger N. Holden, *Stott and Sons: Architects of the Lancashire Cotton Mill* (Lancaster: Carnegie Publishing, 1998), especially p. 43.

33. 'New Secondary School', *Wiltshire Times*, 8 September 1906, p. 8; 'Lord Bath at Devizes', *Bath Chronicle*, 13 September 1906, p. 3; 'Devizes Secondary School', *Building News and Engineering Journal*, 15 June 1906, 838–9 and plate – the illustrations have clear similarities with those of Thomas's Merthyr Tydfil YMCA

competition entry and Designing Club drawings, so there seems every reason to attribute this building to him.

34. Karol, *Charles Holden*, pp. 57–8.

35. '"Building News" Designing Club', *Building News and Engineering Journal*, 8 April 1904, pp. 507–8; '"Building News" Designing Club', *Building News and Engineering Journal*, 20 November 1903, pp. 683–5.

36. 'Art Exhibition: The Awards', *Llanelly Mercury*, 6 August 1903, p. 3.

37. Reilly, 'Percy Thomas', p. 61; for example, 'Proposed Welsh National Memorial Buildings, Cardiff', *Builder*, 9 January 1931, p. 118; Basil Oliver, 'English Inns', *RIBA Journal*, 14 May 1932, pp. 545–67 (533).

38. 'Our Secretaries: Ivor P. Jones, South Wales Institute of Architects', *Architects' Journal*, 21 September 1933, p. 366; 'The Welsh School of Architecture', *Architects' Journal*, 4 September 1929, pp. 361–2.

39. 'Announcements', *Architects' Journal*, 12 September 1935, p. 392; 'Announcements', *Architects' Journal*, 24 December 1936, pp. 867–8.

40. Correspondence over the Swinton and Pendlebury civic centre is headed 'Percy Thomas & Ernest Prestwich Architects, Bradshawgate Chambers, Leigh, Lancashire (and at Cardiff)', and Prestwich attended meetings: Salford Local History Library, Salford (henceforth SLHL), BSP/CL11/1, letter of 5 September 1938 to William Carter (Town Clerk); SLHL, Swinton and Pendlebury Council Minutes 1937–38, Municipal Buildings Sub-Committee of the General Purposes Committee, 11 July 1938.

41. For example, Local History Library, Museum of Wigan Life, Wigan (LHLW), County Borough of Wigan Minutes 1956–57, Joint Meeting of Representatives of the Finance, Planning and Development, Estates, Baths, and Markets and Parks Committees, 23 July 1956.

42. William Holford, 'Percy Thomas', *RIBA Journal*, October 1969, p. 408.

43. 'RIBA', *Architects' Journal*, 16 January 1936, pp. 78–80 (79); Frederick S. Jennett, 'Obituaries: Norman Percy Thomas', *RIBA Journal*, January 1990, p. 114.

44. Jennett, 'Norman Percy Thomas'.

45. Nicholas Adams, *Skidmore, Owings & Merrill: SOM Since 1936* (Milan: Electa, 2006), pp. 21–2.

46. The earliest published use of this practice name appears to be 'Factory for Gnome Photographic Products Ltd., Cardiff, Designed by Sir Percy Thomas and Son', *Architects' Journal*, 4 September 1947, pp. 207–10.

47. Glamorgan Archives, Cardiff (GAC), D900/U/6, folder 'Letters & Odds', IDO [Ivan Dale Owen] to anonymous recipient, 16 May 1963.

48. 'Announcements', *Architects' Journal*, 5 July 1961, pp. 35–6; Wyndham Powell, interview with the author and Michael Sweet, Cardiff, 4 February 2023.

49. Tony Aldous, 'Portrait of a Practice: Percy Thomas Partnership', *Building Design*, 2 December 1977, pp. 13–16 (13).

50. RIBA Library, London (henceforth RIBAL), William Marsden Biographical File, Nomination Papers for William Marsden, 1934; 'Architect of Modern Wales', *South Wales Evening Post*, 14 November 1962, in RIBAL, Sir Percy Edward Thomas Biographical File; 'News: Appointments', *Architects' Journal*, 15 August 1940, p. 128; Archive of the Royal Commission on the Historical and Ancient Monuments of Wales, Aberystwyth (henceforth RCAHMW), Percy Thomas Archive (henceforth PTA), 05/04, 'Sir Percy Thomas & Son: Architects and Planning Consultants', n.d. [*c.*1970].

51. 'Announcements', *Architects' Journal*, 1 May 1963, p. 934.

52. 'Announcements', *Architects' Journal*, 10 March 1965, p. 578; Brian H. B. Chambers, 'Obituary: John Francis Vergette', *RIBA Journal*, April 2010, p. 15.

53. Colleen Hope and Claire Clench, video interview with the author, 10 February 2021.

54. Nick Renwick, telephone interview with the author, 8 October 2021.

55. Maureen Kelly Owen, interview with the author, Penarth, 23 June 2017; 'Twenty-One Years with PTP', *Percy Thomas Partnership: Review*, 1985, unpaginated, author's collection.

56. GAC, D900/U/6, 'Letters & Odds', P. R. Rathbone (Secretary, Town Planning Institute) to I. D. Owen, 9 November 1962.

57. Ronald Weeks, 'The Modern Spirit', *Touchstone*, April 1999, pp. 14–15; Kenneth Powell, 'Obituary: Dale Owen', *Independent*, 28 November 1997, p. 19.

58. RCAHMW, PTA 05/04, 'Sir Percy Thomas & Son: Architects and Planning Consultants'.

59. 'Announcements', *Architects' Journal*, 27 January 1971, pp. 184–5.

60. 'Practice Announcements', *Architects' Journal*, 5 February 1992, p. 49.

61. Jo Doyle, *Percy Thomas Partnership HK: Selected and Current Works* (Victoria: The Images Publishing Group, 1998), p. 8; Gerhard Hattingh, video interview with the author, 3 March 2021.

62. Ian Pepperell, telephone interview with the author, 19 February 2021.

63. Ronald Weeks, telephone interview with the author, 9 November 2007.

64. RIBAL, Percy Thomas Partnership Biographical File, 'Management Consultants', *Percy Thomas Partnership: Review*, 1988, unpaginated; 'AJ100', *Architects' Journal*, 27 March 1997, pp. i–xvi (iii, x).

65. 'Traditional Contextual Architecture', leaflet, n.d. [*c.*1994], author's collection.

66. Adams, *Skidmore, Owings & Merrill*, pp. 14–15.

67. Mike Nightingale, video interview with the author, 2 March 2021.

68. Aldous, 'Portrait of a Practice', p. 14; 'Shrewsbury News', *Percy Thomas Partnership Review*, 1 (1985), unpaginated, author's collection.

2

Modern Classicism and Municipal Democracy

Percy Thomas's work contributed to a remarkable flourishing of civic culture in British cities between the wars. From the nineteenth century arose the idea of the town hall as a monument of independent self-government that could forge a sense of pride and belonging, where citizens could gather as one, surrounded by symbols of local identity.[1] From the late nineteenth century, too, came the 'civic socialism' proposed by Joseph Chamberlain, mayor of Birmingham, who described local government as a 'co-operative enterprise in which every citizen is a shareholder, and of which the dividends are received in the improved health and the increase in the comfort and happiness of the community', justifying the city's ownership of vital services.[2] Consensus over these ideas developed in the early twentieth century with a new politics of idealism, which saw the state as responsible for encouraging citizens to participate in society in return for significant rights. Some viewed welfare as a tool to develop active citizenship, while others argued its necessity for the full participation of all. Idealism influenced politicians on all sides and philanthropic social reformers. Meanwhile ordinary people encountered the idea through 'civics', classes mapping out an interconnected society, and through rituals and events designed to infuse them with a civic spirit and educate them about local government.[3]

In national politics, such principles influenced the expansion of the vote as fundamental to citizenship, and the rapid extension of welfare, notably David Lloyd George's institution of state pensions in 1906 and national insurance in 1911, granting unemployment support and improving access to medical treatment. Governments after the First World War increased state provision of unemployment compensation, healthcare, housing and education.[4] Though initiated in Westminster, much of this new state provision fell to local authorities, whose bureaucratic duties increased dramatically. Councils embraced these responsibilities as intrinsic to their democratic purpose. Philanthropic and private organisations also contributed to welfare, some co-opted by government, such as the friendly societies and insurance companies that administered national insurance.[5]

Managing this expanding welfare activity required new buildings combining bureaucratic functions with symbolic expressions of their noble purpose. Councils also had to cater for populations that had grown precipitously in the nineteenth century: Swansea and Cardiff, for example, were essentially products of Victorian industry and commerce; Swansea was considered large enough to become a county borough in 1889, and Cardiff was made a city in 1905. Competition between cities also motivated new buildings, most notably at Cardiff's Civic Centre, planned to support its claim to capital city status for Wales.[6]

Councils often sought to centralise administrative functions after piecemeal expansion left offices scattered across multiple sites, claiming improved efficiency, but also attracted to the symbolism of prominent new buildings demonstrating local government activity. Unlike today, municipal offices were bustling with the public - plans incorporated waiting rooms for departments, as Thomas noted in a lecture on municipal buildings, because welfare decisions often followed interviews with council staff.[7] Many political commentators viewed this personal element as bringing recipients into a reciprocal relationship with society to appreciate their duties as citizens.[8]

Moreover, councils wanted administrative buildings linked to the spaces of democratic decision-making, council chambers and committee rooms; the rates hall, where ratepayers made their contributions in person; and assembly halls, where citizens could gather for edifying civic events. Fire and police stations, also council responsibilities, could be included, and often law courts, libraries, clinics or schools. Complexes of buildings demonstrating this new understanding of citizenship, democracy and welfare were a new phenomenon in the early twentieth century, distinguished from town halls by the phrase 'civic centre'.[9] The idea of a centre as a focal point for gathering and cementing communities outside commercial imperatives was an important contemporary notion.[10]

Architects explicitly articulated these concepts. Thomas argued that councils' desires for coordinated groups of buildings showed that they were 'reaching out for something more worthy of their town'. 'A civic pride has been created', he said; they wanted buildings that could 'reflect the higher aims and aspirations of the citizens'.[11] Architects had to express these ideals, particularly in elevations, the aspect most evident to 'the ordinary citizen', wrote one author arguing for impressive 'symbols of civic dignity' such as towers.[12] Architects and clients often favoured classicism to express such aspirations, leading to family resemblances between civic buildings across

Britain, evoking the coherence of local government in a national state, even an imperial nation, as Thomas's Swansea Guildhall shows.

Forming the Citizen

Percy Thomas's first two commissioned buildings with Ivor Jones had educational functions, expressed architecturally as civic welfare, combined with a social purpose going beyond education, encompassing the wider formation of the citizen. While the YMCA building in Merthyr Tydfil was a charitable educational endeavour with civic aspirations, Cardiff Technical College was a municipal project, run by Cardiff Corporation and sited in the city's Civic Centre to enshrine it as a state project.

The YMCA had become an international charity with an extensive network of urban centres in Britain, aimed at occupying boys and men in gainful social, sporting and educational activities. It shared in the ethos of civic idealism, aiming to cultivate responsible citizenship, often partnering with local councils.[13] In 1899 it began extending its educational programmes, with a substantial building campaign to provide multifunctional buildings for education and recreation.[14] Merthyr Tydfil's YMCA resulted from the efforts of recently appointed Secretary for Wales Gwilym James to develop urban centres while extending the YMCA's reach into smaller towns, especially in industrial areas.[15] These included a prominent building in Swansea; similar but uncompleted buildings at Pontypridd, where Jones and Thomas came second in the architectural competition in 1907; and Merthyr Tydfil, for which they won the competition in 1909 (see Figure 2.1).[16]

2.1 YMCA, Merthyr Tydfil, 1909–11, viewed when derelict in 2021, chimneys and semi-circular pediment removed (photo: author).

The Merthyr Tydfil branch had a prominent, elevated site at the head of the town's High Street on Pontmorlais Road. The first two of an intended three phases were completed in 1911, an imposing four-storey building squeezing in a variety of spaces for many different activities. These included a library, reading room and lecture hall, the latter the primary public space, reached by a grand staircase. The staircase continued upwards, oriel windows forming landings where members could encounter each other. A broad reception hall, 'Conversation & Smoke Room' and café gave further space for socialisation; games rooms and a rifle range in the attic encouraged social entertainment.[17]

Thomas's elevations used a material palette of red brick and terracotta that also characterised the recent town hall, giving the two a marked affinity. Stylistically, the YMCA is Edwardian free classical, while E. A. Johnson's Victorian town hall is neo-Jacobean, but Thomas seems to have chosen style and material to convey a civic relationship. This civic character was justified by the building's role in the town. The mayor and mayoress supported YMCA fundraising activities in both the town hall and the completed building.[18] YMCA events such as public lectures were open to townspeople; external organisations often hired the building; and YMCA members formed sports teams and a male voice choir, participating in the life of the town.[19] Yet its core mission remained the cultivation of young men as good citizens: as a visitor from the Swansea YMCA explained to Merthyr members in 1912, 'the most important asset to this and other nations was the character of its manhood, and the Association was doing its level best to rear good, healthy, cultured, religious men'.[20] His words echo wider concerns over the moral and physical conditions of working-class men that motivated early twentieth-century government welfare legislation.[21]

Architecturally and institutionally, Thomas's Cardiff Technical College was very different, though aimed equally at making young people productive members of society (see Figure 2.2). The council allocated the college a site in the Civic Centre layout at Cathays Park of 1899, intending to grant the institution a prestigious status related to surrounding buildings for local government offices, law courts, the Welsh Museum and the University College of South Wales and Monmouthshire. By 1911, when Jones and Thomas won the competition, Portland stone and classical styles had become conventional for the Civic Centre's buildings, inspired partly by the contemporary American City Beautiful movement.[22] The Technical College's architecture conformed to this collective language, while politely expressing its relatively modest position in the hierarchy of buildings in Cathays Park.

The Technical College originated in the 1860s with classes at the Cardiff library, taken over by the council as the Central Technical School using powers in the Technical Instruction Act of 1889. Art, music, science and commerce were taught in a former school building but also scattered elsewhere. The rationale for a new building echoes that for many civic buildings of the period; that is, that dispersed activities prevented the organisation from cohering as a single body. Philip Magnus, reporting on the council's education provision in 1907, lamented that 'there is no building in the city which stands out prominently as the Technical School'.[23] Charles Coles, appointed to reform the institution, reaffirmed the need for a single building 'where provision is made for some corporate life, and not a number of scattered and unconnected groups

2.2 Cardiff Technical College (now Bute Building, Cardiff University), 1911–16, extended 1936 (photo: author).

of classes'.[24] Hence, at the centre of Jones and Thomas's plan was a large 'assembly hall' where large numbers of students could attend communal events, and student common rooms encouraged socialisation within the college.

The building raised the level and scope of technical education in the city, including advanced technical and laboratory facilities. Courses concentrated on applied and professional subjects including architecture and engineering, building trades and marine navigation.[25] Opened in 1916 during the war, rhetoric around industrial education took on a patriotic fervour. The Lord Mayor of Cardiff, R. J. Smith, called at the opening ceremony for intensive industrial development to compete with German exports, pioneered by state technical education in partnership with industry: 'the nation should lay down its plan of campaign and carry on the commercial and industrial warfare which would follow the cessation of hostilities,' he urged; 'it was time for the nation to awake and realise its responsibilities and its obligations'.[26] The *Architectural Review* saw the building as contributing to a rise in the prestige of practical subjects conducive to forming the citizen as 'a profitable asset', and argued for state funding of technical education as a 'national investment'.[27]

Jones and Thomas's design helped to express as well as enable this noble purpose. Its planning was lucid and straightforward, blocks of classrooms surrounding the central assembly hall. The principal lecture theatre's position on the main frontage logically suggested a central feature on the elevation, marked by a Roman Doric colonnade framed in rusticated piers, hinting at the gathered institutional body. The elevation was 'simple and dignified', wrote a critic, economical and suited to its serious purpose, in part achieved by placing second-floor rooms in a top-lit attic behind a deep, blank parapet; other competitors' elevations, though similarly classical, were complicated or unmemorable.[28] As built, the elevations were even simpler than the competition drawings, fussier motifs removed, retaining simpler classical elements; crisp details such as the column capitals contrasted with daring omissions, including an almost blank entablature. The main entrance received the densest ornament, carved by Albert H. Hodge with an Egyptian winged sun symbolising the enlightenment bestowed inside.

The College's 'severe' classicism - to use Thomas's own description - later described by William Purchon, the college's head of architecture, as 'Neo-Grec', was based on American architecture following the principles of the École des Beaux-Arts in Paris where many leading American architects studied.[29] Its refined approach to classicism was advocated by Charles Reilly at the Liverpool University School of Architecture and in the architectural press, and practised by architects such as J. J. Burnet, who had studied in Paris.[30] E. Vincent Harris, one of Thomas's rivals throughout his career, sometimes also took this approach. His Glamorgan County Hall alongside the Technical College had a richer and more sculptural Corinthian treatment befitting its higher purpose, and Thomas clearly designed the college in deference to it. Both buildings departed from the elaborate eclectic Edwardian architecture of the Civic Centre's earlier buildings, including W. D. Caroë's University College opposite. Logically organised, easily understood and with bold simplified classical elevations, this modern classical approach characterised Thomas's future civic buildings and much twentieth-century civic architecture in Britain.

Jones and Thomas returned several times to enlarge the building in a consistent style as the college expanded, adding workshops at the rear in 1919, two upper floors of lecture theatres, laboratories and architecture studios in 1927, and a further addition over the assembly hall.[31] Expansion was accompanied by increasing prestige, as the University of Wales accredited courses and students increasingly attended from across south Wales, drawing neighbouring local authorities into its funding.[32] After the Second World War, Thomas would return to develop the college with a new building marking a shift from regional to national status.

Local Government and the State

More than any other building type, town halls embodied concepts of democracy and the state. Local and national politics did not always coincide, however, and local debates about the role of the state, municipal government and conceptions of civic identity influenced municipal buildings. Three of Percy Thomas's town halls show two divergent attitudes. At Swansea and at Swinton and Pendlebury in Salford, local Liberal and Labour parties agreed about state intervention to improve citizens' lives through local government, and wanted buildings to celebrate that role, even presenting new buildings as acts of welfare and drawing national government into their funding. In Tunbridge Wells, however, the council's attempts to build a civic centre engendered heated debate about the nature of the state. Thomas's pragmatic architecture eased tensions in Kent, and enshrined political narratives in Lancashire and Swansea.

A formal modernised classicism ennobled the space of governance, giving imposing backdrops for the everyday interactions of officials and citizens and appropriate settings for ceremonials. All three buildings shared similarities in form and had much in common with town halls across Britain, participating in a national movement, while local inflections in materials and iconography situated buildings in specific civic cultures. These three civic complexes were Thomas's most important interwar buildings, and Swansea Guildhall remains one of the finest twentieth-century town halls in Britain.[33]

At Swansea, the council passed from Liberal to Labour control during construction, but both parties agreed to cooperate in building the Guildhall at the mayor's behest; when the local Chamber of Commerce urged deferral in 1931, the council voted overwhelmingly to continue.[34] Swansea's council was zealous in wider municipal planning and infrastructure. Projects included the Townhill housing estate, planned by borough architect Ernest Morgan with 3,000 workers' houses and a pioneering open-air school.[35] The council built a 600-bed psychiatric hospital at Cefn Coed; it acquired Singleton Park for the recently founded University College of Swansea; it was draining land for industrial expansion; it owned water and electricity companies, gained government funding for a 'super-electricity' station, and even ran a colliery.[36] At the Guildhall's opening ceremony in 1934, the souvenir booklet, newspaper reports and even the builder's advertising celebrated these activities alongside Thomas's building.[37] After the Duke of Kent opened the Guildhall, he was shown around Townhill and met the council's Education Committee, linking the Guildhall with welfare.[38] The Guildhall was also intended to stimulate further urban improvements, with plans for an axial boulevard between the Guildhall and the commercial centre.[39] The local Labour party announced that the building's opening demonstrated 'an awakened civic patriotism', proposing continued developments to engender 'a happy and efficient citizenship equal in nobility to its Guildhall'.[40]

Before running the architectural competition in 1929, Morgan sought information on recent town halls and civic centres from the RIBA, which advised that Cardiff had 'the best example in this country'.[41] Swansea's councillors described their project as 'Civic Buildings' or a 'Civic Centre', until the title 'Guildhall' was transferred from the old building in 1934. Though theirs lacked the scale of Cathays Park, they undoubtedly sought to rival Cardiff, a competitor for trade and cultural status. Swansea's civic centre committee also toured town halls in England. They admired the clarity of planning of ceremonial and committee rooms around grand staircases at Edwin Cooper's neoclassical Marylebone Town Hall and E. W. Mountford's Edwardian Sheffield Town Hall, and advocated the 'Greek Theatre' arrangement of Nottingham's recent council chamber by T. Cecil Howitt. This tour also prompted the committee's insistence on facades of white Portland stone.[42] Swansea's councillors evidently wanted their building to excel within a British movement in municipal architecture.

The competition conditions suggested a contemporary classical approach. Portland stone implied this, as did requirements for elevations of 'a restrained and dignified manner', with 'good proportion and fitting architectural expression rather than ... elaborate decoration and detail'. Plans had to be 'straightforward and economical', although 'a Tower, or other dominating architectural feature' was recommended.[43] The complex brief including law courts, assembly hall, offices and ceremonial spaces were 'to form one architectural group', uniting all aspects as inherent to the council's purpose.[44]

Jones and Thomas defeated seventy architects to win the competition, including experts in the field such as Howitt.[45] The assessor H. V. Ashley chose Thomas's design for its efficient planning, but also because it expressed the council's aspirations. He had organised the complex around a large courtyard (whereas others had narrower courts or light wells), allowing all elements to be appreciated from one place, contributing to Ashley's view that the design formed 'one homogeneous group', although internal elevations were faced in yellow brick. The external elevations had 'an Architectural treatment expressing the Civic purpose of the undertaking'.[46] Thomas adopted a simplified Greek style, plain walls without cornices complemented by a richer Ionic order at important points, a pedimented portico for the main entrance under a pylon-like tower, and a colonnade across the assembly hall (see Figure 2.3). Critics agreed with Ashley, praising the building's division into distinct functional elements, each with its own massing and expression, yet all related through a shared architectural language, exceeding other schemes in clarity and coherence.[47]

While councillors were enthusiastic, the gathering economic depression gave political narratives around the building new purposes. One response to the depression advocated by Liberal and Labour politicians was state intervention to boost the economy, following John Maynard Keynes's principles. At the 1929 election, David Lloyd George advocated government schemes of public works to employ the manual labourers vulnerable to unemployment while investing in infrastructure.[48] Ramsay MacDonald won a minority Labour government on a similar campaign, and supercharged a fund administered by the Unemployment Grants Committee, inviting local authorities to apply for government grants towards projects of 'public utility' and 'economic development'.[49] For the first two years, buildings for municipal government were eligible, and many local authorities applied, though only 'strictly utilitarian' buildings were allowed, and applicants had to demonstrate 'substantial economy and improved efficiency in local government'.[50]

2.3 Swansea Guildhall, perspective of original competition design, *c.*1930 (West Glamorgan Archive Service; courtesy of the estate of Sir Percy Thomas).

Swansea was an early beneficiary of this scheme, after David Williams, MP for Swansea East and an alderman enthusiastic for the new building, encouraged the council to apply and exerted pressure within government.[51] The council argued that the new buildings would increase its efficiency, and that construction would relieve Swansea's severe unemployment.[52] Thomas advised the council on its case, quantifying the effect on local employment of the construction work and orders for building materials, and calculating the volume entitled to a grant.[53] The government awarded around a fifth of the Guildhall's cost in 1930, and its insistence on completion within three years ensured the council proceeded quickly.[54] The council featured this state support in newspapers and the souvenir booklet of the opening, framing Thomas's architecture with a political narrative.[55] This connection was also made at the ceremony: on his tour of council projects, the Duke of Kent visited its Unemployment Welfare Centre; and at the ceremony itself, the Bishop of Swansea and Brecon dedicated the building with a prayer for the unemployed.[56] The Guildhall was presented as having an active role in welfare, and its construction articulated as an act of welfare in its own right.

Thomas changed some aspects of the Guildhall from the competition design, apparently to enhance the building's expression of democracy and citizenship. Several critics questioned his Ionic portico: Reilly found it incongruous in a modern building without conventional mouldings, urging him to eliminate it.[57] This he did, replacing it with a rectangular pavilion pierced with a giant arch (see Figure 2.4).[58]

This improved space and light at the grand staircase leading to the council chamber and offices. But Thomas also suggested a symbolic purpose. Formerly, he noted, main entrances were reserved for ceremonial functions, but he commended a recent tendency towards everyday use: 'If the architecture is to have any effect

2.4 Swansea Guildhall, 1930–4, main entrance façade (photo: author).

upon the civic pride of the citizens', he said, 'the more they use the entrance hall and grand staircase the better'.[59] The arch perhaps symbolised this equality of citizens and council, the citizen's right of access to power and the state's dependency on the citizen. Visitors entering through the arch proceeded downwards to the rates hall, where there was also a public post office, or ascended the monumental barrel-vaulted stair to the municipal offices to meet officials. Thomas similarly revised the assembly hall elevation, defining its entrance with three great arches over a cascade of steps, perhaps influenced by Daniel H. Burnham's Union Station in Washington DC, whose arches suggested a gateway into the heart of American democracy.[60] The imagery of public access extended also to the Guildhall's landscaping, which dispensed with railings and flower beds in favour of plain, open lawns.[61]

Classical orders remained at key points inside to ennoble ceremonial spaces. Thomas imaginatively adapted the classical language to expressions of functional character, drawing on British neo-classical influences including Robert Adam, John Soane, Charles Cockerell and even Alexander Thomson, whom Thomas had long admired, in an approach that Reilly described as 'classic very freely handled, and unhampered by academic rules'.[62] Rich effects of colour also contributed to character with guidance from architectural illustrator William Walcot.[63] The council chamber was sombre and rich, panelled in wood, the seating surrounded by timber Ionic columns with gilded capitals based on the Greek Temple at Bassae, a skylight evoking a temple interior (see Figure 2.5). The assize hall was a cool barrel-vaulted public space subdivided by paired Doric columns in Portland stone (see Figure 2.6). Their entablatures were ingeniously designed as bridges carrying spectators into the public galleries of the two courts, so that ordinary people experienced this dramatic space from above.[64] Reilly

2.5 Swansea Guildhall, 1930–4, council chamber (photo: author).

2.6 Swansea Guildhall, 1930–4, assize hall preceding courtrooms (photo: author).

praised the assize hall as unusually solemn, with 'the right atmosphere for serious affairs'.[65] Meanwhile, the assembly hall and adjacent banqueting room adopted a freer, festive, more distinctly Art Deco classicism.

Throughout the building, iconography conveyed a notion of concentric rings of citizenship. Swansea's mercantilism was emphasised through ships' prows on the tower. The entrance hall took a Viking theme, the bronze handrails of the grand staircase formed into galleys, keystones over secondary stairs carved by Gilbert Seale & Son with the heads of 'Sweyn and his warriors', mythical founders of the town.[66] Over the building's subsidiary entrances were carved the borough's historical seals, and above office doors the arms of figures in Swansea's history.[67] Welsh national identity was celebrated throughout. A lunette relief in the assize hall depicted an ancient Welsh trial based on a medieval account.[68] The council chamber's tapestry frieze showed an imagined Celtic Gorsedd procession, adapting paintings by Grant Murray of Swansea Art School, and goats and leeks animated bronze heating grilles. Secondary entrances to the council suite had carved discs showing St David and a druid.[69] Henry Lewis, Professor of Welsh at University College, Swansea, advised on the symbolic programme.[70]

British elements formed an overall framework, as the Guildhall's Portland stone classicism allied the building with contemporary British civic architecture. The tower, mostly blank and with subtle entasis, emulated First World War memorials, especially Lutyens's Whitehall cenotaph. One reporter saw the Guildhall as symbolic of 'a new Britain' arising after the depression, its 'chaste, severe beauty' a model to other towns.[71] This Britishness also had imperial connotations, for a town claiming to be the empire's 'metallurgical metropolis'.[72] A condition of the government grant was to use materials from Britain and the empire, on which the council took advice from the Empire Marketing Board.[73] Panelling, floors and decorative features employed colonial hardwoods including Australian walnut, Indian laurel and Burmese teak.[74] Lustrously polished and prominently publicised, they evoked Swansea's participation in British imperial trade.

So too did Frank Brangwyn's paintings in the assembly hall (see Colour Plate 1). These were originally commissioned for the House of Lords as a memorial to the empire's role in the First World War, but the Royal Fine Art Commission rejected them, and Swansea applied to receive them instead.[75] Thomas adapted the assembly hall's proportions to accommodate the sixteen canvases and incorporated recesses so that they appeared flush with the walls and integral to the design, resembling murals as Brangwyn intended.[76] The paintings depict the diverse peoples of the empire in settings of luxuriant and exotic plant and animal life.[77] Races and species randomly combined to represent 'the unity of the Empire', they suggest a harmonious global paradise bursting with produce, without violence or politics.[78] Colonial intrusion is harmlessly present - a surveyor using a theodolite; a merchant carrying a carpet; a tree felled, destined perhaps for this building. Swansea's citizens gathering for events in the Brangwyn Hall, as it was named in 1934, were enveloped within this propagandistic Arcadian imperial vision, with images of contented white, Black and Asian British subjects in settings innocent of exploitation.

Swansea Guildhall thus reinforced an idea of the beneficent state as an apparently seamless entity, from the large scale of empire to the small scale of the town, administering law, welfare and edification. The building's architecture encouraged public democratic participation and belonging, so that citizens could feel part of the corporate body of the town, of Wales, and of the empire as a whole.

Just as Swansea Guildhall was being completed in 1934, Percy Thomas and Ernest Prestwich won the competition for Swinton and Pendlebury Town Hall with a design based closely on Swansea's eastern block, but more prosaically clad in brick with a plain neo-Georgian classicism increasingly prevalent by then for government buildings and even social housing (see Figure 2.7).[79] Economy and simplicity also defined its interiors: even the council chamber was 'severely simple', the architects wrote, and they pointed out that the council chamber ante-room's columns were of 'synthetic marble' (see Figure 2.8).[80] Swinton and Pendlebury town hall was meant to commence a civic centre, never built as planned, for which Thomas and Prestwich sketched plans grouping an assembly hall, library, police headquarters, law courts and medical centre alongside the town hall.[81] The Labour council's attitude to welfare and state intervention here mirrored Swansea's, and it chose Arthur Greenwood, former Labour Minister of Health, to open the building, the mayor praising his 1930 Housing Act that enabled the council to undertake slum clearances and build social housing.[82]

Tunbridge Wells Civic Centre, while similar in form, was markedly different in political atmosphere, with a Conservative MP, Robert Gower, also an alderman,

2.7 Swinton and Pendlebury Town Hall, 1934–8 (now Salford Civic Centre) (photo: author).

2.8 Swinton and Pendlebury Town Hall, 1934–8 (now Salford Civic Centre), ante-room to council chamber (photo: author).

2.9 Tunbridge Wells Civic Centre, 1934–41 (photo: author).

and most councillors supported by the Conservative Association.[83] Before the 1934 competition, debate raged in public over a design by Vincent Harris with giant Corinthian columns and elegant baroque details: some councillors condemned it along with excessive government spending, associating the building project with national debates about the role of the state. Gower, for example, argued that 'Unless the State and municipalities exercised the greatest possible economy the financial position of the country would shortly become most critical.'[84] Vocal opponents even stood successfully in council elections specifically to try to block the project from within the council.[85] 'Progressive' councillors promoting the building outnumbered their opponents, but accepted calls for economy, and used an architectural competition to seek consensus. Thomas and Prestwich's design of severe cubic brick blocks with repeated sash windows, only subtly relieved with stone details, looked reassuringly inexpensive and helped to assuage such political conflict (see Figure 2.9).[86] An entrance arch without a tower, set above street level and angled to the crossroads, made an economical landmark. The scheme included municipal offices and council suite, police station and law court, assembly hall, showrooms for the council's electricity department, a library and museum (eventually omitting a planned fire station and child welfare and maternity centre). It was opened in phases from 1939 to 1941.[87]

Compared to these three civic centres, Percy Thomas's other significant building for local government was strikingly eccentric. Carmarthenshire County Hall, designed in 1935, is best explained as a response to its extraordinary location, inside the walls of a ruined medieval castle atop a picturesque bastion overlooking the river Towy at the entrance to Carmarthen.[88] Thomas was told to use local stone, and design 'in harmony with the colour and simplicity of the architectural character of Carmarthen'.[89] The building also had to be 'in keeping' with the new bridge below it, which Clough Williams-Ellis designed as a modernised version of the medieval bridge due for demolition.[90] The County Hall's elevations used rusticated brown Forest of Dean sandstone complementing the castle walls; a steep roof rose over corner turrets; tall chimneys and mullioned casement windows suggested a baronial keep (see Figure 2.10). The only significant interior space, the council chamber, which doubled as an assize court, sat between two courtyards, its jauntily painted neo-Tudor ceiling completed in 1955 after wartime delays (see Colour Plate 2).[91]

The building romantically suggested a historical ancestry for the county council, with painted heraldic shields gracing the council chamber.[92] Carmarthenshire County Council was a modern institution, however, founded like other county councils after the 1888 Local Government Act, and responsible for roads and bridges and vehicle licensing, education, aspects of public health, and, increasingly, benefits and housing.[93] David Evans carved relief sculptures around the entrance to Thomas's building depicting these activities, including a motor car, a marriage register, medical implements, and hands receiving coins (see Figure 2.11). Significant increases in these duties required new office space; the eighteenth-century town hall was inadequate, and several offices were in other towns.[94] Thomas persuaded the council to continue with the site for its

2.10 Carmarthenshire County Hall, Carmarthen, 1936–46 (photo: author).

2.11 Carmarthenshire County Hall, Carmarthen, 1936–46, entrance sculpture by David Evans (photo: author).

beauty, even though its constraints prevented the inclusion of a police station, library and museum.[95] Perched at the town's summit commanding the river and commercial centre, his building transformed Carmarthen's image, defining its character by the weighty presence of local government.

Less distinctive and prominent was Jones and Thomas's extension to Vincent Harris's Glamorgan County Hall in Cardiff Civic Centre, consisting of offices around a courtyard. This building, larger than Harris's, accommodated the county's vastly increased staff since County Hall was opened two decades before. It was built rapidly from 1931 to 1932 to access the government's unemployment grant, though the eastern wing was postponed until the 1950s.[96] Despite its straightforward bureaucratic function, Thomas designed it to complement the Civic Centre, facing its steel frame in Portland stone with chunky Renaissance detailing following the proportions of County Hall's rear elevation.[97]

Civic Services: Police and Fire Stations

Tunbridge Wells Civic Centre demonstrates the importance of police and fire stations to councils, designed as intrinsic aspects of this local government complex. One of few sculptural elements at Tunbridge Wells, by Gilbert Seale & Son probably to Thomas's

2.12 Tunbridge Wells Civic Centre, 1934–41, sculpture over police station by Gilbert Seale & Son (photo: author).

design, adorns the police station: the seated figure of Law regards the viewer like a judge, attended by Justice and a beard-stroking Government; a water carrier symbolises the town (see Figure 2.12).[98] Police and fire services were run by municipal councils, which wanted the public to appreciate their role. The police often participated in civic events: Swansea's Police Orchestral Band played at the Guildhall opening ceremony, for example.[99] Central government, the Home Office, took ultimate responsibility for police forces, however, inspecting facilities, checking building plans and subsidising improvements.

Percy Thomas built three combined police and fire stations. Those at Bristol and Accrington were won through competitions of 1924 and 1930, and at Worcester he was commissioned in 1936, apparently recommended by the Home Office.[100] His architecture and its surrounding political discourse maintained similar themes to civic centres, articulating these services as welfare activities, while accommodating complex functions. New fire stations were often needed in the twentieth century for new motorised fire engines, and incorporated other technologies to improve the service. Their modernity was celebrated, and indicated with a stark, simplified classical architecture, a contrast to the highly decorated police and fire stations of previous generations, and harmonising with other civic architecture.[101]

The Bristol Police and Fire Station, opened in 1930, was Jones and Thomas's first major public building outside Wales (see Figures 2.13 and 2.14). Their plan best satisfied the complex functional demands on an awkward site incorporating a Victorian magistrates' court and other buildings.[102] The assessors praised their elevations as 'scholarly and refined' while expressive of function, their 'neo-Grec' style varying around the block.[103] The fire station's tall engine house doors, stepped lintels and dividing piers

2.13 Bristol Police Station, 1924–9 (photo: author).

2.14 Bristol Fire Station, 1924–30 (photo: author).

gave a monumental feel through simple means, while a corner rotunda with heraldic device signalled its presence. The fire and police station was a major civic development for Bristol's council, motivated by pressure from central government, which granted half the cost of the police buildings.[104] Most significantly, the police station's parade room allowed the force to gather as a corporate body for the first time.[105] Fire service improvements were council funded, and included modern flats for firemen and technology allowing faster response times, with centralised control of alarms, lights and doors.[106] Thomas's architecture accommodated this modern technology within an architecture of civic nobility connecting it to the wider work of the state.

Accrington's fire and police station and magistrates' court, opened in 1935, used similar technology, its fire engines even starting automatically, enabling crews to depart forty seconds after a call.[107] Firemen's welfare was also important, with twelve houses for staff. The buildings' civic quality is evident in the stripped neo-Georgian approach used at Bristol - even the fire station's hose-drying tower forms a classical landmark with a temple pediment (see Figure 2.15).[108] Councillors insisted on using stone despite its cost, resisting calls to use brick to support the famous local industry in the depression, because they considered stone to give qualities of 'nobleness', 'grandeur' and 'beauty' appropriate to a public building that should be 'a credit to the citizens of a town'.[109] At the opening ceremony in 1935, alderman Thomas Higham described the buildings as 'the beginning of the new Accrington', and later that year the council sought Thomas's advice on further civic buildings and a planning scheme.[110]

In contrast, Percy Thomas designed the fire and police stations and courts at Worcester in brick (see Figure 2.16), but here the material derived from the historic and civic context: the site was behind the city's early eighteenth-century red-brick baroque

2.15 Accrington Police and Fire Stations, 1930–5 (photo: author).

2.16 Worcester Police Headquarters and Fire Station, 1935–43 (photo: author).

Guildhall, and brick was Worcester's customary building material. Explaining his simplified neo-Georgian elevations, Thomas said they were designed 'in harmony with the Guildhall'; and the police station's roof lantern echoes that of its historic neighbour.[111] Nevertheless the council expropriated and demolished many old houses and shops on the site to create a new, wide road through the city centre onto which Thomas's buildings faced, allowing fire engines rapid egress from the centre, a modernity of intervention in the city that Thomas's architecture helped to ennoble as a civic project continuous with Worcester's history.[112]

The mayor, William Moore Ede, explained at the foundation stone ceremony in 1939 that the project demonstrated the council's progressivism 'in slum clearance and other modern improvements'. The Archbishop of Canterbury Cosmo Lang, coincidentally visiting, laid the stone, and extolled British democracy and the constitutional relationship of church and state.[113] At the police station opening in 1941, the police chaplain dedicated it as a 'hall of justice, of mercy, and of service'.[114] Such comments emphasising an active and beneficent role for the state, its democratic nature and national character, reveal the attitudes of Thomas's clients and the values he sought to embody.

Competitions and Plans

Competitions were Thomas's route to success since his apprenticeship, and he ardently supported the competition system.[115] Most large civic schemes in the period used competitions, as councillors sought the best possible designs for prestigious buildings. The RIBA nominated assessors and oversaw competition regulations, supplying local government with a service to promote good design. As RIBA president, previously on the Institute's Competitions Committee, Thomas contributed to this approach, arguing that competitions democratised the profession, allowing young architects to obtain work through talent rather than contacts. Furthermore, they served the national interest, he thought, by improving the overall quality of design.[116] On important later occasions, assessing competitions for the Trades Union Congress building in London in 1947 and Coventry Cathedral in 1951, Thomas selected modern designs from younger architects, suggesting an undogmatic and generous attitude. Competitions wasted much labour on failed entries and dissenting clients, turning some against them.[117] Thomas had many disappointments; but architectural journals published commended entries, helping to raise his profile. These creative exercises often stimulated his subsequent work and give further insights into his approaches to civic architecture.

Early in his career in 1913, Thomas entered a competition with Jones and Prestwich for the Board of Trade offices at Whitehall overlooking the Thames, a project that brought them attention among architects and a design approach that they developed elsewhere. Vincent Harris won the competition, though his project was shelved due to the war.[118] Most entrants adopted a baroque classicism to articulate the bulk of the building and appeal to the assessors, but Thomas, Prestwich and Jones were unusual among finalists in incorporating no orders or vertical motifs across storeys on the river elevation other than rusticated quoins, and on the Whitehall frontage only a two-storey rusticated arch (see Figure 2.17). Their design had a pronounced horizontality and severity compared to others. Banded rustication, a deep cornice and recessed attic gave subtle articulation to otherwise boxy elevations eschewing columns or pilasters. Reilly thought the river elevation's 'massiveness and strength ... remarkable for 1913'; critics praised its 'commendable restraint', expressing the building's bureaucratic function.[119] It closely resembled the Cunard building in Liverpool, then being designed, and may even have influenced it.[120] Both borrowed the modernity of American Beaux-Arts architecture, combined with the imperial connotations of Portland stone baroque deemed apt for buildings administering aspects of international trade.

2.17 Board of Trade Offices, London, competition design elevation of 1915 by Percy Thomas, Ernest Prestwich and Ivor Jones (source: *The Builder*, 12 February 1915; courtesy of the estate of Sir Percy Thomas).

In 1925 Thomas used a very similar style for his shortlisted entry for the Masonic Peace Memorial building near Covent Garden.[121] He and Prestwich adopted this severe baroque approach for their second-placed entry for the Birmingham municipal buildings competition of 1935, for an extension of council offices in the newly created civic square west of the Town Hall, in what one critic thought was the 'most monumental' of the commended designs, though they lost to Howitt.[122] The only built application of this approach was for the Glamorgan County Hall extension in Cardiff, where it suited the context of Harris's neo-baroque building.

Thomas and Jones came second in the competition for the Westgate Street fire station in Cardiff in 1912, losing to Harris, but their design seems never to have been published.[123] Following their success in Bristol, they also won the competition for a combined fire station, police station and courts at Newcastle-upon-Tyne. This would have occupied a substantial city block with four storeys of rusticated neoclassical elevations; but after delays and a change of site, the council commissioned a local firm instead.[124] Other notable competition misses, all with Prestwich, included those for the RIBA headquarters building at Portland Place of 1932, placed third with an urbanely reticent neo-Georgian design; Hornsey Town Hall of 1933; Bury Town Hall and Bolton Technical College in 1935, the latter Thomas's first to adopt a more overtly modern style with long horizontal windows and an Art Deco entrance section.[125]

The Second World War ended several important schemes at an early stage, including two significant projects in London. One of these was a scheme for Kensington Borough Council from 1937 to extend and refurbish its Victorian town hall, to build eight storeys of new offices alongside it to replace the former vestry hall and adding a central library nearby.[126] Thomas exhibited his library design, closely resembling Tunbridge Wells Civic Centre, at the Royal Academy in 1939; but after the war the council changed the site and architect, giving the job to Harris.[127] These unbuilt projects demonstrate the nationwide scale of Thomas's ambition; the persistence of classical themes in varied modes, often reworked across different projects; and a repeated concern with the planning of coherent municipal schemes.

The Temple of Peace

The Welsh National Temple of Peace and Health in Cardiff Civic Centre (see Figure 2.18) summarises the interwar politics of citizenship and the state, while also presaging the long-term transformations to follow the Second World War. Its main function was the administration of healthcare, as the headquarters of the King Edward VII Welsh National Memorial Association, typifying the interwar mixed economy combining local and national state welfare with philanthropy. To this were added offices and a hall for the Welsh League of Nations Union, which promoted international democratic citizenship through education and campaigns for world peace. The building related these two aims of peace and health to the First World War as the inspiration for social and political change. Behind both organisations was Liberal politician and philanthropist David Davies of Llandinam. He was president, co-founder in 1911 and sponsor of the Memorial Association; vice-president of the Welsh League of Nations Union, which he

2.18 Welsh National Temple of Peace and Health, Cardiff, 1936–8 (photo: author).

founded as an offshoot of the British League of Nations Union in 1922; and he became Thomas's client for the Temple of Peace.

The Memorial Association aimed to treat and eliminate tuberculosis throughout Wales, in partnership with the state. The 1921 Public Health (Tuberculosis) Act charged the Memorial Association officially with that role in Wales on councils' behalf, so that it could proudly describe itself as 'a rate-aided and State-aided concern'.[128] This fact convinced Davies that the Temple of Peace should obtain the same unemployment subsidy as municipal buildings. The Association's secretary F. J. Alban argued that a 'National Building in Cathays Park, Cardiff ... would be an architectural asset belonging to the whole nation - in the creation of which the State, the Cardiff City Council, the Welsh Local Authorities, and private benevolence would all have played a part'; though a grant was ultimately refused.[129] Nevertheless, Davies and his colleagues wanted the building to express an authoritative, quasi-official status. While the Association built the first tuberculosis sanatorium in Wales at Sully in a modernist style with white-painted flat-roofed wards and big windows evoking a modern scientific rationalism, the Temple of Peace had to convey a wider range of ideas, including connections to the Welsh League of Nations Union.[130]

The Union campaigned for world peace through international cooperation, supporting the League of Nations, organising conferences and lectures on international affairs throughout Wales, popular activities including a children's radio message to the world, and teacher and student visits to the League of Nations headquarters in Geneva.[131] Educational activities included advice to schools on 'civics', with lesson plans exploring the interconnectedness of communities, towns and nations, levels of government, and international cooperation.[132] The Union's international concept of citizenship opposed the narrow nationalisms of European dictatorships while maintaining Welsh national identity.[133] Davies hoped the architecture could express this internationalist vision. 'National character is expressed in institutions', he wrote, 'institutions represent ideas; ideas may mature ... into State and semi-State institutions; architecture may become the visible symbol of ideas and aspirations, expressing the character of institutions and, therefore, indirectly, of the nation itself'. The Temple of Peace, therefore, ought to express 'our national character in its aspirations for international peace and the eradication of the scourge of tuberculosis from our country'.[134]

Both the Association and the Union, however, experienced uncertainties over their purposes. The cause of peace looked hopeless by the late 1930s with the rise of fascist powers.[135] Local authorities questioned the Memorial Association's absorption of their health budgets, and a Ministry of Health inquiry into tuberculosis in Wales later recommended reducing the Association's powers.[136] Thomas's reassuring neoclassical building could help bolster these causes against such doubts, evoking an image of authority and permanence. The building was also a war memorial, complementing J. Ninian Comper's nearby Welsh National War Memorial, unveiled in 1928: Davies offered a space for the Book of Remembrance containing the name of every Welsh soldier killed in the First World War, a page turned every day, honoured at Cardiff's Remembrance Day service. The Temple of Peace would give it suitable surroundings, and thereby symbolically associate the memory of war with the activities of the Association and the Union promoting peace and health.

Davies approached Percy Thomas in 1929, by which time the city council had already agreed to locate the Temple of Peace in the Civic Centre, offering it a plot. Initially it earmarked a prominent site axially north of Queen Alexandra Gardens, a location that would have strengthened the Temple's link to Comper's war memorial, and Thomas may have designed the building for that position.[137] During delays, however, the council awarded the site to the Welsh Board of Health, relegating the Temple of Peace to a subsidiary position beside the Technical College.[138]

Thomas's initial design of 1931 included a Greek Ionic classical temple front flanked by office wings (see Figure 2.19). This order, Thomas argued, 'marked the summit of attainment in the Arts of Peace by the Ancient Greeks'.[139] The design resembles Arnold Thornely's Northern Ireland Parliament building at Stormont, completed later that year, another civic building embodying national identity within the British state.[140] In Thomas's first design, the hall – later sometimes called the 'Hall of Nations' – was to have aisles formed of giant Ionic columns based on the Erechtheion, made of black marble and bronze, with a sculptural frieze, and would be crowded with statues celebrating 'famous men who have done most for the cause of Peace'. At the far end, Thomas suggested a 'symbolical statue of Peace' like a classical temple god. The Book of Remembrance was to be placed in the crypt below the hall, and on the first floor over the vestibule a double-height galleried top-lit meeting room would serve as a 'Council Chamber' and library for the two organisations. A model was commissioned and exhibited in City Hall.[141]

Thomas radically simplified the scheme around 1936, largely to reduce its cost, removing most of its ornamentation. The portico lost its pediment, and the columns became square piers under a solid entablature. While black marble was

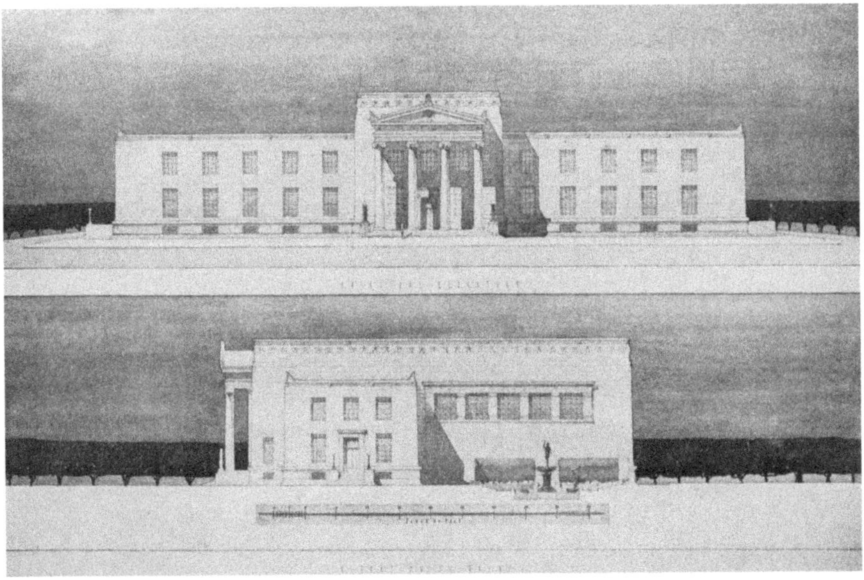

2.19 Welsh National Temple of Peace and Health, Cardiff, design elevations of 1930 by Percy Thomas (source: *The Builder*, 9 January 1931; courtesy of the estate of Sir Percy Thomas).

adopted in the hall as intended, the columns became square fluted piers without capitals (see Colour Plate 3), and the council chamber lost its upper storey.[142] These changes parallel Thomas's elimination of classical details at Swansea Guildhall, and show his engagement with contemporary architecture, but also had relevant symbolic meanings. Paul Cret's Federal Reserve Board building in Washington DC could have influenced Thomas's design changes, as its design was published in 1935, and Thomas visited Washington on a tour of America in 1936, when Cret's building was under construction.[143] A simplified, astylar classicism was then often adopted in civic buildings in Britain, such as E. Berry Webber's Dagenham Civic Centre and P. D. Hepworth's Walthamstow Town Hall. Such buildings showed how modernity could be evoked by simplified forms, while maintaining the civic associations of classicism, 'a modern adaptation of the classic', as Thomas wrote.[144] In a speech after the Temple of Peace's opening ceremony, Davies highlighted an even more relevant precedent: the Palais des Nations housing the League of Nations in Geneva, built by a team of architects from 1929 to 1938.[145] This building also used simplified layers of planes in white stone to suggest classical forms.

The theme of international harmony suggested the diversity of materials inside the Temple of Peace, explained at the opening day, with stone from across Europe, including, pointedly, Italy and Germany, and wood from Austria, Russia and British colonies.[146] The Temple of Peace also evoked the British union, discs on its portico depicting the arms of the four nations.[147] Proposing a toast to Wales and its people following the opening ceremony, Professor Gilbert Murray of the League of Nations Union praised Wales's 'great' but not extremist 'national consciousness'.[148] Davies argued that 'national sovereignties can be merged into a United Federal Sovereignty' in the cause of peace.[149] But this Liberal view could coexist with national expression, strongly evoked in the crypt, with symbols of Welsh counties in its frieze.

Besides symbolic and functional purposes, the Temple of Peace suited solemn events, beginning with its elaborate opening ceremony. Davies designed this occasion to encapsulate his philosophy. He sought an ordinary citizen to open the building, finding Minnie James of Dowlais, whose three sons had died in the First World War, who accepted on behalf of 'the mothers of Wales'.[150] She dedicated the building to the memory of those of all nations lost in the war.[151] James and women representing different nations processed through the hall and read statements from the platform. Llandaff Cathedral choir sang hymns; Anglican, Nonconformist and Jewish leaders gave readings and prayers; Welsh and British national anthems were sung.[152]

Later that day, Davies urged Welsh people to 'visit the building on a pilgrimage'.[153] Thousands of people did so on organised trips throughout the Second World War, holding ceremonies of dedication following an order of service written by Davies's sisters Gwendoline and Margaret Davies.[154] After the war the United Nations Association replaced the Union and continued its work in the Temple, while the Welsh National Memorial Association was absorbed into the National Health Service (NHS), and the Temple of Peace became the headquarters of the Welsh Hospital Board.[155] The Association had in a limited way, for Wales and for one medical purpose, sought to offer a free, universal service with state funding; and in the post-war welfare state in which the NHS became one part of a comprehensive national plan of welfare, Percy Thomas and his practice would continue to play a significant role. ■

02

Modern Classicism and Municipal Democracy

References

1. Colin Cunningham, *Victorian and Edwardian Town Halls* (London: Routledge & Kegan Paul, 1981), for example, pp. 55-7, 89, 215-16.
2. David Marquand, *Decline of the Public: The Hollowing-Out of Citizenship* (Cambridge: Polity Press, 2004), pp. 52-3.
3. Jose Harris, 'Political Thought and the Welfare State 1870-1940: An Intellectual Framework for British Social Policy', in David Gladstone (ed.), *Before Beveridge: Welfare Before the Welfare State* (London: Institute of Economic Affairs, 1999), pp. 43-63; Elizabeth Darling, *Re-Forming Britain: Narratives of Modernity Before Reconstruction* (London: Routledge, 2007), p. 23; Tom Hulme, *After the Shock City: Urban Culture and the Making of Modern Citizenship* (Woodbridge: Royal Historical Society and The Boydell Press, 2019), for example, pp. 77, 100.
4. Bernard Harris, *The Origins of the British Welfare State: Society, State and Social Welfare* (Basingstoke: Palgrave Macmillan, 2004), for example, p. 113.
5. Jane Lewis, 'The Voluntary Sector in the Mixed Economy', and Noel Whiteside, 'Private Provision and Public Welfare: Health Insurance Between the Wars', in Gladstone (ed.), *Before Beveridge*, pp. 10-17 and 26-42, respectively.
6. Neil Evans, 'The Welsh Victorian City: The Middle Class and Civic and National Consciousness in Cardiff, 1850-1914', *Welsh History Review*, 12 (1984), 350-87; John B. Hilling, *The History and Architecture of Cardiff Civic Centre: Black Gold, White City* (Cardiff: University of Wales Press, 2016), pp. 57-8, 83.
7. Percy Thomas, 'The Planning of Municipal Buildings', *Architect & Building News*, 15 February 1935, pp. 217-18 (218); also A. Calveley Cotton, *Town Halls* (London: Architectural Press, 1936), pp. 12, 29.
8. Harris, 'Political Thought', pp. 56-7.
9. Cotton, *Town Halls*, pp. 18-19, 21-2; N. E. Shasore, 'Southampton Civic Centre: Patronage and Place in the Interwar Architecture of Public Service', and Johanna Roethe, '"A Pretty Toy" or "Purely Functional"? Town, City and County Halls in the Interwar Period', *Twentieth Century Architecture*, 13 'The Architecture of Public Service' (2018), 41-61 (58) and 25-39, respectively.
10. Elizabeth Darling and Alistair Fair, '"The Core": The Centre as a Concept in Twentieth-Century British Planning and Architecture, Part One: The Emergence of the Idea', *Planning Perspectives*, 38/1 (2023), 69-98.
11. Percy Thomas, 'The Planning of Municipal Buildings', *Journal of the Royal Institute of British Architects*, 23 February 1935, pp. 469-87 (469).
12. 'Town Halls: Practical Notes on Design and Planning', in Percy E. Thomas (ed.), *Modern Building Practice*, vol. 1 (London: George Newnes Ltd, 1935), pp. 33-48

(34-9); the essay includes passages from various sources, probably by Charles Reilly.

13. Hulme, *After the Shock City*, pp. 136-8, 150-3.

14. William Jones Pate, *The History of the YMCA in Wales, 1852-1972* (The Welsh National Council of YMCAs, 1981), pp. 2-4; 11-13; 24.

15. Pate, *YMCA in Wales*, pp. 24-5.

16. 'Our YMCA', *Pontypridd Observer*, 5 October 1907, p. 6.

17. 'YMCA Merthyr', *Building News and Engineering Journal*, 9 April 1909, p. 541; Edward Holland, *YMCA, Pontmorlais, Merthyr Tydfil: Conservation Statement* (Abergavenny: Cambrian Heritage Regeneration Trust, February 2016).

18. Arthur Young, 'Correspondence: Merthyr YMCA', *Merthyr Express*, 26 February 1910, p. 10; 'Loved His Fellows: Late Col. Lewis and Merthyr YMCA', *Merthyr Express*, 23 May 1914, p. 11.

19. 'Merthyr & District YMCA: Annual Report, 1913-14', *Merthyr Express*, 5 December 1914, p. 10; 'A Tea', *Merthyr Express*, 19 December 1914, p. 9; 'Weekly Meeting', *Merthyr Express*, 1 November 1913, p. 7.

20. 'Merthyr YMCA: Members Entertained', *Merthyr Express*, 19 October 1912, p. 10.

21. Harris, *Origins of the British Welfare State*, p. 156.

22. Hilling, *Cardiff Civic Centre*, pp. 93-4, 134, 182-4.

23. Alexander Harvey, 'One Hundred Years of Technical Education in Cardiff', *Glamorgan Historian*, 9 (1973), 173-90 (175-7); Cardiff University Special Collections and Archives (CUSCA), 103/1, Charles Coles, *Draft of Paper to Be Read at the Summer Meeting, June 28th and 29th, 1928 on 'The Development of Technical Education in Cardiff'* (Loughborough: Association of Technical Institutions, 1928).

24. CUSCA, 103/1, Charles Coles, *Report on the Reorganisation of Technical Education in Cardiff* (Cardiff: Cardiff Education Committee, 1908).

25. Harvey, 'One Hundred Years', p. 179.

26. 'Cardiff's Example: Opening of Technical College', *Western Mail*, 14 March 1916, p. 7.

27. 'Current Architecture: The Cardiff Technical Institute', *Architectural Review*, May 1916, pp. 105-10 (107-8).

28. 'Cardiff Technical Institute Competition', *The Builder*, 22 December 1911, pp. 737-41.

29. 'Current Architecture: The Cardiff Technical Institute', *Architectural Review*, May 1916, pp. 105-10 (105); W. S. Purchon, 'The Public Buildings of Cardiff', *RIBA Journal*, 6 May 1922, pp. 385-95 (390); Percy Thomas, 'The Architecture of Cardiff', in Christopher J. Evans (ed.), *The Book of Cardiff: Presented to the Delegates at the Annual Conference of the National Association of Head Teachers* (London: Oxford University Press, 1937), pp. 72-9 (75).

30. Alan Powers, 'British Architecture Before the Great War', *Architectural Review*, 11 November 2014, *www.architectural-review.com/places/united-kingdom/part-one-british-architecture-before-the-great-war* (accessed 25 May 2021).

31. Hilling, *Cardiff Civic Centre*, p. 135; CUSCA, 103/1, Coles, *Draft of Paper*, pp. 2, 4 and Ministry of Education, *Report by H.M. Inspectors on Cardiff College of Technology and Commerce* (London, 1951), p. 7; 'Cardiff Technical College Completed from the Designs of Ivor Jones and Percy Thomas', *Architects' Journal*, 28 September 1932, pp. 401–3.

32. W. J. Williams, 'Education in Cardiff', in Evans (ed.), *The Book of Cardiff*, pp. 108–17 (115–16).

33. For more detail on this and the following section, see Robert Proctor, 'Citizenship: Welfare and the Democratic State in Percy Thomas's Civic Architecture', in Neal Shasore and Jessica Kelly (eds), *Reconstruction: Architecture, Society and the Aftermath of the First World War* (London: Bloomsbury, 2023), pp. 267–94.

34. West Glamorgan Archive Service, Swansea (WGAS), D 97/15, Mayor to W. D. Rees, 6 April 1925; WGAS, TC 2/7, Swansea Council, 15 April 1931.

35. E. E. M. [Ernest Morgan], 'Architectural Features of Swansea', in *Souvenir of the Opening of the Guildhall, Swansea* (Swansea: Swansea Borough Council, 1934), pp. 31–6.

36. J. R. Alban, 'Preface', in J. R. Alban (ed.), *The Guildhall, Swansea: Essays to Commemorate the Fiftieth Anniversary of Its Opening* (Swansea: Swansea City Council, 1984), pp. vii–viii (vii); H. L. Lang-Coath, 'Swansea Municipal Government', and Ernest E. Morgan, 'The Story of Swansea Told in Its Architecture', *South Wales Evening Post*, 23 October 1934, Guildhall supplement, pp. 25 and 22, respectively; 'Swansea's New Guildhall Opened', *Municipal Review*, 26 October 1934, pp. 1457–8.

37. Advertisement for Turner & Sons, *South Wales Evening Post*, 23 October 1934, Guildhall supplement, p. 19.

38. WGAS, BA 2/15, 'County Borough of Swansea: Opening of New Guildhall, Tuesday, October 23rd, 1934, by HRH The Duke of Kent; Programme of Proceedings', p. 3.

39. David Matthews, 'Story of the Great Scheme: How an Ideal of 1903 Was Realised', *South Wales Evening Post*, 23 October 1934, Guildhall supplement, p. 18; WGAS, TC 53/9097/4, Parliamentary and General Purposes Committee, 25 September 1933; WGAS, PL 301/1, post-war reconstruction drawing, n.d.

40. D. J. Davies, 'The Labour Party and the Future of Swansea', *South Wales Evening Post*, 23 October 1934, Guildhall supplement, p. 16.

41. WGAS, TC 53/9097/2, MacAlister to Ernest E. Morgan, 12 March 1929.

42. WGAS, BA 2/15, 'Report on Visit of the Sub-Committee of the Parliamentary and General Purposes Committee to Various Civic Centres', April 1929.

43. WGAS, BA 2/15, competition conditions, July 1929.

44. WGAS, BA 2/15, H. L. Lang Coath (Town Clerk) and H. V. Ashley, response to competitors' questions, September 1929.

45. WGAS, TC 53/9097/3, list of competitors, n.d. [1929].

46. WGAS, TC 53/9097/1, Ashley to Parliamentary and General Purposes Committee, 17 February 1930.

47. 'Swansea Civic Centre Competition: The Winning Design by Ivor Jones and Percy Thomas', *Architects' Journal*, 26 February 1930, pp. 360–3; W. S. Purchon, 'Swansea Civic Buildings Competition', *The Builder*, 28 February 1930, pp. 429–30.

48. David Lloyd George, *We Can Conquer Unemployment* (London: Cassell & Company, 1929).

49. Martin Pugh, *State and Society: A Social and Political History of Britain, 1870–1997* (London: Arnold, 2003), pp. 208–9; James E. Cronin, *The Politics of State Expansion: War, State and Society in Twentieth-Century Britain* (London: Routledge, 1991), pp. 119–21; 'Unemployment Relief Schemes: Concessions Granted by the Government', *Municipal Review*, July 1930, pp. 257–8; 'Unemployment Grants: Report of Committee', *Municipal Review*, January 1931, p. 13.

50. The National Archives, London (TNA), LAB 4/194, 'Unemployment Grants Committee: Grants in Aid of the Erection of Town Halls', May 1930; TNA, LAB 4/194, J. A. N. Barlow to E. H. Rhodes (Ministry of Health), 1 May 1931 and G. H. Ince to H. D. Hancock (Treasury), 6 May 1931; 'Unemployment Grants Committee', *Municipal Review*, April 1932, p. 148; Roethe, '"A Pretty Toy"', p. 27.

51. W. C. Rogers, 'The Guildhall and Local Government in Swansea', in Alban (ed.), *The Guildhall, Swansea*, pp. 13–32 (14); Edward Harris, untitled essay in *Souvenir of the Opening of the Guildhall*, pp. 2–4 (3); WGAS, TC 53/9097/3, David Williams to Lang-Coath, 26 March 1930; TNA, LAB 4/258, GWI to Hetherington (Ministry of Health), 8 October 1930.

52. WGAS, D 266/1/4/4, 'Proposed New Civic Buildings; Application for Grant Towards Cost of Scheme', n.d. [c. March 1930].

53. WGAS, TC 53/8891/2, note of telephone message from Percy Thomas, n.d. [c. April 1930]; WGAS, TC 53/9097/1, [Lang-Coath] to Ivor Jones & Percy Thomas, 4 May 1931 and Thomas to Lang-Coath, 7 May 1931.

54. Matthews, 'Story of the Great Scheme'; TNA, LAB 4/258, various correspondence; WGAS, TC 53/8891/2, 'New Municipal Buildings: Notes on Notice of Motion of Alderman G. Arbour Stephens to defer the inviting of Tenders for 2 Years; Council of 18th March, 1931'; WGAS, TC 53/9097/1, Thomas to Lang-Coath, 20 March 1931.

55. 'Magnificence of the New Guildhall', *South Wales Evening Post*, 23 October 1934, Guildhall supplement, pp. 19, 21 (19); Harris, untitled essay in *Souvenir of the Opening of the Guildhall*, pp. 2–4 (3).

56. WGAS, BA 2/15, 'Opening of New Guildhall: ... Programme of Proceedings', pp. 3, 8.

57. 'Swansea Civic Centre Competition: The Winning Design by Ivor Jones and Percy Thomas', *Architects' Journal*, 26 February 1930, pp. 360–3 (361); Charles Reilly, 'Some Younger Architects of Today: Percy Thomas', *Building*, February 1931, pp. 60–5 (64); Charles Reilly, 'Expression in Municipal Architecture Today', *Building*, April 1931, pp. 158–65 (165).

58. WGAS, TC 53/9097/4, 'Parliamentary 16 June 1931', extract from the Parliamentary and General Purposes Committee, suggests date for approval of alteration.

59. Thomas, 'Planning of Municipal Buildings', p. 470.

60. WGAS, TC 53/9097/4, Civic Centre Sub-Committee of the Parliamentary and General Purposes Committee, 18 February 1932; 'Societies and Institutions', *Architects' Journal*, 19 October 1932, pp. 505–6 (506); 'Swansea Civic Centre', *The Builder*, 9 June 1933, p. 924.

61. 'Preparing the Setting for Swansea's Civic Centre', *South Wales Evening Post*, 31 October 1933, p. 8.

62. Reilly, 'Percy Thomas', p. 65; 'The Conference Banquet', *Architects' Journal*, 27 June 1935, p. 983.

63. 'Swansea', *The Builder*, 19 October 1934, p. 675; 'The New Guildhall, Swansea', *Architect & Building News*, 19 October 1934, pp. 67–74.

64. 'The Guildhall, Swansea: Designed by Percy Thomas', *Architects' Journal*, 11 October 1934, pp. 522–7 (526); 'The Guildhall, Swansea', *Journal of the Royal Institute of British Architects*, 23 February 1935, pp. 488–99 (496).

65. C. H. Reilly, 'The Year's Work', *Architects' Journal*, 10 January 1935, pp. 69–76 (75); Charles Reilly, 'Percy Thomas', p. 62.

66. WGAS, BA 2/1, 'Guildhall - Swansea: An Architectural Description', April 1940; I. J. Campbell, 'An Architectural Appreciation of the Guildhall', in Alban (ed.), *The Guildhall, Swansea*, pp. 33–53 (43).

67. 'Magnificence of the New Guildhall', p. 21; WGAS, 2/1, Ernest E. Morgan, 'Heraldic Shields in Grand Corridor, Guildhall, Swansea', March 1936.

68. Hilary Woolley, 'Art and Design in the Guildhall', in Alban (ed.), *The Guildhall, Swansea*, pp. 85–108 (86).

69. Campbell, 'Architectural Appreciation', p. 45; WGAS, BA 2/1, 'Guildhall - Swansea: An Architectural Description', April 1940.

70. 'Magnificence of the New Guildhall', p. 21.

71. 'Our Great Day', *South Wales Evening Post* (Swansea), 23 October 1934, p. 8.

72. 'Civic Administration: New Headquarters for Swansea, Camberwell and Hackney', *Municipal Review*, November 1934, pp. 423–6 (423).

73. 'Magnificence of the New Guildhall', p. 19; WGAS, TC 53/9097/3, J. H. Thomas (Empire Marketing Board) to Mayor of Swansea, 11 August 1930 and Town Clerk to J. H. Thomas, 19 September 1930.

74. 'The New Guildhall, Swansea', *Architect & Building News*, 19 October 1934, pp. 67–74 (70); 'The Civic Centre at Swansea', *Official Architect*, December 1937, pp. 100–3 (101–2); advertisement for Burma Teak, *Architectural Review*, May 1940, p. xxiii.

75. Rogers, 'The Guildhall and Local Government', pp. 15–16; H. L. L.-C. [Lang-Coath], 'The British Empire Panels', in *Souvenir of the Opening of the Guildhall Swansea*, pp. 24–30.

76. 'Swansea Civic Centre', *The Builder*, 26 October 1934, p. 702; Matthews, 'Story of the Great Scheme'.

77. Woolley, 'Art and Design in the Guildhall', pp. 90–1.

78. Frank Rutter, *The British Empire Panels Designed for the House of Lords by Frank Brangwyn RA* (Benfleet: F. Lewis, 1933), pp. 23–4.

79. E. & O. E., 'Competition for Municipal Offices for Swinton and Pendlebury U.D.C.', *Architect & Building News*, 1 June 1934, pp. 246–7; 'Swinton and Pendlebury Competition', *Architects' Journal*, 20 September 1934, pp. 421–2; 'Swinton and Pendlebury Municipal Buildings Competition', *The Builder*, 14 September 1934, supplement; on the style, Alan Powers, 'The Architecture of Public Service', *Twentieth Century Architecture*, 13, 'The Architecture of Public Service' (2018), 7–23; Alan Powers, 'Quality in Quality Street: Neo-Georgian and Its Place in Architectural History', and Julian Holder, 'A State of Approval: Neo-Georgian Architecture and His Majesty's Office of Works, 1914–1939', in Julian Holder and Elizabeth McKellar (eds), *Neo-Georgian Architecture 1880–1970: A Reappraisal* (Swindon: Historic England, 2016), pp. 13–24 (18–19) and 122–35.

80. Salford Local History Library, Salford, Percy Thomas and Ernest Prestwich, 'Description of the Building by the Architects', in *Official Opening of the New Town Hall, Swinton*; similar descriptions, for example, 'Swinton & Pendlebury Town Hall', *Architect & Building News*, 30 December 1938, pp. 356–60; 'New Municipal Buildings for Swinton & Pendlebury', *The Builder*, 23 December 1938, pp. 1206–10; 'Swinton Town Hall', *National Builder*, November 1938, pp. 126–8.

81. 'Swinton's New Town Hall: First Portion of a Notable Civic Centre Opened', *Local Government Journal*, November 1938, pp. 347–8 (347); 'Swinton and Pendlebury Municipal Buildings Competition', *The Builder*, 14 September 1934, supplement.

82. 'New Swinton Town Hall', *Eccles and Patricroft Journal*, 22 September 1938, p. 10; for more details, see Proctor, 'Citizenship', pp. 275–8.

83. 'The New Town Hall Inquiry', *Kent & Sussex Courier*, 9 January 1931, pp. 2–3 and 9 (9); Tunbridge Wells Borough Archives (TWBA), 549, 'Dissension Among Members of Chamber of Trade', *Kent & Sussex Courier*, 16 January 1931, unpaginated; TWBA, 800, 'Swept by the Board', *Tunbridge Wells Advertiser*, 6 November 1931, unpaginated.

84. 'Council Discusses Town Hall Scheme', *Kent & Sussex Courier*, 19 September 1930, p. 3; Reilly, 'Expression in Municipal Architecture Today', pp. 159, 162, TWBA, 549, 'The New Town Hall', *Tunbridge Wells Advertiser*, 8 August 1930, unpaginated.

85. TWBA, 800, 'Municipal Bombshell', *Kent & Sussex Courier*, 6 November 1931, unpaginated.

86. Julian Holder and Nick Holmes, 'Emanuel Vincent Harris: Civic, Civil and Sane', in Holder and McKellar (eds), *Neo-Georgian Architecture*, pp. 65–80 (74–5).

87. 'Civic Centre, Tunbridge Wells', *Architects' Journal*, 25 May 1939, pp. 871–5; 'Assembly Hall and Police Court, Tunbridge Wells', *Architect & Building News*, 9 June 1939, pp. 261–4; TWBA, 84/93 (2) and (3), newspaper supplements for 'The Jubilee of Incorporation of Royal Tunbridge Wells', *Tunbridge Wells Advertiser*, 19 and 26 May 1939; 'Opening of the New Town Hall', *Kent & Sussex Courier*, 21 March 1941, p. 5; Proctor, 'Citizenship', pp. 285–8.

88. Carmarthenshire Archives Holdings, held at GAC at time of research (CAHGA), CCC, New County Buildings Committee, 3 July 1935, Percy Thomas, 'Carmarthen County Council Proposed New Offices: Report on Preliminary Plans', 2 July 1935.

89. CAHGA, CCC, Old Prison Committee, 21 January 1935, 'Report of the County Architect on the Proposed New County Buildings'; 'Proposed New County Offices, Carmarthen', *The Builder*, 10 January 1936, p. 97.

90. CAHGA, CCC, Old Prison Committee, 12 September 1934.

91. CAHGA, CCC/CL/76, Articles of Agreement, 3 September 1954; Carmarthen Library, *Official Opening of the County Hall, Carmarthen* (Carmarthen: Carmarthen County Council, 1956).

92. CAHGA, CCC, Percy Thomas, 'Carmarthen County Council Proposed New Offices'.

93. CAHGA, CCC/CL/32, *The Jubilee of County Councils, 1889–1939; Carmarthenshire: Fifty Years of Local Government* (London: County Councils Association, 1939), pp. 21–42, 73.

94. CAHGA, CCC/CL/10, J. W. Nicholas (County Clerk) to Ministry of Health, 23 December 1927.

95. CAHGA, CCC, New County Buildings Committee, 7 December 1937, reported at County Council (Special Meeting), 15 December 1937; CAHGA, CCC/CL/10, correspondence in 'New County Buildings' folder; CAHGA, CCC, New County Buildings Committee, 19 October 1936, Percy Thomas, report on proposed sites, 17 September 1936 (and subsequent meetings).

96. 'County Hall Extensions: Foundation Stone Laid', *Western Mail & South Wales News*, 20 May 1931, p. 11; 'Glamorgan's New £54,000 Building', *Western Mail & South Wales News*, 23 September 1932, p. 11; Hilling, *Cardiff Civic Centre*, p. 147.

97. 'Extension to County-Hall: New Building in Cathays Park', *Western Mail & South Wales News*, 19 May 1931, p. 8.

98. TWBA, 84/93 (2), 'The New Police Buildings', *Tunbridge Wells Advertiser*, 26 May 1939, 'Jubilee of Incorporation of Royal Tunbridge Wells', supplement, p. 4.

99. WGAS, BA 2/15, 'Opening of New Guildhall ... Programme of Proceedings', 1934.

100. 'Worcester's Plan for Civic Offices', *Worcester Evening News*, 3 January 1936, pp. 1, 9 (1).

101. Billy Reading, *Fire Stations* (Stroud: Amberley Publishing, 2017), p. 44.

102. 'Bristol Police and Fire Stations Competition', *The Builder*, 11 April 1924, p. 575 and plates.

103. 'Bristol Fire Station', *Architect & Building News*, 7 November 1930, pp. 622–7 (626); windows were added to the top storey later; as built, see Bristol Archives, Bristol (BA), 39864/2/197, photograph of c.1950; 'The New Police Station at Bristol: An Interesting Treatment of a Two Story Building', *Architect & Building News*, 4 January 1929, pp. 3–7 (3).

104. BA, FB/Adm/M/1/2, Fire Brigade Sub-Committee, 1914–24, Watch (Fire Brigade Sub-Committee), 16 January 1923.

105. BA, M/BCC/WAT/2/30, Watch Committee, 25 April 1923, Draft Report of the Watch Committee [n. d., c. April 1923]; 'Bristol Police and Fire Brigade Premises', *Architecture*, December 1930, pp. 144–7 (146).

106. BA, M/BCC/WAT/2/30, Watch Committee, 25 April 1923, Draft Report of the Watch Committee [n. d., c. April 1923]; Dennis Hill, *Bristol Fire Brigade 1877–1974: An Illustrated History* (Bristol: Redcliffe Press, 1999), p. 82; 'Bristol Fire Station', p. 623; 'Bristol Fire and Police Stations: Completion of £130,000 Scheme', *Municipal Review*, December 1930, pp. 503–4 (504).

107. 'New Courts, Police Station and Fire Station, Accrington', *Architect & Building News*, 28 June 1935, pp. 367–73 (372); 'Developments at Accrington: New Law Courts and Headquarters for Police and Fire Brigade', *Municipal Review*, March 1936, pp. 71–2 (72); 'Accrington Law Courts and Fire Station', *Building*, March 1935, pp. 90–6 (90).

108. 'Police and Fire Station: Accrington', *Architects' Journal*, 4 June 1930, pp. 862–3; 'Accrington Fire and Police Station Competition', *The Builder*, 6 June 1930, pp. 1078–90.

109. 'Stately New Home of Police and Fire Brigade', *Accrington Observer*, 11 May 1935, p. 15.

110. 'Stately New Home', p. 15; Community History Library, Accrington, uncatalogued, Public Buildings Committee, 20 May 1935 and 4 June 1935; 'The Week's Building News', *Architects' Journal*, 30 January 1936, p. 213; 'Accrington Plans for the Future', *Lancashire Evening Post*, 4 June 1935, p. 4; 'Accrington Centre', *Lancashire Evening Post*, 21 December 1935, p. 7.

111. 'Worcester City Council: Building Scheme Explained', *Worcester Evening News*, 4 May 1937, pp. 1 and 10 (1); 'New Fire Station', *Architect & Building News*, 23 April 1943, pp. 57–9 (58); 'Worcester Police Headquarters', *Architect & Building News*, 14 November 1941, pp. 100–3.

112. Worcester Archive and Archaeology Service, Worcester (henceforth WAAS): 496.5/BA11241/E5/Box 4/1, Special Sub-Committee of the Watch & Lighting Committee re Police and Fire Brigade Accommodation, 17 December 1935; 496.5 BA9360/Cab22/25/53, Watch and Lighting Committee, 4 June 1935 and Property and Cemeteries Committee report at council meeting, 7 January 1936; 496.5 BA9360/Cab 22/23/50, Health Committee, 6 September 1933; 496.5 BA9360/Cab 22/24/52: Special Sub-Committee of the Watch and Lighting Committee in Regard to Fire Brigade Accommodation, 28 November 1934; Streets Committee, 10 December 1934; Watch and Lighting Committee, 21 May 1935; 'Worcester's Plan for Civic Offices', *Worcester Evening News*, 3 January 1936, pp. 1, 9; 'Worcester City Scheme for New Civic Offices', *Worcester Evening News*, 8 January 1936, pagination illegible; 'Jottings', *Berrow's Worcester Journal*, 11 January 1936, p. 9; 'Worcester City Council: New Police and Fire Brigade Premises', *Berrow's Worcester Journal*, 11 January 1936, p. 4; 'New Civic Centre', *Berrow's Worcester Journal*, 4 January 1936, pagination illegible.

113. 'Archbishop and the "Menace to Civilised Order"', *Evening News & Times* (Worcestershire and West Midlands), 27 March 1939, p. 5.

114. 'City's New Police Headquarters: Official Opening', *Evening News & Times* (Worcestershire and West Midlands), 12 September 1941, p. 3.

115. Percy E. Thomas and H. V. Lanchester, 'Competitions Past and Present', *RIBA Journal*, 13 May 1933, pp. 525–42; H. V. Lanchester and Percy E. Thomas, 'Competitions Past and Present', *Architects' Journal*, 26 April 1933, pp. 561–2.

116. Kenneth M. B. Cross, 'Letters: Future of Competitions', *Architects' Journal*, 18 October 1945, pp. 275–6; Astragal, 'Notes & Topics', *Architects' Journal*, 24 October 1935, pp. 580–1; Percy Edward Thomas, *Pupil to President: Memoirs of an Architect* (Leigh-on-Sea: F. Lewis, 1963), p. 34; Thomas and Lanchester, 'Competitions Past and Present', pp. 530, 532, 538.

117. 'Future of Competitions', *Architects' Journal*, 6 September 1945, pp. 165–6.

118. TNA, WORK 12/207, [W. A. H.?] to E. Vincent Harris, 4 February 1915.

119. Reilly, 'Percy Thomas', p. 65; 'Board of Trade New Offices Competition', p. 268.

120. Peter De Figueiredo, 'Symbols of Empire: The Buildings of the Liverpool Waterfront', *Architectural History*, 46 (2003), 229–54 (243–7).

121. Reilly, 'Percy Thomas', p. 65; H. P. Cart De Lafontaine, 'The Ten Finalists', *Architects' Journal*, 2 June 1926, pp. 1–8 (7); Library and Museum of Freemasonry, London, BE 64 UNI fol and GBR 1991 PA/23, photographs of second-stage competition entries, *c*.1926.

122. William T. Benslyn, 'Birmingham Municipal Offices Competition', *The Builder*, 19 July 1935, pp. 99, 110–2 (99); Reginald Blomfield, 'Birmingham Civic Centre Competition: Report of the Assessor', *Architect & Building News*, 19 July 1935, pp. 75–80.

123. 'A Masterly Design: Award for the New Fire Station at Cardiff', *Western Mail*, 24 September 1912, p. 4; 'Competitions', *Architect & Building News*, 27 September 1912, p. 434.

124. 'Competition News', *The Builder*, 18 December 1925, pp. 872, 878; 'Big Plan of Police Reorganisation', *Newcastle Evening Chronicle*, 20 February 1926, p. 4; 'Justices Discuss City Schemes: Police Buildings and Fire Station', *Newcastle Evening Chronicle*, 5 January 1926, p. 10; 'Council to Decide on Newcastle Police and Fire Station Scheme', *Newcastle Evening Chronicle*, 1 May 1926, p. 1; 'Newcastle Plans: Police and Fire Station to Cost £134,000', *Yorkshire Post*, 5 May 1927, p. 12.

125. E. Maxwell Fry, 'The Designs Discussed', *Architects' Journal*, 4 May 1932, pp. 608–9; Robert Atkinson, 'R.I.B.A. New Building', *Architects' Journal*, 7 December 1932, pp. 733–4; Iodos, 'The Hornsey Competition: The Designs Reviewed', *Architects' Journal*, 19 October 1933, pp. 479–84 (482); W. G. Holford, 'The Bury Competition', *Architects' Journal*, 13 February 1936, pp. 260–1 (260); 'Bolton Municipal Technical College Competition: A Review of the Designs', *The Builder*, 17 January 1936, pp. 143, 156 (156); 'Bolton Municipal Technical College Competition', *The Builder*, 13 December 1935, pp. 1065–8.

126. 'News: New Municipal Centre for Kensington', *Architects' Journal*, 21 January 1937, p. 130; 'Proposed New Municipal Buildings for Kensington: Council Approves Big Scheme', *West London Observer*, 29 July 1938, p. 9; 'News: Municipal Buildings, Kensington', *Architects' Journal*, 3 November 1938, p. 712; 'News in Brief', *Architects' Journal*, 24 August 1939, p. 263.

127. 'Architecture at the Royal Academy: Review of Exhibits', *The Builder*, 5 May 1939, pp. 836–49 (840).

128. National Library of Wales Archives, Aberystwyth (NLWA), Welsh National Memorial Association Records (WNMAR), Box 33, 'Hall of Nations and WNMA Offices: Opening Ceremony', 'Press Notes: Hall of Nations', n.d. [1938]; Linda Bryder, 'The King Edward VII Welsh National Memorial Association and its Policy Towards Tuberculosis, 1910–1948', *Welsh History Review*, 13 (1986), 194–216 (194–8).

129. NLWA, WNMAR, Box 31, 'Calculations of Interest, etc.', F. J. Alban (WNMA) to Sir William Jenkins MP, 9 March 1931; David Davies to Sir William Jenkins, MP, 9 February 1931.

130. Pyrs Gruffudd, '"A Crusade Against Consumption": Environment, Health and Social Reform in Wales, 1900–1939', *Journal of Historical Geography*, 21/1 (1995), 39–54 (49); Monica Cherry, *Building Wales* (Cardiff: Arts Council of Wales, 2005), p. 12.

131. CUSCA, Temple of Peace Box, *Wales and World Peace, 1936–1937* (Cardiff: League of Nations Union, Welsh National Council, 1937); Robert Laker, 'Wales and the 1935 Peace Ballot' and Craig Owen, 'A History of Welsh Internationalism', papers at seminar, 'The Interwar Peace Movement in Wales' organised by Llafur: The Welsh People's History Society, 2020, *https://youtu.be/47hSZza88i0* (accessed 7 September 2021).

132. CUSCA, Temple of Peace Box, *Teachers and World Peace* (Cardiff: League of Nations Union, Welsh National Council, 1928).

133. Chris Williams, 'The Dilemmas of Nation and Class in Wales, 1914–45', in Duncan Tanner, Chris Williams, W. P. Griffith and Andrew Edwards (eds), *Debating Nationhood and Governance in Britain, 1885–1945: Perspectives from the 'Four Nations'* (Manchester: Manchester University Press, 2006), pp. 146–68; Morgan, *Rebirth of a Nation*, pp. 200–3.

134. [David] Davies, 'Welsh Temple of Peace and Health a National Symbol', *Western Mail & South Wales News*, 6 November 1936, p. 8.

135. Tommaso Milani, 'Retreat from the Global? European Unity and British Progressive Intellectuals, 1930–1945', *The International History Review*, 42/1 (2020), 99–116 (104); Kenneth O. Morgan, *Modern Wales: Politics, Places and People* (Cardiff: University of Wales Press, 1995), p. 105.

136. Bryder, 'Welsh National Memorial Association', pp. 207–11.

137. 'Temple of Peace & Health: Another Fine Building for Cardiff?', *Western Mail & South Wales News*, 2 August 1930, p. 11; 'Cardiff's Temple of Peace', *Western Mail & South Wales News*, 12 September 1930, p. 10; NLWA, WNMAR, Box 32, folder 'New Offices and Temple of Peace, etc.: Public Inquiry by the Ministry of Health', [Alban] (WNMA Secretary) to unnamed addressees, 9 November 1936; Hilling, *Cardiff Civic Centre*, pp. 148–9.

138. 'New Government Buildings for Cardiff Approved', *Western Mail & South Wales News*, 9 August 1934, p. 10.

139. 'Proposed Welsh National Memorial Buildings, Cardiff', *The Builder*, 9 January 1931, p. 118.

140. David Officer, 'In Search of Order, Permanence and Stability: Building Stormont 1921–32', in Richard English and Graham Walker (eds), *Unionism in Modern Ireland: New Perspectives on Politics and Culture* (Basingstoke: Macmillan, 1996), pp. 130–47; Alan Greer, 'Sir James Craig and the Construction of Parliament Buildings at Stormont', *Irish Historical Studies*, 31/123 (1999), 373–88.

141. NLWA, Lord David Davies of Llandinam Papers, D14/5, Temple of Peace, Percy Thomas, 'King Edward VII Memorial Association Proposed Buildings, Cathays Park, Cardiff: Architects' Report', October 1929 (quotations from pp. 3, 6–7 and 11); 'Proposed Welsh National Memorial Buildings, Cardiff', *The Builder*, 9 January 1931, p. 118; 'Cardiff's Temple of Peace', *Western Mail & South Wales News*, 12 September 1930, p. 10; 'Erection of Temple of Peace for Wales', *Western Mail & South Wales News*, 21 January 1933, pp. 8, 10.

142. 'The Hall of Nations, Cardiff: Architect Percy Thomas', *Architect & Building News*, 28 October 1938, pp. 91–5; 'The Hall of Nations, Cardiff', *National Builder*, November 1938, p. 129; 'Temple of Peace and Health, Cardiff', *The Builder*, 4 November 1938, pp. 879–83; 'Temple of Peace and Health, Cardiff, Designed by Percy Thomas', *Architects' Journal*, 17 November 1938, pp. 807–10.

143. Hilling, *Cardiff Civic Centre*, p. 151; 'Periodicals: June and July Anthology', *Architects' Journal*, 22 August 1935, pp. 273–4 (273); 'The Architectural Association: Mr Percy Thomas's Impressions of America', *The Builder*, 19 March 1937, pp. 635–6.

144. 'The Architect's Modern Adaptation of the Classic', *Western Mail & South Wales News*, 23 November 1938, Temple of Peace and Health supplement, p. 3.

145. David Davies, 'Welsh National Temple of Peace and Health', in *Wales and World Peace, 1936–1937* (Cardiff: League of Nations Union, Welsh National Council, 1937), pp. 4–5 (5); '"House Warming" at the Hall of Justice', *Western Mail & South Wales News*, 24 November 1938, p. 7.

146. '"House Warming" at the Hall of Justice'.

147. 'Temple of Peace and Health, Cardiff', *The Builder*, 4 November 1938, pp. 879–83.

148. CUSCA, Temple of Peace Box, *A New Mecca: An Account of the Opening Ceremony of the Welsh National Temple of Peace and Health* ([Cardiff], 1938), p. 11; 'Professor Gilbert Murray on Great Achievement of Wales', *Western Mail & South Wales News*, 24 November 1938, p. 7.

149. David Davies, 'Temple an Expression of Two Ideals', *Western Mail & South Wales News*, 23 November 1938, Temple of Peace and Health supplement, p. 2.

150. Emma West, 'The Opening of the Temple of Peace: Minnie James and the "Mothers of the World"', at seminar, 'The Interwar Peace Movement in Wales', Llafur: The Welsh People's History Society, 2020, *https://youtu.be/47hSZza88i0*, accessed 7 September 2021; 'A Mother of Wales Will Unlock the Temple Door', *Western Mail & South Wales News*, 23 November 1938, Temple of Peace and Health supplement, p. 7.

151. 'Wales's Tragic Mother Opens the Temple of Peace', *Western Mail & South Wales News*, 24 November 1938, p. 7.

152. CUSCA, Temple of Peace and Health box, 'The Welsh National Temple of Peace and Health, Cathays Park, Cardiff: Opening Ceremony and Service of Dedication', 23 November 1938 (Cardiff, Western Mail and Echo Ltd).

153. '"House Warming" at the Hall of Justice'.

154. West, 'The Opening of the Temple of Peace'; CUSCA, Temple of Peace Box, *Wales and the World, 1939–1940* (Cardiff: League of Nations Union, Welsh National Council, 1940), pp. 3–4.

155. For example, CUSCA, Temple of Peace box, *21st Anniversary of the Signing of the Charter of the United Nations: Ceremony of Re-Dedication at the Temple of Peace, Cathays Park, Cardiff* (Cardiff: United Nations Association, Welsh National Council, 1966); 'Welcome Party', *Western Mail*, 5 January 1957, p. 2.

3

Commerce, Consumption and Community: The City and the Suburb

While Percy Thomas's reputation was built on local government municipal architecture, his practice undertook many smaller-scale private and commercial buildings, from department stores to pubs and from churches to houses, most in Cardiff. Large civic projects were sporadic and risky, and private work formed the practice's bread and butter. Yet Thomas's architectural outlook remained informed by civic architecture: his argument for architects' responsibility to wider society applied to all building work, perhaps especially to those forming the setting for citizens' daily lives. Thomas's clients often shared this civic ethos, or hoped to benefit from it.

There was much debate between the wars about how architectural design could improve the urban environment through a civic mentality. Arthur Trystan Edwards, appreciating Georgian architecture, argued that architects should accept a hierarchy of building types, private buildings showing deference to public buildings, and relating harmoniously to neighbouring buildings of similar status through reticence and restraint, suppressing commercial advertising and private expressions of individuality to promote 'civic order'.[1] Edwards participated in a wider discourse of planning and architecture as 'civic design', having studied that subject at Liverpool under Charles Reilly and Patrick Abercrombie. This emerging discipline was influenced by the American 'City Beautiful' movement of the early twentieth century, which promoted ordered cities with regular boulevards, great public spaces, classical monuments and carefully designed street furnishings.[2] Its adherents often juxtaposed this urban vision with the Garden City model: some writers, such as Thomas Sharp and Clough Williams-Ellis, preferred clear distinctions between urban and rural contexts rather than low-density planning and developers' suburbs.[3]

Thomas's practice was, however, pragmatic and responsive to clients, and he was rarely involved in planning or housing. He did not dismiss suburbia but contributed to it, consolidating its character as a distinct, modern environment, not so much halfway between town and country as urban in a new way, with an informal and domestic character in deference to the centre's formality. City Beautiful advocates wanted to distinguish business from residential districts, promoting green landscaping in the latter and applying principles of 'civic art' to houses where they engaged with the street.[4] Suburban taste and the standard builder's semi-detached house were much derided in interwar architectural discourse and wider culture, and Thomas's engagement with the suburb, as with his involvement in commercial building types, suggests his participation in ideas of design reform, which aimed to disseminate refined, even austere, contemporary design in everyday settings and objects. This movement resonated with City Beautiful ideas because of the latter's preference for harmony and deference in architecture, contrary to the supposed individualism of suburbia.[5]

Closely following City Beautiful principles, Thomas helped found the Cardiff Civic Society in 1933 'To Make Cardiff More Beautiful' and stimulate civic consciousness among citizens. Thomas, having proposed such an organisation years before, joined its committee, though its leading voices were J. F. Rees, Principal of the University College of South Wales and Monmouthshire, and architect T. Alwyn Lloyd; W. S. Purchon, head of the Welsh School of Architecture, Cyril Fox of the National Museum of Wales and Ivor Jones were also active.[6] Its varied work in the 1930s included surveys of Cardiff and its surroundings, and a competition for street decorations for the 1937 coronation.[7] It commented on planning applications and council projects. When it demanded improvements to the Central Station area, the council sought Thomas's advice.[8] The Civic Society also staged public lectures: both Abercrombie and his successor as Professor of Civic Design at Liverpool, William Holford, visited. Holford condemned Cardiff's suburban housing, no doubt causing some embarrassment.[9] The Civic Society had, however, already published a booklet on small house design to elevate the tastes of consumers and builders.[10]

Cardiff then was a new city, awarded that status in 1905; a humble market town that rapidly became a cosmopolitan centre dominating the world's coal trade. A self-conscious, confident middle class shaped the city's cultural and social life, anglicised but also proudly Welsh, connected with global fashion and modernity, constructing corporate governance in the Civic Centre.[11] Thomas, son of a trading ship's captain, was one of them, and well equipped to articulate middle-class desires. Swansea, similarly, though industrial since the eighteenth century, grew enormously in the nineteenth century as an industrial and commercial centre and port, a magnet for trade from the countryside. By the 1930s, however, Welsh coal was in severe decline and economic shocks intensely evident, but despite unemployment and poverty for many, this period's suburban expansions also testify to the prosperity of small businessmen, artisans and administrators, moving to spacious city fringes, shopping in fashionable stores, and providing Thomas's practice with a steady stream of work. This chapter considers the public nature of private and commercial work, concluding with a major unbuilt scheme in London. It moves forward from the interwar period to the 1950s and 1960s, as such work continued as the practice grew, gradually changing with the wider architectural acceptance of modernism.

Civic Commerce

In Cardiff, Thomas designed several notable shops and offices as well as smaller commercial buildings, where his use of a restrained but modern American style of neoclassicism imparted civic qualities alongside a conspicuous modernity. Some businesses emulated official institutions to convey authority or status, and evidently commissioned Thomas for his expertise in public buildings. Department stores embraced modernity in business methods, including a large scale and speed of operations, while commercial success gave their owners status in the city's social and political life that came with a certain perceived duty to contribute to the city's improvement. Moreover, the sphere of business and commerce was not always entirely separate from the state, but in certain situations could be brought into partnership with it, and business premises therefore linked directly to local or national government; and at such moments, a visual association with state architecture could express a real institutional relationship. Commissioning a respected architect for a commercial building represented a desire for distinction above the norm of brash commercial culture.

Thomas's addition to the James Howell and Company department store on Cardiff's main shopping artery, St Mary Street, opened in the depression in 1931, received the first RIBA bronze medal for a building in Wales (see Figure 3.1).[12] A four-storey block with basement and attics, the building was no taller than its neighbours, but visually dominated the street with a bold monumental design, contrasting markedly with Howell's adjacent more intricately ornamented Victorian building.

Thomas's extension had a three-storey Greek Ionic order of Portland stone carrying a bold cornice. Its steel frame allowed glazed curtain walls behind the columns. Reliefs depicted producers bringing their wares to market. Spandrel panels and the bronze frames of the plate-glass display windows had elegant but simple classical details relating to the overall design. The style was American Beaux-Arts, and the building emulated the earlier Selfridges building in London, designed by American architect and City Beautiful proponent Daniel Burnham with a similar three-storey Roman Ionic order and full-height glazing. The Cardiff store's owners undoubtedly desired such an association: Hugh Howell explained that his store's expansion would dissuade Cardiff consumers from shopping in London, benefiting the city's economy,

3.1 James Howell & Co. Department Store, Cardiff, 1925–31 (photo: author).

and hoped to attract Americans arriving on Cardiff's new transatlantic liner service.[13] The architecture targeted mobile, affluent consumers and the aspirational middle classes who understood its fashionable associations.

Inside, lifts and terrazzo-lined stairs distributed customers to high, open sales floors where goods were tastefully displayed in oak cases. A third floor 'salon' could stage fashion parades to large audiences. Ostentatious technology included pneumatic tubes sending receipts from tills to attic offices, and chutes where goods were sent to basement conveyor belts for delivery.[14] The business, founded by James Howell in 1865, followed the principles of modern department stores developed in nineteenth-century France.[15] These methods centred on high turnover speeds to maximise profits while enabling competitive prices. As much stock as possible was displayed to generate sales, minimising storage; increasing floor area thus directly boosted income. Big display windows and exciting events kept crowds flowing in.[16]

Department stores were also defined by aggressive expansion: Howells released public shares in 1920 explicitly to fund new extensions and accelerate business.[17] Like other department stores, Howells targeted property acquisitions throughout its urban block, absorbing new premises into the store.[18] The directors hired Ivor Jones and Percy Thomas to alter newly-acquired buildings soon after this share issue, starting with a new section with top-lit galleries on Trinity Street, designed in 1922.[19] This three-bay section had a three-storey neoclassical facade of Portland stone pilasters, contrasting with older brick neighbours, anticipating the St Mary Street block.[20] The curved corners of this later monumental landmark block suggest the Victorian neighbour was intended pragmatically to remain, though much of the site was to be developed with a coordinated neoclassical architecture as a commercial monument.

This use of neoclassicism supported the store's ambition to emulate official architecture, though it ran contrary to Trystan Edwards's criticism of giant classical orders for shops as detracting from their proper use in public buildings.[21] Just as Selfridges declared itself 'London's Civic Centre', publicity for the Howells extensions claimed a public-spirited contribution to Cardiff.[22] A newspaper advertisement for the opening ceremony declared under a perspective of the building that 'A Great City Needs A Great Store!', invoking the founder's intention 'to provide a service which would do honour to Cardiff'.[23] The Lord Mayor, Robert Hill-Snook, spoke at the opening, linking the store's extensions to the city's prosperity. Company chairman T. Francis Howell noted that its builders, E. Turner & Sons, had also built much of the Civic Centre. He urged his audience to shop in Cardiff to support the local and national economy during the depression, another speaker emphasising the store's 800-strong workforce. Thomas's design evidently aimed to pioneer a new look for the whole street: Howell urged other shops to follow suit 'and make St. Mary Street, which is the principal street of Cardiff, one worthy of the city'.[24] Thomas's corner building therefore suggested how the street might be coherently reworked as a boulevard between commercial core and Civic Centre, modelled perhaps on the neoclassical Kingsway in London.

Thomas and Jones designed a further extension, opened in 1937 for new acquisitions around the corner on Wharton Street.[25] This section maintained the corner block's lines and materials in more modern style, with bands of Art Deco fluting and astylar piers formed with stepped lintels, a motif from the Accrington and Bristol fire stations, also recalling J. J. Burnet's austere Kodak House on the London Kingsway.[26] The new section enticed consumers into this secondary street with broad window displays. Howells lacked the capital for a total rebuilding, opening up its interiors incrementally with iron and steel, solid walls awkwardly remaining, including those of a Victorian chapel absorbed in the extension; but Thomas's architecture unified phases, conveying a consistent surface image with an authoritative civic feeling.

Thomas had previously designed a smaller rival department store in Cardiff. Founded in 1879 in Duke Street but expropriated by the city for road widening in the early 1920s, Marments built a new shop in nearby Queen Street.[27] Thomas's elevation used the same approach as for Howells, smaller and more spartan, but equally dominant on a street of narrow frontages, with five bays of three-storey Portland stone Doric columns (see Figure 3.2).[28] The display windows formed a recessed arcade, and inside were multi-storey top-lit atria surrounded by balconies, impressive spaces modelled on Parisian department stores.[29]

After the Second World War, Sir Percy Thomas & Son designed two department stores for the Lewis's chain, one in Hanley in Stoke-on-Trent and a larger store in Bristol. While these stores grew the company and rewarded shareholders, Lewis's also prided itself on its contributions to cities.[30] A civic consciousness was evident in these buildings, although Thomas's delegation of design to younger colleagues shifted its expression away from classicism. The Bristol store, completed in 1957 by Norman Thomas, Wallace Sweet and A. Poniatowski, was plain but classically proportioned

3.2 Marments Department Store, Cardiff, *c.*1922–5 (photo: author).

and clad in Portland stone (see Figure 3.3).[31] A curved, prow-like frontage with grids of windows addressed its prominent site at the gateway to the new Broadmead, a controversial reconstruction of the bombed commercial quarter in a new location. The council wanted to attract flagship stores to boost confidence in the new development, and Lewis's, not previously present in Bristol, was one of the first shops built, alongside local department store, Jones's.[32] The city engineer planned Broadmead on loosely classical lines, specifying cornice heights, but granted these buildings an exceptional prominence, Lewis's rising six floors in height. The building played an important role, therefore, in Bristol's post-war reconstruction, promoting optimism in the city's future.

Inside, fashionable public areas drew on the popular modernism of the Festival of Britain, including staircases with jazzy railings, a restaurant like a cruise liner's in the fourth floor prow and rooftop tea rooms with a garden.[33] From these public meeting spaces, customers could look out over the city to observe the new Bristol rising around them.[34] Reinforcing this relationship to the city, the architects and the Society of Mural Painters ran a competition for a restaurant mural, judged by Percy Thomas and Lewis's chairman S. H. Leake. The winner, Mary Adshead, painted a joyful, colourful modern frieze depicting Bristol life in the Middle Ages.[35]

The Hanley Lewis's, opened by the Lord Mayor of Stoke-on-Trent in phases from 1962, was smaller, replacing a pre-war store opposite, and designed by the Shrewsbury

3.3 Lewis's Department Store, Bristol, 1956–7 (unknown photographer; from the Collections of the National Monuments Records of Wales; courtesy of the estate of Sir Percy Thomas and WSP UK Ltd).

office in more modernist form.[36] Blank walls clad in blue mosaic panels were punctuated with projecting concave black stone screens intended for public artworks, though only one was commissioned: David Wynne's spiky metal figure representing fire, symbolising Stoke-on-Trent's industrial past. On the old site, Lewis's also commissioned the architects for a three-storey modern building for offices and shops, complementing the council's wider developments modernising the shopping centre.[37]

Councils themselves actively intervened in the commercial sphere, even undertaking forms of retail. Many local authorities ran electricity supply companies, and built shop-like showrooms to sell domestic appliances and enrol customers. At Worcester, Percy Thomas advised the council on converting a shop near the Guildhall; and at Tunbridge Wells, he designed a showroom within the Civic Centre.[38] The electricity showroom Thomas designed in Cardiff, opened in 1937, was unusually substantial, and sited provocatively among shops on the Hayes.[39] Thomas's architecture softened controversy with a more monumental than commercial character. Adapting an Edwardian fish market, Thomas wrapped it in cast stone and simplified its mouldings, creating a sober neo-Georgian box with arched display windows. In the arches facing the Hayes, display cases formed an arcade, and displays inside surrounded columns. The building included a demonstration theatre and an electric kitchen to educate consumers in electricity's domestic uses.[40] Traders objected to the council's incursion into their domain with 'magnificent buildings', but the city argued that profits from its electricity department subsidised rates, lowered supply tariffs for businesses and improved citizens' lives.[41]

A more traditional form of state intervention in commerce was the market hall. Although Percy Thomas had no formal role in Swansea's post-war reconstruction, his practice designed and built its new market from 1955 to 1961 as part of the new shopping centre, replacing the bombed Victorian market building. While the council's borough engineers who developed the reconstruction plans wanted to relocate the market to a marginal position near a planned road, others, including market traders, argued for retaining its central site as a symbolically important element of the town.[42] The council agreed to keep it in Oxford Street, and added a public hall and hotel to the scheme.[43] Bomb-damage compensation funded the building, but the council invited proposals from private developers in 1955. The successful bidder, Bonville Investments, presented a brick neo-Georgian scheme by Thomas with a central arched market hall and a tall arched entrance on Oxford Street.[44] His practice redesigned the elevations in 1959 in a simpler modern approach, allowing bigger display windows; the Dolphin hotel on the east side had a Portland stone façade; the public hall was omitted, and the market entrance reduced to a concrete canopy (see Figure 3.4).[45]

These stylistic changes aligned with the rebuilt shopping area's prevailing modernism, and were likely made by the practice's Swansea office, where John Vergette had recently arrived. The market's interior was a showpiece of Swansea's reconstruction, with tapered steel arches spanning almost sixty metres of open floor space, reinforced concrete frames housing stalls along the edges. The architects designed tasteful market stalls with a coherent colour scheme giving a popular, festive character (see Figure 3.5).[46] Like the department stores, this careful design deliberately suppressed commercial individualism and extravagance for a more harmonious appearance expressing participation in a collective endeavour.

3.4 Swansea Market, 1959–61 (unknown photographer; West Glamorgan Archive Service).

3.5 Swansea Market, 1959–61 (unknown photographer; West Glamorgan Archive Service).

Office Work

Percy Thomas designed two notable office buildings in Cardiff for companies seeking an authoritative but modern image. Both also illustrate the complex interrelationships of business and government. 'Empire House' in Mount Stuart Square was at the heart of the merchant quarter, opposite the Coal Exchange, alongside other office buildings for coal and shipping businesses, close to the docks, and, as its name suggests, was bound up with the British Empire through trade (see Figure 3.6).[47] Its street elevation was sober, a flat brick sash-windowed façade, its ground floor faced in Portland stone. Its seven-storey height was softened by setting two storeys into a dormered attic. It resembled a Georgian terrace, eschewing the grandiose orders of nearby older buildings. The Georgian style continued inside with a barrel-vaulted entrance hall panelled in mahogany. This genteel, urbane appearance belied the modernity of the building's Hennebique reinforced concrete frame, though at the rear its structure was exposed, filled with glazing to maximise daylight. Its façade also belied the crude commercialism of the company that built it.[48]

The Evans & Reid Coal Company, a coal merchant, though named on the building, was only a minor participant. It founded the 'Georgian Company' in 1914 to develop and let what it originally proposed to call 'Georgian Buildings', but the company and project were later largely taken over by Elder Dempster and Company, which proceeded to build Empire House for its Cardiff branch office from 1928 to 1929, assigning rooms to Evans & Reid and letting others.[49] Elder Dempster was a shipping company based in Liverpool that operated mail and passenger ships, but its most lucrative business was freight, a large proportion through Cardiff, where new offices were needed for proliferating paperwork. Elder Dempster's ships ferried goods

3.6 Empire House, Cardiff, 1928–9 (photo: author).

between Britain, British colonies in West Africa, and North America. From Africa its ships brought palm kernels, cocoa and cotton, returning with Welsh coal and goods such as textiles and cement. Introducing routes between Africa and Canada allowed it to claim a role in 'the development of inter-Imperial trade', and thus the integration of the empire.[50] It had also become a corporate empire itself, moving into palm oil extraction, cement production and banking. It collaborated with other companies and British and colonial governments to stifle competition from African suppliers, and employed African workers in harsh conditions on its ships, many no doubt lodging nearby in Butetown.[51] Empire House's discrete exterior downplayed its presence, while conveying a gentlemanly image of imperial administration to those who knew its purpose. While some of Percy Thomas's civic architecture gave cultural expression to British imperialism, this building also housed part of its commercial infrastructure.

Thomas's other significant office building was another private speculative development involved with the provision of welfare. The Prudential Assurance building in Cardiff was designed largely by the company's surveyor G. A. Coombe in 1947, but because of its location opposite the Civic Centre, the company appointed Thomas for its elevations.[52] On reviewing his drawings in 1950, the city's Public Works Committee urged him 'to incorporate more ornate features', though he indignantly refused.[53] It was neoclassical in conception, with a rounded prow like the Bristol Lewis's store, a rusticated ground floor, simple cornice and Portland stone cladding complementing Civic Centre buildings. Hints of rustication around first floor windows borrowed a motif from Lutyens. The building's flatness and simplicity contrasted with the City Hall's baroque extravagance, and were perceived as modern, 'the H. G. Wells futuristic look', a journalist wrote. Nevertheless, Lord Mayor Robert Bevan claimed at the opening ceremony that the building 'matches those that our forefathers erected many years ago'.[54]

The Prudential had been formally involved in welfare before the Second World War as an 'approved society' for administering national insurance and healthcare, besides its private health insurance.[55] The outbreak of war in 1939 prompted it to decentralise operations from London to the regions, the Cardiff office becoming its headquarters for Wales.[56] The building's plans included a 'Limbs & Appliances Section', suggesting burgeoning work for returning soldiers.[57] The newly formed National Health Service, however, made the Prudential's business almost redundant and the building unnecessarily large; on completion in 1952, the company occupied part of the ground floor and rented out the rest - fittingly, to government departments, some related to the Prudential's original functions, the Ministries of National Insurance and Pensions and the Inland Revenue.[58] These were undoubtedly attracted by the location close to the Civic Centre, and surely also by Thomas's official-looking elevations.

Pubs

Suburban recreation in the form of the public house was a productive field for the practice. British pubs in this period embraced reform from garish Victorian drinking dens towards bourgeois respectability, with space, light and tables for food, attempting to attract women and families. Brewery companies sought middle-class custom through tasteful buildings, commissioning reputed architects. This movement extended brewers' sales to affluent consumers, and curried favour with councils overseeing licensing. Breweries and architects drew on the wartime 'Carlisle experiment', when central government acquired pubs surrounding an ordnance factory and appointed architects for refurbishments producing light, open interiors, short bars to encourage drinkers to sit and dine, and edifying décor.[59] Welsh brewers built very few pubs between the wars, however, and Thomas's pubs suggest limited reform in Wales; nevertheless, they sought to complement their surroundings with sociable spaces for men and women.[60]

Thomas's first such commission dated from around 1915, when he won a competition for a restaurant in central Cardiff, the Louis Café on Duke Street, whose directors included a brewer.[61] Running a competition indicated a desire for a high class of establishment. Thomas's street frontage was 'neo-Grec', a simplified Erechtheion doorcase architrave in Portland stone framing metal windows, the first floor with a bay window. Smart interiors had mahogany and oak panels and screens by H. H. Martyn & Co. of Cheltenham, architectural craftsmen Thomas also used for fittings in civic buildings.[62] With elaborate, white plaster mouldings and Empire style furnishings, it could have been the restaurant of a contemporary liner. Adjacent to it a few years later, on a similarly narrow plot, Thomas rebuilt an old Cardiff pub, the Rummer Tavern, as an upmarket

3.7 Hallinan's Bar and Restaurant and the Louise Café, Cardiff, c.1920 and 1915 respectively (photo: Thomas Lewis; from the Collections of the National Monuments Records of Wales; courtesy of the estate of Sir Percy Thomas and WSP UK Ltd).

bar and restaurant called Hallinan's (see Figure 3.7). It was published in an architectural magazine, which noted that 'unlike modern "gin palaces," it has been designed and carried out entirely after the manner of the old English inn'.[63] Its street elevation had timber framing and an elaborate gable, while its interior simulated seventeenth-century hostelries, with carved oak panels throughout; a half-timbered fireplace gave a homely feel to the first floor 'Jacobean restaurant' and lounge bar, aimed explicitly at women.[64] A lightwell and skylights increased daylight to the deep plan, including leaded stained glass. It was playful pastiche, like a set from a film for fantasy consumption.

From the mid-1920s the S. A. Brain and Company brewery of Cardiff commissioned Jones and Thomas for a wave of new pubs and alterations, aiming for respectability by adopting reforming features, though not to the fullest extent. In the city centre the Westgate Hotel of 1932 replaced an older pub on Lower Cathedral Road with a typical 'Brewers' Georgian' building of thin Roman bricks and Portland stone details, domesticated with a hipped roof turning the corner and cheerful chimney stacks (see Figure 3.8). Inside, there was wood panelling, and painted heraldic emblems of company pubs decorated several bars and a skittle alley.[65] Thomas gave this ordinary building type personal attention, even taking students and staff from the Welsh School of Architecture for a tour.[66]

The Birchgrove Inn, opened in 1930 in the growing Cardiff suburb of that name, was architecturally more impressive, and nominated for the RIBA bronze medal by

3.8 Westgate Hotel, Cardiff, 1932 (photo: author).

the South Wales Institute of Architects (see Figure 3.9).[67] It followed an Arts and Crafts approach, appropriately for its suburban location, adopting the butterfly plan popularised by Lutyens and others, befitting its corner site on Caerphilly Road. Its steep roof cascaded between gables, dormers and chimneys to a welcoming half-timbered entrance. Its accommodation was similar to the Westgate, with a skittle alley and several bars, including one for women, though more progressive pubs were mixing the sexes to improve men's behaviour.[68] One long panopticon-like bar opened into all the public areas, the landlord's surveillance discouraging trouble, pleasing the licensing authority. Yet, the long bar catered to the persistence of working-class drinking culture in Cardiff, resisting the English trend for short bars and table service.[69] The Culverhouse

3.9 Birchgrove Inn, Cardiff, 1930 (photo: author).

Hotel, however, built around 1936 in a plainer vernacular style, was a more substantial and more modern type of inn, a roadhouse, appealing to the affluent new class of suburban, car-driving consumer, sited on Cowbridge Road beyond the suburb of Ely, designed more for meals, families and events than for drinking.[70] Though small, fun projects, Thomas's pubs were urban landmarks that were significant in many people's lives, and their designs sought to elevate the type to respectable urban and suburban institutions.

Churches

As cities expanded into suburbs, churches and chapels also followed their faithful, providing important sites for community formation and the expression of civic identities. Thomas's practice received no significant commissions for this type until after the Second World War, but from the 1950s they designed several churches for Anglicans, Nonconformists and Roman Catholics in Wales and England. The firm's association with secular architecture may have been considered an advantage, as congregations sought to participate in the civic sphere with buildings that could assuage anxieties about the place of religion in the modern world. Church leaders and their architects often debated the suburb's relationships to the city in this period of large-scale urban developments.[71]

Such debates arose at the Anglican town centre church of St Mary, Swansea, whose late Victorian Gothic Revival church by Arthur Blomfield was bombed in the war. The church's location concerned the council, whose comprehensive planning scheme reduced city-centre housing in favour of new suburban estates, diminishing St Mary's parish population. The diocese, considering the new churches needed for such demographic movements, debated whether to rebuild and where.[72] Parishioners and clergy preferred, however, to rebuild on the old church's foundations, and borough engineer J. Richard Heath concurred, intending the church to be a landmark in Swansea's reconstruction, surrounded by modern shopping streets.[73] The site had historical associations as the 'town church' of Swansea, as its vicar Jack Thomas emphasised: 'We are building not simply for the parish but for the town', he told parishioners; 'the rebuilding of Sw[ansea] will not be complete ... until its Church has been rebuilt and become once more the House of God for Sw[ansea] people'.[74]

The clergy wanted to restore Blomfield's church, but the new Swansea's modernity raised questions over the design approach. Encouraged by Heath and Ernest Morgan to obtain 'the best possible architect', the bishop pondered how to address 'the ancient side' and 'the shopping-centre side of our problem', to evoke the historical church while addressing the modern context, at first discounting Percy Thomas and others as 'thorough-paced moderns' and preferring Edward Maufe, designer of Guildford's modern Gothic cathedral. He appointed Gothic revivalist Leslie T. Moore, who resigned in 1949 before plans were complete.[75] The diocese then approached Norman Thomas at the practice's Swansea office, although Percy Thomas undertook much of the design work himself from 1953 until completion in 1959.[76] War damage compensation allowed only a plain replacement, and while the rebuilding improved height and layout, its architecture was simpler than Blomfield's and evidently contemporary (see Figure 3.10). Windows were mostly lancets, only one employing

3.10 Church of St Mary, Swansea, post-war rebuilding, 1953–9 (photo: author).

tracery; complicated stone-carving was minimised; the exposed timber nave trusses disguised a steel structure, and aisles were vaulted in reinforced concrete.[77] Timber choir stalls, transept screen and pulpit were intricately carved, to Percy Thomas's designs.[78] Fundraising attracted donations for embellishments, including a bequest from Morgan, and Thomas commissioned chancel windows from stained glass artist E. Liddall Armitage in a distinctive twentieth-century expressionist style.[79]

St Mary's clergy considered their church close to a cathedral in status, even 'the greatest parish church in Wales'.[80] Belonging to the town and its citizens, the church had civic as well as religious functions, including to represent Swansea's continuity as many traces of its past were effaced: an aim shared by Swansea's planners, and achieved in Thomas's simplified Gothic design. The practice's only other Anglican project in this period was a similar exercise reinstating the bombed late Victorian church of All Saints, Penarth. Its limited budget demanded simplicity, but the interior included richer Gothic detailing, including a vividly painted timber ceiling.[81]

Nonconformism, meanwhile, remained vital to Welsh culture, and in the post-war ferment of building, inevitably some congregations hoped to appoint Thomas for new chapels; yet the practice's first two such commissions were in England, both important enough to be known to south Wales Methodists. The Didsbury Theological College in Westbury-on-Trym, in particular, was a residential seminary sited to serve both Wales and south-west England, including a substantial chapel. The Methodist Church closed its mid-nineteenth-century theological college at Didsbury in Manchester in 1945, moving its staff and students to a house in this Bristol suburb with grounds for a new building, named after its original location.[82] Ernest Prestwich might have recommended Thomas for the project, as he was advising the Methodist

Church in Manchester on its post-war building programme. Prestwich contributed to guidelines for Methodist church building, including model church plans that Thomas's colleagues evidently absorbed.[83]

The new location overlooked its expanding suburban neighbourhood from a steep hillside, making Didsbury College a prominent landmark when completed in 1953. Thomas applied an austere neo-Georgian brick style, closely resembling Neuadd Reichel, student halls that he had recently built at Bangor, with a simple, capacious barrel-vaulted chapel projecting from the rear.[84] The building's plainness was necessitated by post-war restrictions, but also aligned with contemporary Methodist thinking: E. Benson Perkins and Albert Hearn of the Church's General Chapel Committee argued that the period's austerity was a 'salutary factor' that could encourage Methodist architecture to return to the spirit of Wesley and eighteenth-century preaching houses.[85]

Sir Percy Thomas & Son's first Methodist church was also English, replacing the bombed Victorian King Street Methodist Church in Plymouth. Perkins recommended Thomas, who drew up plans in 1949, developed by William Marsden before completion in 1957 (see Figure 3.11).[86] The old King Street church, 'the Cathedral of Western Methodism' seating 1,500 worshippers, was close to the city centre amid dense Victorian terraces.[87] But when Patrick Abercrombie and James Paton Watson published their proposals for rebuilding the centre in 1944, the church's site and surrounding housing were earmarked for new shopping streets. The question of where to rebuild caused much debate before Thomas's appointment. The interwar Methodist Central Hall's prominence made another central church seem unnecessary, and a neighbouring circuit advocated spending King Street's war damage compensation on churches in new suburban estates.[88] The King Street trustees insisted on a central location, but reduced the seating to 500, anticipating a depleted central population.[89]

3.11 King Street Methodist Church, Plymouth, 1949–57 (unknown photographer; The Box, Plymouth).

The city council offered a central site where bombs had destroyed the end of a Regency terrace called the Crescent.[90] Thomas's neo-Georgian design loosely accorded with the council's condition that the new church 'conform in style' to its neighbours.[91] Its scale and use of silver brick contrasted with the stucco-fronted terrace, asserting the building's public function. This extended beyond worship into community activities, especially for the young. The congregation wanted substantial ancillary facilities, including a hall doubling as Sunday school rooms and a 'Church House' for committees and social events. Thomas positioned the more domestically scaled Church House alongside the terrace, and the hall followed. A linking vestibule turned the corner to the church, a tall gabled block with pedimented doorcase and circular window. It, too, followed Perkins and Hearn's principles for a Methodist architecture, and the plan adapted their model design, with passage aisles.[92]

The question of siting in relation to urban developments was resolved in the other direction in Cardiff, where the Wesleyan Methodists of the Roath Circuit decided against rebuilding their grand Gothic Revival church on Newport Road, also bombed, but instead apportioned war damage compensation to three suburban churches in the circuit, all commissioned from Sir Percy Thomas & Son.[93] St Andrew's Church, Birchgrove and Rumney Methodist Church extended earlier buildings with new churches to accommodate Cardiff's growing suburban population; the third arose on a post-war council estate at Llanrumney. All three seem to have been designed largely by William Marsden, and were more modern versions of the Plymouth design.[94]

St Andrew's, Birchgrove, opened in 1956, was largest, linked to its Edwardian chapel, which was converted into a hall, with a block of rooms for a Sunday school and social activities, here also a core Methodist principle. The new building brought the church forward onto Caerphilly Road, presenting its gable to the surrounding suburb (see Figure 3.12).[95] The gable roughly duplicated the outline of end houses on

3.12 St Andrew's Methodist Church, Birchgrove, Cardiff, 1956 (photo: author).

its Victorian terrace, integrating with its surroundings, elevated to a public character with orange brick and simple modern forms. At its opening, superintendent minister A. W. Abbotts wrote, 'With the new church should go a new vision. We must be a missionary church, looking outwards beyond our fellowship towards the churchless multitude ... claiming this neighbourhood of Birchgrove for Christ' - a perspective that the architecture seems designed to express.[96]

The church at Rumney, also of 1956, was similarly planned, and built of grey brick to harmonise with neighbouring buildings.[97] As at Birchgrove, the church arose on the street frontage, linked to the old chapel behind it. Rumney's congregation established the Llanrumney church, and negotiated a site with the council on a prominent junction at the heart of the estate; smaller and simpler than the others, this church opened in 1959.[98]

Although it was institutionally unconnected to the Wesleyan Methodist Church, Sir Percy Thomas & Son's Calvinistic Methodist Trinity Chapel in Swansea was architecturally similar to those in Cardiff (see Figure 3.13). It, too, moved to suburban Sketty from its bombed city centre church, whose site was co-opted by the city for the new Kingsway.[99] Many in its congregation now lived in the western suburbs and, after the chapel's destruction, were worshipping in an interwar schoolroom that they had already built in Sketty. Percy Thomas, first consulted in 1950, convinced them to rebuild there, and Norman Thomas designed the chapel from 1951.[100]

Externally, Trinity Chapel was a plain pitched-roofed box with gable to the street and low projecting side aisles. Its basilican plan departed from the Welsh Nonconformist tradition of wide plans partly because of the restricted site, creating tension within the congregation, many wanting to sustain a distinctive Welsh approach for this Welsh-speaking chapel. Members insisted that there should be no central aisle, nor even an

3.13 Trinity Chapel, Swansea, 1950–5 (photo: author).

axial division in the pews, to avoid emphasising the communion table. Some members argued for a gallery around three sides; space prevented it, but a rear gallery was built, giving additional seating to sustain the Welsh custom of singing festivals with congregations from neighbouring chapels. Some members wanted a traditional *sêt fawr*, prominent elders' seating, but the minister, H. Wynne Griffiths, negotiated a more discrete screened bench between organ console and communion table.[101] A visually dominant central pulpit most strongly manifested Welsh convention. Norman Thomas gave these characteristic Welsh elements a restrained modern form with silver-grey brick, warm oak and a Festival of Britain style in light fittings and timber panelling.

Nearly two decades later, the Percy Thomas Partnership built another Wesleyan Methodist church at Dowlais in Merthyr Tydfil, where the town council had slated Victorian streets for demolition and new social housing, expropriating the existing Methodist church and allocating it a replacement site on the estate.[102] The new building was designed by Dale Owen, Edward Kluge and Roy Page.[103] Rejecting the typological constraints of the 1950s churches, they took a more radical modern approach, compactly integrating sacred and secular functions: a hall sat at the top of the sloping site, separated from the lower church space by a social room and kitchen; a classroom was tucked underneath the hall. Opened in 1972, the church was low and almost domestic, while its inverted sloping roofs, echoing the valley topography, expressed its higher purpose. Its architecture evoked the congregation's desire to participate in the town's contemporary development with a church 'of value and use to the community around'.[104]

The Gwent Crematorium at Croesyceiliog, near Cwmbran New Town, opened in 1960, was a civic rather than religious project, more typical of Thomas's work, though religious in character (see Figure 3.14). Its location was rural when built, sited for road access from the several local authorities that collaborated in building it, and likely

3.14 Gwent Crematorium, Croesyceiliog, Cwmbran, 1955–60 (photo: author).

anticipating Monmouthshire County Council's proposed county hall nearby, promising a new civic complex outside the town.[105] Meanwhile, Thomas designed the crematorium for the site's rural atmosphere, as its committee wanted 'an unobtrusive and tastefully and simply designed building ... that will fit naturally into its rural surroundings'.[106] As built with the involvement of Marsden and Frank Buckley, it was a straightforward pitched-roofed single-room hall fronted with a cloister walkway of cut-out arches and enclosed in stark white-rendered elevations, with a simplified Arts & Crafts feel.

Several Roman Catholic dioceses also commissioned churches from the practice, despite normally preferring specialised church architects: Our Lady Star of the Sea, Burry Port, and Our Lady Help of Christians, Machynlleth, were economical but striking modern buildings, while their Roman Catholic Cathedral of Saints Peter and Paul in Clifton, Bristol, became, remarkably, one of the most significant churches in post-war Britain. The three commissions shared a donor, the Van Neste Foundation of Bristol, which funded both Welsh churches and much of Clifton Cathedral's cost.

Wallace Sweet and another architect, possibly S. G. Howitt, designed the church at Burry Port, opened in 1964, to a meagre budget for a congregation of only 200.[107] Their plan, an elongated hexagon, sought to bring the congregation closer to the altar following new thinking about liturgy and church architecture, with a forward altar to allow the priest to face the people across it, a modern form with a social purpose, encouraging communal participation. The architects gave it direct modern expression through the economical use of ordinary materials, emphasising the virtues of simplicity espoused by other contemporary church architects: a 'simple rugged vernacular' of brick, painted white inside, hexagonal concrete floor tiles and 'robust and simple' joinery. The architects intended the church to harmonise with its surrounding terraces and post-war housing, using warm brick; and they also wanted to demonstrate 'the progressive nature of the Catholic faith ... by designing in a frankly contemporary manner', with a pyramidal roof and flêche as a landmark.[108]

The even smaller church in Machynlleth, which opened the following year, was designed from the practice's Shrewsbury office. The Redemptorist congregation ran the church on the Diocese of Menevia's behalf as a base for its 'Welsh Travelling Mission' to serve the few Catholics of central rural Wales.[109] The building took an equally bold contemporary form, a flat-roofed box on the town's main road, built of buff brick with slot windows and projecting concrete beams, brickwork and concrete exposed inside. It resembled the modest modern civic structures of the welfare state, such as libraries and community centres, suggesting a desire to participate in the modern world. Like Burry Port, it followed liturgical movement ideas, with seating on two sides of an open sanctuary.[110]

Clifton Cathedral, in contrast, had a substantial budget and scale, seating almost 1,000. The bishop chose the architects in late 1965, following recommendations from the RIBA and interviews with several practices.[111] Sir Percy Thomas & Son's background in civic buildings must have counted in their favour, given that the cathedral's purpose went beyond worship, accommodating events with a civic character, welcoming local dignitaries, and representing Catholic identity in Bristol. The practice's new Bristol office was also conveniently close to the deteriorating Victorian pro-Cathedral. The architects helped choose a site for its replacement in a more suburban area of Clifton.

Although less central, it allowed room for a prominent building, and brought it closer to the parish population, including the university, which was building a modern student union nearby.[112]

Frederick Jennett was the practice partner in charge, but Ronald Weeks was the cathedral's principal designer, assisted by Antoni Poremba.[113] They too applied liturgical movement principles, questioning Bishop Joseph Rudderham and his expert committee to develop their understanding of the liturgy.[114] Weeks and Jennett made diagrams of the Mass and its spatial arrangements, proposing a range of configurations for the committee's discussions.[115] Weeks employed a hexagonal geometry in which liturgical elements could be positioned in symbolic, axial relationships: the font, ambo and altar were aligned, while the fan-shaped nave rotated around the sanctuary (see Figure 3.15). The principal doors to the east brought worshippers through a spiral motion from dark to light around the baptistery.

Completed in 1973, the cathedral won a Concrete Society award for its carefully crafted concrete, its formwork designed to a modular geometry by Weeks, and external precast cladding of Aberdeen granite aggregate complementing the local purple stone in surrounding buildings (see Figure 3.16).[116] The few commissioned artworks complemented the material. William Mitchell's bold reliefs of the Stations of the Cross were made in fast-setting cement; and he also designed craggy sculptural doors made of metallic-plated fibreglass, incorporating the arms of Bristol, acknowledging their donation by the city council. Henry Haig created two abstract *dalle de verre* window friezes inspired by the Pembrokeshire coast.[117] Besides this Welsh allusion, however, the cathedral was firmly anchored in its city. Rising over an undercroft and sunken car park, broad steps and bridges formed theatrical public platforms open to surrounding streets,

3.15 Roman Catholic Cathedral Church of Saints Peter and Paul, Clifton, Bristol, 1965–73 (photo: author).

3.16 Roman Catholic Cathedral Church of Saints Peter and Paul, Clifton, Bristol, 1965–73 (photo: author).

suited to large-scale events and civic receptions. Its concrete spire and cross, visible from around the city, conveyed the cathedral's desire to participate in modern life.

The one factor uniting these disparate church buildings is the practice's civic ethos: their design helped religious communities to develop and articulate their identities in generous engagement with the city around them, often in partnership with civic authorities. Within that civic concern was the question of whether to consolidate congregations in the city centre or to build for communities in suburbs – a question the practice helped their clients to resolve empirically according to their individual needs.

Houses and Housing

While the individual house cannot be reasonably called 'civic', it was invested with a certain social duty to convey its owner's position; and when houses were composed as planned streets, 'civic art' entered as an 'expression of civic life', in Raymond Unwin's words.[118] Whereas Cardiff's Victorian upper-middle class of coal barons and associated entrepreneurs had indulged vast profits in displays of excess in their houses, such conspicuous spending was neither possible nor apparently desired after the First World War: tax rises and the coal trade's decline reduced surplus wealth; Liberal politics and depression made ostentatious consumption unseemly; and a more homely image prevailed.[119] Meanwhile a lower-middle class emerged able to afford cars and houses, developing a distinctive 'middlebrow' or 'intermodern' culture, fascinated with avant garde taste and modernity but seeking the reassurances of tradition and domesticity.[120] Between the wars Percy Thomas built neither grand country houses nor workers' housing, but rather, houses for the middle classes, the well-to-do yet thrifty business elite of the Cardiff docks, often politically active as Liberals or Conservatives, commuters into the purer air of the countryside, where they practised golf and hunting.[121]

Thomas's earliest large houses took an Arts & Crafts approach influenced by such architects as M. H. Baillie Scott and C. F. A. Voysey, with playful gables, steep slate roofs and big chimneys, of stone or rendered brick with hints of medievalising details. But Thomas ignored Baillie Scott's innovations in open planning for conventional room divisions, and ignored Voysey's rustic asceticism for bourgeois refinements such as plaster mouldings and, sometimes, neo-Tudor timber panelling. Generous living rooms could be subdivided with furnishings, sometimes graced with large fireplaces and inglenooks, and were sited on corners with varied outlooks, predominantly to the south: looking south over country views, sometimes from sheltered loggias, was clearly an obsession of his clients.

His first in this style seems to have been The Quarry in Fairwater, west of Cardiff, then in the countryside, completed in 1922 (see Figure 3.17).[122] An old quarry behind the house produced stone for its construction, displayed in rugged rustication.[123] Views south embraced the Vale of Glamorgan. Its owner was Roger W. Price, who had just left Cory Brothers, a coal trading and shipping firm, to establish a rival coal and fuel merchant, Llewellyn, Merrett and Price.[124]

Soon after came a commission from Jack W. Duncan, a shipping magnate, for a larger but similar house in Radyr called 'Fairywood' (later 'Fairwood'), designed in 1922, with a viewing loggia, an extra storey accommodating resident maids, and

3.17 The Quarry, Fairwater, house for Roger Price, 1922 (unknown photographer; from the Collections of the National Monuments Records of Wales; courtesy of the estate of Sir Percy Thomas and WSP UK Ltd).

substantial ancillary service buildings.[125] A smaller, more homely version followed in Dinas Powys for Sir Joseph Davies, who had served in Lloyd George's cabinet during the war, resuming business interests in south Wales after losing his seat.[126] He founded the Dinas Powys golf club, and built the house, the 'Long Twyn' (later 'Lon Twyn'), below it in 1928 (see Figure 3.18).[127] Though facing east, the large living room had a south-facing loggia.

Also Arts and Crafts in inspiration, though more typically suburban, with hipped roof, white render and brick and tile details, was a house in Radyr of 1923 to 1927 (see Figure 3.19). It, too, belonged to a golfing couple, D. Rupert and Isabel Phillips, and looked across the road to the Radyr clubhouse, a course founded by Isabel's father E. Franklin Thomas, who employed Phillips in his coal and shipping company.[128] The relatively modest elevations enclosed a spacious interior, with living rooms across the south frontage containing ornate Art Nouveau plasterwork; there was much timber panelling, a sweeping staircase and a servants' attic.

Thomas's two neo-Georgian houses were in more pastoral landscape settings, evoking eighteenth-century manor houses. The neo-Georgian style encouraged compact outlines, so was more economical than gabled houses, conveying a conspicuous frugality. The first was Sant-y-Nyll at St Brides-super-Ely, facing south over a rolling green valley through which ran the Glamorgan Hunt, in which owner Allan Renwick was prominent (see Figure 3.20).

Renwick was director of his father's shipbuilding company, and had recently married Edith Cory of the colliery dynasty, building the house in 1924. The new house was of red brick with sash windows and stone trim, living rooms compactly planned across the south. Doric columns framed the staircase from a reception room to

3.18 The Long Twyn (now Lon Twyn), house for Sir Joseph Davies, Dinas Powys, 1927–8 (photo: author).

3.19 House for D. Rupert and Isabel Phillips, Radyr, 1923–7 (photo: author).

3.20 House for Allan Renwick, Sant-y-Nyll, 1924 (photo: author).

impress on a budget, but rooms were small, servants' quarters modest and ornament restrained.[129] Cwrt-yr-Ala at Michaelstone-le-Pit, another Arcadian rural site in the Vale of Glamorgan, was built for Price's business partner, Sir Herbert Merrett, who left Cory Brothers with him, then moved into coal production, becoming chairman of Powell Duffryn.[130] Merrett bought the Cwrt-yr-Ala estate in 1937 and commissioned Thomas in 1939 to replace its Regency villa with a new house (see Figure 3.21).[131] Cwrt-yr-Ala was unusually generously built for entertaining: U-shaped in plan, a grand staircase at the centre, recycled from its predecessor, with reception rooms across the south overlooking the landscape, a dining room on the west enjoying evening sunlight, and eight bedrooms. Yet its appearance was austere, 'restrained and uncompromising in its severity', one critic thought.[132] Its compact compression pragmatically reduced construction and maintenance costs. Cwrt-yr-Ala and Sant-y-Nyll allowed their industrialist owners to dabble in pastoral lifestyles: Cwrt-yr-Ala resembled the Georgian Gileston Manor a few miles away, borrowing the image of a minor gentry house.

In the 1930s Thomas or his colleagues designed several smaller houses in a simpler, more modern style inspired by Voysey. Whether they drew on the Welsh vernacular is debatable. Iorwerth Peate of the National Museum of Wales had begun to posit the whitewashed Welsh longhouse as a national tradition, but Thomas's use of clay tiles for roofs suggests English models.[133] The Dingle of 1935–6 for the Misses Lewis was at Lisvane, beyond Cardiff's northern fringe: long and thin, lengthened with a built-in garage, white rendered, with deep pitched roof and asymmetrical gable, it had Art Deco detailing in brick at the entrance and in three-stepped mouldings on

3.21 Cwrt-yr-Ala, house for Sir Herbert Merrett, Michaelston-le-Pit, 1938–40 (photo: Stewart Bale; from the Collections of the National Monuments Records of Wales; courtesy of the estate of Sir Percy Thomas and WSP UK Ltd).

skirtings, cills and ceilings.[134] In 1939 the approach was repeated at Cherry Orchard nearby in a larger and more distinctly modern form for timber importer Arthur Meggitt, with rows of casement windows tucked under its eaves and a bowered loggia onto the terrace with panoramic views to the Bristol Channel. An integral garage and three bathrooms catered to middle-class expectations.[135] The third such house arose in the village of St Nicholas west of Cardiff, a striking contrast to surrounding stone cottages, for department store director John Trevil Morgan (see Figure 3.22). A curved turret on the garden front perhaps borrowed from Charles Rennie Mackintosh's Hill House, though incorporated rooms rather than a stair.

Commenting on some of these houses after the war, a critic wistfully recalled the 'generous living standards of the ultimate decade of plenty'; yet they were modest compared to the houses of the same class of owners of previous generations, with cheap materials, straightforward details and economical plans, as the same critic recognised, speculating on the 'money Sir Percy must have saved his clients.'[136] The Dingle appeared in a book of 'small houses' whose author promoted architects' abilities to serve their clients by steering a 'middle way' between modernism and historicism that avoided expensive ornament to increase space and equipment. Simplified Arts and Crafts and neo-Georgian approaches dominated the book.[137] These arguments echoed those of Arts and Crafts architects since the beginning of the century, chiming with clients' desires to express distinction from the speculative builder's semi.[138]

Thomas's only exercise in suburban housing was at Llanishen, beginning this small town's integration into Cardiff. The builder F. & R. Lewis acquired a mansion called the Rise and demolished it, ploughing up its garden for houses. Employing an architect

3.22 House for J. Trevil Morgan, St Nicholas, 1939 (photo: author).

for a speculative estate envisaged a more prestigious than average market, and even the smaller semi-detached houses on the Rise were about twice the standard price of a semi. Those in the first section from 1934 to 1939 had a high specification, with oak floors, electric wiring, fitted kitchens and garages (see Figure 3.23).[139] Some were in red-brick neo-Georgian and others a plainer Arts and Crafts, more restrained than standard developers' houses, but with details hinting at higher status, such as octagonal windows and tiled corbels. Most had broad inglenooks in their living rooms, unusually for houses of this scale. House sizes and types varied along the street, artfully arranged for coherent variety, set behind shallow front gardens, green road verges and street trees, following Unwin's Garden City model.

After the Second World War, Thomas and F. & R. Lewis entered plans for a semi-detached pair to a competition run by the National Federation of Registered House-Builders for small, economical houses to help resolve post-war housing shortages. Thomas's two houses were built at the Rise and opened by the Lord Mayor of Cardiff, W. R. Wills, in 1946, for public viewing as demonstration homes before their sale; several more followed, dotted among larger houses.[140]

Architects often attacked suburban speculative housing in this period for lacking coherent planning and tasteful design, partly out of professional snobbery towards developers and ordinary people.[141] Thomas, however, apparently did not deride the suburb. In the volumes he compiled on *Modern Building Practice* in the 1930s, an essay on 'The Speculative Builder and the Small House' took a positive approach to the semi, admitting its popular appeal and proposing modest improvements to the type.[142] The Rise refuted common criticisms of monotony, sham decoration or excessive individualism, showing how the speculative suburban estate could be improved with concern for civic design.

3.23 The Rise, Llanishen, houses of 1934–9 (photo: author).

London Landmarks

Meanwhile, Thomas was not only concerned to beautify modern Cardiff but also hoped to make his mark with a great public building in London. Besides his unsuccessful projects for local government, he also narrowly failed at two competitions for buildings for private organisations aiming to make important public statements in the city. The first was the Masonic Peace Memorial building near Covent Garden in 1925, for which Thomas's entry was shortlisted in 1926, in a baroque palazzo style.[143] The other was Thomas and Prestwich's entry for the RIBA headquarters at Portland Place, awarded joint third place with two other schemes in 1932. Thomas and Prestwich took a neo-Georgian approach to suit its context as Arthur Trystan Edwards had advocated, while the simplicity of their elevations emulated assessor Charles Holden's London Underground headquarters, with an effect 'simple, direct and, in a brutal way, strong', in Maxwell Fry's opinion. The first-floor library would have had an Ionic temple-like interior.[144] But Thomas's most exciting London project, and the one that came closest to fruition, was the new Euston railway station for the London, Midland & Scottish Railway (LMS) company.

Though also a private project, Euston had significant government backing and an important civic aspect. Since the 1920s the LMS had considered rebuilding Philip Hardwick's Victorian station, rendered confusing by its many accretions.[145] Chairman Josiah Stamp pushed forward with plans for rebuilding in 1935, approaching Thomas as RIBA president to work as consultant with the company's architect William H. Hamlyn, initial designs appearing the following year.[146] The LMS was motivated by a new government facility for low-cost loans for railway improvements, which Stamp discussed with the Chancellor of the Exchequer.[147] Other funded developments included a new streamlined engine, the Coronation Scot, modernising the company's image to entice consumers away from roads; and Euston was thus part of a wider rebranding that included such buildings as the Midland Hotel in Morecambe and Leeds City Station.[148] It participated in the wider design reform movement pioneered by Frank Pick at the London Passenger Transport Board (whose work with Holden and others was more consistent than Stamp's commissions for the LMS).[149] But it was also commercially important to update the railway's dirty Victorian image. As part of that effort, the LMS sent Thomas to America in 1936 to investigate new stations there, though he was seemingly more inspired by modern classical skyscrapers such as the Chicago Daily News Building.[150]

With a new hotel, better vehicle access and new station facilities including restaurants, the LMS argued that rebuilding Euston would lead to 'a distinctly improved public service' and improvements 'to the amenities of the district'.[151] The idea of a station's civic role was articulated by contemporary commentators. Charles Reilly and John Betjeman argued that stations were 'public institutions' that should be built and run by the state. Reilly urged planners to consider stations in relation to the city with generous formal public spaces. Both critics favoured Euston's rebuilding, urging the LMS to hire an outside architect, and Thomas's reputation for civic buildings must therefore have attracted Stamp.[152]

Grand internal and external public spaces were important aspects from the beginning, with a much-extended site involving demolition not only of the old station and its famous 'arch' but also two streets of houses. A forecourt for traffic circulation was to be flanked symmetrically with a hotel and office block, and the station would have had an immense concourse surrounded by modern facilities including shops, a restaurant and a cinema.[153] A large perspective by William Walcot depicted a twelve-storey elevation across the concourse apparently containing a full-height hall behind it lit by vertical windows under a carved frieze, an elevation that can also be read as an astylar classical colonnade (see Colour Plate 4). The offices and hotel were sober eight-storey cubic blocks like Thomas and Prestwich's RIBA building design, set-back upper storeys recalling Holden's London Underground headquarters. Thomas's approach used neoclassical forms to underline the terminal's serious purpose in the national service of public transport, ascetically pared of mouldings to declare its modernity.[154] The building went as far as demolitions and stone quarrying, before the outbreak of war halted work.[155]

Conclusion

Percy Thomas's architecture of the city and suburb, rather than challenging or reforming the modern social and economic order, celebrated and perpetuated it, accommodating contemporary work, leisure, consumption, domesticity and religion. In responding to context and adopting familiar imagery, the practice's architecture maintained an established vision of civic order and hierarchy, following the 'civic values' advocated by Arthur Trystan Edwards and others. Cardiff and Swansea had unique demands: the continuing dominance of the coal trade over Thomas's patronage is notable; the practice's Methodist churches resulted from a continuing strength of Nonconformity in Wales; the pubs suggest legacies of working-class identity in the suburbs. Nevertheless, the practice's models were often English, and sometimes American, bringing a transatlantic visual modernity to its work in both Wales and England. The civic values expressed in Thomas's architecture tamed commercial and private imperatives, showing deference to the greater public realm; and private businesses could seek to demonstrate benevolent contributions to the city through a public style of architecture. Local and national government, meanwhile, extended its reach into these spheres of commerce and religion. This expressive interplay of public and private spheres became especially important after the Second World War with ever more extensive government intervention, when Thomas's practice made significant contributions to the development and expression of the welfare state in Wales and beyond. ■

03

Commerce, Consumption and Community

References

1. A. Trystan Edwards, *Good and Bad Manners in Architecture* (London: Philip Allan & Co., 1924).

2. N. E. Shasore, '"A Stammering Bundle of Welsh Idealism": Arthur Trystan Edwards and Principles of Civic Design in Interwar Britain', *Architectural History*, 61 (2018), 175–203; Charles Mulford Robinson, *Modern Civic Art: or, The City Made Beautiful* (New York: Knickerbocker Press, 1909).

3. E. M. F., 'Town and Countryside', *Architects' Journal*, 5 April 1933, pp. 471–2; John Pendlebury, 'The Urbanism of Thomas Sharp', *Planning Perspectives*, 24/1 (2009), 3–27; Thomas Sharp, *Town and Countryside* (Oxford: Oxford University Press, 1932); Clough Williams-Ellis, *England and the Octopus* (London: Geoffrey Bles, 1929).

4. Robinson, *Modern Civic Art*, pp. 228–43; 'The Town "Cut"', *Architects' Journal*, 27 July 1932, p. 93.

5. Gavin Stamp, 'Neo-Tudor and Its Enemies', *Architectural History*, 49 (2006), 1–33.

6. 'A Shattered Pride', *Western Mail & South Wales News*, 16 March 1928, p. 4; 'Civic Society for Cardiff', *Western Mail & South Wales News*, 23 June 1933, p. 5; 'New Civic Society', *Western Mail & South Wales News*, 28 June 1933, p. 10.

7. 'Surveys of Cardiff', *Western Mail & South Wales News*, 26 July 1934, p. 6; 'Prizes for Plans of Coronation Decorations', *Western Mail & South Wales News*, 30 October 1936, p. 10.

8. 'Future Building Schemes', *Western Mail & South Wales News*, 3 April 1936, p. 10; '"Ridiculous" Rise in Prices of Building Materials', *Western Mail & South Wales News*, 19 March 1937, p. 13; '"Western Mail" Lead on Civic Centre Plan', *Western Mail & South Wales News*, 1 December 1937, p. 11.

9. 'Cardiff Civic Society', *Western Mail & South Wales News*, 11 October 1934, p. 6; 'Prizes for Plans of Coronation Decorations'.

10. 'Civic Society', *Western Mail & South Wales News*, 7 March 1934, p. 14; William Haywood, review of Cardiff Civic Society, *The Lay-out and Design of Small Houses*, in *Town Planning Review*, 16 (1934), 144.

11. Neil Evans, 'The Welsh Victorian City: The Middle Class and Civic and National Consciousness in Cardiff, 1850–1914', *Welsh History Review*, 12 (1984), 350–87.

12. 'Honour for an Architect', *Western Mail & South Wales News*, 17 June 1931, p. 6; 'The First RIBA Medal Building in S. Wales', *Architects' Journal*, 24 June 1931, p. 876; 'South Wales Architect Honoured', *Western Mail & South Wales News*, 30 January 1932, p. 10; 'Societies and Institutions', *Architects' Journal*,

10 February 1932, pp. 226–7; Frederic E. Towndrow, 'A Monthly Review of Current Architecture', *Building*, March 1932, pp. 128–33; 'Illustrations: New Premises, Cardiff', *The Builder*, 19 February 1932, pp. 339, 343–5.

13. 'Traders' Outlook: City of Cardiff Still in Its Infancy', *Western Mail & South Wales News*, 1 May 1929, p. 11.

14. 'James Howell and Company Limited: Description of the New Building', *Western Mail & South Wales News*, 24 April 1931, p. 7; 'Illustrations: New Premises, Cardiff', *The Builder*, 19 February 1932, pp. 339, 343–5 (344).

15. 'James Howell & Co. Ltd.: Romance of a Great Business, 1865 to 1925', *Western Mail & South Wales News*, 19 October 1925, p. 11; GAC, D407/14/1/1, James Howell Ltd, '60 Years', n.d. [1925]; GAC, DAB/44/17, 'A Hundred Years of Service and Achievement, 1865-1965: James Howell & Company Limited, Cardiff', 1965.

16. For example, Michael B. Miller, *The Bon Marché: Bourgeois Culture and the Department Store, 1869–1920* (Princeton NJ: Princeton University Press, 1994); Rosalind Williams, *Dream Worlds: Mass Consumption in Late Nineteenth-Century France* (London: University of California Press, 1982).

17. 'James Howell & Company Limited', advertisement, *Western Mail*, 13 November 1920, p. 14.

18. Robert Proctor, 'Constructing the Retail Monument: The Parisian Department Store and Its Property, 1855-1914', *Urban History*, 33/3 (2006), 393–410.

19. GAC, BC/S/1/21256, BC/S/1/21414 and BC/S/1/22263, Ivor Jones and Percy Thomas, various plans 1922–3.

20. GAC, BC/S/1/24996, various documents; 'Traders' Outlook: City of Cardiff Still in Its Infancy', *Western Mail & South Wales News*, 1 May 1929, p. 11.

21. Edwards, *Good and Bad Manners*, pp. 53–4.

22. Kathryn A. Morrison, *English Shops and Shopping: An Architectural History* (London: Yale University Press, 2003), p. 180.

23. 'A Great City Needs A Great Store!', *Western Mail & South Wales News*, 23 April 1931, p. 6.

24. 'Howell's Extension: Firm's Confidence in Cardiff's Future', *Western Mail & South Wales News*, 24 April 1931, p. 6.

25. 'Howells: Wharton Street Extension', *Western Mail & South Wales News*, 2 April 1937, p. 6; 'Eight Acres Floor Space in Stores', *Western Mail & South Wales News*, 3 April 1937, p. 7.

26. On the Kodak building and Kingsway, Murray Fraser and Joe Kerr, *Architecture and the 'Special Relationship': The American Influence on Post-War British Architecture* (Abingdon: Routledge, 2007), pp. 93–4; Julia Scalzo, 'All a Matter of Taste: The Problem of Victorian and Edwardian Shop Fronts', *Journal of the Society of Architectural Historians*, 68/1 (2009), 52–73 (66–8).

27. 'Duke-St. Upheaval', *Western Mail*, 26 March 1923, p. 9.

28. 'New Business Premises, Cardiff', *The Builder*, 27 October 1922, pp. 617-18.

29. GAC, DSA/12/4804, 'Proposed Mortgage of Nos. 11, 13, 15 & 17, Queen Street, Cardiff. Particulars of Property'; GAC, DX208, 'In Fashion Now - As in 1879: 1879-1979, Marments, Cardiff', souvenir booklet, 1979.

30. 'Lewis's Investment Trust', *Birmingham Daily Post*, 24 March 1959, p. 11.

31. 'Department Store, Bristol, for Lewis's Ltd', *The Builder*, 20 December 1957, pp. 1088-92.

32. Junichi Hasegawa, *Replanning the Blitzed City Centre: A Comparative Study of Bristol, Coventry and Southampton* (Buckingham: Open University Press, 1992), pp. 81, 121; BA, 43980/11, Broadmead press cuttings, *Western Daily Press and Bristol Mirror*, 23 May 1957, advertising supplement for Jones's.

33. 'Roof Garden at Lewis's Store, Haymarket, Bristol', *Architects' Journal*, 27 February 1958, p. 315.

34. BA, 43980/11, Broadmead press cuttings, 'The New Roads Begin to Take Shape', *Bristol Evening Post*, 2 April 1957.

35. 'Announcements: General', *Architects' Journal*, 7 June 1956, pp. 657-8; the painting is now at John Lewis, Cribbs Causeway.

36. Advertisement for Lewis's, Hanley, *Crewe Chronicle*, 27 October 1962, p. 21; RIBAL, BM/COM/7/A-H, 'Views of Modern Buildings in Great Britain: Commercial', photographs of model and drawings, *c.*1959.

37. RIBAL, BM/COM/7/A, photograph of model.

38. On Worcester: WAAS, 496.5 BA9360/Cab 22/24/54, Council meeting, 2 March 1937, 'Report of Special Meeting of Representatives of Finance, Property and Cemeteries, and Electricity Committees Re Provision of Adequate Office Accommodation for City Treasurer', 26 October 1936; WAAS, 496.5 BA9360/Cab 23/182, 'Fire Brigade & Police Accommodation. Progress of Erection. General File', Percy Thomas to C. H. Digby Seymour (Town Clerk, Worcester), 29 January 1942.

39. The scheme was initiated in 1934 and designed in 1935: 'Market Purchase: Electricity Show Rooms Scheme', *Western Mail & South Wales News*, 20 November 1934, p. 11; 'Tenders and Contracts', *Western Mail & South Wales News*, 14 October 1935, p. 1.

40. 'Cardiff Corporation Electricity Department: New Offices and Showroom', *Western Mail & South Wales News*, 12 June 1937, pp. 6-7.

41. 'Sale of Electrical Apparatus', *Western Mail & South Wales News*, 13 July 1937, p. 6; 'Cardiff Corporation Electricity Department' and 'Cardiff's New Electricity Showrooms', *Western Mail & South Wales News*, 12 June 1937, pp. 6-7 and 10, respectively.

42. Dinah Evans, *A New, Even Better, Abertawe: Rebuilding Swansea, 1941-1961* (Llandysul: West Glamorgan Archive Service, 2019), pp. 66, 102; WGAS, BE 52/71, D. Ivor Saunders (Borough Estate Agent) to Chairman and Members of the Parliamentary Committee, 6 October 1947; WGAS,

B/S/170, Parliamentary and General Purposes Committee (Reconstruction Sub-Committee), 12 July 1954; WGAS, TC 4/Parliamentary and General Purposes/14, Reconstruction Sub-Committee, 30 July 1954; WGAS, BE 52/71, 'Reconstruction of Central Town Area: Supplementary Report by Borough Engineer & Planning Officer to Re-Construction Sub-Committee, 10th October 1947, On the Location of Retail Market in the Plan of Central Area'.

43. WGAS, B/S/170, Parliamentary and General Purposes Committee (Reconstruction Sub-Committee), 5 October 1954.

44. Evans, *Rebuilding Swansea*, pp. 87 (facing image), 136–7; WGAS, B/S/171, Parliamentary and General Purposes Committee (Reconstruction Subcommittee), 4 February and 11 July 1955; WGAS, TC 4/Parliamentary and General Purposes/15, Reconstruction Subcommittee, 27 January 1956; WGAS, PL301/22, perspective of 1955, signature illegible.

45. Evans, *Rebuilding Swansea*, pp. 154–5; WGAS, ES1/RCS/3, photograph album.

46. WGAS, TC 227/1/17, 'Swansea Market Reconstruction: Official Reopening Ceremony', souvenir booklet, 1961.

47. Cardiff Council, *Mount Stuart Square: Conservation Area Appraisal* (Cardiff: Cardiff Council, 2009).

48. 'Empire House: The Development of Mount-Stuart Square', *Western Mail & South Wales News*, 30 August 1929, p. 7; this article attributes the design to Ivor Jones.

49. 'Mr. A. Hogan, FICS, Cardiff and Penarth', *Western Mail & South Wales News*, 8 April 1932, p. 12; 'An Imposing Cardiff Building', *Western Mail & South Wales News*, 7 December 1927, p. 5; 'Coal Sales Agency Appointment', *Western Mail & South Wales News*, 23 June 1927, p. 10; 'Mr Stephen B. Reid, Cardiff', *Western Mail & South Wales News*, 21 November 1930, p. 12; 'Certificate of Incorporation of the Georgian Company Limited', Companies House, 1914, *https://find-and-update.company-information.service.gov.uk/company/00136451/filing-history?page=4* (accessed 21 October 2021); 'Empire House: The Development of Mount-Stuart Square', *Western Mail & South Wales News*, 30 August 1929, p. 7; 'Company Meetings: Elder Dempster & Co., Ltd', *The Scotsman*, 8 June 1928, p. 4; 'Company Meetings: Elder, Dempster & Company', *The Scotsman*, 26 June 1929, p. 7; see also Percy Thomas, 'The Architecture of Cardiff', in Christopher J. Evans (ed.), *The Book of Cardiff: Presented to the Delegates at the Annual Conference of the National Association of Head Teachers* (London: Oxford University Press, 1937), pp. 72–9 (78).

50. 'Company Meetings: Elder Dempster & Co., Ltd', *The Scotsman*, 8 June 1928, p. 4.

51. Marika Sherwood, 'Elder Dempster and West Africa, 1891–c.1940: The Genesis of Underdevelopment?', *International Journal of African Historical Studies*, 30/2 (1997), 253–76.

52. GAC, BC/S/1/38780, drawing of July 1947 by Architectural Section of Prudential Estate Department and drawing of August 1949 naming Percy

Thomas as 'Consulting Architect'; 'Office Building for Prudential Assurance Company, Cardiff', *The Builder*, 29 August 1952, pp. 298–301.

53. 'No Change in Plan of New Building', *Western Mail & South Wales News*, 24 March 1950, p. 6.

54. 'Headquarters in Wales for Prudential Assurance Company Ltd Opened', *Western Mail & South Wales News*, 26 April 1952, p. 3.

55. Noel Whiteside, 'Private Provision and Public Welfare: Health Insurance Between the Wars', in David Gladstone (ed.), *Before Beveridge: Welfare Before the Welfare State* (London: Institute of Economic Affairs, 1999), pp. 26–42 (e.g., 34).

56. G. L. Hosking, *Salute to Service: The Prudential in the Second World War* (London: Prudential Assurance Company Ltd, 1947), pp. v, 45–53, 55.

57. GAC, BC/S/1/38780, plan of August 1949, revised June 1950.

58. 'Headquarters in Wales'.

59. Basil Oliver, 'English Inns', *RIBA Journal*, 14 May 1932, pp. 545–67; David W. Gutzke, *Pubs and Progressives: Reinventing the Public House in England, 1896–1960* (DeKalb IL: Northern Illinois University Press, 2006); Julian Holder, 'Public House: The Carlisle Experiment and the Improved Public House', in Neal Shasore and Jessica Kelly (eds), *Reconstruction: Architecture, Society and the Aftermath of the First World War* (London: Bloomsbury, 2023), pp. 143–72.

60. Gutzke, *Pubs and Progressives*, pp. 205, 226.

61. 'New Companies', *Western Mail*, 30 August 1915, p. 10.

62. 'Louis Café, Cardiff', *Architects' and Builders' Journal*, 1 November 1916, pp. 201–2, plates IV, V and XXXII.

63. 'Illustrations', *Architect*, 24 December 1920, pp. 405, 412.

64. 'Cardiff Rendezvous: An Air of Old-World Romance', *Western Mail*, 15 May 1920, p. 9.

65. 'To-Morrow's Opening: The Comforts of a Modern Inn', *Western Mail & South Wales News*, 18 November 1932, p. 6; brick details in 'Westgate Hotel, Cardiff', *Brick Builder*, September 1933, p. 34; 'Illustrations: Westgate Hotel, Cardiff', *The Builder*, 29 December 1933, pp. 1023–5.

66. 'Hotel Design: Welsh Architecture Students' Inspection', *Western Mail & South Wales News*, 11 November 1932, p. 6.

67. 'Honour for an Architect', *Western Mail & South Wales News*, 17 June 1931, p. 6.

68. 'Birchgrove Inn: Ivor Jones and Percy Thomas', *Architects' Journal*, 24 November 1938, p. 881; GAC, BC/S/1/26014, plans dated 1928; Gutzke, *Pubs and Progressives*, p. 179.

69. Oliver, 'English Inns', pp. 557, 559.

70. Attribution unconfirmed; dating from GAC, BC/S/1/31344 and DCONC/6/38a-e, licensing documents.

71. This section is condensed from Robert Proctor, 'Churches for Towns and Suburbs: Sir Percy Thomas & Son and the Percy Thomas Partnership', in Elain Harwood and Alan Powers (eds), *Holy Houses: Places of Worship in Twentieth-Century Britain* (London: The Twentieth Century Society, 2023), pp. 140–61.

72. WGAS, P/123/CW/547, Swansea & Brecon Diocesan War Damage Consultative Committee, 3 March 1949.

73. WGAS, P/123/CW/547, [Edward Williamson] (Bishop of Swansea and Brecon) to D. Edwards-Davies (Diocesan Chancellor), 29 January 1942; Evans, *Rebuilding Swansea*, p. 60.

74. WGAS, P/123/CW/442, PCC minutes, notes on vicar's speech, Annual Easter Vestry meeting, 30 April 1957.

75. WGAS, P/123/CW/547, Williamson to Edwards-Davies, 5 November 1943, Edwards-Davies to Williamson, 24 October 1943, [Edwards-Davies] to Leslie T. Moore, 8 December 1943.

76. WGAS, P/123/CW/547, Swansea & Brecon Diocesan War Damage Consultative Committee, 22 March 1949; WGAS, P/123/CW/500, correspondence over design of 1956–9 mostly with Percy Thomas in person; Thomas, *Pupil to President*, p. 49; WGAS, P/123/CW/663, main drawings of December 1953.

77. WGAS, P/123/CW/663/k, section drawing, Sir Percy Thomas & Son, 15 December 1953.

78. WGAS, P/123/CW/550, correspondence of 1959 on furnishings between Percy Thomas, T. G. Middleton (Sir Percy Thomas & Son) and H. C. Williams (St Mary's, Swansea).

79. WGAS, P/123/CW/441, Annual Easter Vestry, 22 April 1955; WGAS, P/123/CW/563, E. Liddall Armitage (Whitefriars Stained Glass Studios) to J. J. A. [Jack] Thomas (Archdeacon of Gower and Vicar of St Mary's, Swansea), 26 March 1957, and further correspondence between Armitage and Thomas.

80. WGAS, P/123/CW/547, PCC minutes, [Edwards-Davies] to Moore, 11 December 1943; WGAS, P/123/CW/441, PCC minutes, Annual Easter Vestry, 26 April 1943.

81. John Newman, *The Buildings of Wales: Glamorgan* (London: Yale University Press, 2004), p. 491.

82. University of Manchester Library Special Collections, Manchester, Wesley College Archives, A4/9, 'Didsbury College, New Buildings: Didsbury College, Westbury-on-Trym, Bristol', n.d. [c.1950]; 'Didsbury, Past and Future', *Methodist Recorder*, 3 May 1945, p. 1.

83. E. Benson Perkins and Albert Hearn, *The Methodist Church Builds Again: A Consideration of the Purpose, Principles, and Plans for Methodist Church Building* (London: Epworth Press, 1946), p. 10.

84. 'Didsbury Theological College, Bristol', *Architect & Building News*, 4 June 1953, pp. 651–4.

85. Perkins and Hearn, *Methodist Church Builds Again*, pp. 13, 17, 21.

86. Plymouth Archives and Local Studies, Plymouth (PALS), 2597/3, King Street Methodist Church trustees' meetings of 5 April 1948 and 16 December 1949; Marsden first attending at the meeting of 20 April 1955, described as 'the Architect for the new Building'; PALS, PCC/60/1/17169, plans dated 1954–57.

87. PALS, 3878/13, Pauline Raine, *Blitzed Church is Rebuilt: The Story of King Street Methodist Church* (Plymouth: n. pub., n.d. [c.1986]).

88. Jeremy Gould, *Plymouth: Vision of a Modern City* (Swindon: English Heritage, 2010), pp. 5–7 and 13–14; PALS, 2957/3, John E. Trevithick, 'Methodism in the New Plymouth', 30 January 1947, at Quarterly Meeting of the Plymouth and Devonport Mission Circuit, Joint Leaders' and Trustees' Meeting, 26 March 1947.

89. PALS, 2957/3, Trustees' meetings, 10 October 1946, 5 April 1948.

90. PALS, 2957/3, Trustees' meeting, 23 February 1948.

91. PALS, 2957/3, Trustees' meeting, 16 December 1948.

92. PALS, 2957/3, Trustees' meeting, 6 January 1950; Perkins and Hearn, *Methodist Church Builds Again*, p. 54 and plates, for example, plate II.

93. GAC, DWESCR/20/2, G. P. Williams, 'Acorn-Oak, 1742–1956', in 'Saint Andrew's Methodist Church, Birchgrove: Opening Ceremony', 1956, pp. 5–7 (6).

94. GAC, D761/7/1, photograph of opening ceremony shows Marsden attending, and he is named in written documentation at GAC.

95. GAC, BC/S/1/44594, drawings of 1954.

96. GAC, DWESCR/20/2, A. W. Abbotts in 'Saint Andrew's Methodist Church, Birchgrove: Opening Ceremony', 1956, p. 4.

97. GAC, BC/S/1/44149, drawings of 1954; GAC, D761/1/4, trustees' meeting, 1 April 1954; GAC, D761/7/1, 'Souvenir: Opening and Consecration of the New Methodist Church at Rumney, Cardiff', 1956.

98. GAC, D761/1/2, Rumney Methodist Church Leaders' meeting, 1 September 1952 and 'The Methodist Church, Cardiff (Roath) Circuit: Opening and Dedication of the New Church at Llanrumney', 1959; GAC, D761/1/3, Rumney Methodist Church Leaders' meetings, 29 November 1954 and 7 March 1955; GAC, D761/1/4, trustees' meeting, 11 June 1953.

99. NLWA, Calvinistic Methodist Archives (CMA), EZ1/85/33, 'Capel y Trinity: Adeiladau Newydd. Gohebiaethau Cofnodion', E. Llewellyn John to Regional Licensing Officer, Ministry of Works, Cardiff, 3 May 1952.

100. NLWA, CMA, EZ1/85/33, report of 25 October 1950; NLWA, CMA, EZ1/85/29, for example, New Chapel Building Committee meeting of 7 November 1951 and 'Eglwys Methodistiaid Calfinaidd Y Trinity, Glanmor Park Road, Abertawe: Rhaglen Cyfarfodydd Agoriadol, Mawrth 15, 16 a 17, 1955'; Percy Thomas is depicted in a photograph of the event: Rhidian Griffiths, correspondence with the author, 9 July 2018.

101. NLWA, CMA, EZ1/85/33, for example, Norman Thomas to G. Stanley Howells (Chapel Building Committee), 8 February 1952; Howells to Sir Percy Thomas & Son, 14 November 1952; Howel Mendus to Howells, 13 April 1953 and 9 July 1954; anonymous letter [Howells] to Sir Percy Thomas & Son, 4 February 1955; for information on Welsh custom, I am grateful to Rhidian Griffiths and Jill-Hailey Harries.

102. 'Merthyr's Chapels: Wesley Chapel, Dowlais', The Melting Pot: The Heritage and Culture of Merthyr Tydfil, 2020, *www.merthyr-history.com/?p=3804* (accessed 10 November 2021).

103. GAC, DWES/MT/144/1/4, for example, Sir Percy Thomas & Son, 'Notes of Meeting held in the Architect's Offices on Friday 3rd May, 1968'; GAC, DWES/MT/144/1/1, George Graham (minister at Dowlais) to Herbert Simpson (Department for Chapel Affairs, Methodist Church), 15 January 1971.

104. GAC, DWES/MT/144/1/2, 'History of Dowlais "Wesley" Methodist Church, 1932-1972: 40 Years', 1972.

105. 'Local Authorities Confer at Newport', *South Wales Gazette*, 16 July 1943, p. 7; 'County's 20-Year Development Plan', *Western Mail & South Wales News*, 20 October 1955, p. 8; Gwent Crematorium Archives, Croesyceiliog (GCA), uncatalogued, Monmouthshire and Newport Joint Cremation Committee, 15 November 1954 and 13 May 1955.

106. GCA, Monmouthshire and Newport Joint Cremation Committee, 24 June 1955.

107. Menevia Roman Catholic Diocesan Archives, Swansea (MDA), parish file James Howard (parish priest, Burry Port) to John Edward Petit (Bishop of Menevia), 2 April 1963; Wallace Sweet (Sir Percy Thomas & Son) to Petit, 2 April 1963.

108. MDA, parish file, Sweet to Petit, 16 May 1963 and accompanying report.

109. Christopher Magner, 'Sant Mair, Machynlleth: A Parish History, 1927 to 1997', 1997, *https://fliphtml5.com/aqap/eeiw/* (accessed 15 November 2021); 'Redemptorists Take Over Travelling Mission', *Catholic Standard*, 30 March 1951, p. 3; H. W. J. Edwards, 'The Roman Church in Wales To-Day', *Western Mail & South Wales News*, 19 January 1952, p. 4; 'Machynlleth – St Mair (Our Lady Help of Christians)', Taking Stock: Catholic Churches of England & Wales, n.d., *https://taking-stock.org.uk/building/machynlleth-st-mair-our-lady-help-of-christians/* (accessed 12 November 2021); the church's dedication was changed to St Mair.

110. *Catholic Building Review*, Northern Edition, 1965, pp. 159–61.

111. Peter Ansdell Evans, 'Clifton's Catholic Cathedral', *Architects' Journal*, 11 July 1973, pp. 70–2 (71).

112. Kenneth Nugent, 'Clifton Cathedral Church of SS Peter and Paul', *Clergy Review*, September 1973, 737–44 (739–40).

113. Tony Aldous, 'Portrait of a Practice: Percy Thomas Partnership', *Building Design*, 2 December 1977, pp. 13–16 (15); Ronald Weeks, 'The Design and Construction of the Cathedral Church of SS. Peter and Paul, Clifton', *Pax: The Review of the Benedictine Monks of Prinknash*, 63/2 (1973), 60–9; Kate Wharton, 'Genesis of

a Cathedral', *Architect & Building News*, 1 January 1969, pp. 22–9; Kate Wharton and Ronald Weeks, 'Architectural Heritage Year 2075 ... ?', *The Architect*, May 1975, pp. 24–5.

114. Robert Proctor, 'Uncertainty and the Modern Church: Two Roman Catholic Cathedrals in Britain', in Vladimir Kuliç, Timothy Parker and Monica Penick (eds), *Sanctioning Modernism: Architecture and the Making of Postwar Identities* (Austin TX: University of Texas Press, 2015), pp. 113–38; Robert Proctor, *Building the Modern Church: Roman Catholic Church Architecture in Britain, 1955 to 1975* (Farnham: Ashgate, 2014), for example, p. 160.

115. Robert Proctor, 'Modern Church Architect as Ritual Anthropologist: Architecture and Liturgy at Clifton Cathedral', *ARQ*, 15 (2011), 359–72; Clifton Roman Catholic Diocesan Archive, Bristol (CDA), cathedral box, 'Plans & Construction Details of Clifton Cathedral', drawings of High Mass and Pontifical High Mass of 29 November 1965 and 2 December 1965; CDA, cathedral box, 'R. C. Cathedral Bristol Liturgical Brief (rev. Dec'65)' and similar undated; Ronald Weeks, telephone interviews with the author, 9 November 2007 and 24 September 2008.

116. George Perkin, 'Cathedral Craft: Cathedral Church of SS. Peter and Paul, Clifton, Bristol', *Concrete Quarterly*, January to March 1974, pp. 22–32; 'Concrete Society Award 1974', *Architects' Journal*, 5 June 1974, pp. 1250–2; 'RIBA Awards', *Architects' Journal*, 7 August 1974, pp. 317–20.

117. Henry Haig, 'Clifton Cathedral: Designing and Making the Windows', *Clergy Review*, January 1974, pp. 81–8.

118. Raymond Unwin, *Town Planning in Practice: An Introduction to the Art of Designing Cities and Suburbs* (London: T. Fisher Unwin, 1911), p. 2.

119. Peter Scott and James T. Walker, 'The Comfortable, the Rich, and the Super-Rich: What Really Happened to Top British Incomes during the First Half of the Twentieth Century?', *Journal of Economic History*, 80/1 (2020), 38–68.

120. Ross McKibbin, *Classes and Cultures: England 1918–1951* (Oxford: Oxford University Press, 1998); Nicola Humble, *The Feminine Middlebrow Novel, 1920s to 1950s: Class, Domesticity, and Bohemianism* (Oxford: Oxford University Press, 2001); Faye Hammill, 'Stella Gibbons, Ex-Centricity and the Suburb', in Kristin Bluemel (ed.), *Intermodernism: Literary Culture in Mid-Twentieth-Century Britain* (Edinburgh: Edinburgh University Press, 2009), pp. 75–92.

121. Timothy Brittain-Catlin, *The Edwardians and Their Houses: The New Life of Old England* (London: Lund Humphries, 2020), for example, p. 14; Matthew Cragoe, 'Conservatives, "Englishness" and "Civic Nationalism" Between the Wars', in Duncan Tanner, Chris Williams, Wil Griffith and Andrew Edwards (eds), *Debating Nationhood and Governance in Britain, 1885–1945: Perspectives from the 'Four Nations'* (Manchester: Manchester University Press, 2006), pp. 192–210 (e.g., 205).

122. GAC, RDC/S/2/1920/12, drawings of 27 March 1920.

123. RCAHMW, PTA, 01/12, loose photographs.

124. 'South Wales Coal Annual', *Western Mail & South Wales News*, 3 January 1921, p. 15; 'Welsh Coal Merge: Gueret and Llewellyn, Merrett & Price', *Western Mail & South Wales News*, 3 December 1926, p. 9.

125. GAC, RDC/S/2/1922/35, drawings of 23 September 1922; GAC, RDC/S/2/1923/16 and RDC/S/2/1923/2, lodge drawings, 27 January and 26 May 1923.

126. 'Death of Sir Joseph Davies', *Western Mail & South Wales News*, 6 December 1954, p. 4.

127. J. V. Moody, 'Welsh Golf Courses No. 18: Dinas Powis', *Western Mail & South Wales News*, 18 October 1951, p. 3; 'Social & Personal', *Western Mail & South Wales News*, 2 April 1928, p. 7.

128. GAC, RDC/S/2/1923/68, drawings of 22 January 1923; ARCA, PTA, 01/12, interior photographs; 'Cardiff Pitwood Importers: Well-Known Golfer as Chairman-Elect', *Western Mail & South Wales News*, 28 March 1925, p. 14; 'New High Sheriffs', *Brecon County Times*, 24 March 1932, p. 6.

129. 'Late Wing-Commander A. E. Renwick', *Western Mail & South Wales News*, 11 May 1954, p. 3; GAC, RDC/S/2/1923/17, plans of 10 and 12 March 1923; Edward Holland, 'Sant y Nyll, St Brides Super Ely: Statement of Significance', 2021; Nick Renwick, telephone interview with the author, 8 October 2021.

130. 'Welsh Coal Merge'; 'Leaders of Commerce', *Western Mail & South Wales News*, 20 March 1934, p. 14; 'Site Record: Cwrt-Yr-Ala', Coflein, *https://coflein.gov.uk/en/site/18502* (accessed 2 December 2021).

131. RCAHMW, PTA, 01/12, attributed to Norman Thomas on photograph album; repeated thereafter, for example, at 'Site Record: Cwrt-Yr-Ala'; but GAC, RDC/S/2/1939/1, plans, 20 and 29 March 1939, do not name him.

132. J. R. Leathart, 'Current Architecture', *Building*, March 1942, pp. 58–61 (58); 'Three Pre-War Houses', *Building*, June 1952, pp. 224–7.

133. Iorwerth Peate, *The Welsh House: A Study in Folk Culture* (Liverpool: Hugh Evans & Sons Ltd, 1944).

134. GAC, RDC/S/2/1936/2, plans of 12 December 1935.

135. GAC, RDC/S2/1939/104, plans of 10 May 1939; 'Three Pre-War Houses', pp. 225–6; 'Timber Trade Change: Watsons Acquired by Meggitt & Jones Ltd', *Western Mail & South Wales News*, 31 January 1925, p. 7; Graham Emery, 'Welsh Golf Notes: Amateur Championship Meeting', *Western Mail & South Wales News*, 22 August 1933, p. 3.

136. 'Three Pre-War Houses', p. 227.

137. H. Myles Wright (ed.), *Small Houses £500–2500 Pre-War Costs* (London: Architectural Press, 1946) (reprint of 1937 edition); reviewed at R. Gardner-Medwin, 'The Rational House', *Architects' Journal*, 8 July 1937, pp. 75–6.

138. For example, Barry Parker and Raymond Unwin, *The Art of Building a Home* (London: Longmans, Green & Co., 1901).

139. Lionel East, 'The Rise, Llanishen: A Personal History of The Rise Estate', unpublished memoir, 2020; GAC, BC/S/1/31358, drawings of 15 July 1936.

140. 'HBISC Competition', *Architects' Journal*, 10 May 1945, pp. 359–60; 'From an Architect's Commonplace Book', *Architects' Journal*, 12 July 1945, p. 19; 'News', *Architects' Journal*, 13 December 1945, pp. 423–4; 'Demonstration Permanent Houses', *Western Mail & South Wales News*, 1 June 1946, p. 3.

141. Williams-Ellis, *England and the Octopus*; Paul Oliver, Ian Davis and Ian Bentley, *Dunroamin: The Suburban Semi and Its Enemies* (London: Barrie and Jenkins, 1981), for example, pp. 27–53; Gavin Stamp, 'Neo-Tudor and Its Enemies', *Architectural History*, 49 (2006), 1–33; Deborah Sugg Ryan, 'Living in a "Half-Baked Pageant"', *Home Cultures*, 8/3 (2011), 217–44.

142. 'The Speculative Builder and the Small House', in Percy E. Thomas (ed.), *Modern Building Practice*, 4 vols (London: George Newnes Ltd, 1935), I, pp. 241–56.

143. Library and Museum of Freemasonry, London, BE 64 UNI fol and GBR 1991 PA/23, competition entry photographs, *c.*1926; H. P. Cart De Lafontaine, 'The Ten Finalists', *Architects' Journal*, 2 June 1926, pp. 1–8 (7).

144. A. Trystan Edwards and Frederic Towndrow, 'Style v. Style: From Which Side Should the RIBA Jury Be Picked?', *Architects' Journal*, 14 May 1930, p. 745; 'The R.I.B.A. Competition: Some Opinions, i', *Architects' Journal*, 11 May 1932, pp. 623–5 (625); E. Maxwell Fry, 'The Designs Discussed', *Architects' Journal*, 4 May 1932, pp. 608–9; Robert Atkinson, 'RIBA New Building', *Architects' Journal*, 7 December 1932, pp. 733–34; 'The New Building Competition', *RIBA Journal*, 14 May 1932, pp. 568–83.

145. Gavin Stamp, 'Early Twentieth-Century Stations', in Julian Holder and Steven Parissien (eds), *The Architecture of British Transport in the Twentieth Century* (London: Yale University Press, 2004), pp. 23–46 (41).

146. TNA, RAIL 418/9, London, Midland and Scottish Railway Company Board of Directors meetings, 24 October 1935 and 19 December 1935; 'Euston Station', *Architects' Journal*, 16 January 1936, p. 78; W. W. Sharp, untitled article, *LMS Magazine*, February 1936, p. 53; TNA, RAIL 418/109/13, 'Reconstruction of Euston Station: Present Position', July 1936.

147. TNA, RAIL 418/108/22, Chairman [Josiah Stamp] to Sir Arthur Rose, 15 October 1935; TNA, RAIL 418/159, 13th Ordinary General Meeting of Proprietors, 28 February 1936.

148. 'The Coronation Scot Express', *LMS Magazine*, July 1937, pp. 316–17; Stamp, 'Early Twentieth-Century Stations', pp. 36–40.

149. Michael T. Saler, *The Avant-Garde in Interwar England: Medieval Modernism and the London Underground* (New York: Oxford University Press, 1999), for example, pp. 92–117.

150. TNA, RAIL 418/109/13, [Stamp] to Directors, 28 July 1936; 'The Architectural Association: Mr Percy Thomas's Impressions of America', *The Builder*, 19 March 1937, pp. 635–6; Stamp, 'Early Twentieth Century Stations', p. 46; Thomas, *Pupil to President*, pp. 36–7.

151. TNA, RAIL 418/108/19, E. J. H. Lemon, 'Proposed Loan for New Works: Euston Station Reconstruction', October 1935.

152. John Betjeman, 'Dictating to the Railways', *Architectural Review*, September 1933, p. 84; C. H. Reilly, 'Criticism: 7. Railway Stations, Terminal and Otherwise', *Architectural Review*, October 1935, pp. 147–9; Stamp, 'Early Twentieth Century Stations', pp. 41–2.

153. TNA, RAIL 418/110/12, Memorandum: Euston Re-Construction', 17 June 1937.

154. National Railway Museum, York, 1977-5720, n.d.

155. TNA, RAIL 418/109/13, 'Reconstruction of Euston Station: Present Position', July 1936; TNA, RAIL 418/111/5, 'Memorandum to the Board from the Executive: Euston New Station', January 1938; 'In the News', *LMS Magazine*, November 1937, pp. 541–2; 'Giant Blast at Caldon Low', *LMS Magazine*, August 1938, p. 379; 'Picture News', *LMS Magazine*, May 1939, p. 229; TNA, RAIL 418/112/14, 'Memorandum from the Executive to the Board, November 1939'.

4

Industry and Infrastructure in the Welfare State

The post-war period saw a huge shift in the nature of the practice's work with the advent of the welfare state. Thomas's interwar municipal work shows significant state intervention in welfare and education, undertaken by local authorities through central government legislation and funding. But in several speeches in 1937, Thomas foresaw more expansive government action, in which architects could play a role. 'We are at the dawn of a new era when planning will be the keynote of human progress and when the whole system of roads, towns, and industries will be planned not only in themselves but in their relation to the needs of the people and the preservation of the countryside', he told the RIBA annual conference at Leeds.[1] At the Liverpool Architectural Society, he argued that 'the outlook on national life was changing', and this new era would soon arrive.[2] In London, he said that the new concept of citizenship made 'service to the State' an essential duty, and architects should be 'the pioneers, the missionaries, to preach to our national and municipal leaders of the benefits which ordered planning can bring to the nation'.[3] He already had personal involvement in such work, and his practice would soon be at the forefront of this movement, particularly in Wales.

'Planning' was a constantly reiterated theme in mid-twentieth-century discourse.[4] Planning linked economic and spatial spheres, as Keynesian investment in public works increased in scale, encompassing transport and industry, healthcare and education. The 1940 Barlow Report on the Distribution of the Industrial Population argued for state intervention to plan industrial development across Britain more equitably, benefiting areas of unemployment.[5] Politicians debated the state's relationship to industrial production, Labour arguing for nationalisation of many industries.[6] Concern with welfare accompanied these arguments. William Beveridge's 1942 report argued for comprehensive state benefits and universal free healthcare, both promised by Clement Attlee's post-war Labour government. Local government-led planning of cities and regions was made obligatory through the New Towns Act of 1946 and the Town and Country Planning Act of 1947. The Conservative Party also accepted the state planning of welfare, its government's 1962 hospital plan significantly developing the National Health Service.[7] Harold Wilson's subsequent Labour government advocated renewed state investment in technology, industry, training and research and a dramatic expansion of higher education.[8] In taking over from his father in the 1950s, Norman Thomas understood the architectural opportunities of such political projects, and decided to specialise in health and education alongside Sir Percy Thomas & Son's growing expertise in industrial buildings.

Governments enlisted private companies to achieve this planned state.[9] Labour retained a capitalist state modified by government intervention, promoting high employment, and national income generated by production and trade: a developmental state that funded welfare.[10] Economic planning involved a 'spatial Keynesianism' that shifted the state's scale from local to national government, using regional policies of industrial and infrastructure investment to organise capitalist development.[11] Viewed from Wales through the lens of Thomas's practice, such transformations suggest a move towards greater unification of the British state, but they were also locally distinctive, often celebrated as distinctively Welsh, and often resulted from Welsh initiatives. The practice's work demonstrates that questions of Welsh national identity and agency in British modernity cannot be resolved through binary distinctions.[12]

Architectural modernism has often been seen as intrinsic to welfare state modernity, especially as architects committed to modernism gravitated towards public bodies such as local authorities.[13] Yet much of the practice's post-war work maintained a lingering classicism, suggesting the continuing appeal of that style's symbols of collective endeavour. There were, however, moments when such design methods proved incapable of accommodating contemporary demands, and younger architects trained in modern approaches took over. Modernism came to dominate the practice's work, with new and changing styles and spatial approaches, a frank acceptance of new building technologies, and the careful study and expression of buildings' functions. Sir Percy Thomas & Son's work came to define the concrete spatial and visual forms of the welfare state, especially as they were experienced in Wales.

States of Industrial Production

An experiment in government direction of industry in south Wales in the 1930s proved so successful that it became a major instrument of government influence over industry after the war, and involved Percy Thomas and his practice throughout, making them leading industrial architects in Wales. Government-appointed commissioners investigating regions with high unemployment designated as Special Areas argued for the diversification of industry to reduce dependence on steel and coal, and proposed government trading estates modelled on commercial pioneers at Trafford Park and Slough, where sites had been planned and serviced for industrial occupants.[14] Three national government-backed trading estates followed in 1936, designed on similar lines: Team Valley in Gateshead, designed by William Holford; Hillington in Glasgow; and Treforest, run by the South Wales and Monmouthshire Trading Estates company, which appointed Thomas as consultant architect in December 1936.[15]

Treforest, sited between Cardiff and Merthyr Tydfil for road and rail access and close to populations of redundant miners, was started before Thomas's appointment, laid out with a central boulevard and a grid of roads between loops of the river Taff. Thomas designed the estate company headquarters in an idiosyncratic modern neo-Georgian style (see Figure 4.1), and several service buildings, including restaurants, banks and a post office.[16] Engineers Sir Alexander Gibb and Partners created a standardised modular factory template that companies could adapt and expand, for which Thomas designed customised office frontages with brightly glazed reception areas (see Figure 4.2).[17] The convenience of the estate services and attractiveness of its modern design, pleasant landscaping and favourable financial terms, attracted manufacturing companies making such commodities as aircraft parts, paper and buttons, employing more than 2,500 workers within three years, and continuing to develop after the war.[18]

4.1 Estate Office, Treforest Industrial Estate, *c.*1938 (unknown photographer; from the Collections of the National Monuments Records of Wales; courtesy of the estate of Sir Percy Thomas and WSP UK Ltd).

4.2 Factory frontage, Treforest Industrial Estate, *c.*1950s (photo: author).

Treforest demonstrated how government action could change the industrial landscape, giving a model for more far-reaching post-war transformations. It aimed to change Welsh industry's reputation for hardy but restive workers by bringing skilled jobs in modern industries.[19] It brought rational planning to industry, countering perceptions of Victorian mining towns as squalid and chaotic.[20] Thomas's architecture thus had a polemical purpose, making this modern approach evident and convincing. The success of industrial estates led to more comprehensive government intervention to control industrial location, enabled by the Distribution of Industry Act of 1945.[21]

By then, controlling industrial location had become pragmatic policy during the war as the government took control of military equipment production, dispersing it into the regions to reduce the impact of air raids.[22] Percy Thomas became embedded in the administration of this effort in 1940 when the Ministry of Supply appointed him Area Officer for Wales to mediate between government and industry: Thomas reported to the Ministry on factory capacity, received production requests from government, and persuaded businesses to fulfil them.[23] Minister of Production Oliver Lyttelton created more formal regional boards in 1942 involving government, businesses and trade unions, led by regional controllers, Thomas becoming Regional Controller for Wales.[24] At meetings in London, the Ministry presented operational needs for equipment, labour, or other instructions to industry for controllers to implement through local offices.[25]

Lyttelton and the controllers discussed how this new state machinery could be repurposed in peacetime in the national interest.[26] Treforest's trading estate company assumed this role for Wales, reinvented after the war as Wales and Monmouthshire Industrial Estates (WMIE), and retaining Thomas as its architect. It converted Royal Ordnance Factories into trading estates and worked with the Board of Trade to attract manufacturers into Wales.[27] Meanwhile, Board of Trade president Stafford Cripps reformed regional boards as advisory committees in 1945, appointing Thomas to chair the Welsh Board for Industry for a further ten years.[28] Representing businesses, trade unions and local authorities, he pressed for government urgency over factory building in 1945; urged the Chancellor of the Exchequer to provide work for the disabled; and campaigned for road improvements.[29] He therefore contributed to the design of industry in Wales not only through buildings but also in terms of policy, from the wartime state to the post-war welfare state.

Meanwhile the government applied its main tool of locational control over industry through the Board of Trade by extending wartime licensing: companies building new facilities had to request Industrial Development Certificates (IDCs), enabling government to coerce them into designated Development Areas. The WMIE offered businesses incentives, such as accommodation in standardised factories, built to Thomas's design throughout south Wales.[30] It acquired sites and built specially-designed factories to companies' requirements, renting them back to recoup the capital. Sometimes a business would ask the WMIE to employ their preferred architect, as did Hoover when Wallis, Gilbert & Partners designed its washing-machine factory at Merthyr Tydfil, and the WMIE also built the well-known Brynmawr rubber factory, originally for Enfield Cables, to the designs of the Architects' Co-Partnership.[31]

Hence, Thomas designed one of the most important factories in Wales, for the British Nylon Spinners (BNS) at Mamhilad near Pontypool, an early symbol of welfare-state intervention in industry. The Board of Trade insisted that the company choose a Development Area rather than extend its original site at Banbury, and the WMIE offered a redundant Royal Ordnance Factory hostel at Mamhilad in 1945.[32] Managing director of BNS F. C. Bagnall, who commuted to Pontypool from the Cotswolds, long remained 'resentful' and complained of difficulties recruiting scientists to the rural location (though many workers lived nearby at Cwmbran New Town).[33] This tension was suppressed in public, while a photograph of Thomas's monumental factory against its bucolic backdrop advertised Development Areas to businesses.[34]

The BNS was founded in 1940 by Imperial Chemical Industries (ICI) and Courtaulds to produce nylon under licence from its American inventor, DuPont, which also supplied its machinery.[35] The Pontypool factory produced all nylon yarn in Britain until the 1960s, becoming literally part of the fabric of everyday modernity. Nylon's raw material, however, was coal, made into polymer chips at the ICI plant in Billingham, near Middlesborough, dispatched to Pontypool for conversion into thread, wound onto giant bobbins and sent to textile factories, mostly in the English midlands.[36]

Thomas and colleagues including Frank Buckley designed the factory in a monumental brick style, with 'solid simplicity ... a complete elimination of the unnecessary, creating dignity, nobility, and a cold perfection', as one contemporary writer enthused (see Figure 4.3 and Figure 4.4).[37] Its sharp outlines, visible from the road and railway, created a recognisable image, with a red-brick tower fronting a vast expanse of factory floors.[38] The tower was functional, vats hoisted up inside it to release polymer into machines, but cast stone mullions implied a temple front, hinting at an official character. The factory demanded complex services, but its rooftop plant was hidden behind parapets forming three simple raised blocks. The thin architectural skin

4.3 BNS factory, Mamhilad, perspective by R. F. Buckley, 1947 (Amgueddfa Torfaen Museum; courtesy of the estates of Sir Percy Thomas and R. F. Buckley and of WSP UK Ltd).

4.4 BNS factory, Mamhilad, 1947–9 (unknown photographer; Amgueddfa Torfaen Museum).

of brick on a steel frame gave an illusion of monumentality, by then an old-fashioned approach. In contrast, both the structural dynamism of the Brynmawr Rubber Factory's reinforced concrete vaults and the lighter Bauhaus-inspired approach of architects such as Yorke, Rosenberg and Mardall were increasingly preferred to articulate the liberal social democratic values of the post-war world over the classical monumentality redolent of a previous era.

The main block opened in 1949 and nylon's popularity soon led to expansion, but whereas the architects envisaged a second identical factory beside the original, the company preferred rearward extensions.[39] Meanwhile, the practice designed a campus for administrative, marketing and research departments including testing and development laboratories alongside the factory in the 1950s, adopting a simpler modern style.[40] The welfare of the company's 6,000 employees was overseen in departments set around courtyards on one side of the factory, including clinics, canteens and training facilities, and Thomas designed a social club nearby.[41]

Sir Percy Thomas & Son built smaller factories across south Wales for the WMIE in the 1940s and 1950s, and occasional commissions in England.[42] Harold Wilson gave new impetus to Development Area policy in the 1960s, strengthening industrial estate corporations.[43] The WMIE became the Welsh Industrial Estate Corporation and its work proliferated, including new industrial estates in south Wales. Keith Mainstone led Sir Percy Thomas & Son's new Industrial Planning Group, designing factories in this second wave. Most significant was the Parke-Davis pharmaceutical plant next to the BNS at Mamhilad (see Figure 4.5).

Designed at speed by Mainstone, Owen, Vergette and Poremba and completed in 1971, this complex adopted a new campus style of planning associated with technology firms and corporation headquarters, following American models, and indeed it housed this American firm's British headquarters, relocated from Hounslow.[44] The manufacturing block was programmatically complex, accommodating specialised processes within a single serviced envelope. Administrative, research and welfare buildings were dotted informally around a picturesque landscape with a lake, harmonised with a uniform palette of grey brick, windows almost to the ground and projecting fascias.[45] Shunning Thomas's monumentality, it marked a new high-technology direction for Welsh industry.

4.5 Parke-Davis pharmaceutical plant, Mamhilad, 1969–71 (photo: Jonathan Vining).

Meanwhile, Sir Percy Thomas & Son also gave architectural expression to the modernisation of the older industry of steel. State involvement was crucial to the steel industry's survival, and steel was crucial to the state. Welsh steelworks produced sheets for consumer objects such as washing machines, tinned food and cars, whose exports generated Treasury income. Small-scale Welsh artisan mills produced expensive, uneven steel, while giant American and European steelworks with new machinery made cheaper and better material, threatening British exports. Attlee's government fleetingly nationalised much of the industry in 1951.[46] But even before that, the threat of nationalisation stimulated companies to modernise, and to publicise their progress as a national service.

In 1945 the British Iron and Steel Federation presented the Board of Trade with a 'Five-Year Plan' for reorganisation and new plants to be funded by substantial government loans. Four Welsh companies combined as the Steel Company of Wales (SCOW) to build their share. A completely new steelworks, the Abbey Works, opened alongside existing mills at Margam in 1951, making sheet steel from pig iron from Port Talbot blast furnaces by 'hot rolling' into sheets. Some of these went to new mills at Trostre near Llanelli, opened in phases from 1951 to 1954, and Felindre north of Swansea, completed in 1956, for 'cold-reduction', rolling into thinner sections, and tinplating for packaging.[47] Percy Thomas was SCOW's architectural consultant, and his practice designed many of the buildings.

The most prominent features of the new plants were long bars of giant sheds housing the linear flow of steel production (see Figure 4.6 and Figure 4.7). SCOW's engineers modelled these buildings on American mills, and acquired machinery from American companies with Marshall aid.[48] Engineers W. S. Atkins & Partners gave Thomas limited scope for exterior design at Abbey Works: he decided on vertical slot

4.6 Abbey Works, Margam, perspective by R. F. Buckley, n.d. (*c.*1946) (private collection; courtesy of the estates of Sir Percy Thomas and R. F. Buckley and of WSP UK Ltd).

4.7 Abbey Works Melting Shop and ancillary buildings, Margam, 1951 (photographer unknown; from The Steel Company of Wales Limited, *Port Talbot, Margam and Abbey Works*, n.d.; West Glamorgan Archive Service).

windows curved at the top corresponding to the roofline of transverse clerestories, and designed details giving sharp, uncluttered outlines.[49] This bold treatment gave the Welsh steelworks a family resemblance as cubic modern objects, contrasting with chaotic, soot-blackened older mills. Thomas chose their colours: Abbey Works had steel cladding painted yellow to echo surrounding sand dunes; Trostre had monumental brick cladding (see Figure 4.8); the Felindre buildings were blueish grey.[50]

These buildings became icons of the Welsh steel industry's cooperation with the post-war state, depicted in newspapers, newsreels and booklets.[51] Interior photographs showed vast open spaces containing giant machines, workers undertaking modern forms of labour, pressing buttons or pulling levers without manual effort, 'a complete upheaval in our mode of working', one steelworker recalled.[52] Chancellor Hugh Gaitskell opened Abbey Works in 1951, sending the first ingot on its journey to become a gleaming steel coil exhibited at the Festival of Britain. SCOW's chairman E. H. Lever told him that 'There can be no doubt of the contribution which this great project will make to the nation's economy'; and Gaitskell acknowledged that its workers 'will be doing a job for the nation as important as any in the country'.[53] The visible scale and modernity of the plant, amplified by Thomas's interventions, supported such heroic rhetoric. Nevertheless, the new steelworks depended on the old fuel of Welsh coal, which they consumed in vast quantities. Abbey Works was also achieved through environmental devastation, replacing wetlands at Margam with a raised platform comprising 5 million tons of sand, slag and concrete.

4.8 Trostre Cold Reduction Tinplate Plant, 1947–54 (photographer unknown; from the Collections of the National Monuments Records of Wales; courtesy of the estate of Sir Percy Thomas and WSP UK Ltd).

The steelworks supported plentiful work and brought stability and a strong identity and community to the area for generations. SCOW and its constituent companies applied politically strategic philanthropic concerns for workers' welfare to retain labour and deter strikes.[54] Percy Thomas's Swansea office, especially Norman Thomas, Howel Mendus and later Vergette, designed ancillary buildings. A substantial brick building at Abbey Works housed SCOW's headquarters, including marketing and engineering departments, combining modern ribbon windows and flat roofs with a simplified classical temple front and sculptural symbols, sustaining a pre-war civic language implying a noble purpose (see Figure 4.9).[55] Employees were assigned to

4.9 Steel Company of Wales Headquarters, Margam, *c.*1950 (photographer unknown; from the Collections of the National Monuments Records of Wales; courtesy of the estate of Sir Percy Thomas and WSP UK Ltd).

smaller, informal brick amenity buildings around each site containing dining rooms, medical facilities and offices.[56] Near Margam the practice designed a generously provisioned workers' sports centre in a gentle modern style more in tune with contemporary modernism, and at Ebbw Vale a substantial 'Community Centre' with a hall and restaurant, aiming to develop strong corporate allegiances.[57]

In the 1960s, Richard Thomas & Baldwins built the new Spencer Works at Llanwern, combining blast furnaces, hot strip mill and cold reduction mill. It, too, depended on government funding for more than half its cost, allocated by Harold Macmillan alongside a similar plant at Ravenscraig.[58] Sir Percy Thomas & Son were architectural consultants with Gollins, Melvin, Ward & Partners: Dale Owen worked on site planning and landscaping, and his colleagues oversaw construction.[59] They applied similar principles of visual simplicity of form and use of colour as at Abbey Works, but with a more dynamic, sculptural effect - a 'new look' in steelworks, one journalist wrote.[60] Miesian steel and glass buildings housed administrative functions.[61] Composed for the view from the railway, the plant gave a memorable public image as a symbol of Welsh industrial modernisation.[62]

Infrastructures of Power and Movement

While steelworks tended to reinforce the dependence of south Wales on limited heavy industries, to entice more diverse companies into the south Wales valleys the state planned new infrastructures of coal-fired electrical power generation and petrol-fuelled traffic movement, in which Thomas and his practice took a significant role. Like steelworks, power stations were immense engineering structures in often sensitive landscapes, which architects could help make palatable to public opinion and comprehensible as symbols of national modernity. Attlee's government brought electrical generation and supply within the state under the British Electricity Authority (BEA) in 1948, partly to build large new generators.[63] Despite the national grid, the distance electricity was transmitted affected efficiency. Wales in the early 1950s inefficiently exported coal to English stations and re-imported electricity from England, while new stations in Wales were needed for rising industrial demand; the BNS was a major consumer, highlighted on the BEA's network maps.[64]

The BEA appointed Sir Percy Thomas its architectural advisor for Wales, and commissioned three power stations from his practice. Employing Thomas helped convey a consistent image across state-sponsored Welsh developments in industry and infrastructure. He had already designed Carmarthen Bay power station at Burry Port for a private company in 1948, taken over by the BEA. Frank Buckley's stunning perspectives were exhibited at the Royal Academy, a severe, cubic design contrasting with old-fashioned neo-Georgian station designs displayed alongside.[65] Partially opened in 1953, Carmarthen Bay accommodated its generating equipment in tiered brick boxes under three tapered boiler house chimneys; the lower turbine hall had high-low roofs and vertical windows much like the Trostre steelworks; porthole windows added a nautical character (see Figure 4.10). Subtle classical references followed Giles Gilbert Scott's 'brick cathedral' power stations, the chimneys evoking classical columns.[66]

4.10 Carmarthen Bay power station, Burry Port, 1947–54 (photo: © Vernon D. Emmanuel; from the Collections of the National Monuments Records of Wales).

Classical hints gradually faded in Thomas's subsequent power stations. Aberthaw near Barry (designed around 1953, opened from 1960 to 1963) was clad in brick with vertical slot windows.[67] At Uskmouth in 1957–60 Thomas extended an earlier station with a more contemporary brick turbine hall with horizontal strip windows.[68] Rogerstone, west of Newport, opened in 1958, was the only one requiring cooling towers, given an angular, vase-like shape. Its boiler and turbine rooms formed an axial assemblage of simple cuboids, and it departed from the brick box style with aluminium cladding, following Farmer & Dark's power station at Marchwood. An innovation was a single central control room, apparently the first in Britain, giving a distinctly modern form of technical control over its machinery.[69]

The practice's expertise brought work in England, when the BEA's successor, the Central Electricity Generating Board (CEGB), commissioned Sir Percy Thomas & Son for two simultaneous coal-fired power stations hoping to link the designs, with the same engineers, Rendel, Palmer & Tritton, and builders. They were designed around 1962 and opened in 1970. George Hooper was project architect for Eggborough, and William Marsden and Allan Clark designed Ironbridge station from the Shrewsbury office, exchanging drawings and information. Materials and details were shared – aluminium cladding on upper parts, green aggregate-faced precast panels below, ribbon windows and glazed curtain walls; and as each housed the same equipment, the main volumes were also alike. But their layouts were very different: Eggborough was largely symmetrical, with eight cooling towers in two straight rows across the turbine hall; whereas, on a picturesque site next to the River Severn, Ironbridge's cooling towers plotted an arc (see Colour Plate 5). Both were bold compositions within the landscape, juxtaposing curved towers and rectangular buildings.[70] The practice's power stations demonstrated the link between state planning and industrial development. Opening Rogerstone in 1958, CEGB chairman Christopher Hinton celebrated the connection between England and Wales through the national grid, and the relationship between power and industry: while Wales now exported electricity to England, he said, surplus power enabled further Welsh industrial expansion.[71]

Even more potently, post-war road-building programmes aimed to bind Wales into the economic fabric of Britain while encouraging industrial diversification and accelerating commodity circulation in a post-war 'spatial Keynesianism' or 'state productivism'.[72] Nevertheless such developments were prompted by Welsh interests, and for key elements Thomas was consultant architect. He ennobled the economic and political functions of this infrastructure as an incontestable element of the modern nation.

The idea for a bridge over the Severn estuary preceded plans for a motorway system, and was tied to south Wales's Special Area status and the promotion of industry. Malcolm Stewart, the Special Areas commissioner, and Welsh economist Hilary Marquand argued for a Severn crossing to attract companies across the river.[73] Monmouthshire and Gloucestershire county councils promoted a parliamentary bill for a bridge in 1935, and when it stalled they recruited other councils to lobby the government, arguing its importance for industrial diversification.[74]

After the war, Attlee's government planned a national motorway network in which the Severn Bridge was prominent. Alfred Barnes, Minister of War Transport, announced the Severn Bridge in 1945 as highest priority - the 'king-pin' of the British road programme.[75] This plan was linked to distribution of industry policies, aiming to reduce travel times and costs between industrial locations.[76] Haulage costs affected product prices, whether Margam steel in Birmingham cars or Pontypool nylon in Leicester fabrics; motorways could lower prices and increase exports. Hugh Dalton, President of the Board of Trade in the 1940s, thought new roads would also help in 'cancelling out the Isolation Complex' of south Wales, linking 'this basic industry Region and the fabricating Midlands, thus creating one almost self-supporting industrial complex'. 'Could we not then put South Wales on the Midland map, or, if you prefer, put Birmingham on the South Wales map?' he asked.[77] The bridge was commissioned in 1945 and tenders invited in 1946, before Treasury retrenchment cancelled it the following year.[78]

By then Thomas's design with engineers David Anderson of Mott, Hay & Anderson and Ralph Freeman of Freeman, Fox & Partners was widely published in Buckley's perspectives, stirring enthusiasm (See Figure 4.11). With a central span of over 1,000 metres from the Beachley headland to clifftops at Aust, it would have been the 'largest suspension bridge in Europe' in 1946, and the third longest spanning suspension bridge in the world.[79] Thomas and Buckley modified overall proportions and forms and designed detailed architectural treatments of principal elements. Steel towers had layered modelling and a gentle taper, broad inserts over the roadway for bracing suggesting neoclassical forms. Doubled piers below the trussed deck emphasised solidity. The concrete cable anchors took subtle pylon forms with vertical modelling.[80] A further smaller bridge crossed the Wye to the west, and both were designed together, the Wye Bridge a simple viaduct.[81] Buckley's perspective of the enormous Severn Bridge

4.11 Severn Bridge, perspective by R. F. Buckley of initial design, 1946 (from the Collections of the National Monuments Records of Wales; courtesy of the estates of Sir Percy Thomas and R. F. Buckley and of WSP UK Ltd).

structure launched across the tranquil estuary was a powerful statement of government modernisation of Britain and its concern for Wales in that project.

Local authorities and industrialists in Wales and western England continued campaigning for the bridge. As chairman of the Welsh Board for Industry, Thomas assembled supporters and cultivated government contacts, including ministers (although he did not sit on the Severn Bridge sub-committee).[82] He retired from the board before it submitted its joint report with the South Western Regional Board for Industry in 1955. This document, proposing toll charges to reimburse Treasury funding, reinforced the bridge's urgency to 'remove ... a severe hindrance to industrial development in South Wales'.[83] In 1956, however, the Conservative government announced instead construction of the Forth Road Bridge in Scotland, partly because the party's election prospects there were stronger, only authorising the Severn Bridge in 1961.[84]

The engineers then proposed innovations that made the Severn Bridge unique in the world. After gales destroyed the Tacoma Narrows Bridge, near Seattle, in 1940, suspension bridges had adopted heavy trussed decks for stiffness. The Severn Bridge engineers, now led by Gilbert Roberts with W. C. Brown and Michael Parsons, instead designed a thin, aerodynamic roadway to reduce wind forces, bicycle tracks each side cantilevering out like aeroplane wings. Stiffening came from its construction as welded steel box sections and by changing supporting cables from vertical to V-shaped hangers.[85] These decisions reduced steelwork, so Thomas refined his design (see Figure 4.12).

The Royal Fine Art Commission, meanwhile, insisted on eliminating unnecessary features, simplifying anchorages and towers.[86] Engineers and architect redesigned the Wye Bridge with a novel cable-stayed structure as a foil to its companion, its cables running from two piers splitting into legs below the roadway.[87] As built by

4.12 Severn Bridge, perspective by R. F. Buckley of final design, 1961 (The National Archives; courtesy of the estates of Sir Percy Thomas and R. F. Buckley and of WSP UK Ltd).

Sir William Arrol and Company and the Fairfield Shipbuilding and Engineering Company of Glasgow, Dorman Long of Teesside, and the Cleveland Bridge and Engineering Company of Darlington, painted battleship grey and opened in 1966, the two bridges looked astonishingly delicate, their decks a single blade of metal (see Figure 4.13).

4.13 Severn Bridge, view from Beachley, 1961–6 (photo: author).

Thomas tried hard to retain a significant feature, eventually vetoed by government officials. His designs depicted heraldic emblems in the bracing panels, intended as colourful sculptures of the 'Arms of England' facing drivers from Wales and the 'Arms of Wales' facing those going west.[88] These emblems would heighten the bridge's impression of a gateway between two countries; indeed Ministry of Transport official H. E. Aldington argued in 1946 that the bridge would 'make a wonderful entry into the Principality of Wales'.[89] Objections proliferated, however: that England and Wales did not actually have arms; that the Severn Bridge did not mark the border, which ran along the Wye; and that the Wye Bridge landed in Monmouthshire, its Welsh status disputed.[90] Finally, the Ministry of Transport insisted on leaving the panels blank.[91] Thus the potential for designing the bridge as a threshold between countries was rejected for national homogeneity. Nevertheless, the dramatic experience of the crossing encouraged drivers' perceptions of a transition between England and Wales, making it a significant point of heightened Welsh national consciousness.[92]

Thomas's work extended beyond the bridge to its surroundings and other sections of the M4 motorway. He was consultant architect for the Aust service station, advising on its layout and design.[93] He designed a toll collection building, although Frederick Jennett and Ronald Weeks substituted a more contemporary design when the planning officer and ministry officials found Thomas's proposal too old-fashioned.[94] The Ministry of Transport also appointed Thomas as consultant architect for motorway bridges from the Severn Bridge to Newport, combining rubble stonework walls and elegant reinforced concrete spans.[95] With Owen Williams as engineer Thomas designed the Newport bypass over the River Usk and the rusticated cuttings of the Crindau tunnel entrances, planned in 1946 but begun only in 1962.[96] With Rendel, Palmer & Tritton, he designed the bridge over the River Neath at Briton Ferry, monumental concrete goalpost piers meeting steel spans at delicate joints, completed in 1955, carrying traffic from the Abbey Works.[97] Though pieced together over decades, the M4 gave powerful visual evidence of south Wales's petrol-fuelled modernisation and its integration into the nation, linked to state-sponsored industrial expansion, and constituting part of the everyday life of many in the region.[98]

Less extensive but politically similar was the A55 along the north Wales coast from Chester to Bangor, where a pinch point at Conwy gave Thomas another significant bridge project, considered in the following chapter. Thomas's association with Freeman, Fox & Partners led, furthermore, to an international project for the Auckland Harbour Bridge in New Zealand in 1951. While the engineers advised an economical low-arched cantilevered steel truss form, Thomas advocated a taller, more semicircular tied arch, both illustrated by Buckley. The New Zealand government rejected his preference because of its cost, but Thomas advised on the tapering of trusses and treatments of piers and anchorages. Constructed by some of the Severn Bridge's building companies, it was a triumph for the export of British engineering and design.[99]

State Education

Universities maintained their pre-war semi-autonomous status in the welfare state, but government policies drove their expansion, funded by central government through the University Grants Committee (UGC). Percy Thomas and Sir Percy Thomas & Son designed most post-war buildings for the University of Wales colleges at Cardiff, Swansea, Aberystwyth and Bangor until the 1970s, a further defining feature of modern Wales; and they were also involved in some English universities. Each Welsh college commissioned the practice independently, sometimes also hiring other architects. Technical colleges and schools, continuing under local government but likewise expanded by national policies, were more occasional practice projects.

Between the wars, the University Colleges of Wales had expanded with funding from various sources, including local industries, whose patronage they cultivated. This distinctive local patronage continued after the war: donors to University College, Swansea's post-war development included many Percy Thomas clients, such as the Steel Company of Wales, S. A. Brain, ICI, Gnome Photographic Products and BNS.[100] At Cardiff, the University College of South Wales and Monmouthshire also obtained funding from SCOW and the BNS, which paid for Thomas's stark modern engineering building on Newport Road of 1958.[101] In the welfare state, however, universities expected and depended on state funding. 'The Universities either have or have not an essential contribution to make to the life of the nation', wrote Aberystwyth's principal Ifor L. Evans in 1944; 'If they do perform a national service, then they qualify for national support'.[102] John Fulton of Swansea appealed for state investment to form graduates for industry and the welfare state's administration and social services.[103] Rapid expansion within stringent government cost limits encouraged more flexible modern design methods than the rigid symmetries of pre-war neoclassicism, and, more symbolically, modernism conveyed associations of technical progress linking universities to other manifestations of the welfare state, including industry.[104] The shift from neoclassicism to modernism occurring in Percy Thomas's practice in this period was often motivated by the desires of his clients, and universities articulated those desires particularly well.

Percy Thomas's first university commission was for the University College of Wales, Aberystwyth, which, having outgrown its Victorian seafront building, acquired a large site on the Penglais hillside above the new National Library. Evans, its dynamic principal from 1934, dismissed H. V. Lanchester's first neoclassical campus plan and appointed Thomas instead.[105] Thomas's 1936 plan was also symmetrical but more informal than Lanchester's, with long rows of buildings rising up the hill, subsidiary groups for halls of residence and a more economical modern style (see Figure 4.14).[106]

Thomas designed the first two buildings for Aberystwyth's specialisation in farming: the Agricultural Research Block, intended as one wing to a future great hall, and a dairy some distance away, both completed by 1940.[107] The Agricultural Block housed the Welsh Plant Breeding Station offices and the Imperial Bureau of Plant Genetics (described by Evans as 'a government office, in effect'), and the Ministry of Agriculture and Fisheries granted half the building's cost.[108] It was architecturally distinguished, loosely Arts & Crafts in style, faced in Forest of Dean rubble stonework with a hipped roof containing seed stores (see Figure 4.15). David Evans enlivened it with modern sculpture, including figures in traditional Welsh costume demonstrating wheat production around the entrance.[109]

From 1938 Thomas designed two further buildings at Penglais, delayed by war. The UGC almost wholly funded a hall of residence for men, Pantycelyn, for the

4.14 Penglais campus plan, University College of Wales, Aberystwyth, perspective of Percy Thomas's design by J. D. M. Harvey, 1943 (Aberystwyth University Archives).

4.15 Agricultural Research Block, University College of Wales, Aberystwyth, 1936–40 (photo: author).

many students from rural mid-Wales. This hall, completed in 1951 and expanded in 1957, took a traditional and generous approach with live-in domestic servants, though later phases increased the proportion of student rooms.[110] Pitched roofs and dormers emphasised a residential character on otherwise simple neo-Georgian blocks faced in stone. More modern in style were a swimming pool and sports centre, funded mostly by the National Fitness Council through the UGC.[111]

Such slow, incremental development gave way after the war to vast building campaigns and constant crises of accommodation, in which neoclassicism was not only symbolically relegated to an earlier age but also simply incapable of the fast building and constantly changing requirements of new campuses. The Penglais plan's anticipated target of 1,000 students was already breached by 1948 thanks to generous new student grants. Thomas's symmetrical plan was difficult to adapt to a new institutional scale, and Principal Goronwy Rees commissioned William Holford for a new, denser, campus design.[112] Thomas's practice was then commissioned for individual buildings 'on condition that the work be undertaken by Mr. William Marsden', indicating a preference for the latter's modernist approach.[113]

Meanwhile the University College of North Wales, Bangor employed various architects without much coordination. Thomas designed a hall of residence for men, Neuadd Reichel, completed in 1942, a plain neo-Georgian brick block with student rooms over ground-floor communal spaces, a flat roof imposed by wartime restrictions (see Figure 4.16).[114] The most prominent early post-war building at the college, probably by Marsden, was the Botany and Forestry building on Deiniol Road (see Figure 4.17). Opened in 1955 by Keith Murray of the UGC, it housed two of Bangor's distinctive disciplines, including a museum and library, in an asymmetrical design inspired by European modern architecture, perhaps especially Willem Dudok. Its entrance hall was clad didactically with timber veneers from around the world.[115] By then Marsden attended committee meetings, overseeing the rest of the practice's work at Bangor until 1970.[116]

4.16 Neuadd Reichel (men's hall of residence), University College of North Wales, Bangor, 1942 (photo: author).

4.17 Botany and Forestry Building (now Thoday Building), University College of North Wales, Bangor, 1949–54 (photo: author).

Thomas undertook consultancy work for two universities in England. For the University of Bristol, he proposed a development plan in 1948 for St Michael's Hill. Three open squares connected by grand staircases would rise up the hill on an axis towards the eighteenth-century Royal Fort House; long bars of symmetrical buildings cranked around the contours gave fortress-like massing. The university invited local architect George Oatley to build Thomas's plan, but his modifications undermined its coherence, and it remained unfinished when plans were changed in the late 1950s.[117] Sir Percy Thomas & Son returned in 1962, however, for Badock and Hiatt Baker men's halls, designed by Jennett, Poremba and J. Rewse at the Bristol office. Clusters of low-rise blocks and longer rows of rooms with Scandinavian-style brick elevations surrounded communal facilities, notably a dining hall with an expressive roof structure.[118]

The University of Nottingham's vice-chancellor Bertrand Hallward appointed Thomas for a development plan in 1949, and Thomas nominated other architects to build it. He advised preserving the university's parkland site as an American-style campus, appointing landscape architect Geoffrey Jellicoe. Morley Horder's interwar building was extended by T. Cecil Howitt.[119] Thomas favoured modernist architects for science buildings, appointing David du R. Aberdeen and Basil Spence & Partners.[120] Halls of residence by various architects were disposed in clusters around the park's edges, planned loosely around quadrangles, mostly of brick and vaguely neo-Georgian.[121] Thomas's approach was coherent if eclectic; but as at Aberystwyth, Holford took over in 1962 to oversee much bigger growth.[122]

University College, Swansea also had a parkland campus, granted by the council in 1923.[123] Thomas drew up a development plan in 1949 for another low-rise campus (see Figure 4.18). Four main teaching buildings west of the 1930s library surrounded a new social centre along orthogonal streets. Unlike Nottingham's plan, Swansea's halls were close to teaching buildings, following Fulton's vision for a close-knit residential university.[124]

The Swansea office began with the Natural Sciences building designed by Percy Thomas and Alan West-Jones, a long three-storey range with central lecture theatre opened in 1956, soon extended (see Figure 4.19).[125] It was a modern flat-roofed steel-framed brick-faced block. Cast stone panels depicted symbols of its subjects, and travertine and marble graced the entrance hall. The building's complex

4.18 Campus plan for University College of Swansea, perspective of Percy Thomas's design by J. D. M. Harvey, 1949 (Richard Burton Archives, Swansea University; courtesy of the estate of Sir Percy Thomas).

4.19 Natural Sciences building, University College of Swansea, 1953–6, wings added 1958–9 (photo: author).

functions included museums for geology, botany and zoology, sample storage from Welsh coalfields, an aquarium and a library.[126] Also following the original plan was College House, completed in 1961, a steel-framed brick and glass block, conceived as the college's social heart, with dining facilities for staff and students, a medical centre, shops and recreational rooms (see Figure 4.20). Floor-to-ceiling windows gave views south to the sea, and interior decoration by the pioneering Design Research Unit (under Misha Black) was elegant and fashionably modern.[127] These were the only two buildings following Thomas's plan, however.

While the Chemistry building of 1957-60 was sited as proposed, its central spine and perpendicular wings adopted modern planning for increased density.[128] By then the masterplan was demonstrably inadequate for projected student numbers, and in 1958 Dale Owen drew up a new one. Respecting the cross-shaped campus as begun, it enabled denser development with interlinked square courtyards punctuated by high buildings, student residences now envisaged as tower blocks (see Figure 4.21).[129] Even this plan had to be revised six years later, almost doubling its capacity.[130]

The University College of South Wales and Monmouthshire employed Thomas regularly at Cardiff from the mid-1950s. To fill the triangular site north of W. D. Caroë's Edwardian building in the Civic Centre, Thomas planned a four-storey perimeter block for Arts and Social Science departments, the first phase designed by Norman Thomas, Wallace Sweet and others and completed in 1962. Though a flat-roofed steel structure, it had Portland stone facing with fluted panels giving an Art Deco feel, particularly on the rounded corner lecture theatre, like a Doric column drum.[131] While the Arts building was in progress, however, Professor of Economics and Social Sciences Brinley Thomas criticised its plan, prompting architect and client to explore an alternative approach. He argued that the design was incapable of accommodating growth and change, and,

4.20 College House, University College of Swansea, 1958–61 (photo: author).

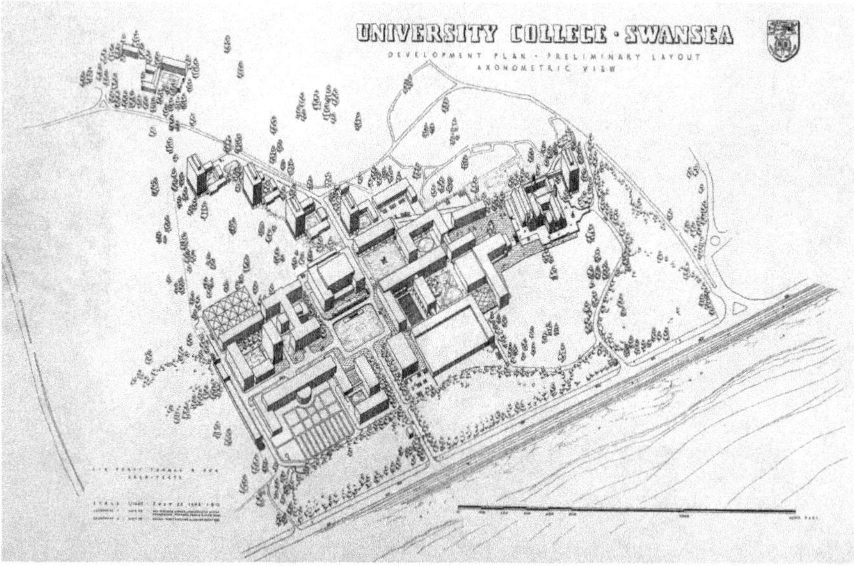

4.21 Development Plan for University College of Swansea, axonometric by Ivan Dale Owen, 1958 (Richard Burton Archives, Swansea University; courtesy of the estates of Sir Percy Thomas and Ivan Dale Owen and of WSP UK Ltd).

moreover, was spatially and socially inappropriate: 'The community of staff and students which makes a modern non-residential university college should not feel confined and enclosed', he wrote. Instead he advocated 'open planning' with greater spatial variety, praising Owen's Swansea plan.[132] A few years later, the architects presented a revised design adopting this advice, arranging modern slab blocks and a tower around a precinct (see Figure 4.22).[133] Despite concerns that this plan's radical nature would raise public objections, city councillors proved favourable, and it was followed throughout the 1960s.[134] Thus, at each college of the University of Wales and elsewhere, Percy Thomas's approaches became incapable of accommodating the university's scale and communicating its role in the welfare state, motivating a shift around 1960 towards modernism, led by younger architects, notably Marsden and Owen.

Each of the Welsh colleges developed further with fully fledged modernist approaches. At Bangor, under Marsden's oversight, a new quadrangle for arts provision was added to Henry Hare's Edwardian college, beginning with a new library wing, a long contemporary box contrasting with Hare's building, clad with slate blocks as the college insisted on using stone.[135] In a similar contemporary style, Marsden designed the students' union with a curved glazed common room perched on pilotis over the path below the college, opened in phases from 1963 to 1970.[136] Marsden presented a development plan for the sciences site on Deiniol Road in 1961 proposing a multilevel complex of precincts with a ten-storey tower block and octagonal library in a sunken garden. Only isolated buildings were built, notably the tower block.[137] The college continued to employ other architects, but Sir Percy Thomas & Son designed the largest student hall, Neuadd Emrys Evans, a row of four and five-storey blocks cranked at angles through a landscaped park.[138]

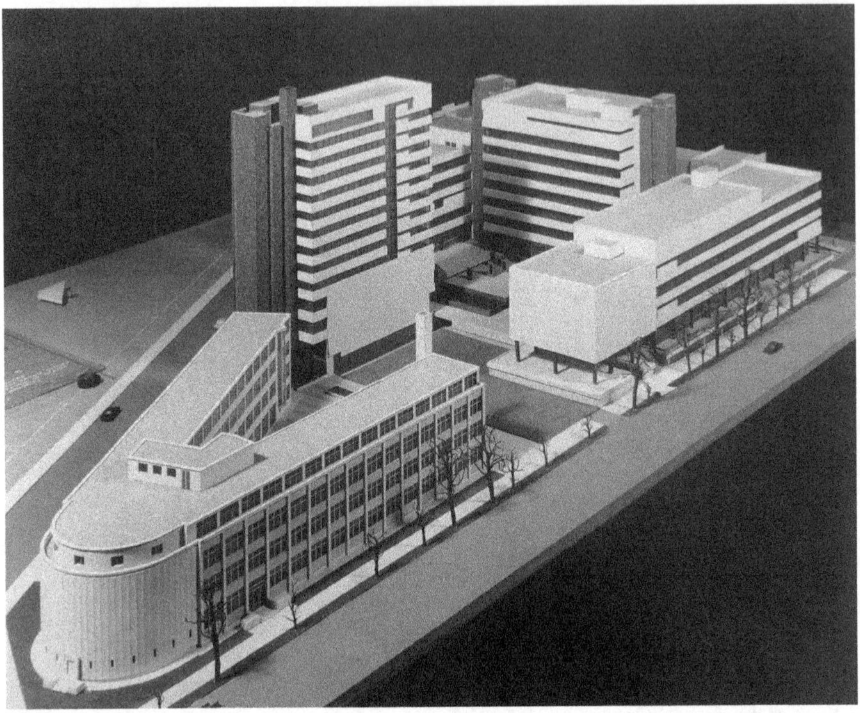

4.22 University College of South Wales and Monmouthshire, Cardiff, model of existing Arts building with proposed Pre-Clinical and other departments, *c.*1961 (photo: Terence Soames/Mike Woodward; from the Collections of the National Monuments Records of Wales; courtesy of WSP UK Ltd).

At Aberystwyth, the practice designed teaching buildings in Holford's masterplan. Most notable was the Physics and Mathematics building of 1959 to 1963 by Marsden and Vergette, consisting of intersecting rectilinear steel-framed blocks clad in red and purple mosaic, a six-storey curved tower astride a projecting rubble-stone lecture theatre forming a dynamic, colourful composition (see Colour Plate 6).[139] Next to it the Llandinam building for Geography, Geology and Social Sciences followed, completed in 1965: a tower block floated over a landscaped courtyard, with bands of glazing and sparkling white aggregate panels (see Figure 4.23).[140] One section's vertical slot windows expressed the library and lecture theatre inside, its roofline of clerestories lighting top-floor laboratories much like Thomas's steelworks buildings.[141]

Owen and colleagues spent a £2 million allocation from the UGC at Swansea from 1960.[142] Work included three residential tower blocks, each given communal facilities around courtyards at its base (see Figure 4.24).[143] Owen and Stephen James designed a library extension, completed in 1963, with a two-storey catalogue hall of card indexes, two airy reading rooms with illuminated ceilings and double-height windows overlooking the park. The college's structural engineering professor Bernard Neal advised on its unusual external steel portal frames, spanning over a podium clad in layered grey aggregate and Portland stone.[144] New courts were added for Applied Sciences and Physics and Mathematics departments, the latter with a ten-storey tower

4.23 Geography, Geology and Social Studies Building (Llandinam Building), University College of Wales, Aberystwyth, 1961–5 (photographer unknown; Aberystwyth University Archives).

4.24 Singleton Halls of Residence, University College of Swansea, *c.*1960–6 (photographer unknown; Richard Burton Archives, Swansea University).

clad in Portland stone, designed by Owen and Vergette. Singleton Abbey's outbuildings became another courtyard enclosed by a Social Sciences building, sensitively designed in brick with a colonnaded walkway, completed in 1963.[145] Swansea's campus was dense but coherent, with linear streets and landscaped squares, scaled and varied like Oxford quads, which Owen argued generated a civic environment promoting social cohesion and identity (see Figure 4.25).[146]

The University College at Cardiff followed Owen's revised plan for a range of science, medical and social science departments, built in phases throughout the 1960s. A lower frontage to the Civic Centre was faced with Portland stone, and three tall blocks behind it enclosed a raised courtyard, including a twelve-storey tower block, positioned on the furthest corner from the Civic Centre to reduce its impact on Cathays Park, designed by Owen with Stephen James, Roy Page, John Hilling and Kerry Veale (see Figure 4.26). Lecture theatres and laboratories were articulated at lower levels.[147] As at Swansea, Owen and colleagues experimented with verticality for student accommodation, with an eleven-storey men's hall of residence, University Hall in Penylan, by Owen, Maureen Kelly and Norman Thomas, completed in 1968.[148]

Students at this period must have spent their entire degrees surrounded by construction sites, but in 1963 economist Lord Robbins recommended even more growth to broaden higher education, and Harold Wilson then made university expansion central to Labour's proposed 'scientific revolution'.[149] 'Needs must where Robbins drives', said principal Anthony Steel, justifying expansion at Cardiff.[150] This new phase was characterised throughout Britain by the sculptural monumentality of brutalism.

4.25 University College of Swansea, aerial photograph of *c.*1970 (photo: Tempest Ltd; Richard Burton Archives, Swansea University).

4.26 University College of South Wales and Monmouthshire, Cardiff, Pre-Clinical departments, Economics, Social Studies and Mathematics, *c.*1961–73 (photo: Terence Soames; from the Collections of the National Monuments Records of Wales; courtesy of WSP UK Ltd).

Steel's successor at Cardiff turned to other architects, but Aberystwyth returned to Percy Thomas, appointing Marsden and Owen as 'Co-ordinators' at Penglais in 1963, and insisting that Marsden and Stephen James design new buildings, Vergette also taking a key role.[151] Owen drew up a comprehensive development plan for this phase in 1965, proposing a new strip of development above Marsden's teaching buildings, centred on a raised three-sided courtyard open to the view, surrounded by a great hall, library and students' union forming the college's core. A chapel (never built) would sit behind the hall, its detached bell tower forming a focal point in the court. The new complex would extend in horizontal terraces across the hillside with networks of covered walkways.[152]

Of this scheme, the three central buildings with the campanile (doubling as a boiler-house flue) and one wing for the library and Arts departments were constructed over the following decade, sharing a monumental language of large simple blocks clad in warm grey precast panels (see Figure 4.27). The auditorium of the great hall cantilevered boldly over an open three-storey foyer and stair, designed by Owen, James and Vergette and completed in 1971.[153] The Hugh Owen Library was designed by Vergette and Neil Graham and completed last, opening in 1977 (see Figure 4.28). Set behind a sheltering colonnade, it was woven into the Arts teaching areas with a courtyard and walkways.[154] This complex, though unfinished, made Penglais a fully fledged university campus with a distinctive civic heart.

At Bangor, three individual buildings adopted this monumental approach, as Malcolm Lovibond and Keith Maplestone joined Marsden. The Arts building completed the Edwardian college's modern quadrangle, with expressive ribbed-concrete precast panels, the windows marked with vertical fins, projecting over a recessed ground floor of purple slate walls. Materially and formally rich, monumental but permeable, it made

4.27 Great Hall and Students' Union, University College of Wales, Aberystwyth, 1966–70; Theatr y Werin to left by Alex Gordon and Partners, 1972 (photographer unknown; Aberystwyth University Archives).

4.28 Hugh Owen Library and Arts buildings, University College of Wales, Aberystwyth, c.1970–7 (photo: author).

a dramatic contemporary feature of the college's main street frontage when opened in 1968 (see Figure 4.29).[155]

The Theatr Gwynedd at Bangor had a more civic function, hosting touring theatre as well as educational uses, and attracted funding from the Welsh Arts Council, local authorities and private donors. It participated in a movement in the early 1970s for university theatres and arts centres able to link town and gown, as also seen at the theatres at Aberystwyth and Cardiff by Alex Gordon and Partners.[156] Sited below the

4.29 Arts building, University College of North Wales, Bangor, 1964–9 (photo: author).

old college facing the town centre, the Theatr Gwynedd adopted a stylistically soft form of brutalism, an orange brick cube on a raised platform, with colonnaded entrance and lead-covered flytower, completed in 1974 (see Figure 4.30).[157]

Equally imposing was the Zoology building, completed around 1970 on Dieniol Road (see Figure 4.31). This extraordinary, deliberately ungainly building drew stylistically on the brutalism of Le Corbusier and Paul Rudolph, and especially the New Museums building at Cambridge by Arup Associates. A double-height galleried specimen museum displayed large mammal skeletons, surely inspiring the building's unusual concrete rib cage.[158] It was remarkably playful, though consistent with university architecture throughout Britain.

Thus, in three waves of building activity stimulated by political ambitions to make universities engines of social mobility and technical and industrial development, Percy Thomas and his practice built much of the Welsh infrastructure of higher education. Just as government roads policies brought Wales into closer relationship with England, however, so did welfare state policies in education. University of Wales colleges became subject to central government and dependent on Treasury funding. Moreover, student grants encouraged geographical mobility. Welsh students attended English universities, and academics with expertise in Welsh culture and locally relevant sciences felt vulnerable: compared to over 90 per cent Welsh students at University of Wales colleges in the 1930s, only 34 per cent were Welsh at Bangor in 1963, around 50 per cent elsewhere.[159] The practice's modern architecture perhaps emphasised this participation in a wider British project; yet, particularly in Owen's work at Aberystwyth, the architects often did consider a distinctive Welsh identity, as the following chapter explores.

Technical colleges, meanwhile, remained under local authority control with the 1944 Education Act, but received increasing direction from central government, as the

4.30 Theatr Gwynedd, University College of North Wales, Bangor, 1970–5 (photo: Dave Bower; Bangor University Archives and Special Collections).

4.31 Zoology building (now Brambell Building), University College of North Wales, Bangor, 1967–70 (photo: author).

Ministry of Education determined budgets and building standards. Before the war, most technical college students attended evening classes, but day and full-time courses became increasingly popular, leading colleges to enhance their social provision with leisure and recreation facilities.[160] Colleges in south Wales taught subjects related to the nationalised industries and newly diversified industries, often in close collaboration with companies.

Sir Percy Thomas & Son designed the new Technical College at Newport, a joint project between Newport Borough Council and Monmouthshire County Council requested and funded by the Ministry of Education following pressure from local industrialists.[161] Its buildings provided advanced facilities in science and engineering for 2,000 students.[162] Described as a 'Spaceship Age College' by the press on its opening in 1958, it was a flat-roofed steel-framed brick complex with four interconnected blocks, visually similar to the practice's industrial buildings: 'It could be the administrative centre of a great industry', claimed the *Western Mail*.[163] Besides teaching spaces it included common rooms and a dining room to generate a sense of communal life. In 1968, the practice extended the college by inserting a three-storey rectangular courtyard building between two wings, adding laboratories, computer facilities, a lecture theatre and library, and extending social amenities.[164]

The government's White Paper on Technical Education of 1956 proposed that a select group of colleges should be developed as colleges of advanced technology with enhanced funding.[165] Cardiff Technical College was the only one so designated in Wales, becoming the Welsh College of Advanced Technology. Though it remained under council control, its governance was reorganised to include local authorities and industry throughout Wales, to make it, as the city's director of education Robert Presswood wrote, 'a truly national institution'.[166] Quintin Hogg, Conservative Minister of Education, told its governors in 1957 that 'Wales must not depend on England and Scotland to produce the first-class scientists and technologists the nation so vitally needs', but that 'The Principality must produce them itself – and as quickly as possible'.[167] With a new national mission, the college commissioned Sir Percy Thomas & Son for a new building, completed in 1960 (see Figure 4.32).

With no space to expand Thomas's original building, the college acquired a new site in Cathays Park beside the Temple of Peace.[168] It was a plain flat-roofed box clad in Portland stone, conventionally planned around a central courtyard. A giant relief sculpture over the main entrance by Bainbridge Copnall represented 'Chemistry, Pharmacy, Navigation, Biology, Public Hall and Students Community Centre', reflecting the departments and amenities inside.[169] At the north end was a large 'assembly hall' and refectory, those in the old building now inadequate for the college's scale. Another section housed the students' union, including a chapel.[170] A sober, conservative building for its time, it conveyed little sense of the modernity of the institution's development, and attracted a student 'anti-ugly' protest on nearing completion. The college's principal Alexander Harvey, however, defended its 'good manners' as a contribution to the Civic Centre.[171]

Besides these Welsh colleges, Sir Percy Thomas & Son also maintained a long-standing relationship with Oldham College of Technology in Lancashire, designing several blocks from the early 1950s, when Thomas collaborated with Prestwich, and

4.32 Welsh College of Advanced Technology, Cardiff (now Redwood Building, Cardiff University), 1960 (photo: author).

in the 1960s under Marsden, when the college's most prominent buildings took a light, modern approach similar to the work of that period at Aberystwyth.[172]

Schools, meanwhile, were relatively unusual in the practice. Notable work included an early comprehensive school, the Upper Rhondda Comprehensive at Treorchy, its first phase designed by Wyndham Powell in the Cardiff office and

4.33 Barry Girls' Comprehensive School, 1973 (unknown photographer; from the Collections of the National Monuments Records of Wales; courtesy of WSP UK Ltd).

completed in 1964. Old mine workings informed its dispersed, low-rise plan of independent blocks; a light modern appearance followed contemporary school architecture elsewhere.[173] Most innovative was Bryn Hafren Girls' Comprehensive School at Barry of 1969-73, attributed to Dale Owen (see Figure 4.33).[174] A two-storey steel-framed building stepping across site contours, its delicate curtain-walled exterior based on a rigorous modular geometry, it extended over a large area around a series of square courtyards, each giving individual identity to a subject domain.[175] These humanised an otherwise large, complex building, an approach related both to Owen's university planning, and also to the practice's hospital architecture - a field that became one of their most important areas of work in the second half of the twentieth century.

A Service to National Health

Unlike the nylon factory or the suspension bridge, the modern hospital has always been seen as a defining feature of the welfare state, as the new NHS instituted the principle of free healthcare for all, and brought most medical services under state control, promising a healthier and happier population. Remarkably, however, the architectural history of the NHS has not yet been written, and as the most complex and specialised building type of the twentieth century, hospitals are the most difficult aspect of Percy Thomas's post-war work to understand. Here I sketch briefly some key principles of their hospital work up to the 1970s, returning to the subsequent period in the final chapter.

The enormous cost of hospitals meant that new buildings were long delayed, until in 1962 Macmillan's Conservative government unveiled a decade-long programme of modernisation, 'A Hospital Plan for England and Wales', assembled largely from proposals submitted by regional hospital boards. Although some important hospitals were built before then (one by Sir Percy Thomas & Son), most capital funding in the 1950s went towards repairing, modernising and extending existing buildings. The Hospital Plan established a comprehensive new system centring on large District General Hospitals of 600-800 beds, their modernity of scale and planning intended to generate cost efficiencies while accommodating medical advances for more effective treatment.[176]

The Ministry of Health and regional hospital boards sought to perfect and economise hospital design through research, partly conducted within the Ministry, disseminated in *Hospital Building Notes*; partly by the Nuffield Provincial Hospitals Trust, which conducted influential studies and designed experimental buildings for the NHS; partly in the work of hospital architects, almost every building an experiment developing the type. Concern with efficiency of operation meant studying hospitals in use and rethinking their planning, prioritising functional analysis, so that architectural modernism became fundamentally embedded in the hospital project. To reduce building costs, architects adopted new construction methods, so hospitals visually conveyed their modernity and their relationship with the wider welfare state. As the most successful plans became apparent, ministry publications began to standardise them. An architectural form that became common in the 1960s was the tower on a podium or 'matchbox on a muffin', derived from American models. It was also a symbolic marker of modernity, evoking popular associations with progress, efficiency and science.[177]

Percy Thomas had little involvement in hospital design until the 1950s, when his inexperience became embarrassingly evident. In 1938, Cardiff Royal Infirmary's Board of Governors commissioned him for the Cardiff Maternity Hospital near its existing hospital. The steel frame was built, but war interrupted construction, resumed in 1950 under the NHS. It was completed with an adjacent block of nurses' housing in 1955, looking two decades out of date, clad in brick with Portland stone trim, six storeys high. It nevertheless housed up-to-date facilities, including a central sterilising room and complex services. Thomas had revised its ward plans after the war, subdividing long open wards into four-bed clusters, the basis of most post-war hospital planning. Old-fashioned on the outside, therefore, it included elements that became standard NHS features.[178]

Since 1948 Thomas had been consultant architect for the United Cardiff Hospitals, the Welsh Regional Health Board and the University of Wales on preparations for an 800-bed teaching hospital in Cardiff. He assigned a colleague to develop a competition brief with a sub-committee, consulting medical staff to plan model wards and departments.[179] Thomas himself sat on the 1960 competition jury, however, and its choice of a scheme by S. W. Milburn & Partners with M. Harding and J. Surtees was roundly condemned by architectural critics. As the first competition for a hospital since the NHS's foundation, it was an important opportunity to demonstrate new thinking; but the *Architects' Journal* complained that the shortlisted schemes were 'pedestrian', with 'little if any architectural merit', and that the winner was 'medically an antique and architecturally a disaster', blaming the jury and its over-prescriptive brief. 'This hospital is a mistake which must not be built', it concluded.[180] The architects reworked their design, but it must have been another prompt to Thomas to cede to the next generation.

A younger generation of architects in the practice, apparently Norman Thomas and Allan Clark, designed the first new post-war hospital in Wales, the West Wales General Hospital at Glangwili, Carmarthen, planned from 1954 and built in phases, the first opened by the Queen Mother in 1959.[181] The hospital had 300 standard beds and a further 100 or so geriatric and psychiatric beds, with a nurses' training school and all the departments expected of a general hospital.[182] Three three-storey ward blocks of ninety-six beds each faced south over a wooded landscape, backing onto a central core containing specialist, service and outpatients' departments. A 'spine' corridor linked ward blocks to operating theatres, other facilities and the main entrance. T-shaped ward blocks adopted some Nuffield Trust ideas: a day-room on each level encouraged 'early ambulation' to improve patient recovery; the thirty-two-bed ward on each floor was thought to maximise staffing efficiency, subdivided into clusters mostly of three beds; a treatment room in every ward improved infection control and privacy. In the medical diagnostic blocks, waiting rooms were dispersed between departments, a feature the Nuffield researchers found could combine with new appointment systems to reduce patient waiting times.[183] American innovations of central sterilised equipment supply and central kitchens lowered operating costs and reduced nurses' workloads.

This hospital's development plan did not consider flexibility and expansion, however, key aspects in recent thinking. It retained an older 'linked pavilion' plan form, and the positions of subsequent ward blocks would terminate the spine corridor.[184] Nevertheless, its elevations gave visual expression to the modernity expected of NHS treatment, with flat-roofed blocks of precast reinforced concrete frames, large windows, and rubble stone end walls. Inside, public areas and staff facilities had modern furniture, Festival of Britain style patterns and stylish fittings, demonstrating the value accorded to patients in the welfare state.[185]

Nevill Hall Hospital at Abergavenny was part of the national hospital plan and typical of the 1960s. A small hospital in a Victorian mansion already existed there, and its convenient site for south Wales valleys between Merthyr Tydfil and Monmouth led the Welsh Hospital Board to earmark it for a 400-bed general hospital.[186] Design began in 1963, and the first phase with 192 beds opened to patients in 1969 (see Figure 4.34). Nevill Hall took the 'matchbox on a muffin' form, a slab of wards over an extended low-rise courtyard-punctured podium containing diagnosis, operating theatres, outpatients, casualty and other services. The H-shaped ward block efficiently sandwiched services and lifts between two lengths of wards. A second identical ward tower was added in the 1970s. The towers rose only four storeys over the lower blocks, but the hospital's location on the main road into Abergavenny made it visually prominent, its modernity striking in the rural context, enhanced by Sylvia Crowe's landscape design.[187] Publicity used the hospital's visual modernity as a sign of medical progress, highlighting 'a far more streamlined efficiency' in 'modern and spacious surroundings' with 'the most modern medical equipment'.[188]

The architects, Jennett and Sweet with Peter Hughes and R. Welton, engaged in thorough discussions with consultants and other staff, and every department had a unique, carefully considered plan. For the x-ray department, Hughes studied staff and patient movements, creating an octagon-in-square plan through which patients would

4.34 Nevill Hall Hospital, Abergavenny, 1966–70 (photo: Hylton Warner & Co. Ltd; author's collection, from practice; courtesy of WSP UK Ltd).

follow a circular route from admission to diagnosis.[189] While such functional analysis was a modern design principle, it slowed hospital planning and risked increasing costs, conflicting with the Ministry of Health's preference for standardisation and uniformity, which it increasingly encouraged over the 1960s, disseminating its own standard ward and department plans. When Nevill Hall's hospital management committee complained that in the second phase the architects were not properly consulting staff, the Welsh Health Board insisted that stricter cost control meant that 'standardisation and loss of individuality becomes an absolute necessity'.[190]

This led to an experiment in the practice's two subsequent Welsh hospitals, the Prince Charles Hospital at Merthyr Tydfil (see Figure 4.35) and the Glan Clwyd Hospital at Rhyl, beginning in 1965 and opening after delays in 1978. To save costs, the two hospitals were designed together to be almost identical.[191] They were larger versions of Nevill Hall, with longer H-shaped ward towers over medical accommodation, each tower for 360 patients, capable of doubling in a second phase.[192] Rather than Abergavenny's light brick exteriors, they used precast concrete cladding with a more severe modern appearance. A disadvantage of this coupled design became evident when similar construction defects were found in both buildings, leading to delays and litigation, a problem that seems to have lost the practice further hospital work in Wales.[193]

The modernity of planning behind these hospitals had upsetting effects on communities whose long-established healthcare facilities were slated for closure. Small towns and villages had nostalgic attachments to local hospitals now absorbed into the national service.[194] A hospital in Crickhowell, closed for Nevill Hall, commemorated First World War casualties and was built with public donations.[195] Caerphilly District Miners' Hospital was founded by miners themselves, whose descendants expressed 'profound disquiet' at plans to close it.[196] When Prince Charles opened the hospital at Merthyr, placard-wielding protestors explained their dismay at losing Aberdare's casualty department.[197] The modernity of Percy Thomas's post-war hospitals in Wales

4.35 Prince Charles Hospital, Merthyr Tydfil, 1965–78 (photo: David Yates; author's collection, from practice; courtesy of WSP UK Ltd).

also therefore represented a loss of local identity and agency, in favour of participation in a uniform, rationally planned welfare state.

By then Sir Percy Thomas & Son were also designing English hospitals. The Bristol office (Jennett, Patricia Townsend and others) designed Yeovil District Hospital from the mid-1960s to 1973 with a ten-storey slab block oversailing lower medical departments, all clad in buff brick. Wards followed a standard plan determined by the South West Regional Hospital Board.[198] More importantly, however, the practice played a significant role in establishing new standardised forms for national use, as the Department of Health and Social Security (DHSS, as the Ministry became in 1968) developed its Harness and later Nucleus systems. Outline modules of identical size and cruciform shape contained layouts for each department or ward type, to be selected by individual hospitals as needed, arranged on the site, stacked up, and linked with corridors and services. The original Harness system included a central spine corridor carrying a service zone above. The DHSS also considered standardising construction so hospitals could be assembled from fully predesigned elements. Only two experimental Harness hospitals were built in Britain, both for the Birmingham Regional Hospital Board: Stafford District General Hospital by the Building Design Partnership, and Dudley District General, later called Russells Hall, by the Percy Thomas Partnership (PTP).

The practice's Birmingham office, where Allan Clark was a hospital specialist, designed Dudley with input from Derek Stow and the DHSS architects, contributing to the development of these systems (see Figure 4.36).[199] The DHSS decided to try

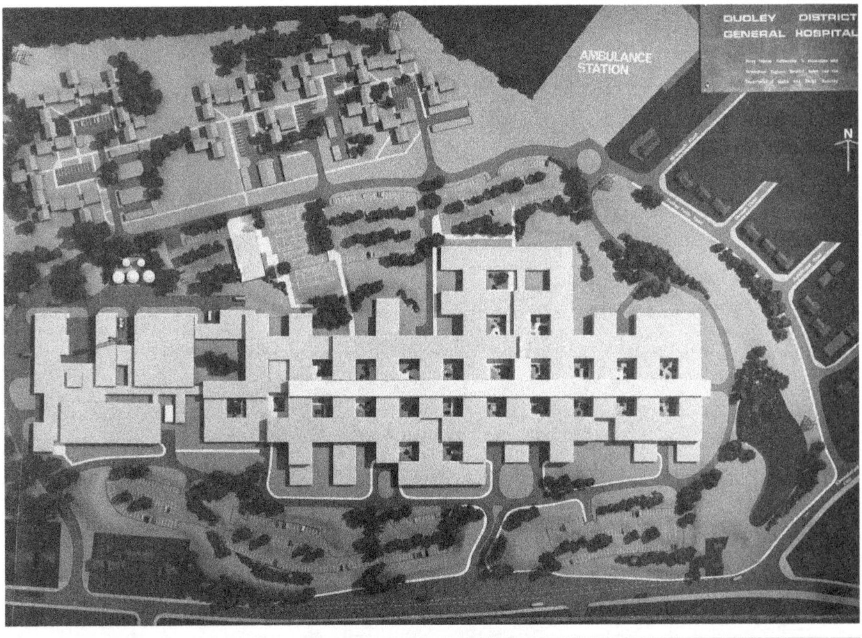

4.36 Dudley District General Hospital (now Russells Hall Hospital), Dudley, 1970–83, design model *c.*1977 (unknown photographer; from *Percy Thomas Partnership Architects & Planning Consultants: Composite Brochure No. 2*, n.d.; author's collection; courtesy of WSP UK Ltd).

Harness there around 1970 (though the hospital was only completed in 1983), and the architects' experiences with the modular system fed back into government policy.[200] Originally planned for over 1,000 beds (scaled back to 400), the architects considered reconciling it to human scale, designing cladding with projecting windows in white concrete for surface articulation alongside brown concrete wall panels; using pastel colours inside with areas of contrasting vivid colour with interior design by Irena Weeks and John Holt of PTP; and through Sue Radley's landscaping giving differentiated characters to courtyards between the modules.[201]

The Harness system was deemed expensive and soon discarded, replaced with the more modest Nucleus system, but Harness nevertheless found continued application in hospitals overseas. The practice of Percy Thomas therefore not only shaped the experience of the NHS for many in Wales but also took a significant role in developing government standards applied to hospitals across Britain.

Conclusion

Between the late 1930s and the 1970s, the practice's work went through several phases: from simplified classical forms to plain surfaces with sharp edges and vestigial hints of classical elements, retaining symmetry and monumentality; a technical modernism comprising light frame structures, curtain walls and thin brick, stone or mosaic cladding, suiting complex and high-density uses through asymmetrical planning, from the 1950s to the 1960s; and in the 1960s and 1970s, brutalism's reintroduction of weighty materials in new spatial forms. The standardisation and prefabrication associated with hospitals, schools and some factories forms a further strand, participating in changing architectural culture. Moments of crisis sometimes precipitated shifts between forms, when an older approach became inadequate for modern realities. Modern architecture responded to new scales and complexities of institution attempting to widen social benefits. Clients and architects sought a visual modernity, often linked across institutions and building types to demonstrate participation in a national project of modernisation. The expression of modernity was intrinsically unstable, however, having to deal with changing technical, institutional, cultural and political factors.

Though the practice's work in this field extended beyond Wales, it had most impact here, and suggests a distinctive Welsh experience of the welfare state predicated on industrial development. It was an experience of big new scales overriding the local, from giant bridges to complex hospitals; of new technologies; of coal-fuelled and petrol-based infrastructures fixing modes of production and consumption for generations to come, rendered seductive through dramatic visual forms in sharp outlines. Nevertheless, the practice's work participated in the greater integration of Wales into the United Kingdom and enabled the growth of important Welsh institutions dependent on central government and contributing to British development. Yet, as the next chapter explores, even in the practice's fully fledged modernism of the 1960s, the architects became increasingly concerned with articulating a sense of place and regional or national identity as the century unfolded. ■

04
Industry and Infrastructure in the Welfare State
References

1. 'RIBA Conference at Leeds: The Banquet', *Architects' Journal*, 1 July 1937, p. 14.
2. 'Societies and Institutions: Liverpool Architectural Society', *Architects' Journal*, 15 April 1937, p. 648.
3. 'RIBA Annual Dinner', *Architects' Journal*, 11 February 1937, p. 263.
4. Glen O'Hara, *From Dreams to Disillusionment: Economic and Social Planning in 1960s Britain* (Basingstoke: Palgrave Macmillan, 2007), for example, pp. 5-17.
5. Bernard Harris, *The Origins of the British Welfare State: Society, State and Social Welfare* (Basingstoke: Palgrave Macmillan, 2004), p. 297.
6. Sam Wetherell, *Foundations: How the Built Environment Made Twentieth-Century Britain* (Princeton NJ: Princeton University Press, 2020), pp. 19, 37.
7. Alistair Fair, '"Modernization of Our Hospital System": The National Health Service, the Hospital Plan, and the "Harness" Programme, 1962-77', *Twentieth Century British History*, 29/4 (2018), 547-75 (548-9), citing Tony Cutler, 'Economic Liberal or Arch Planner? Enoch Powell and the Political Economy of the Hospital Plan', *Contemporary British History*, 25/4 (2011), 469-89, and Rodney Lowe, 'The Replanning of the Welfare State', in Martin Francis and Ina Zweiniger-Bargielowska (eds), *The Conservatives and British Society, 1880-1990* (Cardiff: University of Wales Press, 1996), pp. 255-73.
8. Ben Pimlott, *Harold Wilson* (London: William Collins, 2016), for example, p. 513.
9. Greg Hise, 'Architecture as State Building: A Challenge to the Field', *Journal of the Society of Architectural Historians*, 67/2 (2008), 173-7 (173-4).
10. James E. Cronin, *The Politics of State Expansion: War, State and Society in Twentieth-Century Britain* (London: Routledge, 1991); Martin Chick, *Industrial Policy in Britain, 1945-1951: Economic Planning, Nationalisation and the Labour Governments* (Cambridge: Cambridge University Press, 1998); David Edgerton, *The Rise and Fall of the British Nation: A Twentieth-Century History* (London: Penguin, 2019).
11. Neil Brenner, *New State Spaces: Urban Governance and the Rescaling of Statehood* (Oxford: Oxford University Press, 2004), for example, pp. 99, 108-30.
12. Elaine Davey and Huw Thomas, '"Chief Creator of Modern Wales": The Neglected Legacy of Percy Thomas', *North American Journal of Welsh Studies*, 9 (2014), 54-70; Elaine Davey, 'A National Architect? The Percy Thomas Practice and Welsh National Identity' (unpublished PhD thesis, Cardiff University, 2013).

13. Guy Ortolano, *Thatcher's Progress: From Social Democracy to Market Liberalism through an English New Town* (Cambridge: Cambridge University Press, 2019), pp. 111–19; Elizabeth Darling, *Re-Forming Britain: Narratives of Modernity Before Reconstruction* (London: Routledge, 2007).

14. Geoffrey Percival, *The Government's Industrial Estates in Wales, 1936–1975* ([Cardiff]: Welsh Development Agency, 1978), pp. 4–5; on these precursors: Wetherell, *Foundations*, pp. 18–25.

15. Percival, *Industrial Estates*, p. 14; 'Architect to Trading Estate', *Western Mail & South Wales News*, 30 December 1936, p. 12.

16. RCAHMW, PTA, 01/06, 'Photographs of Work by Percy Thomas', vol. 6, pp. 48–52.

17. Percival, *Industrial Estates*, pp. 17–23; 'Treforest', *Architects' Journal*, 20 May 1937, p. 877; 'Treforest Trading Estate', *The Builder*, 14 January 1938, p. 134; 'The Treforest Trading Estate', *National Builder*, November 1938, p. 130.

18. Percival, *Industrial Estates*, pp. 47, 53; 'Treforest's New Paper Mill Opened', *Western Mail & South Wales News*, 4 August 1938, p. 10.

19. Percival, *Industrial Estates*, p. 2.

20. Wetherell, *Foundations*, p. 45; Hugh Quigley, 'The Facts', *Architects' Journal*, 20 May 1937, pp. 859–61; G. Gillett, 'Foreword', *Architects' Journal*, 20 May 1937, pp. 857–8; 'Industry in Rural Valley', *Western Mail & South Wales News*, 1 January 1937, p. 10.

21. Wetherell, *Foundations*, pp. 37–8.

22. TNA, BT 168/12, Oliver Lyttelton, 'Production Plans for 1944', 9 March 1944.

23. 'News: Appointments', *Architects' Journal*, 15 August 1940, p. 128; Thomas, *Pupil to President*, pp. 41–2.

24. Leon Gooberman, 'Public Governance of Private Munitions Businesses in Regional Britain: The Case of Wales, 1938 to 1945', *Business History*, 66/1 (2024), 201–20; 'Regional Controller for Wales', *Architects' Journal*, 30 July 1942, p. 66.

25. TNA, BT 168/12, for example, Regional Controllers' Conference, 10–11 May 1944 and other documents.

26. TNA, BT 168/12, Regional Controllers' Conference, 13–14 October 1943; TNA, BT 168/13, Regional Controllers' Conferences of 1945 and other documents.

27. Percival, *Industrial Estates*, pp. 48–51.

28. TNA, BT 168/13, Conference of Chairmen of Regional Boards, 22 August 1945.

29. TNA, BT 168/13, Regional Controllers' Conference, 13 June 1945 and 'The Programme of Factory Building', 15 June 1945; TNA, BT 170/224, activities of Welsh Board for Industry, 30 November 1954; TNA, BT 194/50, various Welsh Board for Industry documents of 1948–9.

30. TNA, BT 194/50, Welsh Board for Industry, Sub-Committee on the Industrial Situation in South Wales, n.d. [1949].

31. Leon Gooberman and Ben Curtis, 'The Age of Factories: The Rise and Fall of Manufacturing in South Wales, 1945-1985', in Louise Miskell (ed.), *New Perspectives on Welsh Industrial History* (Cardiff: University of Wales Press, 2020), pp. 181-204 (199); Percival, *Industrial Estates*, pp. 63-4; Victoria Perry, *Built for a Better Future: The Brynmawr Rubber Factory* (Oxford: White Cockade Publishing, 1994).

32. Elaine Davey, 'Something Must Be Done', in David Drake (ed.), *Diffusion Extra: Revolution* (Cardiff: Ffotogallery Wales, 2017), pp. 5-10 (6); TNA, BT 177/1684, T. K. Rees, 'British Nylon Spinners Ltd: Proposed New Factory ... Brief on Distribution of Industry Aspects', 5 May 1958; TNA, BT 208/59, 'Official Committee on the Balanced Distribution of Industry, Panel A, New Building Work: Application to Panel A for Approval of Scheme from Location Aspect', n.d. [1945].

33. TNA, BT 177/1684, for example, A. E. Welch to T. K. Rees, 10 February 1958, 17 March 1958, 19 March 1958; F. C. Bagnall (BNS) to Sir Frank Lee (Permanent Secretary, Board of Trade), 1 May 1958; J. A. R. Pimlott to Welch, 14 March 1958; TNA, BT 177/1685, for example, 'British Nylon Spinners Limited', 31 July 1958; Rees to Welch, 'British Nylon Spinners Ltd. Application for an IDC for a Factory at Havant', 14 August 1958; G. H. Andrew to Sharp and Neale, 18 August 1958; TNA, HLG 79/1488, C. G. Parry to Research Officer, Wales and Controller, Wales, 11 July 1950.

34. Board of Trade, *Room to Expand: Factories and Facilities in the Development Areas and Northern Ireland* (London: Board of Trade, 1955), p. 9.

35. Arthur Elliot, *History of British Nylon Spinners* (Abertillery: Old Bakehouse Publications, 2009), pp. 4-7, 15.

36. 'The Pontypool Factory of British Nylon Spinners Ltd', in Eric L. Bird (ed.), *Industrial Architecture*, (London: RIBA, 1949), pp. 6-9; Elliot, *British Nylon Spinners*, p. 19; G. Collin, 'Polymer Beginnings', *BNS Magazine*, January 1965, pp. 42-3; 'Twenty-Five Years of British Nylon', *BNS Magazine*, January 1965, pp. 5-14.

37. G. B. R., 'Makers of Industrial Wales: Sir Percy Thomas', *Western Mail & South Wales News*, 3 February 1955, p. 8.

38. Amgueddfa Torfaen Museum, Pontypool, perspective by R. F. Buckley of 1947.

39. 'Industrial Building Part Two', *Architectural Design*, March 1949, pp. 54-70 (59); 'Factory at Pontypool for British Nylon Spinners Ltd', *Architectural Review*, May 1949, pp. 216-22. 'The Factory of British Nylon Spinners Ltd, Pontypool, Glam.', *RIBA Journal*, June 1949, pp. 353-9; 'Factory at Pontypool', *Architects' Journal*, 11 August 1949, pp. 144-50; 'Notes on the Factory Extension', *BNS Magazine*, February 1952, pp. 1-3.

40. 'The Yarn Test Room', *BNS Magazine*, January 1952, pp. 1-3; R. M. Lodge, 'Evolution of Research', *BNS Magazine*, January 1965, pp. 45-50; Elliot, *British Nylon Spinners*, pp. 45-51; TNA, BT 177/1684, IDC applications, 1951-6.

41. 'Portrait of a Job: Factory Doctor', *BNS Magazine*, August 1952, pp. 4-5; 'Portrait of a Job: Welfare Officer', *BNS Magazine*, April 1952, pp. 5-6; 'The New Pavilion',

BNS Magazine, July 1952, p. 13; GAC, Dale Owen Papers, D900/U/6, 'British Architects' Conference, Cardiff 1959', booklet, p. 20.

42. 'At the Industrial Architecture Exhibition', *Architects' Journal*, 3 March 1949, p. 200; 'News and Notes', *Architectural Design*, February 1949, pp. 50-1.

43. Percival, *Industrial Estates*, pp. 103-8.

44. Elain Harwood, *Space, Hope and Brutalism: English Architecture, 1945-1975* (London: Yale University Press, 2015), pp. 358-67; Murray Fraser and Joe Kerr, *Architecture and the 'Special Relationship': The American Influence on Post-War British Architecture* (Abingdon: Routledge, 2007), pp. 229-39.

45. 'Building Study: Parke-Davis Plant, Pontypool', *Architects' Journal*, 31 July 1974, pp. 267-85; 'Letters', *Architects' Journal*, 14 August 1974, pp. 370-1; 'Letters', *Architects' Journal*, 21 August 1974, pp. 425-6; 'Excellent of Its Kind', *Architects' Journal*, 4 July 1973, pp. 2-5.

46. Robert Millward and John Singleton, 'The Ownership of British Industry in the Post-War Era: An Explanation' and Ruggero Ranieri, 'Partners and Enemies: The Government's Decision to Nationalise Steel 1944-8', in Robert Millward and John Singleton (eds), *The Political Economy of Nationalisation in Britain 1920-50* (Cambridge: Cambridge University Press, 1995), pp. 309-20 and 275-305; Chick, *Industrial Policy in Britain*, for example, pp. 83, 195.

47. H. Leighton Davies, 'Trostre Works: The General Plan', in *A Technical Survey of the Abbey, Margam, Trostre and Newport Plants of The Steel Company of Wales* (London: Industrial Newspapers, 1952), pp. 169-71; WGAS, D/D Z 208/11, The Steel Company of Wales (Tinplate Division), *Trostre Works* (n. pub., 1962).

48. Louise Miskell, 'Doing It for Themselves: The Steel Company of Wales and the Study of American Industrial Productivity, 1945-1955', *Enterprise & Society*, 18/1 (2017), 184-213.

49. W. S. Atkins & Partners, 'The Work of the Consulting Engineers: Civil and Engineering Buildings', in *Technical Survey*, pp. 35-56 (especially p. 37); Sir Percy Thomas & Son, 'The Work of the Consulting Engineers: Architectural Design', in *Technical Survey*, pp. 80-1.

50. S. H. Haden & Sons Ltd, advertisement, *Architectural Review*, December 1960, p. xv; A. J. Williams, 'Trostre Works - Engineering Background: Civil Engineering and Superstructures', in *Technical Survey*, pp. 172-6, 212 (175-6); National Museum of Wales, paintings of 1950s by Charles Ernest Cundall, via *https://museum.wales/collections* (accessed 1 February 2022).

51. Miskell, 'Doing it for Themselves', p. 193.

52. WGAS, PL 11/22/15, Meirion Bell, 'Velindre Tinplate Works 1956-1989', 8 June 1996; typical images, for example, WGAS, D/D X105/28/22/2, The Steel Company of Wales Limited, *Trostre Works* (n. pub., 1952); WGAS, D/D Xlm 185, 'The Steel Company of Wales Limited. Abbey Works. Port Talbot', 'Margam in Action', from *Future*, 6/5, October/November 1951, pp. 53-60; WGAS, D/D Z 208/74, The Steel Company of Wales Limited, *Port Talbot, Margam and Abbey Works* (n. pub., n.d.); WGAS, D/D Z 375/1, The Steel Division of the Steel

1 Swansea Guildhall, 1930–4, assembly hall (now Brangwyn Hall), with paintings by Frank Brangwyn (Photo: author; courtesy of the Glynn Vivian Gallery, Swansea and the estate of Sir Frank Brangwyn).

2 Carmarthenshire County Hall, Carmarthen, 1936–46, council chamber, completed 1950s (Photo: author).

3 Welsh National Temple of Peace and Health, Cardiff, 1936–8, Hall of Nations (Photo: author).

4 William Walcot, presentation perspective of design by Percy Thomas for Euston Station, London, c.1937 (National Railway Museum, York; courtesy of Science Museum Group and the estate of Sir Percy Thomas).

5 Ironbridge B Power Station, 1963–9 (Photo: Countrywide Images / Alamy).

6 Physics and Mathematics building, University College of Wales, Aberystwyth, 1960–2 (Photo: author).

7 Symphony Hall, Birmingham, 1983–90 (Photo: author).

8 Wales Millennium Centre, Cardiff, 1996–2004 (Photo: author).

Company of Wales Limited, *Port Talbot, Margam and Abbey Works: An Illustrated Description of Plant and Processes* (Port Talbot: Steel Company of Wales, 1957).

53. WGAS, D/D LE 127, A. Leslie Evans, cuttings book, 'Abbey Works; Local Industries', 'Mighty New Abbey Works May Roll Out 2,000,000 Tons of Steel a Year', *Western Mail & South Wales News*, 18 July 1951 and K. S. Price, 'The Story of the Abbey Strip Mill', *Western Mail & South Wales News*, 17 July 1951 and 18 July 1951.

54. Miskell, 'Doing it for Themselves', pp. 201–2; Bleddyn Penny, 'The Affluent Striker: Industrial Disputes in the Port Talbot Steelworks', in Miskell (ed.), *New Perspectives*, pp. 127–53 (134).

55. RCAHMW, PTA, 01/07, 'Photographs of Work by Percy Thomas', vol. 7, pp. 22–7.

56. 'Steel Works at Margam, Port Talbot, South Wales', *Architects' Journal*, 16 August 1951, pp. 195–202; 'The Steel Company of Wales: Abbey Works, Port Talbot', *Architect & Building News*, 16 August 1951, pp. 179–87; 'Abbey Works, Port Talbot for the Steel Company of Wales, Limited', *The Builder*, 24 August 1951, pp. 256–64; 'Current Architecture: Steelworks at Port Talbot, South Wales', *Architectural Review*, February 1952, pp. 115–16; 'New Buildings in Wales', *Architects' Journal*, 11 June 1959, pp. 884–91 (889).

57. WGAS, D/D LE 127, Evans cuttings, 'Margam on the Sports Map', *Evening Post*, 28 November 1952; C. H. Reilly, 'The Next 5 or 50 Years' Work', *Architects' Journal*, 16 January 1947, pp. 54–76 (56, 71).

58. Kenneth O. Morgan, *Rebirth of a Nation: Wales 1880–1980* (Oxford: Clarendon Press, 1981), p. 315; David Kynaston, *Modernity Britain, 1957–62* (London: Bloomsbury, 2015), pp. 255–6.

59. GAC, D900/U/6, 'Letters & Odds', details of Dale Owen's career with P. R. Rathbone (Secretary, Town Planning Institute) to I. D. Owen, 9 November 1962; Ian Pepperell, email to the author, 2 February 2022; Peter Q. Kendall, letter to the author, 28 June 2021; Kerry Veale, telephone interview with the author, 7 February 2022.

60. 'Modest Start to £100m Giant', *Western Mail*, 10 September 1959, p. 8.

61. 'Industrial', *Architectural Review*, January 1962, pp. 65–70; 'Criticism: This Month's Buildings', *Architectural Review*, August 1963, pp. 121–2; 'Steelworks, Newport, Mon.', *Architectural Review*, August 1963, pp. 123–8.

62. Dale Owen, 'Getting Better by Design', in David Cole (ed.), *The New Wales* (Cardiff: University of Wales Press, 1990), pp. 70–90 (77–8).

63. Martin Chick, 'The Political Economy of Nationalisation: The Electricity Industry', in Millward and Singleton (eds), *Political Economy of Nationalisation*, pp. 257–74.

64. TNA, BD 24/220, H. W. Grimmett, 'Report of Public Inquiry ... into the Proposed Aberthaw Generating Station', 1955, pp. 5–9.

65. 'The Royal Academy Exhibition', *Architects' Journal*, 6 May 1948, pp. 413–17; 'Carmarthen Bay Power Station', *RIBA Journal*, October 1947, pp. 598–9.

66. Harwood, *Space, Hope and Brutalism*, pp. 337–40.

67. TNA, POWE 73/2, Central Electricity Generating Board, South Wales Division, Press Statement, 24 May 1961; TNA, POWE 14/687, various documents including drawings by Sir Percy Thomas & Son of 1954–5.

68. John Sheail, 'Power to the People: Power Stations and the National Grid', in Paul Brassley, Jeremy Burchardt, and Karen Sayer (eds), *Transforming the Countryside: The Electrification of Rural Britain* (Abingdon: Routledge, 2017), pp. 38–50 (42–4); 'The Uskmouth Power Station Will Be the Biggest in Europe', *Western Mail & South Wales News*, 7 October 1953, p. 7; 'Site Record: Uskmouth Power Station', Coflein, n.d., *https://coflein.gov.uk/en/site/305883/images?term=uskmouth* (accessed 9 February 2022).

69. TNA, POWE 14/689, '120MW Station Inland of Cardiff-Newport', September 1953; TNA, POWE 14/690, H. W. Grimmitt to Geoffrey Lloyd (Minister of Fuel and Power), 25 May 1954 and drawings by Percy Thomas and Kennedy & Donkin, n.d.; Alec McKinty, 'New Giant Took Four Years to Complete', *Western Mail & South Wales News*, 31 October 1958, pp. 12–13; 'South Wales Institute of Architects' Recent Work in the Area', *Architect & Building News*, 10 June 1959, pp. 749–68 (763); advertisement for Robertson Q-Panel, *Architects' Journal*, 25 December 1958, p. 30.

70. Michael Stratton, *Ironbridge and the Electric Revolution: The History of Electricity Generation at Ironbridge A and B Power Stations* (London: John Murray, 1994); Ric Tyler, 'Ironbridge Power Station: Historic Building Record, 2017', Archaeology Data Service, 3 May 2017, *https://doi.org/10.5284/1043137* (accessed 9 February 2022); Ric Tyler, 'Eggborough Power Station: Historic Building Record 2020', Archaeology Data Service, 2020, *https://doi.org/10.5284/1083523* (accessed 8 February 2022).

71. 'Rogerstone Helps Wales to "Export" Power to England', *Western Mail & South Wales News*, 31 October 1958, p. 11.

72. Brenner, *New State Spaces*, pp. 78–9; Neil Brenner and Stuart Elden, 'Introduction: State, Space, World; Lefebvre and the Survival of Capitalism', in Henri Lefebvre, *State, Space, World: Selected Essays* (Minneapolis MN: University of Minnesota Press, 2009), pp. 1–48; David Harvey, *The Condition of Postmodernity: An Enquiry into the Origins of Cultural Change* (Cambridge MA: Blackwell, 1990), pp. 132, 229–32.

73. Marquand, *South Wales Needs a Plan* (London: George Allen & Unwin, 1936), pp. 93, 191.

74. 'Bridge Over the Severn: Local Authorities' Views', *Local Government Journal*, January 1938, p. 28; TNA, MT 39/280, Ministry of Transport, press release, 'Proposed Severn Bridge', 16 December 1937.

75. James Drake, H. L. Yeadon, and D. L. Evans, *Motorways* (London: Faber & Faber, 1969), pp. 34–40, 43–4; Kathryn A. Morrison and John Minnis, *Carscapes: The Motor Car, Architecture and Landscape in England* (London: Yale University Press, 2012), pp. 257–8; TNA, BD 30/16, 'Severn Bridge "King-Pin" of Road Plans', *Western Mail & South Wales News*, 25 September 1946, cutting.

76. David Starkie, *The Motorway Age: Road and Traffic Policies in Post-War Britain* (Oxford: Pergamon Press, 1982), pp. 1-3.

77. TNA, BT 64/3358, Hugh Dalton (Board of Trade) to C. E. Hollinghurst (Ministry of War Transport), 16 February 1944 and Dalton to Phil J. Noel-Baker (Ministry of War Transport), 27 January 1944.

78. TNA, BD 30/16: H. E. Aldington (Ministry of War Transport) to E. B. Hugh-Jones (Divisional Road Engineer, Wales & Monmouthshire), 9 June 1945; 'Severn Bridge Plan', *Western Mail & South Wales News*, 6 December 1946, cutting; 'Work on Severn Bridge to Begin This Year', *Western Mail & South Wales News*, 25 March 1947, cutting.

79. 'The Severn Road Bridge', *The Builder*, 27 September 1946, pp. 314–15; 'Severn Road Bridge', *Architect & Building News*, 27 September 1946, pp. 188–9; TNA, BD 30/16, Ministry of Transport, 'Severn Road Bridge: General Description of Works', September 1946.

80. TNA, MT 95/818: 'How the New Severn Bridge Will Appear', *Gloucester Citizen*, 1 August 1947, cutting, and 'Severn Bridge Plan Approved', *The Telegraph*, 1 July 1947, cutting; Percy Thomas, 'My Work as the Consultant Architect', *Birmingham Post*, 8 September 1966, Severn Bridge Supplement, p. III.

81. TNA, BD 31/97, 'Trunk Roads North of Almondsbury [etc.]', (London: HMSO, 1947); TNA, MT 39/606, drawing, Percy Thomas, 'Proposed Bridge over River Wye', n.d.

82. For example, TNA, BT 170/224, Welsh Board for Industry, 30 March 1954, 27 April 1954, 27 July 1954, 28 September 1954; TNA, BT 1954/52, Severn Bridge Sub-Committee, 1954–6; quotation: TNA, MT 121/3, J. R. Willis to A. W. Peterson (Home Office), 11 March 1954.

83. TNA, BT 170/225, Welsh Board for Industry and South Western Regional Board for Industry, 'Joint Submission to the Minister for Transport and Civil Aviation of the Views of the Two Boards that a Road Bridge over the River Severn between Beachley and Aust Should be Constructed as Soon as Possible', n.d. [1955].

84. Martin Johnes, '"M4 to Wales - and Prosper!" A History of a Motorway', *Historical Research*, 87/237 (2014), 556–73 (560); TNA, BD 30/68, 'Squabbles Lose the Severn Bridge for Wales', *Western Mail*, 20 June 1956, cutting and David G. Rosser, 'Construction of Severn Bridge Cannot Start Before Late 1960', *Western Mail*, 13 November 1958, cutting; TNA, BD 40/90, 'Draft Press Notice: Severn Bridge Contract for Superstructure Let', with Callum B. (Ministry of Transport) to Gilbert J. Shoebridge (Ministry of Housing and Local Government), 13 April 1962; TNA, MT 123/292, R. B. Lang, memo to Heston, 21 March 1963; TNA, MT 123/293, J. Ford, memo to E. F. Fairbrother, 30 April 1968.

85. Associated Bridge Builders Ltd, *The Severn Bridge Superstructure* (Birmingham: The Kynoch Press, 1966), for example, pp. 25-9, 61-2, 95; James Sutherland, 'Long Span Bridges', *Architectural Review*, September 1966, pp. 176–83; TNA, BD 40/90, 'Hollow Box Cuts Costs on Bridge', *Western Mail*, 11 January 1963, cutting; Dorothy Henry and J. A. Jerome, *Modern British Bridges* (London:

Applied Science Publishers Ltd, 1965), pp. 19–33; Tony Hunt, 'Engineering: Michael Parsons Obituary', *Guardian*, 2 June 2021, *www.theguardian.com/technology/2021/jun/02/michael-parsons-obituary* (accessed 10 May 2022).

86. TNA, MT 95/820: Godfrey Samuel (Secretary, Royal Fine Art Commission) to [H. C. Adams (Assistant Chief Engineer (Bridges), Ministry of Transport)], 19 October 1960; Samuel to [Adams], 15 December 1960; Adams to Percy Thomas, 23 December 1960; TNA, MT 118/8, Samuel to Assistant Chief Engineer (Bridges) (Ministry of Transport), 19 October 1960; Ministry of Transport, *The Appearance of Bridges* (London: HMSO, 1964), pp. 38–41; 'The Royal Academy', *Architects' Journal*, 4 May 1961, pp. 638–43 (642); TNA, BD 40/90, reproductions of perspective drawings by R. F. Buckley, 1960 and 1961.

87. Henry and Jerome, *Modern British Bridges*, p. 37.

88. 'Notes and News: The Severn Road Bridge', *The Builder*, 27 September 1946, pp. 314–15; TNA, MT 95/824, perspective by R. F. Buckley, 1961.

89. TNA, BD 30/69, Ministry of Transport, public inquiry minutes, 24–5 September 1946, p. 7.

90. TNA, BD 40/90, various correspondence, 1962; TNA, MT 95/818, various correspondence, 1946.

91. TNA, BD 40/90, Judd to Evans, 15 February 1963; TNA, MT 95/821, T. R. Newman to A. E. Coombs (Chief Road Engineer, Welsh Office), 22 July 1965 and Newman to Parr, 7 July 1965.

92. Peter Merriman and Rhys Jones, 'Nations, Materialities and Affects', *Progress in Human Geography*, 41/5 (2017), 600–17.

93. TNA, MT 121/400, Percy Thomas to T. R. Newman, 24 July 1965.

94. TNA, MT 121/400: drawings, Percy Thomas, n.d.; T. R. Newman to Dickinson, 15 July 1965; drawings, Sir Percy Thomas & Son, 'Severn Bridge: Gloucester Approach', 24 May 1965; TNA, MT 121/402: M. R. Porter to Barnett, 15 January 1964; TNA, MT 95/821: 'Severn Bridge Tolls Administration Building: Record of Meeting at Thornbury on 16th February 1965'; A. F. Parr (MOT) to Clerk (Gloucestershire County Council), 2 February 1965; H. G. Barnett to A. D. Holland, 24 August 1965.

95. Henry and Jerome, *Modern British Bridges*, pp. 26, 119.

96. TNA, MT 121/154, 'Contracts: Sir Robert McAlpine's £1.5m Award in S. Wales', *Financial Times*, 13 July 1962, cutting, and E. A. Bibby to Bristow (Treasury Chambers), 29 September 1961.

97. Robert Peel Mears and Ernest Edward Pool, 'Road Paper No. 54: The Design of Neath and Briton Ferry Viaducts', *Proceedings of the Institution of Civil Engineers*, 7/3 (1957), pp. 465–90; TNA, BD 31/80, David J. Young (Steel Company of Wales) to Divisional Road Engineer (Ministry of Transport, Cardiff), 26 April 1951,; TNA, BD 31/81, J. E. Jones (for Divisional Road Engineer) to J. B. H. Skinner (Construction Section, Highways (Engineering) Division), 7 July 1952.

98. Johnes, 'M4 to Wales'; Peter Merriman, '"A Power for Good or Evil": Geographies of the M1 in Late Fifties Britain', in David Gilbert, David Matless and Brian Short (eds), *Geographies of British Modernity: Space and Society in the Twentieth Century* (Malden: Blackwell, 2003), pp. 115–31.

99. 'Auckland Harbour Bridge: Report by Freeman, Fox and Partners' (London, n. pub., 1951), *https://kura.aucklandlibraries.govt.nz/digital/collection/rarebooks/id/7878* (accessed 3 March 2022); '£6m Bridge Opened at Auckland', *Shields Daily News*, 30 May 1959, p. 3; Gilbert Roberts and Oleg Alexander Kerensky, 'Auckland Harbour Bridge: Design', *Proceedings of the Institution of Civil Engineers*, 18/4 (1961), 423–58.

100. Richard Burton Archives, Swansea University, Swansea (RBAS), Box 4, 2017/11, Development Appeal Fund, 'Progress Report 2', 1962.

101. CUSCA, UCC/CL+CM/M/10, Council, 26 November 1957.

102. AUA, CAC/1/16, Court of Governors, 25 October 1944, Principal's Report.

103. RBAS, Box 664, 1/213/6, Court of Governors, 18 November 1949, 'Extract from an Address by Principal J. S. Fulton'.

104. William Whyte, 'Neo-Georgian: The Other Style in Britain's 20th-Century University Architecture?', in Julian Holder and Elizabeth McKellar (eds), *Neo-Georgian Architecture 1880–1970: A Reappraisal* (Swindon: Historic England, 2016), pp. 136–49.

105. AUA, C/BLDC/BUS, 'Sir Percy Thomas & Son 1936–1956': 'H. V. Lanchester's Report', n.d. [*c.*1931]; Needs Sub-Committee, 5 December 1934; Ifor L. Evans, 'Note to Lord Davies on Priority of Buildings on Penglais', November 1934; AUA, Photographs A(vii)/4/a, perspective, n.d.; AUA, CNL/1/A6, UCW Council Minutes, 13 March 1931, Report of Needs Committee, 9 January 1931; AUA, C/BLDC/BUS, 'Sir Percy Thomas & Son', Ifor L. Evans, 'New College Buildings', 29 January 1935; Edward Lewis Ellis, 'Evans, Ifor (Ivor) Leslie (1897–1952), Principal of the University College of Wales, Aberystwyth', Dictionary of Welsh Biography, 2001, *https://biography.wales/article/s2-EVAN-LES-1897* (accessed 7 March 2022).

106. AUA, Photographs, A(vii)/4/b, perspective, n.d.; reproduced at 'RA Exhibition: General Architectural Exhibits', *Architects' Journal*, 18 May 1944, pp. 371–4 (372).

107. AUA, CAC/1/11, Court of Governors, 18 October 1939, Principal's Report.

108. AUA, CAC/1/8, Court of Governors, 21 October 1936, Principal's Report, and Report of the Agricultural Executive Committee to Council, 2 December 1936.

109. 'New Buildings for The University College of Wales, Aberystwyth', *Architect & Building News*, 8 October 1943, pp. 26–32.

110. AUA, CAC/1/18, College Council, 18 July 1947; AUA, UWA/C/6/4, 'Report on the Work and Needs of the College', March 1944; AUA, CAC/1/23, Report of New Buildings Committee, 3 August 1951; AUA, CAC/1/9, College Council, 29 June 1938, Percy Thomas, 'Description of the Proposed Buildings', 27 May 1938; AUA, P/BLD, Percy Thomas, 'University College of Wales, Aberystwyth:

Proposed Hostel for Men', 28 May 1943, and ILE [Evans], 'University College of Wales, Aberystwyth: Halls of Residence for Men Students', May 1947, p. 36.

111. AUA, CAC/1/9, College Council, 27 April 1938, John Beresford (UGC) to Pro-Chancellor (University of Wales), 14 April 1938, and College Council 27 April 1938, report by Percy Thomas on swimming bath; 'New Swimming Bath, University College of Wales: Aberystwyth', *Architect & Building News*, 24 September 1943, pp. 183–6.

112. AUA, CAC/1/16, Court of Governors, 28 October 1949, Principal's Report; AUA, CAC/1/28, New Buildings Committee, 23 March and 23 April 1957; AUA, CAC/1/29, New Buildings Committee, 28 June 1957 and 31 October 1957.

113. AUA, CAC/1/29, New Buildings Committee, 8 February 1958, 27 June 1958 and 24 July 1958.

114. BUASC, Council, 22 June and 14 December 1938, Hall of Residence for Men Committee reports; BUASC, Council, 7 February 1940, Developments Committee report.

115. 'Botany and Forestry: Veneers Picked from Main Timbers of World', *North Wales Weekly News*, 26 May 1955, p. 6.

116. BUASC, Development Committee, 24 September 1970.

117. 'Development Plan', *Western Daily Press and Bristol Mirror*, 22 July 1948, p. 3; 'Bristol University', *Architects' Journal*, 9 January 1958, pp. 40–1; John Jordan, 'AJ Information Library: College and University Buildings', *Architects' Journal*, 31 January 1968, pp. 311–20 (318–20); Andrew Foyle, *Bristol* (London: Yale University Press, 2004), pp. 246–7.

118. Langley London Ltd, advertisement, *Architectural Review*, October 1963, p. 169; 'Percy Thomas Partnership Architects & Planning Consultants: Composite Brochure No. 2', n.d. [c.1972], unpaginated, author's collection; 'Halls of Residence, Bristol', *Architect & Building News*, 4 October 1967, pp. 567–79.

119. 'Nottm University Development-Plans', *Nottingham Journal*, 4 June 1949, p. 6; 'Educational Buildings', *Architectural Review*, January 1956, pp. 61–72; 'Recent Work in Nottingham', *Architects' Journal*, 7 July 1949, pp. 12–21 (15); 'Nottingham University', *Architects' Journal*, 9 January 1958, pp. 61–2.

120. 'Laboratories for Nottingham University by David Du R. Aberdeen', *Architects' Journal*, 7 July 1949, pp. 22–4; 'University Buildings', *Architectural Review*, January 1960, pp. 11–19 (18–19).

121. 'Nottingham University Hostels', *Architects' Journal*, 23 June 1960, pp. 962–3; 'Nottingham University Competition', *Architects' Journal*, 22 September 1949, p. 307; 'Nottingham Hall of Residence', *Architects' Journal*, 4 May 1950, p. 541; 'Hall of Residence for Nottingham University', *Architects' Journal*, 11 May 1950, pp. 566, 573–5.

122. 'New Consultants for Nottingham University', *Architects' Journal*, 5 December 1962, p. 1257; see also Whyte, 'Neo-Georgian', pp. 140–7.

123. David Dykes, *The University College of Swansea: An Illustrated History* (Stroud: Alan Sutton, 1992), p. 94.

124. RBAS, Box 664, 1/213/6, Court of Governors, 18 November 1949, 'Extract from an Address by Principal J. S. Fulton'; RBAS, Box 664, 1/213/6, 'Note in Support of the Application by the University College of Swansea to the Corporation of Swansea for a Grant of Additional Land', with J. S. Fulton (Principal, University College of Swansea) to Town Clerk (Swansea Corporation), 22 June 1949; plan illustrated in Dykes, *University College of Swansea*, p. 156; also RBAS, photograph album, 1997/36, 0004.

125. RBAS, Report of the Council, 1953–4; Geraint John, interview with the author, Bath, 25 April 2017.

126. H. E. Street, 'University College of Swansea. New Science Laboratories', *Nature*, 1957, 124–6; RBAS, Box 584 (1/213/1), 36, 'University College of Swansea: Botany, Geography, Geology, Zoology', n.d. [*c.*1961].

127. RBAS, Ref 2003/10 (Box 1), 1/202/9, 'University College of Swansea: College House and Halls of Residence', n.d. [*c.*1962]; Dykes, *University College of Swansea*, pp. 164–5.

128. RBAS, Reports of the Council, 1955–6 and 1960–1; 'University College, Swansea', *Architects' Journal*, 2 January 1958, pp. 16–17.

129. RBAS, Box 231, 1/215/2, Sir Percy Thomas & Son, 'University College of Swansea: Development Plan Preliminary Report', July 1958; Dykes, *University College of Swansea*, pp. 164–6.

130. RBAS, Box 2003/11, 1/202/7, Sir Percy Thomas & Son, 'University College of Swansea, Singleton and Contiguous Sites: Proposals for the Extension of Academic Studies at Singleton for a Maximum of 4,000 Students and the Possibilities of Contiguous Sites; Preliminary Report', December 1964.

131. Hilling, *Cardiff Civic Centre*, pp. 159–61.

132. CUSCA, 418/31, Brinley Thomas, 'A Note on the Cathays Park Development Plan for the Arts Departments, the Library and the Pre-Clinical Departments of the University College of South Wales and Monmouthshire', 1 August 1959.

133. CUSCA, UCC/CL+CM/M/12, Sites and Buildings Committee, 6 October 1959; CUSCA, UCC/CL+CM/M/13, Sites and Buildings Committee, 6 March 1961; GAC, D/900/U/5, photographic negative of drawing by Dale Owen, 'University College of South Wales and Monmouthshire: Proposed University Precinct, Cathays Park, Cardiff', January 1961.

134. CUSCA, UCC/CL+CM/M/14, Sites and Buildings Committee, 7 November 1961.

135. BUASC, Developments Committee, 5 March 1959, in UCNW Council, 25 April 1956.

136. For example, BUASC, Developments Committee, 14 March 1963, in UCNW Council, 24 April 1963; RCAHMW, PTA 05/05, 'Percy Thomas Partnership: Architects & Planning Consultants' (n.d. [*c.*1977]).

137. BUASC, Developments Committee, 13 December 1961, in UCNW Council, 7 February 1962; BUASC, uncatalogued, Sir Percy Thomas & Son (Shrewsbury), 'UCNW: Development of the Science Buildings Site at Deiniol Road, Bangor', 1961; BUASC, Developments Committee, 14 December 1965, in UCNW Council, 2 February 1966.

138. RCAHMW, PTA 05/05, 'Percy Thomas Partnership: Architects & Planning Consultants' (n.d. [c.1977]).

139. AUA, CAC/1/30, New Buildings Committee, 21 March, 4 May and 23 May 1959 reported in College Council, 26 June 1959; AUA, CAC/1/35, Principal's Report to Court of Governors, 30 October 1963.

140. For example, AUA, CAC/1/33, for example, New Buildings Committee, 18 December 1961 in College Council, 19 December 1961; AUA, CAC/1/37, New Buildings Committee, 13 December 1965.

141. 'Coleg Prifysgol Cymru/University College of Wales, Aberystwyth: The Llandinam Building', n.d. [1965], author's collection.

142. RBAS, 'University College of Swansea: Thirty-Eighth Report of the Council, 1957–58'.

143. RBAS, 2014/1/0, 'University College of Swansea, University of Wales: Halls of Residence', n.d.; RBAS, Ref 2003/10 (Box 1), 1/202/9, 'University College of Swansea: College House and Halls of Residence', n.d. [c.1962], for example, pp. 3, 30–2.

144. 'A View to the Sea: University College of Swansea's Library Extension', *Architect & Building News*, 10 July 1968, pp. 52–9; on Neal, Lucy Chivers, 'Professor Bernard George Neal Obituary', Imperial College London, 2016, *www.imperial.ac.uk/news/172629/professor-bernard-george-neal-obituary* (accessed 11 March 2022).

145. 'School of Social Studies, University College of Swansea, Awarded the RIBA Bronze Medal', *Architecture Wales*, February 1966, pp. 13–14.

146. GAC, D900/U/6, Ivan Dale Owen, 'The Environment of Liberal Studies', *Liberal Education: Journal of the Association for Liberal Education*, January 1967, pp. 14–21.

147. For example, CUSCA, 101/1/4/2/2, Principal's Address to Court of Governors, Special Meeting, 25 March 1966; CUSCA, 101/1/1/1, 'Annual Report of the Council to the Court of Governors', 1 October, 1962 to 30 September 1963 and subsequent reports up to 1969; CUSCA, 101/3/3/1, 'Tower Building. University College Cathays Park Cardiff', n.d. [c.1968]; CUSCA, CLCM/SB/M/2, I. L. Stephen James (Sir Percy Thomas & Son) to E. R. Evans (Registrar), 28 July 1967.

148. CUSCA, 101/1/4/2/2, Principal's Address to Court of Governors, 13 November 1964; CUSCA, UCC/CL+CM/M/14, Sites and Buildings Committee, 6 March 1962, including minutes of Ty Gwyn Court Development Working Party of 5 March 1962.

149. Lionel Charles Robbins, *Higher Education: Report of the Committee* (London: HMSO, 1963); Pimlott, *Harold Wilson*, pp. 302–4.

150. CUSCA, 101/1/4/2/2, Principal's Address to Court of Governors, 13 November 1964.

151. CUSCA, UCC/CL+CM/M/15, Joint Development Committee of the Council and Senate of the College, 26 April 1963; CUSCA, 101/1/4/2/2, Principal's Address to Court of Governors, 10 November 1967; AUA, CAC/1/35, New Buildings Committee, 19 October 1963; AUA, CAC/1/36, New Buildings Committee, 17 December 1964, in College Council, 18 December 1964, and New Buildings Committee, 10 March 1965.

152. AUA, R/Pbi/Misc/2, Sir Percy Thomas & Son, 'University College of Wales Aberystwyth, Development Plan 1', June 1965; R. Meadows, 'Project for University College of Wales, Aberystwyth', *Architect & Building News*, 8 December 1965, pp. 1082–3; Elisabeth Beazley, 'University College of Wales: Development Plan', *Architects' Journal*, 13 April 1966, p. 922.

153. 'Project Design for Great Hall, University College of Wales, Aberystwyth', *Architecture Wales*, April 1967, pp. 13–17; Kate Wharton, 'A Sequence of Spaces', *Architect*, April 1971, pp. 48–51; for awards see: 'Seemly Styling', *Architects' Journal*, 3 May 1972, pp. 930–43; 'Regional Incentives', *Architects' Journal*, 5 July 1972, pp. 2–6; AUA, R/Pbi/Misc 2, Percy Thomas Partnership, 'University College of Wales Aberystwyth, Development Plan 2', June 1974.

154. RIBAL, *Llyfrgell Hugh Owen Library* (Aberystwyth: University College of Wales, Aberystwyth, 1977).

155. BUASC, Developments Committee, 19 January 1965, in UCNW Council Minutes, 3 February 1965; Developments Committee, 22 June 1965, BUASC, UCNW Council Minutes, 29 September 1965; '£500,000 Multistorey Extensions to UCNW', *North Wales Weekly News*, 19 January 1967, p. 17; BUASC, 'Various Plans', Sir Percy Thomas & Son, plans of 12 April and 15 November 1965.

156. Alistair Fair, *Modern Playhouses: An Architectural History of Britain's New Theatres, 1945–1985* (Oxford: Oxford University Press, 2018), pp. 135–8.

157. BUASC, BMSS/40177, 'University College of North Wales/Coleg Prifysgol Gogledd Cymru: Theatr Gwynedd, Official Opening/Agoriad Swyddogol', 7 July 1975; BUASC, BMSS/40175, PHO/5/14, PHO/5/54 and uncatalogued, contemporary photographs.

158. BUASC, Developments Committee, 16 November 1965, in UCNW Council Minutes, 8 December 1965; Developments Committee, 28 February 1967, in UCNW Council Minutes, 28 June 1967; Developments Committee, 27 September 1967; Developments Committee, 24 September 1970, in UCNW Council, 30 September 1970; BUASC, PHO/5/4, photographs of Zoology museum, n.d. [*c.*1970]; 'Education', *Architectural Review*, January 1968, pp. 47–59 (47).

159. BUASC, Annual Report, 1974–5; BUASC, 'University College of North Wales: Number of Welsh Students in the College', 23 March 1965, in Council Minutes, 28 April 1965.

160. Barbara Price, *Technical Colleges and Colleges of Further Education* (London: Batsford, 1959), for example, pp. 25, 28, 46, 56, 73.

161. 'College Governors' First Meeting', *Western Mail & South Wales News*, 7 August 1953, p. 2; 'Education Minister's Visit to Monmouthshire', *Western Mail & South Wales News*, 7 November 1953, p. 5.

162. 'Where Are the Bright Boys of Wales?', *Western Mail*, 4 May 1957, p. 5.

163. John Hunt, 'Youth Learning for Industry's Sake', *Western Mail*, 24 February 1959, p. 7.

164. RCAHMW, PTA 05/05, 'Percy Thomas Partnership Architects & Planning Consultants', n.d. [*c*.1977].

165. Price, *Technical Colleges*, pp. 25–7; CUSCA, 103/14, 'New "University" On Show', unattributed press cutting, 1957.

166. CUSCA, 103/15, Robert E. Presswood, 'New Extension to College Gives Better Facilities', *Western Mail*, 19 September 1960, cutting.

167. 'Boffins Must Be Home-Grown', *Western Mail*, 15 May 1957, p. 7.

168. CUSCA, 103/15, Don Morgan, 'It's Mystery Acre No Longer', *South Wales Echo*, 29 May 1958, cutting.

169. BUASC, BMSS/39192, W. Marsden (Sir Percy Thomas & Son, Cardiff) to Lord Kenyon, 15 December 1959.

170. CUSCA, 103/15, souvenir booklet, 1961.

171. CUSCA, 103/14, 'Anti-Ugly Slogans on New Cardiff College', *South Wales Echo*, 7 April 1959, cutting.

172. Peter Q. Kendall to author, 28 June 2021; RCAHMW, PTA, 05/03, 'Sir Percy Thomas & Son: Architects and Planning Consultants', n.d. [*c*.1968]; RCAHMW, PTA, 05/05, 'Percy Thomas Partnership Architects & Planning Consultants', n.d. [*c*.1977].

173. Wyndham Powell, interview with the author and Michael Sweet, Cardiff, 4 February 2023; RCAHMW, PTA 05/05, 'Percy Thomas Partnership. Architects & Planning Consultants', n.d. [*c*.1977].

174. Ronald Weeks, 'The Modern Spirit', *Touchstone*, April 1999, pp. 14–15 (14).

175. 'Percy Thomas Partnership Architects & Planning Consultants: Composite Brochure No. 2', n.d. [c.1972], author's collection.

176. Alistair Fair, '"Modernization of Our Hospital System"', pp. 548, 551.

177. Jonathan Hughes, 'The "Matchbox on a Muffin": The Design of Hospitals in the Early NHS', *Medical History*, 44/1 (2000), 21-56.

178. Dorothy Dungworth, 'Duchess of Kent's Visit to Cardiff Hospitals', *Western Mail & South Wales News*, 13 July 1955, p. 6; RCAHMW, PTA 01/15, 'Photographs of Work by Percy Thomas', vol. 15; Delme Griffiths, *50 Years of the National Health Service Estate in Wales* (Cardiff: Welsh Health Estates, 1998), p. 47; Thomas, *Pupil to President*, pp. 49–50.

179. D. G. Morgan, 'United Cardiff Hospitals' and A. Trevor Jones, 'University Hospital of Wales: Preparation of the Brief for the Architects', in George H. Bell (ed.), *Hospital and Medical School Design: International Symposium, Dundee 1961*, 2 vols (Edinburgh: E. & S. Livingstone Ltd, 1962), vol. 1, pp. 3-4 and 30-3.

180. 'Competition for Medical Teaching Centre at Cardiff', *Architects' Journal*, 2 June 1960, pp. 825-37; 'Cardiff Competition: A Study of the Entries', *Architects' Journal*, 28 July 1960, pp. 133-40; 'The Wrong Hospital', *Architects' Journal*, 28 July 1960, p. 127.

181. Both architects appear in correspondence at TNA, MH 96/1859, West Wales Hospital Management Committee, 'Special Scheme under Para 3 of HM(55)19: West Wales General Hospital, Glangwili; Proposed Development; Stage 1', 1954-6.

182. David Edmunds, 'From Huts to This', *Western Mail*, 28 May 1959, p. 8; Griffiths, *50 Years*, pp. 47-9.

183. 'West Wales General Hospital, Glangwili', *The Builder*, 5 June 1959, pp. 994-5; 'South Wales Institute of Architects' Recent Work in the Area', *Architect & Building News*, 10 June 1959, pp. 749-68 (767); 'West Wales General Hospital, Redevelopment', *Hospital and Health Management*, March 1962, pp. 228-32; 'West Wales General Hospital, Carmarthen', *The Hospital*, October 1962, pp. 659-65; Hughes, 'Matchbox on a Muffin', pp. 26-31; Nuffield Provincial Hospitals Trust, *Studies in the Function and Design of Hospitals* (London: Oxford University Press, 1960), for example, pp. 7-8, 14-16, 19-20, 28, 53.

184. Sunand Prasad, 'Typology Diagrams', in Sunand Prasad (ed.), *Changing Hospital Architecture* (London: RIBA, 2008), pp. ix-xi (ix).

185. 'West Wales General Hospital, Carmarthen', *The Hospital*, October 1962, pp. 659-65.

186. TNA, BD 18/2145, Chairman (Welsh Board of Health), 5 September 1960, and other documents.

187. TNA, BD 18/2377, Sir Percy Thomas & Son to Welsh Hospital Board, 31 December 1963; TNA, BD 18/2157, 'Nevill Hall, Abergavenny: Official Opening' etc., 10 April 1970; 'Nevill Hall Hospital', *The Hospital*, October 1970, pp. 354-6.

188. TNA, BD 18/2378, Meyrick Phillips, 'Millions Will be Well Spent on Hospital for Three Counties', *Western Mail*, 29 June 1966, cutting; TNA, BD 18/2157, 'Nevill Hall Hospital', n.d. [*c*.1970].

189. A. G. M. Davies, Peter G. Hughes, and L. T. Lewis, 'The X-Ray Department for the District General Hospital at Nevill Hall, Abergavenny', *The Hospital*, November 1962, pp. 739-42.

190. TNA, BD 18/2378, A. G. M. Davies (North Monmouthshire Hospital Management Committee) to P. Alwyn-Smith (Welsh Hospital Board), 24 November 1971 and Alwyn Smith to Davies, 13 December 1971.

191. TNA, BD 18/2153, Norman Thomas to A. E. Newell (Welsh Hospital Board), 29 November 1965.

192. Evan Thompson, 'Prince Charles Opens Hospital', *Pontypridd Observer*, 12 May 1978, p. 7.

193. Griffiths, *50 Years*, pp. 56–7, 89–91.

194. TNA, BD 18/2377, M. Morgan (Breconshire Executive Council, National Health Service) to P. Alwyn-Smith (Welsh Hospital Board), 5 March 1964, and other correspondence.

195. TNA, BD 18/2377, A. Jones (Crickhowell Parish Council) to Welsh Regional Hospital Board, 22 January 1964; TNA, BD 18/2378, 'Crickhowell Fights for Its Hospital', *Abergavenny Chronicle*, 5 December 1968, p. 3.

196. TNA, BD 18/2378, 'Miners Pledge Support to Campaign', cutting, no details.

197. Thompson, 'Prince Charles Opens Hospital'.

198. 'New District Hospital Is Completed', *Wells Journal*, 16 February 1973, p. 17; John R. Guy, *'Y.D.H.': The Story of Yeovil District Hospital* (Yeovil, n. pub.: 1983); 'Twenty-One Years with PTP', *Percy Thomas Partnership: Review*, 1985, unpaginated, author's collection.

199. Fair, 'Modernization of Our Hospital System', pp. 558–64; Derek Stow, 'Transformation in Healthcare Architecture: From the Hospital to a Healthcare Organism', in Prasad (ed.), *Changing Hospital Architecture*, pp. 13–48 (26–9); W. Paul James and William Tatton-Brown, *Hospitals: Design and Development* (Architectural Press, 1986), p. 5; Mike Nightingale, video-interview with the author, 2 March 2021.

200. TNA, MH 166/361, Birmingham Regional Hospital Board, 'The New Dudley District General Hospital', n.d. [*c.*1970], and other documents; TNA, MH 166/658 for Stow's involvement; TNA, MH 166/1129, documents of 1974 for construction details; '£150 Million to Be Spent on Midland Hospitals in Next Nine Years', *Birmingham Daily Post*, 28 July 1973, p. 6; Stanley Slaughter, 'Delay in Building Hospital "Will Lower Standards"', *Birmingham Daily Post*, 6 February 1975, p. 1; 'New Building Schemes to Cost £400m', *Birmingham Daily Post*, 5 July 1978, p. 10.

201. TNA, MH 166/489, 'The New Dudley District General Hospital', n.d. [*c.*1970]; 'How the Hospital Took Shape', *Russells Hall Round-Up*, no. 1, December 1982, unpaginated, *www.facebook.com/photo/?fbid=10222604505614143&set=pcb.1128143470981838* (accessed 29 March 2022); 'Dudley D. G. H. Reaches Completion', *Percy Thomas Partnership: Review*, 1982, unpaginated, from Philip Bintliff.

5

Place, Landscape and Heritage

The work of Sir Percy Thomas & Son and the Percy Thomas Partnership (PTP) was concentrated on large-scale, highly technical modern buildings, dramatic statements of modernity, visibly demonstrating and embodying the achievements of the welfare state, especially in Wales. Yet there is another side to the practice during that period and beyond that considered architecture in relation to place, sometimes articulated as a national concern in Wales, sometimes orientated towards immediate urban or regional contexts, and studying historical precedents, particularly local vernacular forms. This approach arose within modernism, attempting to reconcile the facts and benefits of modernity to the local culture adopting it (a 'Critical Regionalism', rather than simply regional revival).[1] Yet this preference led some in the practice to reject modern movement principles for historical styles, a break in stylistic continuity that nevertheless developed from the same architectural roots. The practice's work included not only new buildings but also historic building restorations, and extended to concern with the landscape - the ways in which architecture could embrace and enhance its environment, in complementary relationships with topography and plants. This sensitivity to site, nature and history overlaps with postmodernism. Unlike some postmodern architecture, however, often characterised by intentional superficiality or arch pastiche, PTP's approach was generally more earnest.[2] Whether modern architecture inspired by tradition or tradition creatively interpreted, this vein of work attempted holistic synthesis and deeply felt engagement with places and their histories.

In Wales this interest in local culture was often articulated as a national concern. Dale Owen's involvement with Iorwerth Peate, curator at the National Museum of Wales, on the project for a Welsh Folk Museum heightened the practice's appreciation of Welsh landscape and building traditions, considered as national characteristics. Peate, drawing on the thinking of H. J. Fleure of University College, Aberystwyth, and Cyril Fox, the National Museum's director, connected upland landscapes to the culture of their people, including Welsh vernacular building, arguing for the longhouse as a national building type. By travelling into the rural heart of the country, Peate thought he had found 'the "refuge" of ancient racial types, of bygone customs and forgotten things'; and hoped to contribute to 'education in the value of the old tradition and in the methods of developing it to suit present social needs'.[3] In 1966 a new, short-lived, architectural journal, *Architecture Wales*, made upland and coastal landscapes and vernacular buildings recurring themes, including an interview with Peate. An article by landscape architect Bodfan Gruffydd urged architects to integrate buildings with the topography and use local natural materials and vernacular forms.[4] Certain kinds of landscape, light and material could stimulate feelings of national sentiment;[5] and for Owen, who enjoyed hillwalking and photography, such feelings increasingly found expression in his work. These concerns arose alongside growing acceptance of Welsh identity, with stronger political representation and official recognition of the language from the 1960s.

In England, too, a desire to consider local identities influenced modern movement architecture after the war. Architect Frederick Gibberd and planner Thomas Sharp studied historic towns such as Bath and Saffron Walden and argued for picturesque planning and the texture and variety of local materials; the *Architectural Review* promoted similar concerns, particularly through Gordon Cullen's 'Townscape' studies; Nikolaus Pevsner defined one aspect of the 'Englishness of English Art' as a picturesque quality inspired by Arcadian lowland landscapes and influenced by a moderate climate.[6] Such regionalism within modernism had become part of international debates even before the war, and remained current into the 1970s.

Many architects then began adopting vernacular and classical revivals as modernism was deemed incapable of adequate regional expression. The Essex county planning authority's *Design Guide for Residential Areas* of 1973 asked developers to respect the county's 'unique building character' and adopt local forms and materials, inspiring a vernacular revival in England with implications also for Wales.[7] This shift was sometimes overtly linked to the decline of a welfare state consensus and the rise of consumerism: if modernism embodied the welfare state, rejecting the style could imply a rejection of the universalising, paternalistic, monolithic notion of the state.[8] Moreover architectural practice in this period increasingly involved the conservation of historic buildings and areas, motivating architects to relearn old materials and techniques. Both modernist and historicist approaches developed in parallel in the Percy Thomas practice. Historically informed design maintained the practice's civic ethos, considering architecture as a service to citizens, reinforcing their understanding and pride in their identity and belonging, with an architecture relating meaningfully to its setting.

Modernism for Welsh Culture

Two post-war buildings by Sir Percy Thomas & Son demonstrate that at first more international forms of modernism could, with modifications, be considered apt assertions of modern national identity, bringing the welfare state into a more nuanced relationship with its local manifestations: Broadcasting House, or Canolfan y BBC, for the British Broadcasting Corporation at Llandaff, and the Welsh Folk Museum at St Fagans. Municipal cultural buildings, particularly libraries and theatres, were conceived of as part of the welfare state, and these two institutions were similarly allied to it; unusually, however, they were national rather than municipal cultural endeavours. Both institutions sought to disseminate Welsh identity and revive and modernise Welsh culture.

The BBC's ethos of 'public service broadcasting' and its educational remit associated it with the welfare state ideal, and central government oversaw its policies. Nevertheless, the distinction between English and Welsh names for the Llandaff buildings emphasised a national purpose in Wales: 'In British terms, here is another Broadcasting House; in Welsh terms, here is a Broadcasting Centre for Wales', wrote the BBC's Controller for Wales, Alun Oldfield-Davies.[9] The opening of prominent, starkly modern buildings by Sir Percy Thomas & Son in 1967 (see Figure 5.1) consolidated a growing autonomy for Welsh broadcasting, with increased programming in Welsh and on Welsh subjects in English, including programmes for schools.

5.1 Canolfan y BBC/Broadcasting House, Llandaff, 1960–7 (photo: author).

In 1962, the Pilkington Committee on Broadcasting had accepted overwhelming demand for greater Welsh content and a dedicated 'National Region', leading to the launch of BBC Cymru Wales in 1964.[10] By then Oldfield-Davies had already pushed the BBC towards increasing Welsh provision.[11] Rivalry with commercial television, also developing Welsh content, gave Oldfield-Davies support for his mission: 'It would seem to be the natural obligation of a public service Corporation to meet the legitimate national needs of Wales', he argued. The architecture of the new buildings helped cement this prestigious status.[12]

The BBC had long hoped to build new studio and broadcasting facilities, acquiring a Victorian mansion and gardens, Baynton House, at Llandaff. Dale Owen drew outline plans in 1960, assisted by Wallace Sweet, Walford Roberts and T. Herridge.[13] Owen's report celebrated the mature garden, including mature trees that he proposed to retain: the building would comprise functionally distinct connected blocks arranged around the trees, new planting added to interweave landscape and architecture. As some trees blocked views from the site, a tall building would peer over them.[14] The initial phase formed a row of buildings prominent along Llantrisant Road, giving a powerful public image to the street, sharp modern architectural forms interspersed with noble pines.[15] Subsequent buildings behind abandoned Owen's plan for a more utilitarian approach.

The first buildings took an international modern character similar to the practice's other work, and similar to other contemporary regional BBC buildings, notably John Madin's Pebble Mill studios in Birmingham. A staff restaurant was set behind a floating concrete balcony and detailed with an external concrete frame, somewhat like the library at University College, Swansea. A six-storey block of administrative offices containing a double-height entrance hall and projecting boardroom was clad in sparkling Carrara marble aggregate panels alternating with ribbon windows, similar to the Llandinam building at Aberystwyth. Sound studios for radio, three small ones on the road frontage and two behind for drama and music, were articulated as projecting blank cubes with a skyline like the Welsh steelworks. A concert studio for the BBC Welsh Orchestra, large enough for public audiences, formed an exposed reinforced concrete box with projecting beam ends rising behind a glazed corridor.[16]

The immediate impression was of a marked modernism that chimed with contemporary welfare state architecture elsewhere in Wales. Yet once plans were approved, Owen and his clients sought to introduce elements evoking Welsh identity. G. Wyn Rowlands, Programme Organiser for Wales, wrote to Oldfield-Davies suggesting symbols of Welsh counties and other emblems for the entrance hall, and it was here that their efforts focused. Owen suggested a steel-ribbed screen enclosing yellow slab glass engraved with the arms of Welsh counties, ultimately made in cheaper plate glass. He proposed a riven slate floor, though this was denied (deemed a trip hazard). He wanted to position a natural Welsh boulder in the entrance hall, set on pebbles and glistening with running water. Suitable rural stones were found, and Welsh artist Jonah Jones advised on their shaping, though the plan was abandoned to reduce costs.[17] The most distinctive symbolic feature was the external concert studio wall, inside and above the glazed corridor, made with round, brown pebbles taken from the river Taff at Aberfan, lit with concealed tubes to heighten its visibility (see

5.2 The 'Pebble Walk', Canolfan y BBC/Broadcasting House, Llandaff, 1960–7 (photo: author).

Figure 5.2). Press announcements highlighted its relationship to a building tradition at Llandaff, and Princess Margaret was filmed processing along it to open the building on St David's Day in 1967.[18] The use of local stone was by then an internationally common modern movement technique to suggest a building's relationship to its location. Here architects and clients used it to articulate a Welsh identity in this otherwise overtly modern building. Broadcasting House thus adopted an outward-facing, internationally aware architecture associated with wider contemporary British (and especially Welsh) developments, alongside symbols of Welsh identity, housing an institution that nurtured the Welsh language and disseminated Welsh music, poetry and drama, unifying an 'imagined community' of Welsh people, helping to forge the very idea of Wales as a nation.[19] The architecture's modernity legitimised this activity within the contemporary state.

The Welsh Folk Museum also adopted an international modernism, but the architects looked instead to Scandinavian models engaging with landscape and national culture. The National Museum of Wales led by Fox had proposed since 1930 an open-air museum to display its folk collection and to show salvaged buildings representing Welsh traditions. Lord Plymouth donated the Elizabethan house and gardens at St Fagans in 1946.[20] Percy Thomas was appointed, and work began with the mansion's conservation, which Iorwerth Peate, the Welsh Folk Museum's curator, regarded as an exhibit of elite Welsh culture complementing the vernacular buildings that he wished to acquire. William Marsden converted the top floor into curators' flats; the first floor, with original timber panelling, exhibited Welsh furniture and decorative arts, installed as period rooms, its long gallery opened up and restored; the ground floor, modestly extended, became a tea-room for the opening in 1948.[21] Marsden approached St Fagans

Castle with reverence, replacing its external render, repairing leaded windows and roof slates, leaving original fabric intact wherever possible.[22] Meanwhile, Thomas advised the museum committee on rescuing a derelict mill as the first open-air exhibit.[23]

Peate and Fox had always intended a large modern building to contain offices for administration and folk culture researchers; exhibition halls displaying scientifically arranged objects, complementing scenographic displays in the transferred buildings; a restaurant and shop; and spaces for lectures and conferences. Peate wanted to create a centre for national culture, 'not only a centre for historical research and a fountain-head of inspiration in architecture, craftsmanship and art but also a social centre for national movements and conferences of all kinds'.[24] In 1953 the architects (Marsden and Norman Thomas) planned a long, low modern building of intersecting blocks, with white walls, large bands of glazing and stone panels.[25]

Its realisation awaited funding, finally granted by Harold Wilson's government in 1964, though phased grants meant building incrementally until 1976, long after Peate's retirement (see Figure 5.3).[26] Owen redesigned the building with Sweet and John Hilling, whose thesis project at the Welsh School of Architecture had been a Welsh folk museum. A later critic of their building complained that it failed to reflect its location and purpose, not seeming to have 'anything to do with either Wales or traditional folk crafts'.[27] The building's modernism indeed frames the site's historical exhibits as a separate nostalgic realm detached from the present, perhaps contradicting Peate's intentions, and the museum originally depicted Welsh history as rural, static and idealised, ignoring political and social change.[28] When designing the museum in the mid-1960s, however, both client and architect rejected any mimicry of vernacular models; Peate wanted to present the study of Welsh culture as a rational, scientific

5.3 Welsh Folk Museum (now St Fagans National Museum of History), St Fagans, 1965–76 (photo: author).

activity informing the contemporary world, the building's modernism a foil to the popular picturesque approach in the park.[29]

Peate was inspired by Scandinavian folk museums, particularly Skansen near Stockholm, a museum of reconstructed vernacular buildings founded in the nineteenth century with similar cultural aims.[30] Skansen's director, Andreas Lindblom, advised him that his new building 'should be completely modern and functional and that no attempt should be made to compromise with past architectural styles'.[31] In 1946, Peate toured Swedish museums, admiring contemporary buildings, especially the Museum of Art at Norrköping and the Technical Museum in Stockholmand. At Peate's suggestion, Owen and Hilling visited museums in Norway, including the Maihaugen open-air folk museum, whose 1950s building by Sverre Fehn and Geir Grung formed a striking group of three low blocks in exposed concrete, terraced gently down a slope. They admired its 'extremely fine' appearance against the woodland backdrop, its manipulation of natural light and orchestrated views into the park.[32] Also influential were the Munch Museum in Oslo and the Louisiana Gallery of Modern Art near Copenhagen, both single-storey crisply detailed buildings conceived as walkways through landscapes.[33]

The Welsh Folk Museum's low, plain reinforced concrete and silver brick bars of accommodation, like these models, deferred to its parkland surroundings and gave a neutral backdrop for varied craft objects and vernacular buildings.[34] The building was arranged around a courtyard exhibiting historic farm equipment. Reinforced concrete roof beams gave continuity throughout, their ends projecting between clerestory glazing lighting the galleries. Darker areas such as a long ramp from entrance to galleries enhanced contrasts of daylighting, stimulating visitor attention and helping to convey a sense of place.

Modernism and Landscape

Meanwhile the practice considered landscape context and design in relation to modern architecture in many other projects. 'Amenity', including the preservation of visual and natural beauty, often had to be considered in infrastructure projects, a concept enshrined in the 1957 Electricity Act.[35] The Central Electricity Generating Board's landscape architect Sylvia Crowe wrote influential books on the treatment of landscapes around such contemporary structures as power stations and roads, arguing that their huge new forms should be accepted and complemented with bold, large-scale landscape design.[36] Her ideas transformed architects' understanding of the role of landscape as integral to architectural conception in the total design of the environment. This concept resonated with Walter Gropius's argument, advocated by Owen, that the architect 'must comprehend land, nature, man and his art, as one great entity'.[37]

Ironbridge power station was a key project where landscape became especially significant to the practice, because of its picturesque setting in the wooded Severn valley. Marsden and Allan Clark worked with landscape architect Kenneth Booth following Crowe's principles. They toured viewpoints several miles from the site to develop the design. Raised platforms positioned the rectangular station volumes in asymmetrical juxtapositions over trees, including new planting; and the four cooling towers followed a curve almost to the river's edge. Booth specified a rusty-red dye for the cooling towers' concrete, making them even more prominent against the woodland while evoking the colour of the local soil (see Colour Plate 5).[38] As Crowe advocated, they both allowed the modern forms to dominate the landscape and artfully integrated them into it.

Owen's approach to landscape was especially thoughtful. His 1965 Penglais development plan for University College, Aberystwyth is rich with romantic appreciation for the hillside site, emphasising that new development must relate to the existing and new landscape as a 'total built environment'.[39] 'Standing on the site at Penglais high above the town there is a strong sensation of being partly on the ground and partly in space', he wrote:

> *This feeling is common to most hills and mountains and although only a few hundred feet above the sea, the sense of physical uplift is emphasised by the ring of surrounding high land encircling the town ... The genius loci of Penglais comes from this sense of being high up in a vast amphitheatre commanding a field of view which seems all but infinite.*[40]

This topography drove his conception of the campus as a series of terraces providing 'viewing platforms'. The buildings were to form horizontal rows faced in a single material, 'Somewhere between light grey and white; local material if possible or at least Welsh', intended to suggest Welsh longhouses (though ultimately a Cornish granite aggregate was chosen). Small trees and shrubs would surround and 'penetrate the site like long fingers between the buildings'.[41]

This concept was never really achieved because so little was built, but the planting at Penglais was innovative because Philip Wareing and Basil Fox of the college's Botany department used the campus to experiment. Brenda Colvin, a landscape architect sharing Crowe's vision, designed broad woodland areas around Pantycelyn and the National Library from 1963; Owen, however, introduced John Ingleby to work with Fox and Wareing.[42] Much of their planting created sheltered enclosures to mitigate harsh weather on the exposed slope.[43] Fox and Wareing chose exotic trees and shrubs clustered in broad masses, and softened walls with climbing plants.[44] While the architecture complemented the landscape, the planting enriched the buildings' austere modernism.

The practice's landscaping for factories, hospitals and other utilitarian buildings followed Crowe's theories, broad swathes of trees emphasising large volumes and intimate planting addressing closer views.[45] By the mid-1970s Frederick Jennett, sharing Owen's convictions, appointed landscape architects and planners within the practice to contribute to projects, developing a specialist group at the Bristol and Birmingham offices. Sue Radley began the group in 1976, followed by David Daniell as urban planner at Bristol in 1982 and Bill Ambridge, Michèle Lavelle, Jane Findlay, Bill Champion and others in the 1980s, when they formed a separate company, PTP Landscape and Urban Design, to undertake independent commissions. Jennett often brought them into projects to inform initial site responses, not merely to add planting at the end.[46]

The latter approach was sometimes necessary but could nevertheless transform buildings. Radley led the landscape design for the practice's Dudley District

General Hospital, which, with its grid of standardised Harness modules, had little scope for adaptation to its site. Planting was added as it neared completion in 1981 to humanise the building for patients, aiming to bestow a sense of place. Each of the hospital's seven internal courtyards received a different treatment giving distinct atmospheres to different areas from inside, assisting orientation: one a Japanese garden; the central larger courtyard more formal with brick planters and a fountain; another marked by red flowers and foliage; one planted with blues and greys spiralling around a circular pool.[47] Not only did the landscaping give unique spaces to a serial architecture, but it was also hoped to have a therapeutic purpose, as Radley and her colleagues were aware of Roger Ulrich's arguments for the effects of nature on patient wellbeing and recovery.[48]

This occasionally profound concern with landscape, topography, the characteristics of a place, and their enhancement through planting, thus emerged from within the post-war modern movement for the welfare state. It was by no means unique to Wales, though developed through Owen's distinctive sensitivity to landscape, and particularly at certain Welsh sites with extraordinary qualities, including others discussed below.

Reconstruction and Conservation

St Fagans was one of numerous projects involving conservation and historic contexts undertaken by the practice. After the war, a growing conservation movement tempered modernist reconstruction, and attention to historic buildings became ever more significant. There are early moments where the practice, in parallel with its modern movement projects, accepted a 'civic' contextualism, acknowledging the historic environment and contributing to its character, and this approach became increasingly important in the practice's work.

Besides his reconstruction of St Mary, Swansea, Thomas also reinstated a bomb-damaged late-Victorian mansion designed by J. L. Pearson for William Waldorf Astor on the Embankment at Temple Place, London, dense with luxurious craftsmanship, including timber panelling and a hall with hammerbeam roof and stained-glass windows. The Society of Incorporated Accountants had acquired it in 1928 for offices, library and events, naming it the Incorporated Accountants' Hall. From 1949 to 1951 Thomas restored the building, redrawing lost details from photographs, though he also 'enhanced' it, adjusting room dimensions.[49] Smith & Nephew later acquired the building for their head office, and returned to Sir Percy Thomas & Son in the late 1960s to add a rear wing continuing Pearson's neo-Gothic elevations, with a new oriel window and leaded glazing (see Figure 5.4). Richly carved timber doors lined a panelled corridor with elegant wrought iron lanterns similar to those of the Victorian house. John Betjeman praised the architects' sensitivity to Pearson's work: 'It is rare today to find modern architects modest enough to continue a building of strong late-Victorian character in the same style', he wrote; 'It is rare too, to find a large commercial firm willing to retain a little masterpiece such as Temple Place and to take so much trouble over having not just the exterior made to harmonise with the design, but also the rooms in the new addition in every detail'.[50]

5.4 Incorporated Accountants' Hall, subsequently Smith & Nephew headquarters (now 2 Temple Place), London, originally J. L. Pearson, 1895; restored after bombing by Sir Percy Thomas, 1948–51; extension on left by Sir Percy Thomas & Son, 1967 (photo: John Bracegirdle/Alamy).

In another extraordinary historic context alongside Conwy Castle, Percy Thomas made a prominent intervention that appears on countless postcards, though its discrete design makes it rarely noticed. The main road between Chester and Bangor (and thence to Holyhead and Ireland) passed alongside the medieval castle and through the picturesque market town after crossing the Conwy River on a suspension bridge built in the 1820s by Thomas Telford. By the 1930s, the Conway Bridge Commissioners' engineer H. W. FitzSimons reported that Telford's bridge was badly deteriorating, and the Ministry of Transport absorbed the project into its national trunk road scheme.[51] The Ministry appointed Percy Thomas with FitzSimons for a new bridge to replace Telford's in 1941.[52] Initial plans by the Ministry of Transport for a town bypass along the harbour wall outraged fishermen, councillors and tourists, concerned about loss of access to the harbour and the destruction of the ancient town walls and cottages.[53] Eventually the Ministry gave up this scheme, and the vociferous reaction reinforced the importance of respecting the historic surroundings.[54] Telford's bridge was listed as a historic monument in 1950, preventing its demolition, and Thomas and FitzSimons's new bridge was narrowed to fit alongside it.[55]

The Ministry reassured objectors about its concern for the historic environment as an 'amenity' in road proposals, 'particularly so with regard to Conway, where it is most essential that the attractions of the unique intermural town should not be adversely affected by any proposals'.[56] Minister of Transport John Boyd-Carpenter, cutting the turf for the new bridge in 1955, reaffirmed this concern, reminding onlookers that 'officials of the Ministry have been particularly anxious that the bridge shall ... be fitting for the historic and lovely setting', and insisting that it 'had to look right against its historic background'.[57] Minister for Welsh Affairs Henry Brooke added a further interpretation on opening the bridge in 1958, arguing that, with the castle, it formed an iconic symbol of Wales, and acted as a 'gateway into Welsh Wales', thus helping 'to bind the whole Welsh nation into one'.[58]

Thomas's first design of 1943 was for a suspension bridge similar to Telford's, with castellated masonry Gothic piers punctured by pointed arches.[59] This design was soon discarded in favour of a broad, low arched bridge, much sleeker and more overtly modern, to be constructed as a steel truss. The cross-braced trusses, however, were evidently considered unfitting for the castle backdrop, so Thomas designed a cast iron façade to conceal it, subtly modelled with a vertical pattern suggesting linenfold panelling. He also designed the abutments and walls for the road as it rose to the height of the bridge, constructed of reinforced concrete but faced with a north Wales stone chosen to harmonise with the castle and to 'satisfy local nationalism', as FitzSimons put it.[60] A series of half cylinders echoed the great towers of the castle. Despite its contemporary form, the bridge, completed in 1958, looks remarkably right for its place, particularly in views towards the castle from the north, along the railway line and river shore (see Figure 5.5). Thomas clearly composed it for these views, the bridge's gentle arc presenting a pedestal for the castle from some angles, setting it off rather than competing for prominence.

The picturesque approach here contrasts with the practice's rigorous modernism elsewhere. Despite the modernity of their university campuses, however, several educational projects involved careful adaptation of historic buildings. At Swansea, the first hall of residence, Neuadd Gilbertson, was housed at the late Georgian Clyne Castle along the coast, and while Sir Percy Thomas & Son designed a simple modern wing

5.5 Road Bridge, Conwy, 1953–8 (photo: author).

in the mid-1950s, they also converted the house into student common rooms, library, refectory and further bedrooms, while conserving historic features such as baronial moulded ceilings and marble fireplaces.[61] Similarly, the practice worked at St Donat's Castle in Glamorgan for the United World College of the Atlantic (or Atlantic College), opened in 1962, an international, private sixth-form college. The buildings centred on a medieval castle extended into a Tudor mansion, fantastically embellished with fragments of historic buildings by American newspaper magnate William Randolph Hearst between the wars. The practice converted the house into communal rooms including library, refectory and hall, and adapted outbuildings into workshops and classrooms.[62]

At Aberystwyth a decade later, the architects took an alternative approach for a small but significant building for which they received a Civic Trust Heritage Award. Among several historic buildings that the practice adapted for University College was a derelict early nineteenth-century farmhouse, Brynamlwg, at the eastern end of the Penglais campus. In the early 1970s, John Vergette and Dale Owen converted and extended it into a staff sports and social club. The buildings comprised two long rubble stone barns at right angles with a cottage forming one end, strikingly like one of Peate's longhouses. The architects retained the stonework and added new walls to match, with sections of sympathetic white-painted render and dark-painted timber weatherboarding (see Figure 5.6). They opened up the interiors and connected them with a new projecting entrance foyer, while the cottage became the steward's residence. Long low slate roofs were added to unify the group, and dormer windows gave a contemporary feel by inverting the roof pitch.[63] It was a subtle and creative

5.6 Brynamlwg Staff Social Club, University College of Wales, Aberystwyth, 1970–5, proposal painting by John Vergette (Aberystwyth University Archives; courtesy of the estate of John Vergette and WSP UK Ltd).

approach going beyond restoration into a reinterpretation of vernacular architecture within modernism.

Modernism, Urban Context and the Vernacular

An interest in historic and vernacular architecture became a core aspect of the modern movement after the war. Younger architects such as those associated with Team 10, led by Alison and Peter Smithson, advocated close attention to historic urban forms as expressions of inhabitants' longstanding social structures, and sought to reinvent these traditions in their work using contemporary technologies and aesthetics.[64] Such an approach appeared in Percy Thomas's practice from the mid-1960s, as in other Welsh architects' work, such as that of Bill Davies.[65]

Dale Owen explicitly based University College, Swansea's courtyard plans on Oxford and Cambridge universities as early as 1958, while evoking eighteenth-century picturesque landscape gardens and pavilions to justify tower block residences.[66] But by the mid-1960s the practice began looking at more local precedents for inspiration. At Aberystwyth, the practice's long, grey buildings in landscape sought to reinterpret the Welsh longhouse.[67] But their Development Plan reports from 1965 to 1970 also discussed Aberystwyth's Victorian terraces, whose 'repetitive bay windows seen from the promenade produce a bold and pleasing architectural rhythm', which they aimed to capture in some buildings, particularly the Cwrt Mawr postgraduate halls by Vergette.[68] These had pitched roofs and a repeated bay window rhythm, though arranged in courts rather than terraces. Aberystwyth's Great Hall, meanwhile, evoked a Welsh Nonconformist chapel in its broad plan.[69]

The practice explored similar intentions at a college campus nearby at Llanbadarn Fawr overlooking the Rheidol valley. This campus, designed in collaboration with Cardiganshire County Council's architect G. R. Bruce, combined Aberystwyth College of Further Education, the College of Librarianship and the Welsh College of Agriculture, providing a library, students' union, teaching spaces and student residences. Planned in 1968 and about two-thirds completed over the following five years, residential buildings formed a staggered series of long bars overlooking the valley, their horizontality emphasised by bands of windows and brick; above them, L-shaped buildings formed landscaped courtyards interwoven with covered walkways, and the area around the entrance became a larger-scaled, central feature for union and library buildings. While the library was almost classical in feel, the other buildings had pitched roofs, many modelled with subsidiary or split slopes giving clerestories. With consistent shapes and materials, grey brick, dark roof tiles and copper panels, the architects wrote that the campus would 'harmonise with the local Welsh vernacular'.[70]

Owen and Kerry Veale designed the Albert Edward Prince of Wales Court care home for the elderly at Porthcawl around the same time, following this modern neo-vernacular approach (see Figure 5.7). It was built for the Royal Masonic Benevolent Institution, as part of its national network of care homes. Partly because of its purpose housing vulnerable people and partly because of its suburban setting, the architects sought a domestic character and scale. A tall central communal hall, externally barn-like, had subsidiary social areas of a more domestic scale within and around it, fitted

5.7 Albert Edward Prince of Wales Court, RMBI Care Co. Home, Porthcawl, 1970–3 (photo: author).

under a balcony, and social spaces were also dispersed among bed-sitting rooms; a tower contained a small sunroom with views to the sea. Pitched roofs expressed a domestic purpose, and conveyed a sheltering atmosphere inside, giving intimate spaces under exposed timber beams. Most rooms were planned around two-storey courtyards, one with an enclosed cloister, recalling old almshouses. Each bed-sitting room had a bay window, and thus the long rows of rooms resembled Victorian terraces, particularly on the street frontage, where three ranges overlooked gardens. Light grey brick and Welsh slate roofs evoked 'the Vale of Glamorgan domestic building vernacular'.[71] It received a RIBA award in 1975 alongside English buildings similarly inspired by vernacular forms, a widespread interest by then.[72]

These complexes were distinct from urban contexts, but the practice also took this approach in urban settings, responding to the historic townscape. The Arts building at Bangor, for example, though essentially brutalist in style, echoed the form and scale of nearby Victorian bay windows, continuing their rhythm along the street. Malcolm Lovibond, one of its architects, explained how the practice had similarly approached a commission in the centre of Shrewsbury for Lloyds Bank. They decided that rebuilding the bank's dilapidated listed building, partly Tudor with a Victorian façade, would be dishonest, and instead replaced it with a modern reinterpretation appropriate for its context. They undertook detailed 'townscape studies' characterising Shrewsbury's vernacular buildings, considering such elements as roof pitches and geometries of timber studding. The bank, completed in 1968 and faced with finely detailed faceted precast concrete, brutalist in style, followed the 'grain' of surrounding buildings' narrow frontages, and took a similar overall form: the two upper storeys were jettied over the ground floor, the first floor with an asymmetrical oriel window; joints between the hipped roof's leadwork sheets continued the vertical rhythm (see Figure 5.8). The building was widely published and well received, winning a Civic Trust Award and an award from the European Cement Association for 'outstanding concrete buildings

5.8 Lloyds Bank, Shrewsbury, 1967 (photo: John Rea Studios; author's collection, from practice; courtesy of WSP UK Ltd).

in old or historic surroundings' in the European Architectural Heritage Year, 1975.[73] Around that time, too, Owen designed a speculative office and housing scheme for the Grosvenor Estate, Portcullis House, overlooking Cardiff Castle in a modern movement approach hinting at castle courtyards and crenellations.

The stereotyped view of the modern movement in architecture as inimical to the historic city has been much revised, and it is now recognised that large-scale urban replanning often included the preservation of historic urban areas, and that modernist interventions in historic contexts could be sensitive in character and scale.[74] Percy Thomas's post-war work rarely involved comprehensive urban planning, but Marsden and colleagues at the Shrewsbury office designed a significant urban development at Chester considering the town's historic fabric. Chester's council had embraced modern planning principles, assembling a ring road with much demolition and building car parks around the centre to reduce congestion.[75] By 1960, residents' disquiet at the loss of historic buildings led to the formation of the Chester Civic Trust.[76] Architect George Grenfell-Baines advised the council, urging careful preservation of the best of old fabric, while encouraging new development that respected the town's historical forms, including narrow plot widths and distinctive materials, accepting exposed concrete if used with care.[77]

Sir Percy Thomas & Son's project was a commercial scheme for the Grosvenor-Laing Development Company, a partnership between the Duke of Westminster's Grosvenor Estate and builder John Laing, for a site almost filling one of Chester's four central urban blocks formed by the Roman crossroads and medieval Rows.[78] While the duke was demolishing his nearby Victorian mansion, Alfred Waterhouse's Eaton Hall, his representative reassured the town that 'while any new development must obviously be consistent with modern standards, the charm of Chester's present architectural character must not be spoiled'.[79] The new development was inserted behind the Rows, leaving the frontages intact, providing a new shopping centre, offices, a multi-storey car park and an extension to the Edwardian Grosvenor Hotel.[80] Completed in 1965, this was a huge and fundamentally modern form of development for the small city, but largely invisible in the historic centre.

The architects stitched the Grosvenor Precinct's internal malls directly back into the pedestrian colonnades of the Rows and into a Victorian arcade, St Michael's Row. At the centre a skylit court provided a focal space, optimistically advertised as an Italian piazza.[81] The council's planning department, with Grenfell-Baines and Marsden, vetted tenants' shopfront proposals for appropriateness to the town.[82] The Civic Trust suggested linking the pedestrian mall to high-level walkways on the medieval city walls, and this the architects did, adding a footbridge from the court. The Civic Trust enthusiastically endorsed the scheme for its 'considerable sympathy with Chester', and councillors declared unanimous satisfaction 'to see Chester's historic Rows extended in this logical and visually exciting way'.[83]

Nevertheless, a Georgian house and most of Newgate Street were erased, and Roman ruins were buried unrecorded.[84] To the rear, the architects designed modern elevations to complement the setting. The council had previously demolished Georgian houses on Pepper Street, so a new three-storey office block and shops surrounded the mall entrance here (see Figure 5.9). The ground floor was set back behind piers like the Rows, and the upper floors had precast concrete cladding marked with projecting

5.9 Grosvenor Precinct, Pepper Street façade, Chester, 1961–5 (photo: author).

mullions of pink concrete; offices staggered forward in narrow bays.[85] Another external access at Newgate Street led to a first-floor pedestrian deck alongside shop windows, emulating the multi-level Rows, a sawtooth plan evoking the city's narrow plots. Though a poor substitute for what had been lost, the aim was to 'interpret the spirit of Chester in modern form', giving this vast corporate development a civic ethos, preserving and connecting with the historic city where feasible, and otherwise emulating it in a modern language.[86]

One of the practice's few modern housing projects emulated but inadvertently marred its urban context. The Billybanks, housing more than 500 residents in Penarth for the Penarth Urban District Council, was designed by Owen with Hilling, Roy Page, John Roberts and others from 1963 and built in phases from 1966 into the early 1970s. It comprised maisonettes in four-storey blocks for families, with small flats for the elderly. The architects appreciated the spectacular site behind Victorian terraces on an escarpment overlooking Cardiff Bay. Surrounding houses informed their design: Penarth, they explained, 'has a fine traditional building vernacular, using the local limestone and dark grey Welsh slate, enriched occasionally by orange-red brick on chimneys, quoins, string courses and surrounds to windows and door openings'. Those materials were unaffordable, so they specified 'matching warm grey brick' and dark grey roof tiles for 'architectural unity with what already exists'. Rows of Victorian terraces following contours 'produce a fine architectural composition', they wrote optimistically, so placing taller maisonette blocks along the site's northern boundary would 'form the westernmost extension of this composition'. Routes into the estate extended existing streets and footpaths.[87] Staircase access to maisonettes rather than decks reflected traditional housing, and permitted living rooms to span the block depth to combine views to the north and sunlight from the south, although access balconies were adopted in the more ungainly final phase. On the sheltered southern side, perpendicular rows of maisonette blocks formed intimate courtyards, stepping down to two-storey blocks scaled to adjacent Victorian houses, giving a sense of community around shared outdoor spaces.[88] A photograph of the scheme on the town's skyline, likely taken by Owen, suggests the desired impression of a new but complementary development, though it was clearly overbearing in scale (see Figure 5.10).

Ominously, the council insisted on materials and details for minimal maintenance, leading to plain elevations without relieving projections, though pitched roofs tempered the estate's modernity with a visual allegiance to older housing. Owen specified profuse planting with areas of grass, shrubs, climbing plants and trees, individually landscaped courtyards for distinct identities and flower boxes for residents. His rich vision was curtailed, however, the council preferring institutional lawns and paving.[89] Neglect and subsequent housing policy changes ultimately led to the Billybanks estate's decline, its reputation as an 'eyesore' and demolition, its civic ambitions forgotten.[90]

Similarly concerned with townscape and heritage combined with modern movement principles were the practice's planning studies for rural Welsh towns Rhayader and Brecon. Owen led both projects with architects across the practice, including Marsden, Roger Owen, Mary E. Kerr, Lovibond and Page. Ian Pepperell made exquisite drawings for the Brecon report. Both plans were for county councils (Radnorshire and Breconshire), following proposals from the Mid-Wales Industrial

5.10 The Billybanks, Penarth, 1965–8, viewed on the horizon from the south (photographer unknown, likely Ivan Dale Owen; author's collection, from practice; courtesy of the estate of Ivan Dale Owen and WSP UK Ltd).

Development Association to reverse depopulation in rural Wales by attracting new industries. The Wilson government endorsed the Association's ideas in the mid-1960s, and, alongside proposals for a mid-Wales new town (later dropped), designated both as 'growth towns' alongside five others. The Association commissioned reports and plans with local authorities to shape their expansion with new infrastructure, industrial estates and housing.[91] The towns' historic architecture and landscapes were important in all their plans, especially to develop tourism and attract incoming workers.

Sir Percy Thomas & Son undertook a pilot study for the series in 1967, envisaging doubling Rhayader's population to 2,500. Their report applied conventional modern planning principles – a ring road and car parks keeping traffic to the periphery; central 'civic and shopping precincts', largely pedestrianised; new zones for factories and housing (see Figure 5.11). But they enthused over Rhayader's 'Urban Character', its Georgian and Victorian buildings, its 'identity and charm'. These were to be emphasised alongside growth, preserving its heritage; and a livestock market would be relocated so that surrounding historic buildings framed a 'civic square', to 'foster a greater civic sense and sense of identity'.[92]

Landscape was also explored: the 'contrast between the remoteness of hills and the intimacy of the centre' was to be maintained and enhanced; tree planting would conceal roads and factories. But there was a marked development in the subsequent 1974 Rhayader report's landscape proposals, with greater appreciation for the existing landscape, particularly nearby wooded hills: more substantial tree planting would intensify the woodland setting, using 'local species of forest trees' to reinforce a natural, regional ecology. This shift of emphasis followed Nan Fairbrother's *New Lives, New*

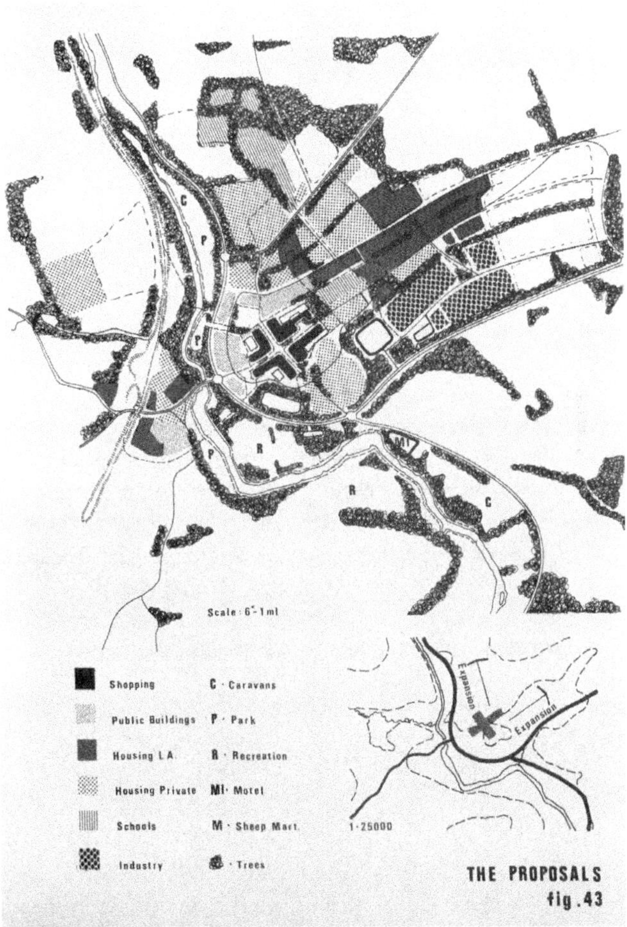

5.11 Outline of proposals for Rhayader, from Sir Percy Thomas & Son, *Expansion of Rhayader: A Pilot Study* (Cardiff: Mid-Wales Industrial Development Association, March 1967) (author's collection; courtesy of WSP UK Ltd).

Landscapes, which explored how modernity could be adapted to local character by using native plants, creating 'a new type of scenery – the man-made wild'.[93]

Similarly, the rise of historic conservation policies such as the government guidance *Historic Towns: Preservation and Change* of 1967 and conservation area legislation gave a strong foundation for the architects' interest in Rhayader's historic fabric.[94] Their 1974 report presented detailed advice for improving and restoring old buildings and proposed designating the town centre as a conservation area. Existing buildings were to influence new developments to reinforce the town's character, as outlined in conservation area policy and the Essex *Design Guide*.[95]

These principles were even stronger in the 1974 Brecon report, for a historic town in a national park. Space was needed for 2,000 new dwellings, new roads and industry, while maintaining Brecon's 'essential character and high townscape qualities' and its relationship to the landscape. Though much of the centre was already a conservation area, the report recommended many buildings for statutory heritage listing. Pepperell's

Townscape-style studies demonstrated how modest improvements to shopfronts and ground surfaces would enhance coherence (see Figure 5.12).

New buildings required strict design control: 'The handsome regional architectural character of the town needs careful analysis', the architects argued, 'and should be used as the basis for selecting materials for all the new work'. Existing landscape features, including hedgerows, would be retained and reinforced with 'indigenous' trees and shrubs, so that nature flowed across the town's edges. The architects found old photographs showing a mature tree, since felled, forming a central landmark, and urged its replacement as 'one of the most important contributions which could be made to restore one of the finest views'.[96] Despite the report's modernity of purpose – planning new industry and tourism, housing and infrastructure, a new road alongside the river – the study shows the architects' depth of feeling for the town and its landscape, rigorously applied.

Little of these proposals ever came to fruition.[97] Only Newtown received substantial investment, under the remit of a new Mid-Wales Development Corporation, developed as a modest New Town. Here PTP undertook a detailed study of local vernacular architecture, particularly Victorian terraces, to inform housing design. Various architects designed new housing groups, PTP allocated the Vaynor area around 1976. Though frugal, it took inspiration from the architects' studies with long rows of pink and grey brick terraces forming curves and enclosed courts, sharing slate roofs, a sense of detail and rhythm conveyed by simple entrance canopies and bay windows.[98]

5.12 Sketch proposal for pedestrianisation of the Bulwark, Brecon, from Percy Thomas Partnership, *Brecon Town Expansion Plan* (Bristol: n. pub., 1974) (author's collection; courtesy of Ian Pepperell and WSP UK Ltd).

Thus, a broad acknowledgement of precedent and context in some of the practice's early post-war work became during the 1960s and into the 1970s a more profound engagement with place, with the characteristics of towns and their environments. The architects hoped to emphasise the social identity of towns by heightening historic and characteristic elements. New architectural contributions maintained twentieth-century forms and materials, adapting forms, colours and scale from the surroundings to reinforce local character - a fundamentally civic idea, close to Trystan Edwards's conception of the civic articulated half a century before.[99]

Traditionalism

This consideration of historic environments led some architects in the practice back to a more overtly historicist approach, drawing more literally on historic context, largely rejecting modern expression to adopt past building styles. From the late 1970s onwards, some of the practice's work may be described as 'postmodernism', but while one of postmodernism's defining features was a playfulness or irony in historical references, evident occasionally in the practice's work, their approach to context more often retained the seriousness of the earlier period, including the thoughtful study of townscape and vernacular forms. The neo-traditional approach became most associated with the Bristol office, especially Peterjohn Smyth, Willie Harbinson and Neil Embleton; but many other architects also worked on conservation projects, historicist designs or buildings with postmodern approaches. Smyth became, however, a vocal opponent of modern movement architecture; and the Bristol office became involved in one of the most significant and contentious traditionalist projects of the late twentieth century at Poundbury in Dorset, a commission whose origins lie in the firm's concern for historic context in the 1970s.

By the 1970s, the Bristol office (then including Antoni Poremba, John Gilmour, Patricia Townsend, David Barnett and others) specialised in housing, including work for Bristol City Council, housing associations and commercial developers.[100] A small housing group in Knowle, Bristol, with deeply pitched roofs almost touching the ground, completed in 1979, shows the Essex *Design Guide*'s influence, but none were particularly local in character or historical in context.[101] The project that changed the Bristol office's approach was for housing in the centre of Southampton. The Third Collingwood Housing Association commissioned PTP in 1977 for nearly 100 small flats, mostly sheltered housing for the elderly, with gardens, meeting rooms and wardens' accommodation. The site fronted onto Upper Bugle Street in the heart of Southampton's old town in a fragment of the city's historic area that had survived wartime bombing. On one side was the impressive timber-framed Tudor House museum of around 1500. Around the site ran the vaulted ruins of the medieval city wall. Surrounding it were fine-grained streetscapes including Georgian houses. Southampton's city council designated the quarter a conservation area in 1972, publishing design guidelines for new buildings. It was also clearing sites for redevelopment, now viewed as opportunities to rebuild in harmony with the historic context, even to recreate aspects of the pre-Victorian town, restoring lost medieval lanes and threading a new 'Town Walk' along the city walls.[102]

The council produced a detailed, unusually prescriptive 'Brief for Redevelopment' for Upper Bugle Street. An existing road bisecting the site was to become a pedestrian lane. The steep, curving Blue Boar Lane alongside the Tudor House was retained, and its 'sense of enclosure' recreated. Housing was to be of high-density low-rise form, street frontages evoking historic forms with facades close to pavements to enclose the street, perhaps staggered to suggest narrow burgage plots. Nevertheless, the planners disparaged revivalism: 'designs should be wholly of this era, but in harmony with their ancient surroundings', though 'traditional materials' had to be used 'where possible, whilst pitched roofs and a varied skyline will be a pre-requisite'.[103] PTP's Bristol office submitted an outline plan in 1977, Gilmour the partner in charge, subsequent outline designs submitted by David Barnett, and the design worked out largely by Harbinson.[104] The initial plans comprised two three-storey perimeter blocks marked by high and low gabled projections, in response to which the City Planning Officer, R. H. Hall, sent numerous critical comments reinforcing the brief: buildings had to be closer to the street, without front gardens, and 'a more varied roof line' was demanded.[105] For a local authority to intervene so strongly with a private housing scheme was then unusual.

As Harbinson developed the design, its relationship to the historic context became richer. Completed in 1982, the Upper Bugle Street project actually borrowed more from adjacent Victorian and Edwardian buildings than from imagined medieval precedents (see Figure 5.13). Bright orange-red brick harmonised with neighbours; pitched roofs were capped with terracotta ornament and dotted with chimneys and tiled turrets; projecting gabled bays gave variety to elevations, with decorative touches in brick; black-and-white timber screens forming porches evoked both the Tudor House

5.13 Upper Bugle Street, Southampton, housing for Third Collingwood Housing Association Ltd, 1977–82 (photo: author).

and the Edwardian neo-Tudor. The buildings deferred to the Tudor House at the adjacent corner, leaving a small public space marked with a tree, jettied projections echoing its oriel window.[106]

The design owes much to the intricacy of scale and use of brick in such earlier high-density housing schemes as Darbourne & Darke's Lillington Gardens in London and Stirling & Gowan's housing project in Preston, inspired by dense Victorian neighbourhoods.[107] Upper Bugle Street was more overtly historicist than those, creatively reworking both the general qualities and the specific details of a Victorian vernacular.

Later, the West Somerset Rural Housing Association commissioned the Bristol office for a cluster of cottages in Luccombe in Exmoor National Park, completed around 1992. White render, exposed timber lintels, tiled roofs and a corner chimney evoked the Devon vernacular.[108] At the heart of the village opposite the medieval church, the houses were gathered closely on the site to avoid suburban dispersion, and close to the street line to maintain the existing village's pattern and enclosure, as advocated for village planning by Sharp.[109]

The architects also extended their approach to other building types. On Hammersmith Broadway in London, Smyth and Ron Morgan designed a speculative office block in 1988 seeking authenticity in solid brick and carved Portland stone masonry in a neoclassical style following nearby Victorian and interwar buildings.[110] Smyth and Harbinson then designed a new headquarters for the Skipton Building Society in North Yorkshire, inspired by local historic industrial buildings while suggesting a Georgian mansion, clad in the area's buff stone, a stylistic dressing of otherwise contemporary offices, like a spartan version of Robert Adam's recent building at Dogmersfield Park. Smyth wrote that the client 'exercised no "stylistic censorship"' and that 'the proposals arose simply from our efforts to build in sympathy with the setting in a fine north Yorkshire town', though the company had chosen them for their historicist approach, bypassing PTP's nearer Manchester office.[111]

By then, the Prince of Wales's antipathy to modern architecture was well established. He delivered his first provocative speech to the RIBA in 1984. When he visited Birmingham a few years later, local councillors proudly showed him a model of the International Convention Centre by PTP and the Renton Howard Wood Levin Partnership, only to be deeply offended when he complained that it resembled 'a concrete missile silo'.[112] He called the Convention Centre 'an unmitigated disaster' in his 1988 television series, *A Vision of Britain*, and its spin-off book.[113] His simplistic polemic angered many architects, who generally shared his appreciation for historic buildings and places.[114] His 'Ten Principles' included respect for the landscape, planning for 'enclosure' and the use of local materials, already widely accepted, as the Percy Thomas practice demonstrates. Indeed, among new buildings that Prince Charles highlighted that met these ideals was the West Dorset General Hospital in Dorchester, which he had opened in 1987, designed by Gilmour, Trevor Martin, Ronnie Rennoldson and others at PTP's Bristol office.[115] He praised its lively 'domestic character' conveyed by 'pitched roofs, attractive brickwork and balconies', its traditional materials, the 'visual pleasure' of its ornament.[116] It was an intricately detailed building, a playful postmodern reinterpretation of Victorian architecture drawing on local precedents and influenced by Jeremy Dixon's work (see Figure 5.14). Smyth and Harbinson's housing scheme at Luccombe probably also came to the prince's attention through a *Country Life* article by his architectural adviser Giles Worsley; and thus, the Bristol office seemed apt for his Poundbury project at Dorchester.[117] PTP were appointed as coordinating architects for Poundbury's first phase in 1992, and Smyth, Embleton and Harbinson designed several housing groups there.

The story of Poundbury has been widely told, but often simplistically so: PTP's involvement is rarely mentioned, and focus on the prince's radical conservatism has obscured deeper historical continuities.[118] Poundbury's development was actually initiated by West Dorset District Council, not the prince. Concerned at Dorchester's housing shortage, the council's Chief Planning Officer Des Derrien outlined three options for enlarging the town, elicited planning ideas from landowners and developers, and undertook a public consultation in 1987. The farm of Poundbury was heavily favoured, with the least impact on surrounding villages and landscapes.[119] It was Duchy of Cornwall land, and Prince Charles seized the opportunity to create his model town. The council, meanwhile, adopted a design policy encouraging 'the creation of environments in character with West Dorset', including design standards and briefs for developers.[120] Poundbury thus began as a council-organised development, and remained subject to council control.

5.14 West Dorset District General Hospital, Dorchester, first phase, 1980–7 (photo: author).

While the prince often criticised American influences, he looked to America for urbanism promoting 'tradition', to the 'New Urbanism' of Andres Duany and Elizabeth Plater-Zyberk and their nostalgic classical clapboard and portico town of Seaside in Florida, where 'codes' controlled house designs for a coherent appearance resembling colonial settlements. Léon Krier had been involved, and the Duchy commissioned him for Poundbury's masterplan in 1988. After public consultation, and with advice from the council's architect David Oliver, Krier changed his original classical scheme of perimeter blocks and avenues to a more picturesque approach.[121] His plan aimed to create a new town rather than a suburban extension, compact and high density, mixing housing with public buildings, shops and workplaces. Krier's plans outlined streets and building plots with heights and approximate volumes of building, and his and Alexander Cresswell's perspectives suggested a mixed neoclassical and vernacular appearance.[122]

The initial phase in the south-east corner formed a pilot exercise in the mid-1990s, but because of its marginal position in the masterplan, it was more village-like than later stages. Narrow, curved streets gave enclosure, intimacy and picturesque views. House façades came to pavement edges, and were grouped for compact coherence, like the Luccombe and Southampton schemes. Smyth, Embleton and Harbinson of PTP and collaborating architects Ken Morgan, Clive Hawkins and Grahame Saunders travelled around Dorset with Oliver's guidance studying vernacular buildings to emulate at Poundbury.[123] PTP assigned plots to architects (giving neighbouring plots to different designers to encourage variety) and assembled their designs into street plans and elevations to be adjusted for overall effect. Smyth presented designs to a review panel including Poundbury director Andrew Hamilton, Oliver, and often Krier and the prince, before they went to the council's planning committee.[124] Though somewhat chaotic in its eclecticism and oddly disjointed into small housing groups, Poundbury's first phase was visually exuberant with rich, absorbing detail and stimulating street scenes.

One of Poundbury's pioneering features was its integration of social housing, for which the Duchy engaged the Guinness Trust Housing Association, which commissioned all its housing in the first phase from PTP.[125] The District Council established a policy in 1989 in which 20 per cent of all new housing was to be rented by housing associations to those on council waiting lists, as 1980s Conservative policy discouraged it from building council housing.[126] The prince's philanthropic interests coincided with this social aim, and Poundbury's social housing far exceeded the council's target proportion from the first phase onwards.[127] Krier and Charles wanted social housing distributed throughout Poundbury to encourage social mixing, so the architects dispersed them around the first phase. These houses were more modest in design than private housing, smaller and in simpler materials, mostly white render, often grouped in rows: one formed a terrace like an eighteenth-century almshouse; another spanned the end of a street vista with an arch to the back court (see Figure 5.15). Eaves details, door canopies, timber lintels and dormers enhanced otherwise straightforward buildings. Private houses, by contrast, were more often brick or stone clad with ornamental or textural treatment.

In the later and much larger second phase in the late 1990s and early 2000s, the Duchy simplified control, allocating larger blocks to single developers and their

5.15 Housing for Guinness Trust, Poundbury phase 1A, *c.*1993–6 (photo: author).

architects.[128] Smyth and Embleton designed two blocks for Westbury Homes.[129] One centred around a square dominated by a Palladian colonnaded office block, surrounded by formal and vernacular house types. Houses were more tightly terraced along streets than before, while maintaining stylistic diversity (see Figure 5.16). Along the broad main road between sections, Peverell Avenue, three-storey neo-Georgian houses gave formality, their style and details derived perhaps from Cheltenham or Clifton. PTP's housing retained its earnest integrity, detail and character following the pilot phase; later, other architects departed from Krier's plan and principles, building luxury flats in steel-framed towers and pseudo-Victorian warehouses, altering Poundbury's character.

Poundbury encapsulates many contradictions yet to be properly explored, between the modernity of its planned mass housing and the historicism of its design; between democratic council control and its archaic feudal conception and symbolism; between an English Conservative national imaginary and a planned social utopia different from contemporary Conservative policy. PTP's architects, however, simply delighted in an opportunity to create coherent places with a civic sensibility that, with largely straightforward stylistic means, attempted to render large-scale urban development palatable in a small market town.

The prince's arguments and Poundbury's example influenced government policy, resonating with a political rhetoric of Englishness embraced by both Conservative and Labour parties: the rural village and market town embodied national character, and New Urbanism promised to create 'urban villages' countering the supposed amorality and despair of the 'inner city'.[130] Some of Poundbury's principles became embedded in government 'Planning Policy Guidance' notes, encouraging local authorities to insist on regional building traditions and materials, high densities and mixed tenures.[131]

5.16 Housing for Westbury Homes, Poundbury phase 2E, 2002–5 (photo: author).

Developers responded by tailoring standard house designs to local contexts. Westbury Homes commissioned PTP for such templates and estate layout advice, undertaken by Embleton. In more sensitive sites, Embleton designed all its housing: a Westbury Homes scheme in the Cotswolds village of Ebrington in the early 2000s received a RIBA housing award for its thoughtful approach to context and vernacular design.[132] He also worked on an army housing project near Salisbury, creating a series of standard house types and elevational variations in brick, flint and render, arranged in picturesque streetscapes.[133]

Other PTP offices adopted historicist approaches less ideologically alongside modernist styles. One extraordinary project transformed a modernist building into a historicist one when the Duke of Westminster appointed the Cardiff office to remodel Eaton Hall from 1988. Keith Mainstone, Elio Leo and Andrew Murray extended and remodelled the 1970s house by John Dennys, adding a French-style attic and chimney stacks, wrapping it in pink sandstone, reworking the garden with terraces, adapting forms and motifs from Waterhouse's surviving buildings. Hugh Casson advised on the work, having as much fun as the Cardiff architects: 'Eaton Hall enlivened!', he scribbled on Leo's sketch.[134] Similarly entertaining was a recreation of a Jacobean manor for Mito golf club near Tokyo in 1992 by Allan Clark and John Elkington of the Nottingham office and the interior design office, PTP Seward (led by Julian Seward), made of British bricks and including rooms modelled on those of historic houses.[135]

In sensitive urban contexts, contextualism, historicism and conservation became common approaches by the 1980s. Public reaction against post-war modernism often centred on conservation campaigns, and conservation became significant to many practices. One such campaign involved Henry Tanner's elaborate

Victorian Post Office in Victoria Square in Birmingham. The Post Office sought complete demolition and redevelopment in the 1970s, arousing a popular revolt that led to the building's listing.[136] A more modest project followed, retaining the building and adding new offices behind it. Vergette had in 1983 designed a speculative office block on Newhall Street in a well-crafted postmodern classical manner sympathetic to Victorian commercial neighbours, with rusticated basement, red brick, a projecting corner rotunda and articulated roofscape, suggesting possibilities for resolving the Post Office controversy.[137] John Gilmour, Steve Monk, Rennoldson and others made detailed studies for the Tanner building's extension in 1986, their townscape drawings analysing Victorian and Edwardian rooflines, corners and facades. Their design, like the Newhall Street offices, was more postmodern and theatrical than historicist, with stripy brickwork, towers of oriel windows and a spiky skyline, eventually abandoned for a blander scheme by another practice.[138] The Post Office had previously gutted the Tanner building's interior, but when it became the TSB bank headquarters in the late 1980s, PTP undertook refurbishment and interior design. While Seward and Joanna Leach designed contemporary offices taking subtle cues from the architecture, Pepperell, Leo and others at the Cardiff office recreated Tanner's entrance hall with classical columns, wrought ironwork and rich materials.[139]

Also neo-Victorian and civic in nature were two hotel projects of 1988 by the Birmingham office (John Gilmour, John Cooke and Jason Tavernor), one for Novotel in Birmingham and a paired complex for Novotel and Ibis in Southampton.[140] All employed a postmodern heritage warehouse style evoking their cities' Victorian mercantilism, now supplanted by business conferences and service industries. Birmingham City Council promoted sites for hotels to attract services companies to the city in the 1980s to replace lost manufacturing, and the Novotel was prominent on Broad Street alongside new offices (see Figure 5.17).[141] The warehouse look followed contemporary international enthusiasm for heritage as a marketing tool, giving a veneer of local character while also logically expressing the serial nature of their internal spaces.[142]

In 1991, PTP merged with a small practice in Edinburgh, Kneale & Russell, then run by James Landels and Clifford Martin, after collaborating on a historicist urban project in the Scottish capital. This was a competition run by the city in 1989 for a large site next to Haymarket railway station, for which developers submitted proposals, many historicist in approach.[143] PTP and Kneale & Russell won the competition for Southwark Investments with a scheme of housing, including social housing, hotels, retail and offices. Axial streets continued those of the surrounding late-Georgian New Town into a new circus around a public park. The buildings were to be faced in sandstone with modernised classical elevations and corner rotundas evoking the Edinburgh tenement vernacular, juxtaposed with modern glazing, steel balconies and sharp-edged volumes.[144] Only the housing was built to their plans, in a more subdued neo-traditional form than originally designed after much public criticism of the original scheme, in cheaper yellow brick and concrete block, with a simple play of rustication and mouldings within the monumental curved terrace form (see Figure 5.18).[145] It participated in a wider movement in Scotland reassessing traditional tenement housing. Martin and Helen Kelly similarly designed a social housing tenement in a neo-vernacular style in a conservation area on Buccleuch Street in Edinburgh's Old Town,

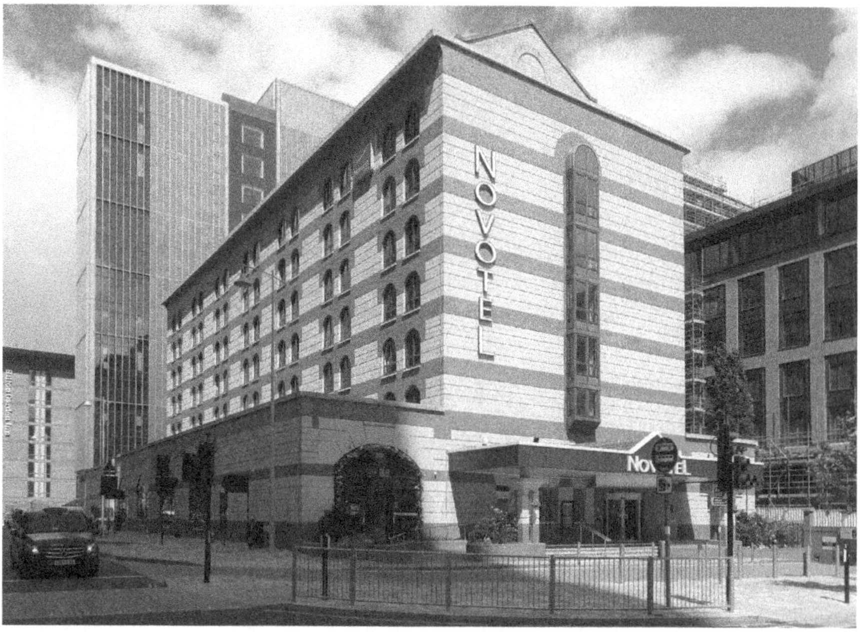

5.17 Novotel, Birmingham, 1988–9 (photo: author).

5.18 Housing at Morrison Circus, Haymarket, Edinburgh, mid-1990s (photo: Alistair Fair).

using Georgian window proportions, yellow blockwork rustication, render and ceramic tile decoration, an economical and clearly contemporary elevation sitting comfortably among rubble stone Georgian and Victorian vernacular tenements, different from the New Town's formal classicism.[146]

This traditionalist mode thus emerged independently in different PTP offices across Britain, pragmatically but creatively responding to places where engagement with local and regional identity was desired. Despite often appearing to reject modernism and sometimes participating in anti-modernist exercises, the architects nevertheless continued modes of analysis of heritage and townscape established within modernism and sustained continuously by the practice. As the following chapter explores, however, such work accompanied a developing mainstream modernism, as industry and the state remained the practice's most important clients. ■

05
Place, Landscape and Heritage
References

1. Kenneth Frampton, 'Towards a Critical Regionalism: Six Points for an Architecture of Resistance', in Hal Foster (ed.), *The Anti-Aesthetic: Essays on Postmodern Culture* (New York: The New Press, 1998), pp. 17–34.

2. For a succinct and nuanced summary of postmodernism, see Geraint Franklin and Elain Harwood, *Post-Modern Buildings in Britain* (London: Batsford, 2017), pp. 8–20.

3. Iorwerth Peate, *The Welsh House: A Study in Folk Culture* (Liverpool: Hugh Evans, 1944), pp. 9 and 4; Eurwyn Wiliam, 'Three Giants: Iorwerth Peate, Cyril Fox and Peter Smith, and the Welsh Contribution to Vernacular Architecture Studies', *Transactions: Ancient Monuments Society*, 61 (2017), 8–33; Neil Evans, 'The Changing Context of Welsh Historiography, 1890–2000', in Helen Brocklehurst and Robert Phillips (eds), *History, Nationhood and the Question of Britain* (Basingstoke: Palgrave Macmillan, 2004), pp. 20–32 (21–2).

4. W. R. Davies, 'Landscape and Tradition: An Interview with Dr Iorwerth Peate', *Architecture Wales*, June 1966, pp. 8–12; Bodfan Gruffydd, 'Landscape and Development', *Architecture Wales*, June 1966, pp. 13–17.

5. Peter Merriman and Rhys Jones, 'Nations, Materialities and Affects', *Progress in Human Geography*, 41/5 (2017), 600–17; Pyrs Gruffudd, 'Prospects of Wales: Contested Geographical Imaginations', in Ralph Fevre and Andrew Thompson (eds), *Nation, Identity and Social Theory: Perspectives from Wales* (Cardiff: University of Wales Press, 1999), pp. 149–67.

6. Christine Hui Lan Manley, *Frederick Gibberd* (Swindon: Historic England, 2017), pp. 24–9, 47; Frederick Gibberd, 'The Design of Residential Areas', and Thomas Sharp, 'The English Village', in Ministry of Housing and Local Government (ed.), *Design in Town and Village* (London: HMSO, 1953), pp. 20–70 and 1–19; Nikolaus Pevsner, *The Englishness of English Art* (New York: Frederick A. Praeger, 1956), chapter 7; Mathew Aitchison, 'Townscape: Scope, Scale and Extent', *The Journal of Architecture*, 17/5 (2021), 621–42; Erdem Erten, 'Thomas Sharp's Collaboration with H. de C. Hastings: The Formulation of Townscape as Urban Design Pedagogy', *Planning Perspectives*, 24/1 (2009), 29–49; David Matless, 'Taking Pleasure in England: Landscape and Citizenship in the 1940s', in Richard Weight and Abigail Beach (eds), *The Right to Belong: Citizenship and National Identity in Britain, 1930–1960* (London: I.B. Tauris, 1998), pp. 181–204.

7. County Council of Essex, *A Design Guide for Residential Areas* (n. pl.: County Council of Essex, 1973), p. 15; Geraint Franklin, 'Pooley's Progress: Towards a Modern Vernacular in Buckinghamshire', *Twentieth Century Architecture*, 13, 'The Architecture of Public Service' (2018), 147–61; Lance Wright, 'Architects in Hiding', *Architectural Review*, January 1976, pp. 3–4.

8. Guy Ortolano, *Thatcher's Progress: From Social Democracy to Market Liberalism through an English New Town* (Cambridge: Cambridge University Press, 2019), pp. 138–41.

9. A. B. Oldfield-Davies, 'New BBC Centre for Wales', *Financial Times*, 13 March 1967, p. 14.

10. Amy Genders, 'An Invisible Nation? The BBC and English-Language Arts Television in Wales', *Journal of British Cinema and Television*, 16/4 (2019), 409–28; Jamie Medhurst, '"Nation Shall Speak Peace Unto Nation"? The BBC and the Nations', *Critical Studies in Television: The International Journal of Television Studies*, 17/1 (2022), 8–23.

11. BBC Written Archives, Reading (BBCR), Loc. 46, 'Regional Development Commitments': A. B. Oldfield-Davies to DDTelB, 11 March 1959; Oldfield-Davies, 'Television in Wales', 5 February 1960; Oldfield-Davies to CTelA and CPSTel, 18 March 1960; 'West Wales TV Development', 21 October 1960; John Davies, *Broadcasting and the BBC in Wales* (Cardiff: University of Wales Press, 1994), pp. 216–18.

12. Davies, *BBC in Wales*, p. 221.

13. BBCR, 213 Loc. 45, 'Building & Services (Major) – Broadcasting Centre', P. A. Florence (Head of Central Services Group) to Cardiff New Headquarters Site Development Sub-Committee, 10 February 1961; architects at New Headquarters Site Development Committee, for example, 1 December 1960, 18 October 1961 and Main Site Meeting, 11 July 1963; BBCR, 'Baynton House File No. 1', Site Development Sub-Committee, 10 September 1959.

14. BBCR, 'Baynton House – Schedules of Requirements', Sir Percy Thomas & Son, 'The British Broadcasting Corporation Welsh Regional Headquarters: Report on the Preliminary Master Plan', September 1960.

15. H. A. N. Brockman, 'Successful Integration with Surroundings', *Financial Times*, 13 March 1967, p. 14.

16. BBC Wales Archive, Cardiff (BBCC), uncatalogued, 'Canolfan y BBC Broadcasting House', 1967, and press release, George Cook, 'Broadcasting House, Llandaff', n. d. [1966–7].

17. BBCR, 'New Headquarters – Baynton House, File No. 2': G. Wyn Rowlands (Programme Organiser, Wales) to [Oldfield-Davies] (Controller, Wales), 24 May 1962; New Headquarters Site Development Sub-Committee, 22 November 1962; BBCR, 'New Headquarters, Baynton House, File 3': 'BBC Headquarters, Llandaff: Summary Notes of a Meeting at Broadcasting House, Park Place, Cardiff on 24th February, 1964'; 'New Headquarters: Meeting on Site 19th October 1964'; 'Cardiff – New Headquarters; Note for File: Meeting in Cardiff 24th February'; New Headquarters Site Development Sub-Committee, 7 October 1964; BBCR, '2.4. New Headquarters': 'Cardiff – New HQ, Notes of a Meeting Held at Sir Percy Thomas & Son's Offices in Cardiff, 28th February 1966' and New Headquarters Site Development Sub-Committee, 17 February 1965 and 2 February 1966.

18. BBCC, uncatalogued, press release, 'New BBC Headquarters for Wales, Llandaff, Cardiff', n. d. [1967]; BBCC, Tape WG443 (Ref PEAA188S), recording of opening ceremony, 1 March 1967.

19. Medhurst, '"Nation Shall Speak Peace"', p. 21, citing Davies, *BBC in Wales*, p. 319.

20. Iorwerth C. Peate, *Amgueddfeydd Gwerin/Folk Museums* (Cardiff: University of Wales Press, 1948), p. 45.

21. St Fagans National Museum of History Archives (SFNMHA), 'Building Specifications', 'WFM Committee Minutes', Folk Life Committee, for example, 11 April, 5 September and 7 November 1947, 5 March 1948; SFNMHA, 'Files from Nat. Museum', 'Director's Report 15 March 1946, St Fagans', [Cyril Fox], 'A Folk Museum for the National Museum of Wales: Director's Report to Council', 7 March 1946; SFNMHA, 'Reports on Fishponds, Building', etc., 'Architects' Corres', Cyril Fox to Percy Thomas, 18 January 1947; SFNMHA, uncatalogued, 'National Museum of Wales, St. Fagans Castle [etc.]: General Specification and Schedule of Approximate Quantities' etc., January 1948.

22. SFNMHA, 'Reports on Fishponds, Building', etc., 'Architects' Corres', William Marsden, 'Report on Progress of Work at St Fagans Castle', 6 November 1947 and W. Marsden (Sir Percy Thomas & Son) to Iorwerth C. Peate, 2 December 1949.

23. SFNMHA, 'Building Specifications', 'WFM Committee Minutes', Welsh Folk Museum Committee, 3 June, 1 July, 2 September and 2 December 1949, 3 February 1950.

24. Peate, *Amgueddfeydd Gwerin*, p. 57, pp. 23–5; SFNMHA, 'Files from Nat. Museum', 'Memo. on Policy & Reconstruction', 'The Welsh Folk Museum: A Memorandum on Policy of Acquisition, Siting and Reconstruction of Buildings', September 1946; SFNMHA, 'Files from Nat. Museum', 'Plymouth Estates Ltd - Gen. Corresp.', untitled statement, n.d.

25. SFNMHA, 'Building Specifications', 'WFM Committee Minutes', Welsh Folk Museum Committee, 1 May 1953; Elaine Davey, 'A National Architect? The Percy Thomas Practice and Welsh National Identity' (unpublished PhD thesis, Cardiff University, 2013), pp. 138, 185.

26. Davey, 'A National Architect?', pp. 190–214.

27. 'Welsh Awards', *Architects' Journal*, 16 August 1978, p. 291.

28. David Adamson, 'The Intellectual and the National Movement in Wales', in Fevre and Thompson (eds), *Nation, Identity and Social Theory*, pp. 48–68 (63); Rhiannon Mason, 'Nation Building at the Museum of Welsh Life', *Museum and Society*, 3 (2005), 18–34 (20–2).

29. SFNMHA, 'Building Specifications', 'WFM Committee Minutes', Cyril Fox, 'The Welsh Folk Museum: A Memorandum on Policy of Acquisition, Siting, and Reconstruction of Buildings', 17 October 1946; Peate, *Amgueddfeydd Gwerin*, pp. 46–51.

30. Peate, *Amgueddfeydd Gwerin*, pp. 15–35.

31. SFNMHA, 'Building Specifications', 'Reports of the Keeper's Tour of the Scandinavian Museums', Iorwerth Peate, 'Report of the Keeper of the Department of Folk Life on His Tour of Scandinavian Museums', September 1946.

32. GAC, D900/U/4, 'Report of Visit by I. D. Owen and J. B. Hilling to the Maihaugen Folk Museum, Lillehammer, Norway, on 8th and 9th June 1965'.

33. John Hilling, interview with the author, Cardiff, 30 January 2018.

34. Deyan Sudjic, 'Space for Folk', *Building Design*, 15 September 1978, p. 36; Dale Owen, 'Getting Better by Design', in David Cole (ed.), *The New Wales* (Cardiff: University of Wales Press, 1990), pp. 70–90 (79).

35. Katrina Navickas, 'Conflicts of Power, Landscape and Amenity in Debates over the British Super Grid in the 1950s', *Rural History*, 30/1 (2019), 87–103.

36. Sylvia Crowe, *Tomorrow's Landscape* (London: Architectural Press, 1956); Sylvia Crowe, *The Landscape of Power* (London: Architectural Press, 1958); Sylvia Crowe, *The Landscape of Roads* (London: Architectural Press, 1960).

37. Walter Gropius, *Scope of Total Architecture* (London: George Allen & Unwin, 1956), p. 159; this recommended by Owen and Jennett: GAC, D900/U/6, IDO and FSJ, 'Design Note 1', n.d. [1964].

38. Michael Stratton, *Ironbridge and the Electric Revolution: The History of Electricity Generation at Ironbridge A and B Power Stations* (London: John Murray, 1994), pp. 81–2.

39. AUA, R/Pbi/Misc 2, Sir Percy Thomas & Son, 'University College of Wales Aberystwyth, Development Plan 1: Stage 1 – Preliminary Report', June 1965, p. 10; Elisabeth Beazley, 'University College of Wales: Development Plan', *Architects' Journal*, 13 April 1966, p. 922.

40. AUA, R/Pbi/Misc 2, Sir Percy Thomas & Son, 'University College of Wales Aberystwyth, Development Plan 1: Stage 1 – Preliminary Report', June 1965, pp. 10–11.

41. AUA, R/Pbi/Misc 2, Sir Percy Thomas & Son, 'University College of Wales Aberystwyth, Development Plan 1: Stage 1 – Preliminary Report', June 1965, pp. 16–19.

42. AUA, CAC/1/34, New Buildings Committee, 22 October 1962; New Buildings Committee, 5 February 1963; AUA, CAC/1/35, New Buildings Committee, 19 October 1963; AUA, CAC/1/38, New Buildings Committee, 18 October 1966.

43. AUA, uncatalogued, New Buildings Committee minutes 1946–8, Grounds Sub-Committee, 2 August 1968 and I. Dale Owen (Percy Thomas & Son) to T. Arfon Owen (Registrar, UCW, Aberystwyth), 7 November 1966.

44. Arthur Hellyer, 'Lessons of a Maritime Garden', *Country Life*, 13 October 1977, pp. 1026–30.

45. Cliff Tandy, 'Landscape: Strategy', *Architects' Journal*, 5 September 1979, pp. 509–15 (511–12).

46. Jane Findlay and Sue Thomas, video interview with the author, 17 March 2021.

47. Sue Radley, 'Dudley District General Hospital', *Landscape Design*, December 1983, pp. 27–9.

48. Jane Findlay and Sue Thomas, video interview with the author, 17 March 2021; for example, Roger S. Ulrich, 'Visual Landscapes and Psychological Well-Being', *Landscape Research*, 4/1 (1979), 17–23.

49. 'The Society of Incorporated Accountants and Auditors: Sixty-Sixth Annual General Meeting', *The Accountant*, 2 June 1951, pp. 544–51 (544); 'The Society of Incorporated Accountants and Auditors: Report for 1950', *The Accountant*, 19 May 1951, pp. 489–93 (491); 'Weekly Notes', *The Accountant*, 26 May 1951, pp. 517–18 (517); A. A. Garrett, *History of the Society of Incorporated Accountants, 1885–1957* (Oxford: Oxford University Press, 1961), pp. 130–1, 227–8, 281–2, 342–3.

50. GAC, D/900/U/4, John Betjeman, foreword to '2 Temple Place', n. d. [1971].

51. Conwy Archives Service, Conwy (CAS), CX155/3, Glyn Griffiths, 'Day to Day in Wales: Welsh Bridge of Sighs', *Liverpool Daily Post*, 26 January 1950, cutting.

52. CAS, COB/389/4, Town Clerk's Office, report of interview, 2 December 1942; TNA, BD 43/97, N. M. Woolger to illegible addressee, 2 August 1962.

53. For example, CAS, COB/389/3, Joseph T. Jones (Mayor of Conwy) to 'The Ratepayers of Conway Borough', 10 September 1938; CAS, COB/389/4, 'Report of Mr. Thomas Owen, PASI, County Surveyor: Borough of Conway, Trunk Road A.55', n.d. [c.1940] and [anon.] to L. H. Macklin (Ministry of War Transport), 1 March 1944; CAS, COB/389/5, Ada M. Rushworth (Southport) to Mayor of Conwy, 3 November 1944, and other correspondence, 1944–5; CAS, CX155/2, Idwal Owen, 'Day to Day in Wales: Waterfront is a Showpiece', unattributed cutting, 28 July 1951.

54. CAS, COB/389/8, 'Report of a Meeting of the Roads and Bridges Committee', County Council, Caernarvonshire, 28 February 1952, and other documents.

55. CAS, COB/389/7, [illegible] (Ministry of Town and Country Planning) to Clerk to the Conway Bridge Commissioners, 30 January 1950.

56. CAS, COB/389/5, A. J. Lyddon (Ministry of Transport) to Mr Sylvester, 22 November 1944.

57. CAS, CX155/2, '"The Need Appreciated for Many Years," says Minister', unattributed cutting, 11 February 1955; TNA, MT 39/950, 'When Chief Constable was Held Up 1½ Hours!', *North Wales Weekly News*, 10 February 1955, cutting.

58. CAS, CX338/10, 'Opening of the New Conway Bridge', *North Wales Weekly News*, 18 December 1958, souvenir supplement, pp. 9–10.

59. TNA, BD 31/218, drawing, Percy Thomas, 'Conway Bridge & By-Pass – Suspension Type Bridge', 24 March 1943.

60. TNA, MT 39/948, H. W. Fitz Simons to C. S. Chettoe (Ministry of Transport), 17 May 1954, and other documents.

61. RBAS, Ref 2003/10 (Box 1), 1/202/9, 'University College of Swansea: Development Appeal', 1960.

62. Tudor Edwards, 'The First Atlantic College', *Birmingham Post*, 20 September 1962, p. 10; Clive Aslet, 'St Donat's Castle, South Glamorgan: The Property of the United World College of the Atlantic', *Country Life*, 18 September 1980, pp. 942-5; booklet, 'The Atlantic College in the United Kingdom' (n. pub., n. d., [c.1960]); John B. Hilling, 'The Buildings of St Donat's', in Roy Denning (ed.), *The Story of St Donat's Castle and Atlantic College* (Cowbridge and Barry: D. Brown & Sons and Stewart Williams, 1983), pp. 1-16.

63. AUA, R/Pbi/Misc 2, Percy Thomas Partnership, 'University College of Wales Aberystwyth, Development Plan 2', June 1974; GAC, D900/U/3, University College of Aberystwyth Grounds Committee, 9 November 1977; Tony Aldous, 'Higher Education at Lower Cost: The New Universities - III', *Country Life*, 12 February 1976, pp. 356-8 (357); David Crawford, 'Keeping a Welcome in the Farmhouse', *Building*, 4 July 1975, pp. 63-6; RCAHMW, PTA, 05/05, 'Percy Thomas Partnership Architects & Planning Consultants', n.d. [c.1977].

64. Robert Proctor, 'Social Structures: Gillespie, Kidd & Coia's Halls of Residence at the University of Hull', *Journal of the Society of Architectural Historians*, 67/1 (2008), 106-29 (116); Eric Mumford, *The CIAM Discourse on Urbanism, 1928-1960* (Cambridge MA: MIT Press, 2000), pp. 225-65.

65. Jonathan Vining, 'A Particular Sense of Place', *C20: The Magazine of the Twentieth Century Society*, no. 1, 2021, pp. 48-3.

66. RBAS, Box 231, 1/215/2, Item 8, Sir Percy Thomas & Son, 'University College of Swansea: Development Plan Preliminary Report', July 1958.

67. AUA, CAC/1/37, Principal's Report to Court of Governors, 27 October 1965.

68. GAC, D900/U/2, Sir Percy Thomas & Son, 'University College of Wales Aberystwyth: Development Plan, Stage 2 Report', October 1970; AUA, R/Pbi/Misc 2, Percy Thomas & Son, 'University College of Wales Aberystwyth, Development Plan 1', June 1965, 'Stage 1 - Preliminary Report', for example, p. 11.

69. AUA, R/Plans, 'Great Hall & Students Union, UCW Aberystwyth: Outline Proposals', April 1966; 'Great Hall, University College of Wales at Aberystwyth', *Building*, 10 December 1971, pp. 61-8; 'The Great Hall at Aberystwyth', *Concrete*, April 1974, p. 42.

70. 'Percy Thomas Partnership Architects & Planning Consultants: Composite Brochure No. 2', n.d. [c.1978], unpaginated, author's collection; RCAHMW, PTA 05/05, 'Percy Thomas Partnership Architects & Planning Consultants', n.d. [c.1977].

71. Kerry Veale, untitled typescript, n.d., sent to author; *The RMBI: Our Purpose, Achievement and Endeavour* (London: The Royal Masonic Benevolent Institution, n.d. [c.1977]), unpaginated, author's collection; Kerry Veale, letter to the author, 25 April 2021; Kerry Veale, video interview with the author, 13 April 2021.

72. 'RIBA Awards 1975', *Architects' Journal*, 30 July 1975, pp. 247-9; 'This Year's RIBA Commendations', *RIBA Journal*, August 1975, pp. 16-23.

73. Malcolm Lovibond, 'Renewal in Historic Towns', *Architecture West Midlands*, December 1970, pp. 12–13; Michael Wright, 'Building with Modesty and Pride: The Civic Trust Awards, 1968', *Country Life*, 6 February 1969, pp. 282–3; 'Awards: 7 United Kingdom Entries for Cembureau', *Building*, 14 February 1975, p. 57; 'Record', *Architects' Journal*, 19 February 1975, pp. 390–1; 'Beast as the Beauty', *Architects' Journal*, 3 September 1975, pp. 452–3; RCAHMW, PTA 05/04, 'Percy Thomas Partnership Architects & Planning Consultants' (n.d.) [*c*.1975]; on wider conservation influences, for example, John R. Gold and John Pendlebury, 'The "Spirit of Living Continuity"? Revisiting the Urban Vision, Methodologies and Influence of the Studies in Conservation', *Town Planning Review*, 90/1 (2019), 33–56.

74. For example, Otto Saumarez Smith, *Boom Cities: Architect-Planners and the Politics of Radical Urban Renewal in 1960s Britain* (Oxford: Oxford University Press, 2019), for example, pp. 8–10, 25–9, 33; John Pendlebury, 'The Modern Historic City: Evolving Ideas in Mid-20th-Century Britain', *Journal of Urban Design*, 10/2 (2005), 253–73.

75. Sidney H. Tasker, 'Chester: The Challenge of Change', *The Town Planning Review*, 37/3 (1966), 189–206.

76. Cheshire Archives and Local Studies, Chester (CALS), ZCR 251/12, J. H. Chandler (Chester Civic Trust), 'The Inner City Plan', press release, 2 December 1964; CALS, ZCR/15, J. H. Chandler, 'The Chester Civic Trust', 20 October 1965.

77. CALS, ZCR 251/72, G. Grenfell-Baines, 'Chester: A Plan for the Central Area', October 1964.

78. 'City Centre Scheme Will Cost Over £2m', *Chester Chronicle*, 8 September 1962, p. 24.

79. 'Eaton Estates Reveal City Plan', *Chester Chronicle*, 17 June 1961, p. 24.

80. George K. Ridley, 'In Business Today', *Chester Chronicle*, 5 November 1965, p. 25; CALS, ZCB/11, Chester City and County Council minutes, 30 April 1958.

81. 'Stroll Into a Gleaming Future', *Chester Chronicle*, 5 December 1964, p. 10; C. P. Lewis and A. T. Thacker (eds), *A History of the County of Chester: Volume 5 Part 1, the City of Chester: General History and Topography* (London: Victoria County History, 2003), pp. 258–61.

82. J. M. V. Cotterell, 'Just One Regret', *Chester Chronicle*, 5 November 1965, p. 39.

83. 'Piazza Plan Gives Pleasure', *Chester Chronicle*, 11 May 1963, p. 20.

84. 'Grosvenor Plan for Chester Is Ripe', *Chester Chronicle*, 13 April 1963, p. 20; John Pratt, 'Behind the Facade', *Cheshire Life*, December 1964, pp. 58–65.

85. Tasker, 'Chester', pp. 199–203.

86. 'In Continental Style But Not Incongruously So', *Chester Chronicle*, 4 May 1963, p. 8; W. Kirby Laing, 'Proud of Their Work', *Chester Chronicle*, 5 November 1965, p. 1; 'Old Into New: Access from the Historic Rows of Chester into a Twentieth-Century Piazza', *Chester Chronicle*, 4 May 1963, p. 8; 'Views – and Questions

- on the Grosvenor-Laing Plan', *Chester Chronicle*, 4 May 1963, p. 21; 'Chester - Central Shopping Development', *Architects' Journal*, 22 May 1963, pp. 1070-1.

87. GAC, UDPE/S/X4, Sir Percy Thomas & Son, 'Penarth Urban District Council, Billybanks Housing Development 3: Final Design Report, December 1965'; GAC, D900/U/1, 'Work Nearly Finished on Billybanks Homes', *South Wales Echo*, 29 March 1968, cutting.

88. GAC, UDPE/S/X4, Sir Percy Thomas & Son, 'Penarth Urban District Council, Billy Banks Housing Development 3: Design Report', October 1965.

89. GAC, UDPE/S/X4, 'Report by Sir Percy Thomas & Son on the Housing Development at Billybanks for Penarth Urban District Council', 23 January 1967 and Sir Percy Thomas & Son, 'Penarth Urban District Council, Billybanks Housing Development 3: Final Design Report, December 1965'; Julian Owen, interview with the author, Bristol, 16 February 2022.

90. Tonia Carless, 'Producing Space, the Confrontation Between Abstract Space and Everyday Life: "I Wunder If Heaven Got a Ghetto"', *ARQ*, 17/2 (2013), 139–47 (141).

91. Ian C. Thomas, 'The Beginnings of an Economic Development Policy in Mid-Wales: The Mid-Wales Industrial Development Association, 1957–1974', *Welsh History Review*, 17/3 (1995), 411–51.

92. RIBAL, Sir Percy Thomas & Son, *Expansion of Rhayader: A Pilot Study* (Cardiff: Mid-Wales Industrial Development Association, March 1967); George Finch, 'Development in Mid-Wales: Expansion of Rhayader', *Architects' Journal*, 10 May 1967, pp. 1108–9; 'Rhayader Development Scheme: Some Notes on the Outline Proposals', *Architecture Wales*, August 1967, pp. 18–19.

93. Nan Fairbrother, *New Lives, New Landscapes* (London: Architectural Press, 1970), pp. 254–5, 340–53.

94. Ministry of Housing and Local Government, *Historic Towns: Preservation and Change* (London: HMSO, 1967).

95. RIBAL, Percy Thomas Partnership, *Rhayader Plan: Final Repot* (Manchester: n. pub., 1974).

96. RIBAL and GAC, D900/U/4, Percy Thomas Partnership, *Brecon Town Expansion Plan* (Bristol: n. pub., 1974), pp. 1, 13–14, 37–8, 79–82, 127, 144.

97. Thomas, 'Beginnings of an Economic Development Policy', pp. 444–7.

98. Tony Aldous, 'Planning: Newtown - Britain's Smallest Town', *Architects' Journal*, 15 September 1976, p. 482; Percy Thomas Partnership, *Vernacular Study: The Domestic Architecture of Newtown Powys* (Cardiff: n. pub., 1975), author's collection; the housing is between Heol Vaynor, Newtown, and the River Severn, and likely also Heol-y-Coleg and Heol-y-Nant.

99. A. Trystan Edwards, *Good and Bad Manners in Architecture* (London: Philip Allan, 1924), p. 163.

100. 'Announcements', *Architects' Journal*, 1 May 1963, p. 934; 'Announcements', *Architects' Journal*, 27 January 1971, pp. 184–5; Tony Aldous, 'Portrait of a

Practice: Percy Thomas Partnership', *Building Design*, 2 December 1977, pp. 13–16 (15).

101. 'Percy Thomas Partnership Architects & Planning Consultants: Composite Brochure No. 2', n.d. [c.1978], author's collection; RCAHMW, PTA, 03/13, practice promotional booklet missing cover, n.d. [c.1985]; 'Sound Barrier', *Building Design*, 5 May 1978, p. 10.

102. Southampton Local Studies and Maritime Library, Southampton (SLS): City Planning Department, Southampton, 'Conservation Areas Report 2: Old Town Area', April 1974, pp. 8–9; Southampton City Planning Office, 'Conservation Areas Report 1', November 1972; City Planning Office Southampton, 'Conservation Areas Report 2: Old Town Area; A Draft for Consultation', June 1973.

103. Southampton Archives, Southampton (SAS), SC 2/13/1, City Planning Office, 'Upper Bugle Street Area: A Brief for Redevelopment', February 1974, p. 12; also SAS, SC/PL 24, R. J. Coles (City Planning Officer), 'Upper Bugle Street Redevelopment', February 1972.

104. Willie Harbinson, video interview with the author, 18 March 2021; Third Collingwood Housing Association Ltd and Percy Thomas Partnership, 'Planning Application 12717/15125/M4', 1977, Southampton City Council, *https://planningpublicaccess.southampton.gov.uk/online-applications/files/B8EDB1B7AD27F73DE646D5E91AAF9E1B/pdf/1525_M4-Historic-767354.pdf* (accessed 7 June 2022); Percy Thomas Partnership, 'Flat Development at Upper Bugle Street', drawings of May and June 1977, Southampton City Council, *https://planningpublicaccess.southampton.gov.uk/online-applications/files/DF1524520702974C2A65A2DC6E96AD8F/pdf/1525_M4-Historic-721173.pdf* (accessed 7 June 2022).

105. R. H. Hall (City Planning Officer) to Percy Thomas Partnership, 13 June 1977 and Percy Thomas Partnership, 'Planning and Housing Group', Bristol, 'Report of Meeting', 'Meeting Held with Planning and City Engineer Officials on Tuesday', 27 September 1977, in Third Collingwood Housing Association Ltd and Percy Thomas Partnership, 'Planning Application 12717/15125/M4', 1977, Southampton City Council, *https://planningpublicaccess.southampton.gov.uk/online-applications/files/B8EDB1B7AD27F73DE646D5E91AAF9E1B/pdf/1525_M4-Historic-767354.pdf* (accessed 7 June 2022).

106. 'Report', *Architects' Journal*, 15 October 1980, p. 737; 'Aspects of an Area', *Architects' Journal*, 14 July 1982, pp. 28–35 (29); RIBAL, Percy Thomas Partnership – Biographical File, 'Upper Bugle Street, Southampton', *Percy Thomas Partnership: Review*, 1984, unpaginated.

107. For example, Mark Crinson, 'The Uses of Nostalgia: Stirling and Gowan's Preston Housing', *Journal of the Society of Architectural Historians*, 65/2 (2006), 216–37.

108. Giles Worsley, 'Cheap But Not Shoddy', *Country Life*, 30 April 1992, pp. 68–70.

109. Sharp, 'The English Village'.

110. Giles Worsley, 'The Style That Dares Not Speak Its Name', *Independent*, 8 August 1990, p. 13; Ron Morgan, video interview with the author, 9 March 2021.

111. Peterjohn Smyth, letter to the editor, *Architects' Journal*, 11 October 1989, p. 21; 'Astragal', *Architects' Journal*, 25 September 1991, pp. 6–7; Percy Thomas Partnership, 'Traditional Contextual Architecture: Percy Thomas Partnership, Bristol', 1994, author's collection; Willie Harbinson, video interview with the author, 8 March 2021; Prince Charles may have indirectly motivated the choice of approach and even architects by criticising the Skipton Building Society's existing headquarters: 'Battle of the Styles', *Architects' Journal*, 20 September 1989, p. 5.

112. Andrew MacLeod, 'Royal Rocket for Centre', [Birmingham] *Evening Mail*, 27 November 1987, in Timothy Ross Hall, 'Urban Regeneration and Cultural Geography: The International Convention Centre, Birmingham' (unpublished PhD thesis, University of Birmingham, 1994), pp. 250, 411.

113. Charles, Prince of Wales, *A Vision of Britain: A Personal View of Architecture* (London: Doubleday, 1989), pp. 32–3.

114. For example, Charles Jencks, 'Ethics and Prince Charles', *Architectural Design*, May 1989, pp. 24–9; Christopher Martin, 'Second Chance', *Architectural Design*, May 1989, pp. 7–15; Richard Rogers, 'Pulling Down the Prince', *Architectural Design*, May 1989, pp. 66–9.

115. 'Ward Cluster Solution at Dorchester', *Architects' Journal*, 23 September 1987, p. 13; RIBAL, Percy Thomas Partnership - Biographical File, 'West Dorset General Hospital', *Percy Thomas Partnership: Review*, 1988, unpaginated; Paul James and Tony Noakes, *Hospital Architecture* (Harlow: Longman, 1994), pp. 130–4; Mark Collyer, *Dorset County Hospital: 175 Years of Rural Healthcare, 1840–2015* (Dorchester: Dorset County NHS Foundation Trust, 2015), pp. 33.

116. Charles, *Vision of Britain*, p. 118.

117. Worsley, 'Cheap But Not Shoddy'.

118. For example, Dennis Hardy, *Poundbury: The Town That Charles Built* (London: Town and Country Planning Association, 2006); Michelle Thompson-Fawcett, '"Urbanist" Lived Experience: Resident Observations on Life in Poundbury', *Urban Design International*, 8 (2003), 67–84; Gillian Darley, 'Poundbury Unpicked', *Architects' Journal*, 13 November 2008, pp. 41–2; Yanhui Lei, 'Urban Village Extension: Design Principles of New Urbanism - The Case Studies of Poundbury and Upton' (unpublished PhD thesis, University of Nottingham, 2014).

119. Dorset History Centre, Dorchester (DHC), DC-WD ACC 9480: D. D. Derrien (Chief Planning Officer), 'Alternative Development Strategies for Dorchester and the Surrounding Area', 2 July 1987; West Dorset District Council, Eastern Area Planning Sub-Committee, special meeting, 23 July 1987; Report of the Chief Planning Officer, 'Alternative Development Strategies for Dorchester and the Surrounding Area: A Summary of the Comments Received', 29 October 1987; DHC, DC-WD ACC 9480, 'Alternative Development Strategies for

Dorchester and Surrounding Area: Report of the Working Party', 3 March 1988 and West Dorset District Council Planning and Development Committee, 25 May 1988 and 8 June 1988.

120. DHC, DC-WD ACC 9480, West Dorset District Council Development and Planning Committee, 28 February 1991.

121. For example, Hardy, *Poundbury*, p. 50; Giles Worsley, 'Pushing Poundbury', *Country Life*, 17 October 1991, pp. 62–3; Léon Krier, 'Master Plan for Poundbury Development in Dorchester', *Architectural Design*, May 1989, pp. 46–55.

122. Léon Krier, *Architecture: Choice or Fate* (Windsor: Andreas Papadakis, 1998), for example, pp. 133–57.

123. Lei, 'Urban Village Extension', p. 347; Simon Conibear, video interview with the author, 6 July 2022.

124. Valerie Elliott and Mira Bar-Hillel, 'Prince Delighted at Advance of His Village of Vision', *Sunday Telegraph*, 28 March 1993, p. 11; James Stamford, 'Town and Country', *Country Life*, 27 May 1993, pp. 58–9; Christine Webb, 'Homes Fit for a Prince', *The Times*, 5 January 1994 (via Nexis); Helena de Bertodano, 'Prince's Neighbours Watch Out as a Royal Dream Takes Shape', *Sunday Telegraph*, 6 February 1994, p. 15; Robert Cowan, 'New For Old', *Architects' Journal*, 3 July 2003, pp. 38–43; Neil Embleton, video interview with the author, 9 March 2021; Willie Harbinson, video interview with the author, 18 March 2021.

125. Harbinson, interview, 2021.

126. DHC, DC-WD ACC 9480, West Dorset District Council Development and Planning Committee, 23 November 1989; DHC, DC-WD ACC 9480, West Dorset District Council Development and Planning Committee, 28 March 1990.

127. Hardy, *Poundbury*, pp. 96–8.

128. Oliver Wainwright, 'Keeping Up Appearances', *Building Design*, 6 July 2012, pp. 8-11 (9); Lei, 'Urban Village Extension', p. 348.

129. Neil Embleton, interview, 2021; Conibear, interview, 2022.

130. Daniel Maudlin, 'Constructing Identity and Tradition: Englishness, Politics and the Neo-Traditional House', *Journal of Architectural Education*, 63/1 (2009), 51–63.

131. Matthew Carmona, 'Design and PPG3: Seven Years On', *Town & Country Planning*, May 1999, pp. 152–3; Matthew Carmona and Andrew Renninger, 'The Royal Fine Art Commission and 75 Years of English Design Review: The Final 15 Years, 1984-1999', *Planning Perspectives*, 32/4 (2017), 577–99.

132. Neil Embleton, 'Village Virtues: Percy Thomas Partnership in Ebrington', *Architecture Today*, May 2005, pp. 50–5.

133. Embleton, interview, 2021.

134. Alastair Stewart, 'Radical Redesign for Controversial Eaton Hall', *Building*, 22 January 1988, p. 7; Hugh Pearman, 'Unmodernise This Eyesore, Says the Duke', *Sunday Times*, 7 February 1988 (Nexis); Alastair Stewart, 'Redesign

Gives Eaton Hall a Rosy Outlook', *Building*, 10 February 1989, p. 9; Paula Bailey and Eileen Simpson, *The Halls of Eaton: Eaton Hall, Chester* (Chester: Grosvenor Estate, 2010), pp. 79–91, 95; Colleen Hope and Claire Clench, video interview with the author, 10 February 2021; Elio Leo, telephone interviews with the author, 22 February 2021 and 4 March 2021.

135. W. A. Clark, 'The English Tradition', *Percy Thomas Partnership: Review*, 1992, unpaginated, author's collection.

136. Ewan Harrison, '"Money Spinners": R. Seifert & Partners, Sir Frank Price and Public-Sector Speculative Development in the 1970s', *Architectural History*, 61 (2018), 259–80.

137. Andy Foster, *Birmingham* (London: Yale University Press, 2005), p. 138; RCAHMW, PTA, 03/13, Percy Thomas Partnership, untitled booklet, n.d. [c.1985]; Andy Foster, email to author, 13 June 2022.

138. Joe Holyoak, 'Urns and Chamberpots', *Architects' Journal*, 18 November 1987, p. 129.

139. Fred Holden, 'TSB New Headquarters in Birmingham', *Percy Thomas Partnership: Review*, 1992, unpaginated, author's collection; Marcus Field, 'TSB Says Yes to Integrating the Traditional and Contemporary', *Architects' Journal*, 4 November 1992, pp. 24–5; Ian Pepperell, telephone interview with the author, 19 February 2021; Elio Leo, telephone interview with the author, 22 February 2021.

140. RIBAL, Percy Thomas Partnership Biographical File, 'Novotel Hotels and Ibis Hotel', *Percy Thomas Partnership: Review*, 1988, unpaginated.

141. Birmingham City Council, *Developing Birmingham, 1889 to 1989: 100 Years of City Planning* (Birmingham: Birmingham City Council, 1989), p. 147.

142. Christine M. Boyer, 'Cities for Sale: Merchandising History at South Street, Seaport', in Michael Sorkin (ed.), *Variations on a Theme Park: The New American City and the End of Public Space* (New York: Hill and Wang, 1992), pp. 181–204.

143. Hugh Anderson, 'Edinburgh Entries', *Architects' Journal*, 13 December 1989, pp. 24–9 (24); 'Wedgwood Peace', *Architects' Journal*, 4 April 1990, p. 13.

144. The Haymarket Partnership, 'Morrison Street, Haymarket, Edinburgh', n.d. [1989], author's collection.

145. Clifford Martin, video interview with the author, 16 April 2021.

146. Clifford Martin, 'Sensitive Infill in Edinburgh', *Percy Thomas Partnership: Review*, 1992, unpaginated, author's collection.

6

Architecture and the Neoliberal State

On becoming leader of the Conservative Party in 1975, Margaret Thatcher announced a philosophy of distributing power and property away from the state and into the hands of citizens. This principle guided her to electoral victory four years later and for over a decade in power as she oversaw the transformation of the economy and government, and changed the terms of debate and action for her successors, including the next Labour administration.[1] This political reorientation has been described as 'neoliberalism', the idea of reducing the state's role and expanding the reach of the capitalist market. These aims applied to the economy, with the privatisation of nationalised organisations and reduced taxation and regulation; and to the welfare state, where reforms introducing the market and market-like characteristics created a 'competition state'.[2] This ideological shift accompanied economic changes towards 'late capitalism': a traumatic decline in manufacturing industries in the west, supplanted by high technology, finance and service industries, new methods of small-scale production, rapid obsolescence driven by consumer marketing, and the globalisation of industry and capital.[3] Politicians sometimes encouraged such changes, sometimes belatedly endorsed them.[4] One response to deindustrialisation was to shift state intervention from regions to cities, with policies aiming to revive their economic and social fortunes by encouraging service industries and commercial speculation.[5]

This grand historical narrative has been questioned and developed. Government ministers and others involved in policy and implementation often differed. Contrary to political rhetoric, the state did not retreat. The welfare state continued, retaining such fundamental principles as free universal education and healthcare, adapted to a changing culture.[6] Such complexities are evident in the work of the Percy Thomas Partnership, which included many large-scale public buildings. And Wales was especially complex: while the narrative describes changes in Wales, with its catastrophic losses in heavy manufacturing, steel and coal, the state's role in diversifying Welsh industry remained important, bringing work for the practice. Gradual devolution allowed Wales to modify British politics, from the establishment of the Welsh Office in 1965 to the National Assembly for Wales (now the Welsh Parliament or Senedd) in 1999.[7] Even in many of PTP's large British and international projects apparently exemplifying neoliberal ideas, closer analysis often reveals a messier reality. This chapter demonstrates that despite rhetoric around the state's retreat, the state remained fundamentally important in producing the spaces of welfare, governance, infrastructure and business. Through architecture, the state moulded the spaces of citizens' everyday lives, though in ways that reframed notions of citizenship and governance. Moreover, PTP's architecture often articulated concepts of citizenship and community that were not clearly aligned with neoliberalism, but rather sought to counter its alienating effects.

The question of whether there was a neoliberal architecture remains contentious. Postmodernism has been interpreted as a response to late capitalism, sometimes critical, sometimes laudatory.[8] Postmodernism as 'Ironic, Iconic and Critical' practice, in Charles Jencks's formulation, was not strongly represented in PTP's architecture, increasingly split between earnest neo-traditionalism and earnest modernism, seeking to resolve clients' and users' desires, while sustaining older architectural and social ideals. Nevertheless, the practice itself became postmodern in its fragmentation, as semi-autonomous offices took different approaches, and even architects favouring modernism dabbled in neoclassicism or heritage styles. PTP became part of the late capitalist order, providing a cultural service, as architects lost their privileged control of construction; and its work became global, with offices in the Middle East and south-east Asia.

Nevertheless, one architectural feature appears consistently across many building types and seems to characterise the period: the atrium, a glazed central hall uniting internal spaces. This spatial form arose in the nineteenth century, but became fashionable again from the 1970s, following American models including John Portman's giant hotel complexes. It tended to imply modernity, often requiring technical innovations; and it also suggested an allegiance to the consumerism of the shopping mall.[9] The atrium in American developments maximised profits in land and building speculation, and created a corporate internalised urbanism cushioning the middle classes from surrounding urban decline.[10] Yet PTP's use of the atrium emerged from welfare state building types as well as commercial models, and often overtly contradicted a supposed contemporary individualism to generate a sense of civic community, a function of the atrium understood at least since Frank Lloyd Wright's early twentieth-century Larkin Building.[11] After an initial section on hospitals, this chapter proceeds by considering the purposes of the atrium and atrium-like spaces where they appear in the various sectors of the practice's late twentieth-century work. It concludes by arriving almost full circle at significant projects that, despite their new contexts and forms, echo the civic ethos espoused by Percy Thomas at the practice's origins.

Welfare States

Thatcher's government was initially wary of challenging the National Health Service (NHS). Building hospitals often took decades, and the Department of Health and Social Security's (DHSS) semi-standardised Nucleus planning system, developed from Harness, remained popular, applying pre-planned hospital departments in cross-shaped modules.[12] This system reduced planning time, encouraging architects to develop elevations, interiors and landscaping, encouraging more diverse appearances.[13] Central government relinquished some control, so regional health authorities could choose their approaches, but state architectural expertise was often lost to private practices.[14] Mike Nightingale, for example, left the Oxford Hospital Board to join Llewelyn Davies & Weeks before moving to PTP's London office in 1978.[15] Frederick Jennett's adoption of an American computer-aided design system in the 1970s streamlined hospital drawing work, storing Nucleus plans and service layouts, and PTP's 'Central Technical Office' at Shrewsbury, run by Keith Cluderay, employed a hospital services engineer.[16] Even NHS estate planning was contracted out: Roger Cockle at the Manchester office designed a computerised system for planning healthcare services in relation to buildings for the Mersey Regional Health Authority, developing it for wider use by the DHSS.[17]

Most of PTP's later hospital work was in England. Postponed 1970s hospitals came to fruition in the 1980s, including the first phase of the Manchester Royal Infirmary, completed in 1981, the Mayday Hospital in Croydon, opened in 1982, and the Glenfield Hospital in Leicester, opened in 1984, all Nucleus hospitals with varied modernist expressions.[18] Colchester District General Hospital, similarly, was planned in 1971, resumed in 1977, and opened in 1984, designed by Julian Cockayne and Nightingale.[19] Here the North East Essex Regional Health Authority departed from Nucleus while retaining its briefing and space standards. Nightingale, following Llewelyn Davies & Weeks's concept of open-ended design, separated functions into expandable blocks. Simple modern elevations were enlivened with bright green glass-reinforced concrete panels and landscape design by Mike Littlewood and Jane Findlay, a footbridge crossing a lake to the entrance.[20]

New 1980s hospitals included Stoke-on-Trent City General of 1982 to 1988, mainly using Nucleus. It extended a Victorian building with a historicist style of red brick and hipped roofs, bay windows giving ward seating areas.[21] Peterjohn Smyth, Patricia Townsend and others in Bristol designed Weston-super-Mare District General, completed in 1986, adopting T-shaped wards designed by the South Western Regional Health Authority's architect Viréndra Sahai. A spine corridor divided the hospital into a ward zone facing south towards a wooded rise, and a clinical zone behind. Pyramidal roofs and buff brick walls suggested a country house, and green-painted

6.1 Weston-super-Mare General Hospital, 1981–5 (photo: author).

steel balconies gave a fun postmodern feel (see Figure 6.1).[22] Similar in layout was the Mid-Sussex Hospital at Haywards Heath of 1985 to 1989, by Ronald Weeks with Roger Bourne, Terry Sullivan and John Deacon (see Figure 6.2). Its elevations adopted a neo-vernacular red brick style with low pitched roofs; wards projected forward on tall pilotis. Although elements were repeated for economy and design coherence, monotony and indefiniteness were avoided by terminating roofs with hips and folding the entrance into an asymmetrical step in the plan.[23]

6.2 Mid-Sussex Hospital (now Princess Royal Hospital), Haywards Heath, *c.*1985–9 (photo: ResilienceUAV/Alamy).

The diversity of design in later hospitals reflects the many architects involved, but also the Thatcher government's concern to reduce centralisation, and to consider patients as consumers making choices in a marketplace, where hospital appearance and patient satisfaction became crucial.[24] Nevertheless, the Conservative Party often reiterated welfare state ideals: its 1987 manifesto boasted of having undertaken the 'biggest hospital building programme in the history of the Health Service', illustrated with a photograph of PTP's Croydon hospital.[25] John Major and Tony Blair introduced more radical market-like mechanisms emphasising patient satisfaction. Renewed concern with design quality followed, and ward plans favoured individual rooms.[26] Major also introduced the Private Finance Initiative (PFI) for new buildings, embraced by Blair's Labour government in a new programme of hospital construction. In this system, developers and banks built hospitals as investments, leased back to hospital trusts with maintenance services. The state offloaded capital costs and risks and hoped for more timely and efficient construction; trusts became locked into potentially expensive long-term contracts. Architects were now employed by developers rather than NHS staff, their designs having to stand out from competitors to win contracts. Yet, PFI could reduce innovation, encouraging standardised planning and conventional construction to mitigate risk and delay.

Some of these factors are evident in PTP's 1990s hospitals. Barnet General Hospital, for example, replacing two older hospitals, received central government funding for the first phase in 1994 on condition of obtaining private finance for the remainder, completed in 2002. While its unexceptional Nucleus plan adapted standard templates, neo-Victorian facades and bright interiors suggested a 'luxury apartment feel'. One-off internal spaces gave enhanced patient and visitor facilities, including a circular reception area with restaurant and café.[27] Wishaw General Hospital at Motherwell by Peter Jarman, Harbinson, Smyth and others at the Cardiff office, was Scotland's first PFI hospital, completed with Sir Robert McAlpine in 2001, planned with a grid of specially designed T-shaped modules around courtyards (see Figure 6.3). Elevations broke down the building's bulk with a creative modern interpretation of a Scottish vernacular with slate roofs, harling and split gables, a central tower providing a 'civic focus'.[28] A second PFI project with McAlpine, meanwhile, doubled the size of Russells Hall Hospital in Dudley in a modernist style. Both, however, lost the practice money, as fees failed to cover the workload.

Glazed atria forming circulation cores characterised some celebrated hospitals; and while PTP's hospitals did not include top-lit atria, some of their circulation spaces approached that model.[29] This was especially true of the Royal Victoria Hospital in Belfast, despite the client's rejection of some neoliberal principles. The head of estate planning in the Health Estates Agency of Northern Ireland, John Cole, was also an architect, advising the RIBA and the Department of the Environment on PFI; but he largely shunned it himself, commissioning hospitals directly.[30] He kept PFI's aspect of design competition for the Royal Victoria, however, won by PTP in 1995 with local practice Ferguson McIlveen.[31] Weeks with Ron Morgan, John Santhanam and others designed the competition submission, and many others became involved; the first phase opened in 2002, Gerhard Hattingh subsequently adding a critical care centre.[32] Weeks's ability to resolve difficult briefs with easily understood diagrammatic plans and his vivid

6.3 Wishaw General Hospital (now University Hospital Wishaw), 1997–2001 (photo: John Guthrie Photography; courtesy of Willie Harbinson).

perspectives attracted the jury, centring planning on a multi-level hospital street linking an Edwardian building with new wards, operating theatres and departments, a long-standing post-war principle of hospital design. Daylight entered this circulation route from courtyards through full-height glazing, some levels two storeys high. Vivid colours and wayfinding symbols by Alice Maher and stained glass by Michael Minnis enlivened these spaces, halfway between a shopping mall and a civic building in feel. Cole wanted to demonstrate a break with older cluttered hospital architecture, an aim ultimately continuous with the post-war NHS, here expressed in late twentieth-century forms.[33]

This period was also characterised by more consumer-orientated healthcare in customised facilities, particularly for the elderly, disabled and mentally unwell, to reduce demand on hospitals. At the Manchester Royal Infirmary in the 1980s, the Manchester office designed a mental health unit and a department for the elderly and severely mentally infirm; the former a cheerful domestically scaled building including a secluded garden, the latter with a cascade of glazing in a brick block.[34] Meanwhile, in Dawlish a GP surgery built and ran a small hospital for the South Devon Healthcare Trust, engaging Sir Robert McAlpine as the PFI provider with PTP's Clifford Martin and others in 1998. It was a picturesque building resembling old-fashioned cottage hospitals, countering the anonymous modernity associated with the NHS.[35]

Private hospitals now proliferated alongside the NHS.[36] Cockayne, Nightingale and Peter Mulrenan designed an early private hospital for Bupa at Harpenden with an unostentatious red-brick courtyard building resembling a hotel or country club in a woodland setting, completed in 1982. Hotel-like wards comprised single en-suite bedrooms, and the double-height colourful reception area gave a welcoming impression, relatively luxurious design and intimate scale distinguishing it from NHS hospitals.[37] Another strand of healthcare work came from the Royal Air Force, which, through the government's Property Services Agency, commissioned PTP for medical and dental clinics on bases at Upwood and Fairford in the 1980s, shared by the United States Air Force. Designed by the Nottingham office (Allan Clark, Chris Coombs and others), they were low, hipped-roof courtyard buildings set into landscaped slopes, Fairford's clad in reconstituted stone suiting its Cotswolds setting.[38]

Thus, hospital architecture burgeoned in the late twentieth century, remaining an important aspect of PTP's practice, as despite changes of type and contract and the dispersion of state power, the political importance of the NHS persisted and approaches to hospital design developed slowly in the new generation.

While government gave up trying to standardise hospitals, it marketed decades of NHS expertise to other countries, promoting British welfare state architecture as a service export for economic and political advantages, often accompanying trade deals.[39] Around 1978 the DHSS established a marketing office, Health Buildings Overseas, assisting construction firms in obtaining work, replaced in 1981 with a similar Health Care Export Team.[40] British officials, even ambassadors, accompanied PTP architects at meetings with overseas governments, reimbursing their expenses. British architects sought overseas work systematically from the 1970s when the oil crisis scuppered much local building while stimulating development in oil-rich nations. Jennett, as PTP chairman, participated in this movement, capturing increasingly substantial work and opening overseas offices, service rewarded with an OBE.

Some newly independent nations sought expertise outside colonial relationships. In the 1970s, PTP's London, Birmingham and Manchester offices planned two teaching hospitals using the Harness system in Algeria.[41] Then, from 1980 to 1986, PTP collaborated with construction company Tarmac to build four identical hospitals in Algeria at Mascara, Tigheniff, Ghriss and Mohammadia. These hospitals used the CLASP industrialised building system invented originally by British local government architects in the 1950s for schools. Most of the Algerian hospitals' materials and components were made in Britain, and British workers flew south to build them. The CLASP system's modular concrete panels were redolent of post-war welfare state modernism; the architects added simple shading devices and shutters for the climate.[42]

Another early project was a 400-bed general hospital in the Cairo suburb of Giza, as PTP won an Egyptian government-run competition in 1976, the brief informed by the DHSS and its jury including British and French assessors. Weeks and Smyth adapted the Harness system to the small site with a high central slab block. Lower ward units ran either side, their stepped-back terraces creating an appropriately pyramidal massing, cantilevered out to shade lower levels. Harness's courtyards suited the climate, allowing shading and natural ventilation; and the architects orientated the building to minimise solar gain while giving views from wards to the ancient pyramids. Construction was postponed, but a British aid agreement of 1983 revived the project, partially completed in 1989 (see Figure 6.4).[43]

Most work flowed from the British government's interests in maintaining relationships with former colonies, as Britain sold them the tools of nation-building

6.4 Pyramids Hospital (now Al Haram Hospital), Cairo, 1976–89 (photo: Jeremy Cockayne; private collection; courtesy of WSP UK Ltd).

that it had forged at home. Hospitals were a key aspect of modern development, visible symbols of beneficent rule. After a hospital project in Kingston, Jamaica in the late 1960s and early 1970s, PTP became heavily involved in Oman with British government support.[44] Oman's ruler, Sultan Qaboos bin Said, educated at Sandhurst, was installed by a British-organised coup that toppled his father in 1970. The British government helped suppress a communist insurgency, and used hospitals to help pacify rebels. As Oman's oil revenues rose, Qaboos planned modernisation, including roads, schools and health centres.[45] In 1981 Thatcher visited him to negotiate work for British companies, one of which, notoriously, employed her son.[46] No such scandal surrounded the work gained by PTP, which was commissioned with John Laing International for a hospital for armed forces and their families at Seeb in Muscat, completed in 1985. This was an expansive two-storey building with barrel-vaulted internal streets, designed in a modernist style by Cockayne and John Rudge with deep overhangs and gridded screens for shade.[47]

In 1982, the DHSS offered to produce a healthcare plan for Muscat, and passed the job to PTP.[48] This plan proposed a district general hospital at Al Ghubrah to the south, which Qaboos nominated a Royal Hospital, to include a ward for his family, and PTP were commissioned to build it with George Wimpey International (see Figure 6.5). The 600-bed hospital on a rocky plain was designed by Cockayne, Rudge, Nightingale and others in London and Pepperell and colleagues in Cardiff; housing for 2,000 hospital workers with a sports centre and mosque were masterplanned in Cardiff and designed by the Bristol office. The hospital was arranged around an H-shaped barrel-vaulted

6.5 Royal Hospital, Al Ghubrah, Oman, 1983–7 (photo: Jeremy Cockayne; from the Collections of the National Monuments Records of Wales; courtesy of WSP UK Ltd).

corridor-street, separating diagnostic and outpatients' blocks from wards facing north to sea views, much like some of PTP's British hospitals. Complete sex segregation meant doubling many facilities, and a local custom of families accompanying patients was accommodated with an outer ring of corridors where they could camp.

Initial designs showed a horizontally layered modernist scheme with stair towers, and external colonnades for shading. During construction, however, the sultan issued a decree imposing a national Omani character on all new buildings, inducing PTP to study Arab forms. Precast concrete pieces with geometrical relief patterns and stylised cut-out arches were added to the exterior. Communal interior spaces, especially the double-height barrel-vaulted reception hall and the royal wards, were lavishly decorated in marble with Arab motifs, many designed somewhat chaotically by PTP's on-site architects Steve Crosland-Mills and Richard Mazuch. The housing also adopted modernised regional features, planned around landscaped courtyards with fountains. From commission to completion took only four years, the hospital opening in 1987.[49] Two further hospital commissions followed.[50]

In a similar diplomatic transfer of welfare state knowledge to a former colony, the DHSS shared the Nucleus system with Malaysia. Malaysia's Ministry of Public Works awarded a contract around 1990 to PTP, John Laing and Malaysian construction firm YTL for eight Nucleus hospitals, later adding another four. Simon Hopcutt, who had worked on healthcare projects in the Manchester office, and Chris Howe of the London office went to Kuala Lumpur, completing all twelve by 1995.[51] Though they were British in planning, the architects wanted them 'to look like a local building', adopting local materials and domestic forms, including pitched tiled roofs with extended eaves, first floor balconies and timber lattice screens in corridors. They adapted Nucleus to local customs, adding space for relatives accompanying patients.[52] This project followed Thatcher's cultivation of British relations with Malaysia through trade agreements and development aid, cemented when Thatcher met Malaysia's prime minister Mahathir bin Mohamad in 1989, stipulating that aid funds were spent with British businesses.[53] The exchange gave Malaysia its own possibilities for global influence, however: YTL announced in 1995 that it would now build Nucleus hospitals overseas for the Malaysian government, repeating British postcolonial policy.[54]

Meanwhile, Hong Kong, continuing as a British colony, also brought hospital work for PTP, as the practice established an office there with local architects Dominic Kwan & Associates in 1987. Howe and Hattingh joined Vincent Ng and Grace Cheng, and Peter Hughes also worked there for several years, designing hospitals in the 1990s, adapting British planning methods. Most were in the New Territories, areas developed as new towns by the Hong Kong government.[55] Funded by the Hospital Authority, they helped to resolve a paucity of welfare provision in the colony. They coincided with the British government's belated moves towards democracy anticipating the handover to China, aiming to reassure residents of Hong Kong's capacity for autonomy under future Chinese rule.[56]

Overseas healthcare work could stimulate further projects. PTP gained a foothold in Kuwait with a military hospital in the 1970s; they were then invited to enter a competition for the State Mosque in 1976; commissions for a shopping centre and private villas followed in the 1980s.[57] Meanwhile, the British Foreign and Commonwealth Office commissioned PTP for an extension to the British Embassy in Kuwait, designed around a shaded courtyard and elegantly detailed in travertine, completed in 1985.

While the British government sought to exploit welfare state knowledge for political and economic advantages, architects found themselves building substantial projects at speed in very different political and cultural contexts. Nevertheless, PTP often maintained a welfare state ethos, designing buildings to resolve complex functional needs and considering qualities of light, climate and culture for patients' benefit.

Education and the Civic Atrium

PTP's educational work dwindled in the 1980s, and in this sphere too it sought overseas work to compensate. The practice built two new university campuses in Hong Kong, both gained through competitions and funded by the Hong Kong government and the Jockey Club (regarded by the colonial government as a proxy welfare provider), aiming to raise citizens' capacity to maintain an autonomous standing in China after 1997.[58] First was the City Polytechnic of Hong Kong, won in 1983 for a new institution for 13,000 students at Kowloon Tong (see Figure 6.6). The rules required a Hong Kong practice's involvement, so Weeks collaborated closely with a former Bartlett friend, Chung Wah Nan of Alan Fitch & W. N. Chung. The Hong Kong University of Science and

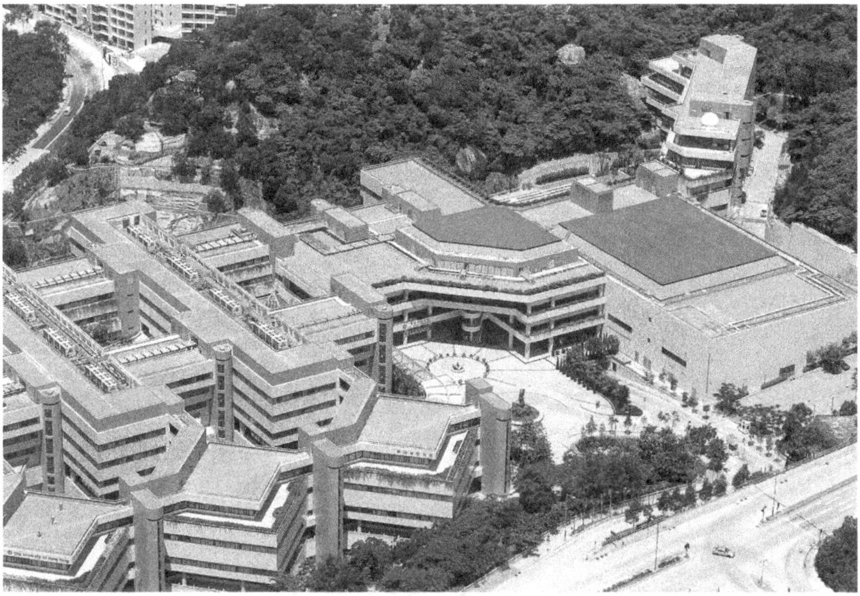

6.6 City Polytechnic (now City University), Hong Kong, 1983–8 (photographer unknown; courtesy of City University of Hong Kong).

Technology (HKUST) competition followed in 1987, for a campus for 10,000 students at a former British military base at Tai Po Tsai, for which Hattingh collaborated with Simon Kwan (see Figure 6.7). Their entry came second, but they were awarded the contract after the client controversially rejected the winning scheme. Both were built in phases into the early 1990s.[59]

Though the City Polytechnic was urban and the HKUST essentially rural on a spectacular coastal hillside, their academic buildings adopted similar design strategies. Both had height limits imposed, and although the HKUST could have been dispersed across the open site, reusing the military base foundations favoured more concentrated planning. Both projects were thus compact, complex, high-density megastructure buildings, organised around linear central routes punctuated by multistorey atria. Their almost classical symmetry and organisational clarity appealed to competition juries, much like Percy Thomas's plans half a century before. This approach magnified the post-war hospital street principle, likewise allowing expansion by envisaging extended axes and multiplied modules; some post-war university precedents may also have been influential.[60]

In both projects, atria provided orientation, circulation and generous social spaces evoking civic qualities. The City Polytechnic led visitors into the central mall under projecting concrete canopies enveloping an entrance courtyard: resembling some of Portman's buildings, it turned away from its surroundings, suggesting an internal urbanism. The HKUST, however, had a more open formal entrance on a circular piazza, bounded by a cut-out postmodern classical colonnade. Visitors entered a large glass-roofed atrium, a sociable entrance space uniting the main north-south

6.7 Hong Kong University of Science and Technology, 1987–91 (first phase) (photo: seaonweb/Shutterstock).

axis through further atria towards lecture theatres and laboratories, and the eastward route along stepped footbridges through the landscape to waterfront residential and amenity buildings. Encouraging student sociability across disciplines was important in both institutions. Chung argued that the City Polytechnic's atria related to Chinese courtyard houses, expansive and open to provide ample meeting places. Writing up the design, Hughes emphasised the HKUST architects' aims 'of providing spaces where nothing happens, where students can sit and argue'.[61] The suggestions of freedom and openness in these large complexes were politically pointed at this threshold between undemocratic British rule and the Chinese takeover. Subsequent education commissions in Hong Kong included the Open University of Hong Kong's teaching and resource centre, commissioned in 1993, and a medical school building for the University of Hong Kong, completed around 2001. Both were modernist in style, split into two parts according to function, and despite intensive density of accommodation, included intimate gardens for social interaction.[62]

In the 1990s, the Conservative government began encouraging British universities to expand competitively, with new buildings enticing students and boosting income. The state withdrew from long-term capital development, however, forcing institutions to seek alternative finance. PTP's work in this sphere was accordingly more sporadic. A new Cheltenham and Gloucester College of Higher Education, formed in 1990 from separate smaller colleges, commissioned the practice for buildings at its Cheltenham campus alongside other architects. The library, or 'learning centre', was hoped to bolster the institution's research credentials in seeking university status. Keith Mainstone, Elio Leo and others in Cardiff designed it in high-tech glass and steel with an airy atrium, but the project was shelved. The more modest Elwes Building was built to PTP's design by Hattingh and Huw Jones.[63] Completed in 1994, it gave the college a distinctive contemporary identity amid older campus buildings. A broad, top-lit double-height atrium between a lecture theatre and students' union created a new campus entrance, a teaching block behind.[64]

Labour's 1997 manifesto made education its priority, and dramatic university expansion followed. Harbinson and Embleton designed chemistry research laboratories for the University of Bristol, completed in 2000 (see Figure 6.8). This building fitted four storeys of laboratories and offices into a narrow site between older buildings on St Michael's Hill. While the laboratories took a glass and steel high-tech appearance, the rest was neoclassical, complementing George Oatley's 1950s modern classicism. While its materials and details sat well in its urban context, its individual character, with a skyline of twisted ventilation chimneys, helped the university market research facilities to students and funders, as an investment that would 'more than pay for itself' (although almost half the cost came from central government).[65]

One of PTP's last buildings was also for higher education, arising not only from Labour's renewed attention to universities but also through its location in Cornwall, a county granted 'Objective 1' status by the European Union, allowing access to regional development grants. A new university campus was a key proposal, for which several

6.8 Synthetic Chemistry Research Laboratories, University of Bristol, 2000 (photo: author).

existing higher education institutions formed a consortium in 1998, the Combined Universities of Cornwall (CUC). Central government gave about a third of initial costs, and the South West Regional Development Agency also contributed.[66] Thus, the project was linked intrinsically to regional development policies similar to those of the post-war period, though now emphasising culture and knowledge and their entrepreneurial offshoots as economic drivers over the manufacturing that previously dominated such policies.

Falmouth College of Art acquired a new site in 1999 in Penryn for the CUC's hub, completed in 2004. Jonathan Adams gave it a dynamic modern form engaging with topography, adopting local materials and considering historic precedents (see Figure 6.9). The buildings emerged from a grassy hill, a green roof intended to form an entrance approach. Under it, art and design studios formed layered terraces curved around a central courtyard, articulating the university's communal endeavour like an Oxbridge quad. Along one side, a glazed bar of teaching accommodation, mainly for sciences, rested on a castle-like bastion incorporating slices of granite boulders from a nearby quarry.[67] It was a visually arresting building promoting the institution's messages of environmental concern, creativity and technology, aimed to attract students, to epitomise a rooted but progressive identity for the county, and serving a political purpose as a regeneration flagship. Nevertheless, it maintained values in common with the post-war welfare state university: interdisciplinary socialisation, gathering spaces sustaining a communal identity; a civic ideal of a university belonging to its place; an overt modernity. Adams's approach perhaps shared much with Dale Owen's at that other hillside campus overlooking the sea arranged in terraces around a court, at Aberystwyth.

The practice's work in schools was also infrequent, but a competition win led to one of its most interesting buildings - one that, like its university work, maintained the welfare state ethos in an architectural form only superficially redolent of neoliberalism.

6.9 Combined Universities in Cornwall (now part of Falmouth University), Penryn, 2001–4 (photo: John Fielding).

The defining feature of Swanlea Secondary School at Whitechapel in London was a three-storey glazed atrium running through the building, its high-tech steel framework suggestive of shopping malls. Shortly before the project began, the Thatcher government's educational reforms encouraged schools to relinquish local authority control, supposedly to stimulate competition and individuality.[68] Tower Hamlets Borough Council, however, opposed the policy, persuading schools to remain in its orbit.[69] In building the new Swanlea school, it sought to demonstrate its willingness to continue investing in education as a fundamental function of civic welfare.

Swanlea was the first new secondary school built in London for a decade, and by this time had become urgent in this deprived borough.[70] The council already owned the site, where a planned shopping centre had stalled, and ran an architectural competition in 1990.[71] Hattingh and Ron Morgan in the PTP's London office collaborated with Hampshire County Architect Colin Stansfield Smith and his staff, then well-known for innovative schools and rigorous design research, sustaining a post-war tradition of local government innovation in school architecture.[72] The design's logical plan arranged around the central atrium and Hampshire County Council's offer of assistance with fittings and furnishings encouraged the project's selection from ninety entries, and the school was completed in 1993.[73]

Several primary schools in the previous decade adopted malls or mall-like aspects, including Hampshire's Netley Abbey Infants' School of the early 1980s, with a long glazed 'conservatory' corridor linking classrooms, forming an environmental buffer and social space. Each classroom had a pitched roof so that the building resembled a cluster of houses.[74] In 1989, meanwhile, a RIBA award went to Nelson Mandela Primary School at Aston, Birmingham by Will Howland of the City Architect's Department, with a broad top-lit atrium throughout the building forming a generous social and teaching space.[75] Swanlea School was similarly planned at a much larger scale for over 1,000 students.

The atrium roof curved over three storeys of classrooms to a two-storey range (see Figure 6.10). Classrooms had doors and windows into the atrium, expressing collaborative endeavour and connections between subjects. Ground-floor art and craft workshops displayed student work in the windows. Stairs, bridges and balconies to upper classrooms kept most circulation in the atrium, encouraging a sense of community identity and allowing supervision. The atrium's generous width gave informal gathering spaces. While elevations used yellow brick to address the hard London context, the end of the atrium projected to the street with a sheltering canopy, a welcoming gesture to encourage extended community use outside teaching times (see Figure 6.11). Boundary walls enclosed courtyards landscaped by Findlay, including an 'amphitheatre'. Stepped out classrooms with curved roofs reduced the volume into domestically scaled elements, as at Netley, though more contemporary in form.[76]

Building the atrium required technical innovations, including special glazing with internal louvres and an automatic smoke ventilation system in case of fire.[77] The elegant structure, engineered by Allan Bernau of YRM Anthony Hunt Associates, was made of tapering curved tubular steel supports, with secondary struts like tree branches. Such studies served the atrium's primary purpose, its social function, bringing the school together as a community, 'a social generator', as the council's chief education officer

6.10 Swanlea School, London, 1990–3 (photo: author).

6.11 Swanlea School, London, 1990–3 (photo: author).

called it.[78] Swanlea School's architecture thus sustained Percy Thomas's civic ethos, adapting contemporary architectural forms to an older purpose.

Infrastructural Continuities

Big government-directed infrastructure projects remained especially important to the practice, particularly in or related to Wales, with a similar political power to demonstrate national modernisation as in the post-war period. Despite increasingly involving the private sector, these projects' architectural design remained largely uncompromised, even sometimes retaining overt continuity with post-war modernism.

PTP's Cardiff office received commissions for telephone exchanges in the late 1960s and early 1970s from the Wales and the Marches Telecommunications Board, projects absorbed by the government's Property Services Agency on its formation in 1972, which then continued patronage of the practice. Large-scale modernisation of the telephone network was needed for ever-increasing telephone lines and new technology. As many exchanges were prominent structures in urban locations, architects were charged with making them more palatable. One in Swansea by Alex Gordon & Partners received heavy criticism for imposing a stark modern tower block beside the historic castle, and because its glazed curtain walls misleadingly resembled commercial office blocks rather than acknowledging its nature as 'a large box of apparatus'.[79] Balancing contextual sensitivity and modern design principles was fundamental to infrastructure projects throughout the second half of the twentieth century.

PTP's Cardiff telephone exchange, completed about 1976 next to the existing post office, occupied a similarly prominent site in the city centre between the rugby stadium and St Mary Street, and a tall building was similarly needed. The architects made it more elemental than Gordon's at Swansea - a simple box on a low plinth, articulated with vertical glazed slots between strips of concrete cladding. More dynamic and almost church-like was their slightly earlier 'Chartist' telephone exchange and engineering services building at Newport, whose open interiors were wrapped in white concrete blockwork with rippling vertical piers.[80] A decade later PTP extended an older exchange in Barnstaple, now for state corporation British Telecom, with an equally inventive oval drum of brick with slot windows, playfully alluding to the Norman castle keep formerly on the hill behind it.[81]

PTP's most important infrastructure project of this period was the Second Severn Crossing. Though initiated by the state, with new approach roads paid for by the Treasury, the bridge was given over to the private sector using PFI. Bridges of the 1960s, including the Severn Bridge, demonstrated that tolls could finance construction, making them potential financial investments. The government even bundled the original Severn Bridge into the Second Severn Crossing's PFI contract, though cannily set terms under which the bridges would return to the state after thirty years. The Conservative government viewed the Second Severn Crossing as a model for future road projects and passed the New Roads and Street Works Act in 1991 to enable private companies to build and manage roads along similar lines.[82] Welsh MPs (including a Conservative) boycotted a ceremony to mark work beginning in 1992, however, decrying increased tolls as 'a uniquely unfair penalty to Wales'.[83]

Like the Severn Bridge, the Second Severn Crossing arose through pressure from Welsh local government and industry. The original bridge often had traffic restrictions, sometimes closing in high winds, and when its engineers discovered in 1983 that heavy modern lorries could induce catastrophic failure, their access was restricted and disruptive strengthening undertaken. Welsh proponents argued that, in a south Wales ravaged by job losses in the recession following Thatcher's election, recovery depended on better road connections, and the promise of a second bridge would stimulate inward investment.[84]

A feasibility study in 1986 recommended the route south of the existing bridge, and engineers G. Maunsell & Partners and W. S. Atkins devised an 'illustrative design', an outline scheme of two long curved approach viaducts flanking a central cable-stayed bridge over the shipping channel.[85] Companies bidding for the contract had to present more developed designs as well as financial arrangements. The winner, announced in 1990, closely adhering to the illustrative design, was a collaborative venture between Laing and French builders GTM, their engineers Sir William Halcrow & Partners (notably David Mizon) and SEEE of France, with PTP as architectural consultants.[86] The crossing was built within budget and on schedule from 1992 to 1996 (see Figure 6.12).

Weeks, with John Santhanam, collaborated with the engineers in refining the design. Weeks's presentation images showing the bridge in its estuary landscape helped reassure residents and local authorities in consultations. The Royal Fine Art Commission commented on design iterations, concerned to ensure a harmonious and coherent form, after the strongly criticised design inconsistencies of the Queen Elizabeth II Bridge at Dartford, another early PFI project completed in 1991.[87] The two different bridge types

6.12 Second Severn Crossing (now Prince of Wales Bridge), 1989–96, viewed from Sudbrook (photo: author).

of which the crossing was composed, the precast viaducts and the cable-stayed centre span, thus had to be unified. Weeks persuaded the engineers to adopt a consistent 33-metre module for pier spacings, using it to drive other aspects of the design, such as cable positions. The form of suspension piers for the cable-stayed bridge helped to provide a unifying feature, with two reinforced-concrete rugby-post piers tapered in two gradients to accentuate their slenderness and emphasise stability, chamfered edges catching lines of light and shade, braced by crossbars with angled ends echoing the viaduct geometry. The viaducts of precast box-beams leaned outwards to emphasise their supporting purpose, their top outside edges inflected inwards to give a continuous light line along the deck. The piers rose from oval caissons, necessary to withstand tidal currents, the transition between piers and foundations modelled with the same pyramidal geometry as other elements. The Commission insisted on maintaining these subtle refinements when the contractors became nervous of their cost.[88]

Colour, too, was important: the cable-stayed bridge's steel deck trusses were a deep blue-green, differentiating them from the concrete viaduct; lamp posts were cyan; the windshield was light green; and the cables were a paler green, a graded colour scheme applied only to metallic elements, complementing the landscape and the warm beige concrete.[89] Weeks and Santhanam also designed the toll booths and control building a mile into Wales reprising aspects of the bridge, with a metallic canopy across the road suspended from doubled piers.[90]

The approach throughout was consistent with post-war architectural modernism and modern motorway infrastructure, gently modulating engineering forms for visual harmony and simplicity, expressing its purpose and structural forces. There is also a notable affinity between the bridge's geometries and those that Weeks employed at Clifton Cathedral. The Royal Fine Art Commission's official oversight encouraged such continuity.[91] The absence of visible signs of the new procurement method for state infrastructure perhaps sought to reassure sceptics that high standards could be maintained. Of similar scale, the PTP submitted three entries to the Department of Transport's competition for a new road bridge in Poole Harbour in 1997. This project was more overtly neoliberal in generating multiple novel and dramatic designs; it was, however, aborted by the following Labour government.[92]

Contractually more conventional was the Flintshire Bridge over the river Dee near Shotton, funded by Clwyd County Council and the Welsh Office and opened by the Queen in 1998 (see Figure 6.13). The bridge created a bypass around Shotton for traffic between Lancashire and north Wales, and gave access to a new business park at Shotton's former steel mill, a victim of the early 1980s recession. This development belonged to a new network of business parks to generate economic revival, overseen by the Welsh Office and the Welsh Development Agency.[93] The bridge had a psychological and symbolic function, therefore, promoting local optimism and indicating a high-skilled industrial future. The county council initiated a competition, selecting engineers Gifford Graham & Partners, who later appointed PTP to refine their design, as they had recently worked with Weeks on the small tubular steel Jackfield Bridge in the Ironbridge Gorge in Shropshire.[94] For Flintshire, the engineers determined an asymmetrical cable-stayed bridge with inverted Y-shaped tower, a landmark against surrounding industrial dereliction. Weeks and Santhanam introduced a three-dimensional taper to the pylon

6.13 Flintshire Bridge, Connah's Quay, 1990–8 (photo: Toby Driver; aerial photograph 6459081 Connah's Quay Road Bridge is Crown copyright and is reproduced with the permission of the Royal Commission on the Ancient and Historical Monuments of Wales (RCAHMW), under delegated authority from the Keeper of Public Records).

and refined the deck profile, made in crisp white concrete. Cables were pastel green and barriers of aluminium. They designed elegant lamps and arranged floodlights in the tower to light the structure, enhancing its visual drama.[95]

One project did suggest a new approach for privatised infrastructure: a sewage treatment works in Swansea. Welsh Water was created from the privatised Welsh Water Authority in 1989, becoming Hyder as it diversified into other utilities. The government imposed on water companies a duty to improve sewage treatment standards after the European Commission notoriously publicised Britain's coastal pollution. Swansea's proposed new treatment works were planned at the eastern end of its docks alongside other regeneration schemes. Residents' concerns about appearance and smell forced Hyder to conceal the works, and they commissioned Pepperell and PTP's Cardiff office to use architecture and landscape to make it palatable. Most of the plant was thus sunk under a landscaped hill against a long retaining wall, the first completely covered sewage plant in Britain when completed in 1998 (see Figure 6.14). A wooded parkland was planted on top, designed by Sue Radley and Findlay, flowing over circular lightwells like half-buried pavilions. A control tower on the wall contained a visitor centre and meeting rooms, acting as a distinctive landmark, pointing south over Swansea Bay and shaped like a ship's bridge (influenced by Nicholas Grimshaw's ship-like Western Morning News and RAC buildings). Hyder used the plant to market its expertise, PTP's landmark element and green landscaping giving it a contemporary image as a form of branding. That commercial function became redundant when Hyder was taken over and broken up and Welsh Water became a non-profit company, while

6.14 Swansea Wastewater Treatment Works, 1994–9 (photo: author).

the role of the architecture and landscape in making public infrastructure partly invisible and, where visible, palatable and meaningful, remained.[96]

Industry, Science and Government

The Cardiff office continued to undertake many industrial projects in Wales, in a relationship with the state that also remained largely continuous. When the Welsh Development Agency (WDA) was founded by the Welsh Office in 1976, it absorbed the Welsh Industrial Estates Corporation, and maintained its aim to diversify industry into highly skilled fields, especially technology, compensating for heavy industry's decline. The WDA's approach shifted from encouraging English firms to open branches to attracting overseas companies while nurturing local enterprise. Independent, but funded by the Welsh Office, it could intervene in the market while allowing government to appear more distant. Thatcher appointed an opponent of her neoliberalism as Secretary of State for Wales in 1979, Nicholas Edwards, who supported the WDA's role. The Development Board for Rural Wales (DBRW) (the Mid-Wales Development Board from the mid-1980s) undertook a similar role in central Wales, and both commissioned work from PTP.[97]

Inherited by the WDA from the Industrial Estates Corporation, one project aimed to offset steel closures by expanding the Hoover factory at Abercanaid. The extension was built opposite the interwar building across the river, linked by a new pedestrian footbridge. Completed in 1980, it comprised a vast open-floored factory, four-storey offices and a cafeteria, designed for new production lines promising 3,000 new jobs. Mainstone and colleagues, with Arup Associates, unified disparate elements with consistent materials of brown brick and upper parts of red-painted metal cladding.[98] Modernist concerns persisted: simple outlines, comprehensible articulation by function, harmonious materials and a memorable image. Hoover, however, changed its mind, announcing several thousand job cuts instead, though it moved its headquarters from Perivale to the new offices. The WDA marketed the empty factory as 'Dragonparc' for several years.[99] This project perhaps warned the WDA that new strategies were needed.

A more postmodern form of creative industry company was Laura Ashley, based at Carno in Powys since the 1960s, selling a nostalgic Victorian lifestyle image through fashion design and textiles, though it also manufactured its own products in Wales and overseas. In 1984 the firm played offers from the Netherlands and Britain against each other for a new textile and wallpaper printing factory, accepting a proposal from the DBRW and the Welsh Office that included construction of the factory in Newtown.[100] The building was designed by Dale Owen with Mainstone and Arnot Hughes: their sketch design contributed to the company's decision to expand in Wales, and it opened in 1987 (see Figure 6.15). Owen argued that the building's design could help create 'a new image in Mid Wales' for the company, which wanted a building of architectural significance.[101] Glazed purple bricks gave monumentality; traditional tile hanging reflected the rustic, patterned aesthetic of the company's products, and related to Newtown's historic buildings. The combination of traditional imagery with

6.15 Laura Ashley factory, Newtown, 1985–7 (photo: Jeremy Cockayne; Glamorgan Archives; courtesy of WSP UK Ltd).

the interior's technological design for advanced machinery satisfied the company's paradoxical modern traditionalism.[102]

The most important of the practice's Welsh industrial buildings of this period originated with a nationalised company in the 1970s, the Radiochemical Centre. Founded in 1940 in Amersham by Patrick Grove and acquired by the government in 1946, the Radiochemical Centre produced radioactive chemicals, mainly for medical and scientific use, especially in hospitals. In 1973 it found a second site for expansion at a planned new motorway junction at Whitchurch north of Cardiff. Grove and Cardiff branch manager John Maynard approached Mainstone that year, and Mainstone appointed Pepperell as job architect. The first phase of building was completed in 1978, and later phases continued into the mid-1980s, Pepperell and younger colleagues taking over (see Figure 6.16). PTP's buildings enabled the company to increase output especially for profitable exports, making it an easy pilot for privatisation in 1982, when it rebranded itself as Amersham International.[103]

The company wanted to demonstrate its modernity to passing motorists. Glass-reinforced plastic cladding gave a smooth, curved-edged outline and distinctive colours, sandy yellow for the main buildings, chocolate brown for the bar of services across the top, a recessed red stripe between, mirrored glazing reflecting lawn and trees, suggesting an advanced scientific character. Three 50-metre chimneys for fume dispersal were gathered into a vertical element as purple tubes supported by a white concrete pylon. Subsidiary buildings also had a shiny, curved modern aesthetic, including two conjoined rotundas housing staff amenities and offices. Finely detailed curved brick stair and service towers punctuated the complex throughout.[104]

6.16 Radiochemical Centre (later Amersham International), Cardiff, first phase, 1975–8 (photo: Hylton Warner; from the Collections of the National Monuments Records of Wales; courtesy of WSP UK Ltd).

The planning was logical and legible. At the company's Amersham site, chaotically accumulated buildings hindered staff interaction. Visiting the government's Atomic Energy Research Establishment at Harwell, to which the Radiochemical Centre was linked, Mainstone and Pepperell discovered a corridor where chalkboards encouraged staff exchange, suggesting the potential to stimulate community and interdisciplinary knowledge.[105] The hospital 'street' principle (also carrying services in the Harness and Nucleus systems) likely also influenced the architects' thinking, and the Cardiff complex centred around a long spine building connecting different elements. Ramps and glazing gave a dynamic interior, dotted with tea bars and informal meeting spaces. The circular office and amenity blocks were at the spine's western 'head', production and laboratory blocks at the centre, and engineering, storage and power units terminated the eastern end. Amersham International became an important symbol of Welsh industry's diversification towards highly specialised technology, alongside Richard Rogers's Inmos microprocessor factory in Newport (the latter a WDA project). The Inmos building was dissimilar, but its externally expressed central spine 'street' echoes PTP's building, and PTP's subsequent 1980s blocks at Amersham International were inspired by it in return.[106]

PTP worked in the following decade for British Airways (BA), another state company privatised by Thatcher's government in 1987.[107] By 1991 significant restructuring projects included moving Boeing 747 aircraft maintenance to Cardiff Airport, and the Avionics Engineering department from Heathrow to Llantrisant, where both became subsidiary companies also servicing other airlines.[108] The WDA offered the Llantrisant site and prepared it for building, probably recommending PTP's Cardiff office and Arup Associates, though John Major misleadingly implied central government responsibility when announcing the project on an election visit to Wales in 1992.[109] Opened from 1992 to 1994, the Avionics Engineering centre repaired and replaced electronic equipment, from flight instruments to catering ovens, using computerised storage and retrieval for rapid turnover. It comprised three buildings designed by Pepperell and colleagues in a curve, each comprising two rectangular wings housing workshops, offices and stores, angled to enclose an atrium (see Figure 6.17). The double-height atria provided informal social spaces including a café and restaurant, threaded together with walkways. Intensive servicing was hidden in roof spaces designed with wing-like sections reflecting the building's purpose; pipes, access stairs and entrances were detailed like sculptural machines. The new buildings contributed to BA's commercial profitability, while their striking appearance raised the WDA's profile as an agent of Welsh modernisation.[110]

More innovative, attempting to nurture Welsh high-technology enterprise, was the WDA's 'Technium' project. The first Technium opened at Swansea in 2001, the WDA collaborating with the University of Wales, Swansea for a building combining small business premises with support services and access to the university's research staff. Designed by the Powell Alport Partnership of Cardiff, its glass-clad modernism gave it a contemporary presence on a 'sexy' docklands site to attract technology and software entrepreneurs.[111] The Welsh government became enthusiastic, allocated funds and obtained European grants, plotting nine further Techniums around Wales.[112] Responding to a cluster of companies specialising in optoelectronics (such as lasers,

6.17 British Airways Avionics Engineering Centre, Llantrisant, 1991–3 (photo: author).

fibre optic cables and photovoltaics), the WDA commissioned PTP for the Optronics Technology and Incubator Centre (or OpTIC) Technium at St Asaph business park in north Wales, partnering with Bangor University and the North East Wales Institute of Higher Education at Wrexham.[113] The WDA demanded a creative, flagship building with an exemplary sustainable approach, to entice youthful entrepreneurs and promote its own image after recent management scandals. Whether Technium costs justified the jobs created was much debated; but the OpTIC's architecture made a visually optimistic statement of the devolved government's interventionist approach, with political and cultural significance (see Figure 6.18).

Matt Jones articulated the building's core functions: business support, a two-storey block projecting over the entrance containing offices, meeting rooms and lecture theatre and a flanking curved café; a technology centre with shared laboratories and workshops; and lettable business spaces disposed along a glazed atrium 'street' where occupants could socialise.[114] A screen wrapped over the frontage forming a service tunnel, clad with solar panels, appropriately for the Technium's specialism, part-funded as an experiment by the Department of Trade and Industry. Although critics wondered whether they were a marketing ploy, the range of sustainable features including water recycling and biodiverse landscaping by Findlay and Radley earned it *Building* magazine's first UK Sustainable Building of the Year award in 2005. Materials included timber cladding and walls of Welsh slate blocks.[115]

PTP occasionally received industrial and laboratory commissions in England. One was a small chemical factory and laboratory complex at Birch Vale near the Peak District for polymer manufacturer Briggs & Townsend, completed around 1980 by Philip Bintliff with an unusually playful postmodern use of ordinary materials, bright

6.18 OpTIC Technium, St Asaph, 2002–4 (photo: the Photolibrary Wales/Alamy).

colours, bubble-shaped windows, and an arched trellis used as applied ornament.[116] Later, the practice's laboratory expertise attracted two English government projects. The first, in the mid-1990s, was a secure, hermetically sealed laboratory building for the Ministry of Defence at Porton Down near Salisbury, by John Garrard, Peter Kendall and others in Cardiff.[117] The second was one of PTP's most complicated and substantial projects, the National Physical Laboratory (NPL) at Teddington, for the Department of Trade and Industry.

The Conservative government privatised the NPL's operation in the 1990s, but advanced laboratories were much needed to replace older buildings, and these remained within the Department of Trade and Industry's ownership.[118] A PFI process that was begun in 1997 was a controversial failure. Serco and John Laing won bidding with a joint company called Laser – Laing as builder and Serco to take over as operator. Laing hired Weeks at PTP's London office, who approached design with his habitual logical rigour: laboratories and offices formed two parallel rows, one canted outwards to fit the site; between them ran a spine containing administration, computing, meeting rooms, library and restaurant. Two unroofed passages separated the spine from the parallel laboratory blocks, planted with trees and crossed by bridges. Weeks used a consistent elevational language of gridded glazing, white-clad blocks and colonnades, curved into a rotunda for the entrance.[119] Modular repetition allowed laboratories to be sequentially completed and occupied. Curved roofs housed servicing, but plant machinery sat in attached units, preventing heat and vibration from entering laboratories.

The NPL's work included sensitive measurement, requiring precise temperatures and minimal sound and vibration, but flaws in the services and construction quality made some laboratories inadequate, and the Department of Trade and Industry imposed remedial measures.[120] By 2000, Laing declared enormous losses, and, incurring similar losses at the Millennium Stadium in Cardiff, it sold its construction business to a rival.[121] The PFI arrangement broke down and the government hired another contractor.[122] While the state obtained a cheap building at the builder's expense, it had to revert to conventional capital funding, and completion was six years late: the National Audit Office concluded that 'All parties got less from the project than they had hoped'.[123] Nevertheless, the NPL was finally completed in 2007, a striking monument to government-sponsored science.

Thus, in its industrial and scientific work PTP depended largely on the welfare state's continuation of government support for industry, while also working for state-owned institutions behaving like companies or undergoing privatisation. The bold modernity of the practice's architecture promoted government agency or a company's purpose, and often both at once.

Corporate Atriums

Much the same was true of the PTP's work in commercial and corporate design, as the state emulated the commercial sphere. Here, too, the atrium came to prominence, as at Swanlea School expected to act as a social condenser, and as at Amersham International knitting together large, complex workplaces. Moreover, commercial and office schemes had important relationships with neoliberal planning policies, stimulated by competing forms of state management of urban space.

The practice undertook much straightforward retail design in this period, including work for Sainsbury's that culminated in a substantial Savacentre hypermarket in 1989.[124] Pepperell and colleagues at Cardiff designed the seventh and hitherto largest branch at London Colney near St Albans, when such out-of-town big-box American-style retail developments proliferated as the Conservative government relaxed planning restrictions. Opened in 1990, the Savacentre's main volume comprised a typically banal shop floor, fronted by a mall running across its width under a glass roof, described as a 'market street' containing smaller shops and a restaurant. Structural glazing and distinctive signage gave a contemporary appearance, attracting consumers, its modernity contrasting with the kitsch aesthetic of the market-style shops.[125]

In this period, new policies of city centre regeneration emerged in which PTP participated. Thatcher's government promoted urban transformation through 'enterprise zones', areas provisionally released from much planning legislation and taxation, where the market was invited to generate wealth through competitive capitalism. Urban Development Corporations oversaw these projects, adapting administrative mechanisms from post-war New Towns, often in uneasy relationships with local authorities, which proposed enterprise zones but often lost power over them.[126] The first round of enterprise zones approved by Secretary of State for the Environment Michael Heseltine in 1981 included Swansea, where PTP were not much involved, and Dudley, where they were. Dudley's Labour council hoped enterprise zone status would revive its steel industry, but instead the steelworks was demolished and replaced with the Merry Hill shopping mall.[127] Its developers Roy and Don Richardson then planned a waterfront project on the adjacent Dudley canal. Their architect Trevor Brown of Level Seven sketched offices and shops in 1988, detailed in cheerful brick and metal ornament by Neil Graham and others of PTP's Birmingham office. Ironically, the recession made it difficult to let, and government agencies moved in, including the Inland Revenue.[128] PTP added a landmark office block in the 1990s, Point North, with a sociable courtyard and multistorey atrium entrances to impress potential tenants.[129]

When the government designated another enterprise zone in Salford and Trafford, Salford City Council added its own competing, complementary development alongside it called Salford Quays in the redundant Manchester Docks, using central government grants for rehabilitating derelict inner-city land to provide roads, bridges and waterfront walkways.[130] PTP's Manchester office won a bid with developer Amec in 1989 for a prominent office complex, the Anchorage, employing a simplified warehouse style in red brick cladding. Sitting between a new tram stop and the dock, it incorporated a nine-storey public atrium on the axis of the basin.[131]

Parc Tawe in Swansea was a small dock development also by its council, largely a banal city centre retail park by PTP for developer Citygrove. As a planning condition, however, the council insisted on a civic element, which the architects designed as a pyramidal glasshouse for the council's use as an indoor botanical garden. Opened in 1989, Plantasia was described as the largest tropical greenhouse in Britain outside Kew. Bintliff designed it with a crystalline form in structural glazing, developed by Mainstone, Arnot Hughes and Glyn Parker with a simpler tubular steel structure (see Figure 6.19).[132] This civic facility looked intrinsically part of its commercial surroundings, characteristically for this council enthusiastic for development schemes, including its local enterprise zone.[133]

Office complexes became a mainstream activity for PTP in the 1980s and 1990s. Most were business offices, but their first and last significant projects of this type were for government ministries. These derived from campaigns to move central government departments from London to provincial towns, programmes started by Labour in the

6.19 Plantasia, Swansea, *c.*1988–90; Swansea telephone exchange in background (photo: author).

1960s and renewed by Thatcher. Such relocations saved money, demonstrated fiscal responsibility for political purposes, and could boost skilled employment in deprived areas. For Conservatives, relocations also helped suggest a slimmer, more businesslike state bureaucracy.[134] Government offices resembling business buildings borrowed aspects of corporate culture, conveying impressions of efficiency and modernity.

When the Board of Trade's Business Statistics Office moved from London to Newport in the early 1970s, the Property Services Agency employed PTP for its offices, designed by Mainstone for phased occupation by 2,500 staff (see Figure 6.20). It was planned on a modular grid as a series of diagonally linked courtyard blocks, with a communal amenity block between them and a separate computer building. Pepperell detailed them with modern ribbon windows flush with brown brick walls, punctuated by stair towers, their interiors sharply contemporary.[135] An angular metal sculpture at the entrance conveyed the image of a corporate headquarters.

Conversely, one commercial office project became more public. Guardian Royal Exchange Assurance acquired Victorian and Edwardian buildings near Queen Street station in Cardiff and hired Weeks and PTP's London staff to replace them, one element an eleven-storey office tower clad in glass curtain walling. Wales Gas, then still a state corporation, decided to make the building its headquarters around 1981, and staff at PTP's Cardiff office designed its interiors and negotiated design elements with Weeks, introducing a regional control centre.[136] Thus, a speculative commercial development became a public utility landmark.

Several office complexes adopted the atrium as the driving planning principle, initially for companies, and then also for the government. One was a new headquarters for Esso, a company that the practice had worked for occasionally since the 1950s, which wanted to expand away from the constraints of its London offices.[137] Weeks and Peter Mulrenan won a competition of six invited architects for a site on the

6.20 Business Statistics Office (now Office for National Statistics), Newport, 1972 (unknown photographer; from *Percy Thomas Partnership Architects & Planning Consultants: Composite Brochure No. 2*, n.d.; author's collection; courtesy of WSP UK Ltd).

6.21 Esso Headquarters, Leatherhead, 1984–90 (photo: Jeremy Cockayne; from the Collections of the National Monuments Records of Wales; courtesy of WSP UK Ltd).

Leatherhead motorway junction in 1984, and it was completed in late 1990, involving others including Pepperell, Santhanam and Steve Crosland-Mills (see Figure 6.21).

The architects justified the atrium as increasing daylight to workspaces and emphasised its social purpose, creating a corporate community culture with a sense of belonging. Mulrenan, a graduate of the Welsh School of Architecture, had experience of office atrium designs from a period of work at Skidmore, Owings & Merrill in America, and architects and clients toured the United States studying similar buildings.[138] The atrium rose between two linear blocks of offices and laboratories, widening in the centre to give social as well as circulation space, including a restaurant, and it was roofed with a glazed tubular steel space frame. This building for an oil company logically extended PTP's work designing the fossil fuel-based industry and infrastructure that enabled the welfare state and twentieth-century economic development; but the Esso headquarters was more typical of post-Fordist capitalism, as a high-skilled scientific and administrative node in a global corporation, set in bright, sociable surroundings largely masking the nature of the company's functions.[139] With a similar use of the atrium as a 'social street', Pepperell and the Cardiff office designed a smaller office building in Little Chalfont for Amersham International's administrative staff in the mid-1980s. Its diagonal atrium opened up the interior of an otherwise low and simply detailed brick block, kept modest to avoid overpowering a residential neighbourhood.[140]

The culmination of these atrium office buildings was a huge project relocating the Ministry of Defence Procurement Executive from several sites across England to Filton near Bristol, supposedly the largest civil service relocation until then, and the biggest office project in Britain since Canary Wharf, accommodating nearly

6,000 staff.[141] The move allowed the government to claim long-term savings and followed defence reductions adjusting to the post-cold-war world, responding to the House of Commons Defence Select Committee report, 'Options for Change' of 1990.[142] The Procurement Executive organised armed forces equipment and supply, from aircraft carriers to catering; its 'New Management Strategy' accepted government policies to increase private sector involvement, and sought to make procurement 'more market-orientated' and businesslike. It proposed restructuring as a smaller, more flexible administration, mixing up staff from different armed services and departments, to be continually reformed into transient teams.[143] Offices were accordingly open plan, designed by PTP Seward with wheeled partitions for rapid layout changes.[144] John Rudge and Clifford Martin led the project from 1992 until completion in 1996 and architects from across the practice were involved. Architects Scott Brownrigg & Turner collaborated on detailed design and construction (see Figure 6.22).

Environmental qualities were carefully studied. Daylight penetration, solar shading, natural ventilation with opening windows, high insulation and long-lived heat-absorbing materials were important and visually evident. Crisp Portland stone cladding on south elevations enclosed bands of deep-set windows, contrasting with ribbon-windowed curtain walls on north sides. The setting by PTP Landscape evoked science parks or university campuses, presenting a friendly outward face, with an elegant white

6.22 Ministry of Defence Procurement Executive offices, Filton, Bristol, 1994–6 (photographer unknown; from the Collections of the National Monuments Records of Wales; courtesy of WSP UK Ltd).

cable-stayed bridge crossing a lake, the attractive water feature doubling as a security barrier.[145]

Four atria placed across the site united clusters of parallel blocks of offices, which extended beyond the atria, some angled to enclose landscaped courts. This arrangement emulated Neils Torp's SAS headquarters in Stockholm of the late 1980s, which Rudge and the client visited, where one irregular street-like atrium connected several U-shaped offices.[146] PTP's atria, though more uniform, provided distinct 'neighbourhoods' with 'central avenues', promoting an intimate sense of community (see Figure 6.23). As at Leatherhead, each atrium widened into a 'piazza' containing a café, complementing the complex's central formal restaurant. Bridges crossed the atria under tent-like canopies, and balconies and meeting spaces opened into them, making them a focus of activity. The atrium could be justified pragmatically through environmental and cost benefits - internal elevations dispensed with watertightness and insulation, and surrounding offices gained daylight. These advantages helped convince the client to adopt it for its social and organisational effects, helping the Ministry of Defence to dissolve departmental silos and encourage new connections.

6.23 Ministry of Defence Procurement Executive offices, Filton, Bristol, 1994–6 (photo: Jeremy Cockayne; from Jo Doyle, *Percy Thomas Partnership HK: Selected and Current Works* (Victoria: The Images Publishing Group, 1998); author's collection; courtesy of WSP UK Ltd).

The Filton complex indicated a new conception of government work as akin to business, 'a new, non-bureaucratic culture', as one critic wrote, emulating post-Fordist flexibility.[147] Nevertheless, the aim of coordinating staff on one site for efficiency recalls the municipal offices Percy Thomas designed several generations earlier. The use of Portland stone, similarly, evoked pre-war government architecture, now detailed unashamedly as thin cladding, and justified as economically and environmentally advantageous.

PTP's work for commerce and corporate administration demonstrates complex relationships between government and the private sector, the state guiding and aiding private development while building for its own administration and emulating corporate practices. Nevertheless, despite political and social change, architects and their clients remained idealistic about the potential of architectural form to achieve social effects. The atrium was redolent of consumerism and modernity and environmentally practical, but organisationally akin to the inward-focused spaces of Percy Thomas's early buildings - and like them, was thought able to stimulate social exchange and shared identity.

Civic Assembly

Two important projects in this neoliberal period between the governments of Thatcher and Blair were civic responses to new political and economic conditions: the International Convention Centre in Birmingham and the Wales Millennium Centre in Cardiff. In this new era of a supposedly shrinking state, free-roaming capitalism, enterprise zones and postmodern neo-historical urban regeneration, municipal authorities adopted new strategies and architectural forms. Nevertheless, both projects suggest more fundamental continuities with Percy Thomas's pre-war civic architecture.

The International Convention Centre (ICC) demonstrates perfectly this dual allegiance: a public institution built for citizens' welfare, promoting new sources of prosperity in a globalised economy. The building manifested this duality and housed the spaces in which both approaches awkwardly converged, appearing both modern and postmodern, socialist and capitalist, monumental and fragmented. It confirms notions of neoliberal entrepreneurial city governance and accompanying postmodern urbanism, while subverting that narrative with a basis in twentieth-century municipal thinking.[148]

The model of an interventionist local government established by Birmingham's late nineteenth-century Liberal mayor Joseph Chamberlain remained especially powerful in his own city, where politicians invoked his memory throughout this period. The ICC, indeed, originated in the expansion of Birmingham's Victorian civic core westwards in the 1930s, when councillors had hoped to build a concert hall.[149] In 1970, John Madin, architect of the Central Library, submitted a sketch design for a 2,500-seat concert hall opposite the new Repertory Theatre, depicting a brutalist building with a public foyer onto the civic square.[150] Even elements of the project more commonly associated with neoliberal attitudes also originated in earlier proposals. The council considered in the 1960s acquiring and rebuilding a commercial Victorian trade exhibition hall just west of the theatre.[151] Bingley Hall burnt down in 1984, freeing the site for the ICC, and as by then the council had built the National Exhibition Centre, a conference venue seemed a more appropriate function.[152] Leisure facilities on the waterways behind the site were also proposed in the 1960s.[153]

The ICC's site and brief were thus largely in place when the new circumstances of the 1980s finally triggered the project. By then Birmingham's economy, dependent on heavy industry, had been devastated by the recession, and the council hoped to diversify it into services and tourism, changing the city's image.[154] Conservative council leader in the early 1980s Bernard Zissman argued that employment in restaurants or hotels was as worthy as factory work; and that while manufacturing moved elsewhere, companies would still need to sell products to western markets. A national shift from manufacturing to services seemed, moreover, part of Thatcher's plan.[155] The convention centre and concert hall were thus loaded with a deeper significance.

Consultants recommended an American convention centre model with integral hotel to attract large businesses, a type not yet built in Europe; they predicted tens of thousands of new jobs and a transformed city image. It would make a continuous loss, however, so had to be regarded as an investment in wider prosperity.[156] The council, with cross-party agreement, decided in 1983 to build the ICC itself, giving the task to its National Exhibition Centre company, overseen by a council committee.[157] Central government refused funding, but classified the city centre as an assisted area to make it eligible for the European Commission's Regional Development Fund, which awarded a grant in 1986.[158] As the European grant covered economic development but not civic projects, the concert hall was disguised as 'Hall 2', described as a venue for speeches seating over 2,200, incidentally suited to music. The ICC was thus fundamentally civic in conception, though adapting to neoliberal culture.

John Vergette of PTP, working initially with Trevor Martin and Hattingh, invited theatre specialists the Renton Howard Wood Levin Partnership (RHWL) (notably architects Robin Derham, Nicholas Thompson and Tony Williams) to form a joint company, the Convention Centre Partnership. The council committee accepted their outline proposals in 1985, narrowly rejecting Richard Rogers.[159] As design work progressed, the partnership deteriorated and roles diverged: Vergette with Rudge, Pepperell and Neil Graham of PTP took over coordination and most of the design, allocating the hotel and several conference halls to RHWL. Graham with Huw Heywood, Rob Firman, Judith Isherwood and others of PTP designed Symphony Hall. Pepperell and colleagues from Cardiff also designed exteriors and many of the canalside buildings. It was an enormous and complex project involving up to eighty architects from each practice at once.[160]

Symphony Hall was the ICC's prestige element when it opened in 1991 (see Colour Plate 7). For acoustic isolation it was sited furthest from an underground railway tunnel, and located to the east to make it prominent on the civic square. Its multistorey foyer looked out over the square through faceted glazing, though the positioning of its main entrance inside the complex gave it an unintentionally inaccessible appearance (partly the reason why this façade was recently demolished). Its interior received the most concentrated design effort of the ICC. American acoustic consultants Artec, led by Russell Johnson, were appointed even before the architects on the advice of City of Birmingham Symphony Orchestra conductor Simon Rattle.[161] Johnson favoured the classical 'shoe-box' form, outlining a symmetrical, tall narrow space with apsidal ends and tiered seating, following his work at Morton H. Meyerson Symphony Hall in Dallas designed by I. M. Pei.[162] Graham and Heywood worked with Johnson and Nicholas Edwards of Artec and Arup Associates as engineers to perfect the acoustic performance through design. Geometries of reflections determined the apsidal plan, and surfaces of concrete, polished plaster and wood reflected sound. Over the stage, concrete doors opened into huge voids to adjust reverberation, positioned over a 'cascade' of shelves reflecting sound back to performers. A movable canopy and wall panels further shaped the sound. Using models and computer studies, Arup's engineers designed silent air conditioning through balcony frontages. The structure was isolated from its surroundings, a double shell of reinforced concrete sitting on neoprene pads on piled foundations, with gaps between all its materials and the rest of the ICC. The hall was silent to the threshold of human hearing, its acclaimed acoustics attracting international musicians.[163] Its interiors were rich in surface treatment, emulating old theatres and referencing musical instruments using wood and chrome; red columns evoked local terracotta and brick; and horizontal banding suggested Art Deco opulence, continued on the ICC's exteriors.[164] Everything else at the ICC was subservient to this impressive civic space.

The other ten halls took a range of sizes and forms: Hall 1, designed by RHWL and PTP, especially Firman, was a large auditorium allowing theatre performances, with raked seating for 1,500, a proscenium stage and flytower; Hall 3, by Pepperell's team with RHWL, was a large octagon suiting exhibitions or banquets, roofed with a steel space frame; PTP's square Hall 4 was for meetings, banquets or dances. The remaining halls, mostly by RHWL, were smaller, including a lecture theatre behind Symphony Hall; four to the west could be let as a separate group. Architecturally, all were rather neutral, with advanced technical facilities to attract international users, and a kitchen serving feasts for thousands of guests besides everyday catering.[165] RHWL's glass-clad tower block hotel for the American Hyatt hotel chain, awkwardly diverging from the ICC's monumentality, connected to the complex by a footbridge (see Figure 6.24).[166]

Running right through the ICC from the civic square to the canal behind it was a glass-roofed mall (see Figure 6.25). Early proposals lined it with shops, restaurants and cafés, but only a handful of outlets were finally included.[167] Diagonal geometries opened out informal social foyer spaces for Symphony Hall and the convention halls, where Piranesian angled staircases and escalators led to a reception area. The mall's tubular steel structure was crossed by diagonal bridges and by Symphony Hall's air conditioning tubes. This space borrowed from the architectural language of shopping malls, positioning Symphony Hall in an apparently commercial setting.[168] Like American convention centres, the mall turned the ICC largely inwards, leaving exteriors oppressively blank. Yet the mall was public-spirited in conception. The council's planners had previously stipulated a public route through the site, and by roofing it and integrating it into the scheme, the architects hoped to 'encourage the maximum use of the Centre by the public as an attraction and amenity'. The council hoped, too, that Symphony Hall would arrange informal musical entertainments in the mall.[169] Once completed, the council insisted on permanent public access, even at night: classifying it as a street necessitated imposed licensing restrictions on its bar, requiring the architects to add barriers to contain drinking. Residents could use the

6.24 International Convention Centre, Birmingham, 1983–90 (photo: Steven Roe/Alamy).

6.25 International Convention Centre, Birmingham, 1983–90 (photo: author).

mall as a shortcut, mingling with concert goers and conference delegates.[170] The mall was part of the city fabric, not a counterpart to it.

The ICC was part of a much larger urban development. It completed the 1930s civic square, renamed Centenary Square in 1989 to celebrate Birmingham's city status, paved in carpet-like patterns by artist Tess Jaray, with further artworks commissioned for the square and the mall in collaboration with the architects, many evoking Birmingham's industrial past.[171] The road separating Centenary Square from the older civic centre was lowered into a cutting, a footbridge over it restoring pedestrian movement along Symphony Hall's axis, unifying a civic complex of monumental buildings of the nineteenth and twentieth centuries.[172] The ICC's grey granite and cast Portland stone cladding, in places articulated as rustication, with continuous horizontal lines in red granite echoing Jaray's paving, gave a monumental presence harmonising with older civic buildings in Portland stone.[173]

To the west, the ICC's character adjusted to the different context of the canal, newly opened up with pedestrian access down steps and ramps designed by Pepperell and PTP Landscape in red brick complementing surviving industrial buildings. Here, urged on by the council's Conservation Areas Advisory Committee, Pepperell's team restored a listed Georgian brewery master's house as a creche. Their red brick Energy Centre aimed to restore the character of Victorian warehouses demolished around it, and a neo-Victorian iron suspension footbridge connected the mall to development sites over the canal. Two Victorian pubs were retained, and the ICC's bulk drawn in around them. Though fundamentally modern, therefore, in its conception of a vast urban intervention optimistically intended to resolve social and economic problems, the ICC also had an opposing aspect, reinventing the city's industrial heritage for picturesque consumption.[174] Beyond the canal, Brindleyplace later bristled with postmodern office blocks and a festival marketplace leisure area of restaurants and cafés, modelled on Baltimore's heritage harbourside, a paradigm of postmodern urbanism, Terry Farrell taking over its masterplan from PTP's initial proposals.[175] PTP were also executive architects to American practice HOK for the National Indoor Arena to the north, a sports venue funded by the Sports Council and the city, also opened in 1991.[176]

The ICC was a relatively early example of the neoliberal and civic postmodern urbanism that became common for post-industrial waterside regeneration, and the template was also followed at Cardiff Bay, where PTP designed one of its last major projects, the Wales Millennium Centre (WMC). The WMC represents a fitting culmination to this history of the practice, and through it of twentieth-century architecture, as a neoliberal flagship project that also represents a moment of national fulfilment in Percy Thomas's hometown, the Welsh capital. Yet this building, too, reveals internal contradictions: it was sited in an enterprise zone, but dependent on state funding; it emerged out of controversy, with an architecture aimed to assuage critics, much like Tunbridge Wells Civic Centre. The WMC's design explored themes of place and community, both civic and national, its architects explicitly recalling Thomas's civic architecture. It too suggests continuities across the practice.

The Thatcher government established the Cardiff Bay enterprise zone in 1986 after a proposal by Glamorgan County Council to the Secretary of State for

Wales, Nicholas Edwards, hoping to revive the redundant Bute docks and surrounding areas. The enterprise zone was managed by the Cardiff Bay Development Corporation, chaired by Geoffrey Inkin. The project was painfully slow because Edwards insisted that central government pay for an expensive, ecologically destructive barrage across the bay to convert its tidal mudflats into a lagoon, considered more appealing to developers and consumers. It was completed only in 1999 against strong opposition.[177]

Edwards and the Development Corporation centred the regeneration scheme on an Opera House for Welsh National Opera.[178] A competition awarded Zaha Hadid the prize in 1994 for a radical design with oblique geometries, and PTP became involved soon after, chosen by her to develop the scheme.[179] Hadid's role ended in 1995 when the Millennium Commission, created by John Major to award large grants from the National Lottery to celebratory schemes for the year 2000, rejected the Cardiff Bay Opera House Trust's bid, leaving a funding gap. A lack of local consensus had been fatal, as key figures including Inkin and local MP Rhodri Morgan opposed the project, and the city council pointedly won a rival bid for the new Cardiff rugby stadium.[180]

A new committee formed the following year to revive the project controversially returned to PTP.[181] The brief remained similar, but rebranding as the WMC suggested a national character and avoided elitist overtones, and the Millennium Commission finally granted funding. PTP, led by Rudge and Graham, sketched a new high-tech design, changing the project's image and quelling controversy.[182] Hadid's basic idea of an auditorium embraced by ancillary buildings remained, without her plan's permeable transparency, and the architects shaped the auditorium and flytower into a single curved volume.[183] The Royal Fine Art Commission condemned it, however, and funding problems forced a rethink.[184] In early 1998, Jonathan Adams approached the practice from Alsop & Störmer, known for its distinctive pop postmodern style, and Rudge appointed him to work on the project. Adams's reshaping of the design inspired public enthusiasm when published that summer.[185] He realised the potential for the building to encapsulate a Welsh identity, just as Welsh devolution had been sanctioned by the Labour government's referendum, promising a new national government.[186] In 1998, the Welsh Assembly building's site was chosen next to that of the WMC, charging the latter with a new national cultural significance.

Adams's design, developed with an extensive project team led by Firman, dramatised the two main elements, the auditorium and its enclosure (see Colour Plate 8).[187] The auditorium was shaped into a beacon-like vessel, tilted forward over the entrance like a canopy, clad in riveted metal sheets evoking the ships and industries of south Wales. Into this surface was cut an inscription in Welsh and English composed by poet Gwyneth Lewis celebrating the building's purpose as a crucible of creativity, the lettering style inspired by David Jones, a reminder of language and literature's significance to Welsh culture.[188]

Surrounding the auditorium was an enclosure of thick stone walls of randomly laid slate blocks, recalling Sir Percy Thomas & Son's slate panels at Bangor, and intended to suggest Glamorgan's coastal cliffs with horizontal lines of strata and vertical breaks between planes. The architects selected stones from north Wales quarries and brought north Wales masons to Cardiff to erect the walls against an inner concrete plane.[189] Running through the slate like quartz seams were translucent structural glass blocks devised by artist Rodney Bender and the Architectural Glass Centre of the Swansea Institute of Higher Education.[190] Adams realised that slate could vividly convey a Welsh identity, influencing many others, including the Richard Rogers Partnership, which adopted it for the Welsh Assembly building's podium.[191] The Welsh theme continued throughout the WMC, with Welsh hardwoods cladding internal balconies and stairs and black metal lamps modelled on fossils of prehistoric plants in Welsh coal mines. The entrance door handles were designed by Ann Catrin Evans to represent farmers' sickles and flowing rivers.[192] The WMC melded romantic Welsh ingredients into an accessible and coherent image. It was, said Adams, 'designed for this place and this time and the language of these people'.[193]

This strength of image bolstered the WMC's funding negotiations. Delays arose as the National Lottery grant was insufficient, site problems became evident, and the contractor withdrew.[194] The architects reduced and simplified the design and the Welsh Assembly was asked for help.[195] Welsh ministers debated the scheme, and as several Assembly members opposed it for concentrating culture in the capital, supporters had to justify its benefits for the wider nation.[196] One of the WMC's occupants was Urdd Gobaith Cymru, a venerable youth organisation promoting Welsh culture and language, allotted its own theatre inside and a hostel wing to accommodate 120 children from across Wales.[197] Geraint Talfan Davies, meanwhile, as chairman of the Welsh National Opera, argued that the opera company was a global cultural ambassador for Wales.[198] Other occupants included Diversions, the national dance company of Wales; and Academi, an organisation promoting Welsh writing.

The civic element, however, remained important, with space for local arts, theatre and dance organisations; and when delays prompted the landowner to sell the site, the city council bought it for the WMC.[199] Adams's design attracted city politicians formerly opposed to the Opera House, as it evoked earlier civic buildings like those of Percy Thomas. The lettering, Adams argued, derived from 'the classical tradition' of texts over civic porticos; and 'to have the necessary civic presence', he wrote, 'it had to be built from stone'.[200] Like Swansea Guildhall's arch and stair, the auditorium sheltered a broad entrance inviting public access to a generous foyer. Inspired by the Royal Festival Hall in London, Adams lifted the auditorium above the ground floor to create this open space.[201] Two three-storey 'concourse' spaces flanked the foyer, wrapped in curved balconies. Both were atrium-like, the deeper north concourse lit with clerestories, creating informal gathering and performance spaces.

The auditorium, designed with theatre consultants Carr & Angier and acoustic advice from Arup, stacked its nearly 2,000 seats intimately around the stage on balconies in a flattened horseshoe configuration (see Figure 6.26). Walls were clad in sculptural gypsum blocks, dispersing sound; their terracotta colour and banded arrangement gave a cave-like interior enveloping the audience as a unified body. The stage could extend over the stalls to bring performers amid the audience. Architects and clients sought forms that encouraged consciousness of participation in a public sphere as a closely bound community.

6.26 Wales Millennium Centre, Cardiff, 1996–2004 (photo: Sarah J. Duncan; courtesy of WSP UK Ltd).

The WMC's directors may have been aware of the ceremonies inaugurating Percy Thomas's Temple of Peace (the Welsh National Opera's chairman until 2000, for example, was David Davies of Llandinam, its founder's grandson). Through similar dramatic events the WMC sought to imbue its building with meaningful associations. The first slate block laid in January 2003 was supposed to travel by boat around the coast from the quarry, encompassing Wales, though bad weather forced a helicopter journey instead. Bryn Terfel, the opera singer and former Urdd member, was greeted by Morgan, now First Minister, and laid the stone; a Cardiff choir sang Welsh folk songs.[202] The Queen, Duke of Edinburgh and Prince Charles attended opening performances in November 2004; but to emphasise popular involvement, the WMC allocated half the first gala performance's seats to the public through a free draw. Morgan declared at the opening ceremony that the Centre was 'not just for the elite but for all of Wales'.[203] Ann Catrin Evans designed the key that opened the building, which arrived in Cardiff after a journey around the world.[204] As at the Temple of Peace, the person who turned the key was a woman representing the ordinary people of Wales, Janet Thickpenny of Barry, chosen through a local newspaper competition.[205] These ceremonies, like PTP's architecture, sought to elide conflicts over place, class and culture to create a broad consensus around a shared Welsh national identity. Although participating in a typical government-orchestrated neoliberal enterprise zone and surrounded by commercial development, therefore, the WMC harked back creatively, architecturally, socially and politically, to a time of civic and national urban institutions.

Conclusion

The atrium and atrium-like focal spaces represented a repeated motif throughout the practice's work in this period, as in much other contemporary architecture. PTP's work demonstrates that this feature had broad origins and purposes that contradict any simplistic reading of the atrium as a neoliberal or commercial form. One origin was the modern movement planning principle of the spine corridor, which helped organise complex plans and made them legible to users, sometimes becoming more expansive in later hospitals and used for similar purposes in industry. But such features had a deeper purpose within modernism that continued into the late twentieth century, of bringing people together at a central core to encounter each other and freely interact during everyday movement, allowing the members of an organisation - and in Birmingham's case the citizens of a city and its visitors - to perceive themselves as a single organism, and thereby to generate a community. PTP's late twentieth-century work demonstrates a persistence of the modernist ethical belief that architecture could perform a socially unifying function.

The neoliberal political shift complicated the background, the ways these aims were effected and some of the reasons behind them. Yet PTP's work, particularly when viewed from Wales, demonstrated deeper continuities in many levels and arms of the state, as the idea that the state should build the spaces of welfare, citizenship and the productive economy remained powerful. The practice's architecture continued to serve the state, therefore; but the question of the nation that it served became far more complex - as the practice worked abroad on behalf of British diplomacy or colonialism; and as Britain, despite ever greater integration in some spheres, became politically and culturally more fragmented. As the idea of a Welsh nation became stronger and more tangible than at any previous time in the century, PTP's architecture helped to articulate its identity and contributed to the spaces in which its own national destiny could be worked out. ■

06
Architecture and the Neoliberal State
References

1. Margaret Thatcher, 'Press Conference after Winning Conservative Leadership', 11 February 1975, Margaret Thatcher Foundation, *www.margaretthatcher.org/document/102487* (accessed 5 July 2022).
2. Neil Brenner, *New State Spaces: Urban Governance and the Rescaling of Statehood* (Oxford: Oxford University Press, 2004), pp. 172–3; Sam Wetherell, *Foundations: How the Built Environment Made Twentieth-Century Britain* (Princeton NJ: Princeton University Press, 2020), pp. 11–12; Kenny Cupers, Catharina Gabrielsson and Helena Mattson, 'Introduction: Undead Neoliberalisms', in Kenny Cupers, Helena Mattsson and Catharina Gabrielsson (eds), *Neoliberalism on the Ground: Architecture and Transformation from the 1960s to the Present* (Pittsburgh PA: University of Pittsburgh Press, 2020), pp. 1–15 (3).
3. Fredric Jameson, *The Cultural Turn: Selected Writings on the Postmodern, 1983–1998* (London: Verso, 1998), for example, pp. 3, 19–20, 141–2, 152–3; Brenner, *New State Spaces*, pp. 161–5; David Harvey, *The Condition of Postmodernity: An Enquiry into the Origins of Cultural Change* (Cambridge MA: Blackwell, 1990), pp. 147, 155–6.
4. For example, Richard Vinen, *Thatcher's Britain: The Politics and Social Upheaval of the 1980s* (London: Simon & Schuster, 2009), p. 285.
5. Brenner, *New State Spaces*, pp. 4, 15–16, 166, 218–19.
6. For example, Emily Robinson and others, 'Telling Stories about Post-War Britain: Popular Individualism and the "Crisis" of the 1970s', *Twentieth Century British History*, 28/2 (2017), 268–304 (268–70, 273–8); Otto Saumarez Smith, 'Action for Cities: The Thatcher Government and Inner-City Policy', *Urban History*, 47/2 (2020), 274–91.
7. Leon Gooberman, *From Depression to Devolution: Economy and Government in Wales, 1934–2006* (Cardiff: University of Wales Press, 2017), pp. 116–18, 123–4, 127; Vinen, *Thatcher's Britain*, pp. 211–14.
8. Jameson, *Cultural Turn*, pp. 159–61; Amy Thomas, 'The Political Economy of Flexibility: Deregulation and the Transformation of Corporate Space in the Postwar City of London', in Cupers, Mattsson and Gabrielsson (eds), *Neoliberalism*, pp. 127–50 (137–8).
9. For example, Margaret Crawford, 'The World in a Shopping Mall', in Michael Sorkin (ed.), *Variations on a Theme Park: The New American City and the End of Public Space* (New York: Hill and Wang, 1992), pp. 3–30 (29).
10. Harvey, *Condition of Postmodernity*, p. 80; Trevor Boddy, 'Underground and Overhead: Building the Analogous City', in Sorkin (ed.), *Variations on a Theme*

Park, pp. 123–53 (138, 140–41); Charles Rice, *Interior Urbanism: Architecture, John Portman and Downtown America* (London: Bloomsbury, 2016), pp. 24, 34, 41.

11. Richard Saxon, *Atrium Buildings: Development and Design* (London: The Architectural Press, 1986).

12. Alistair Fair, '"Modernization of Our Hospital System": The National Health Service, the Hospital Plan, and the "Harness" Programme, 1962–77', *Twentieth Century British History*, 29/4 (2018), 547–75 (575).

13. Paul James and Tony Noakes, *Hospital Architecture* (Harlow: Longman, 1994), p. 140.

14. James and Noakes, *Hospital Architecture*, p. 130.

15. Mike Nightingale, video interview with the author, 2 March 2021.

16. John Knape, video interview with the author, 19 March 2021.

17. Cockle, telephone interview with the author, 28 May 2021.

18. Richard Mazuch, video interview with the author, 15 March 2021; Knape, interview, 2021; Cockle, interview, 2021; RCAHMW, PTA 03/13, practice brochure, n.d. [c.1985]; Nightingale, interview, 2021; Mazuch, interview, 2021; Peter Mulrenan, video interview with the author, 17 December 2021; RCAHMW, PTA 03/05, photograph album, 'MRI Phase II', n.d.

19. 'Colchester Hospital Completed', *Percy Thomas Partnership: Review*, 1985, unpaginated, author's collection.

20. RCAHMW, PTA 03/13, practice brochure, n.d. [c.1985]; 'Hospitals 1: Research and Development – Thinking About Design', *Architects' Journal*, 21 July 1982, pp. 65–71 (66); untitled article, *Architects' Journal*, 18 April 1984, p. 35; 'A Right Royal Day', *Suffolk Free Press*, 23 May 1985, p. 21; Nightingale, interview, 2021; Julian Cockayne, telephone interview with the author, 3 March 2021; Mazuch, interview, 2021.

21. James and Noakes, *Hospital Architecture*, pp. 136–40; Jo Doyle, *Percy Thomas Partnership HK: Selected and Current Works* (Victoria: The Images Publishing Group, 1998), p. 70; RIBAL, Percy Thomas Partnership Biographical File, 'City General Hospital: Stoke-on-Trent', *Percy Thomas Partnership: Review*, 1984, unpaginated.

22. W. Paul James and William Tatton-Brown, *Hospitals: Design and Development* (Architectural Press, 1986), p. 59; 'Hospitals 1: Research and Development – Thinking About Design', *Architects' Journal*, 21 July 1982, pp. 65–71 (65); 'Anthology of British Architecture', *Journal of the Royal Institute of British Architects*, March 1981, pp. 26–61 (51); RCAHMW, PTA 03/13, practice brochure, n.d. [c.1985]; 'Twenty-One Years with PTP', *Percy Thomas Partnership: Review*, 1985, unpaginated, author's collection; 'Hospital Plans Mooted', *Central Somerset Gazette*, 14 May 1981, p. 5; Michael Alford Andrews, 'Viréndra Sahai, 1933–2014', *RIBA Journal*, 15 September 2015, *www.ribaj.com/culture/viren-sahai-1933-2014* (accessed 12 July 2022).

23. RCAHMW, PTA 03/13, practice brochure, n.d. [c.1985]; RIBAL, Percy Thomas Partnership Biographical File, 'Mid-Sussex Hospital Topping Out', *Percy Thomas Partnership: Review*, 1988, unpaginated.

24. Alex Mold, 'Making the Patient-Consumer in Margaret Thatcher's Britain', *The Historical Journal*, 54/2 (2011), 509–28; Victoria Bates, 'Cold White of Day: White, Colour, and Materiality in the Twentieth-Century British Hospital', *Twentieth Century British History*, 34/1 (2023), 1–37.

25. Conservative Party, *Our First Eight Years: The Achievements of the Conservative Government since May 1979* (London: Conservative Central Office, 1979), pp. 12–13.

26. Mold, 'Making the Patient-Consumer', p. 525; Derek Stow, 'Transformation in Healthcare Architecture: From the Hospital to a Healthcare Organism', Michael Davis, 'Financing Hospital Investment' and Paul Hyett and John Jenner, 'Rebuilding Britain's Health Service', in Sunand Prasad (ed.), *Changing Hospital Architecture*, pp. 13–48 (49–45), 65–100; and 101–52; Paul Jones, 'Private Finance Initiative Hospital Architecture: Towards a Political Economy of the Royal Liverpool University Hospital', *Sociology of Health & Illness*, 40/2 (2018), 327–9; Nightingale, interview, 2021; Ian Newton, telephone interview with the author, 11 February 2021.

27. Barnet London Borough Council, *https://publicaccess.barnet.gov.uk/online-applications/files/1C9556298B91227C80930F0382504A0D/pdf/N01070AH-Other_Documents-443531.pdf* and *https://publicaccess.barnet.gov.uk/online-applications/files/3A44D5F864F5B7364D4AEA3B160A5C51/pdf/N01070AH-Other_Documents-454551.pdf*, 1997 (accessed 15 July 2022); Peter Scher, 'Barnet General Hospital, Phase 1A', *Hospital Development*, February 1998, pp. 21–4; Mark Hellowell, 'A Tale of Two Hospitals', *PFI Report*, March 2002, pp. 12–13.

28. 'Scotland's Yards', *Hospital Development*, October 2001, pp. 16–22; Peterjohn Smyth, Curriculum Vitae, n.d. [c.2004], architect's archive; Harbinson, video interview with the author, 18 March 2021; Peter Q. Kendall, correspondence with the author, 28 June 2021.

29. On the atrium hospital and neoliberalism, Robin A. Kearns and J. Ross Barnett, 'Consumerist Ideology and the Symbolic Landscapes of Private Medicine', *Health & Place*, 3/3 (1997), 171–80; Annmarie Adams, David Theodore, Ellie Goldenberg, Coralee McLaren and Patricia McKeever, 'Kids in the Atrium: Comparing Architectural Intentions and Children's Experiences in a Pediatric Hospital Lobby', *Social Science & Medicine*, 70/5 (2010), 658–67.

30. Deborah Singmaster, 'A Vision for Belfast', *Architects' Journal*, 6 March 1997, pp. 22–3.

31. David Taylor, 'Percy Thomas Wins Belfast Royal Victoria Hospital Job', *Architects' Journal*, 21 September 1995, p. 16; David Taylor, 'AJ100', *Architects' Journal*, 21 March 2002, pp. 39–69 (50) (incorrectly stating that this was the PFI).

32. Gerhard Hattingh, video interview with the author, 3 March 2021; Ron Morgan, video interview with the author, 9 March 2021; John Knape, video interview

with the author, 19 March 2021; John Santhanam, telephone interview with the author, 1 April 2021; John Garrard, video interview with the author, 12 May 2021.

33. Paul Larmour, 'The Royal Revolution', *Perspective: The Journal of the Royal Society of Ulster Architects*, February 1996, pp. 37–55; Linda Brooks, 'Royal: A Healthy Improvement', *Perspective: The Journal of the Royal Society of Ulster Architects*, March 2002, pp. 40–9; Tim Graham, 'The Art of the Medic Machine', *Touchstone*, August 2004, pp. 18–21.

34. RCAHMW, PTA 03/05, photograph album, 'MRI ESMI Unit'.

35. 'GPs to Run Private Finance Hospital', *Pulse*, 14 March 1998, p. 8; Clifford Martin, interview with the author, Bristol, 16 April 2021.

36. 'Hospitals 1: Private Sector – Going Private', *Architects' Journal*, 21 July 1982, pp. 71–5; Mike Nightingale, 'Buildings Update: Health-Care Buildings – 1. The NHS in the Market-Place', *Architects' Journal*, 29 March 1989, pp. 65–8.

37. 'BUPA Hospital, Harpenden', *Percy Thomas Partnership: Review*, 1982, unpaginated, Philip Bintliff archive; RIBAL, Percy Thomas Partnership Biographical File, 'BUPA Hospital: Harpenden', *Percy Thomas Partnership: Review*, 1984, unpaginated; Anthony Williams, 'BUPA Hospital, Harpenden', *Building*, 9 March 1984, pp. 35–42.

38. RCAHMW, PTA 03/13, practice brochure, n.d. [c.1985]; RCAHMW, PTA 03/95, photographs of Upwood clinic, 1987; 'A Piece of Cake: United States Air Force Award for RAF Fairford Clinic', *Percy Thomas Partnership: Review*, 1985, unpaginated, author's collection; Chris Coombs, video interview with the author, 22 March 2021.

39. E.g. on Richard Llewelyn Davies and government export of planning expertise, Guy Ortolano, *Thatcher's Progress: From Social Democracy to Market Liberalism through an English New Town* (Cambridge: Cambridge University Press, 2019), pp. 87, 94–5, 184–211.

40. Howard Goodman, 'Health Buildings Overseas', *Architects' Journal*, 21 June 1978, p. 1190; P. Ward, 'Architecture for Export', *Architects' Journal*, 13 September 1978, p. 462; Stephen Games, 'Four Studies Abroad', *Architects' Journal*, 7 July 1982, pp. 38, 43; 'Hospitals 1: Research and Development – Thinking About Design', *Architects' Journal*, 21 July 1982, pp. 65–71 (65).

41. RCAHMW, PTA 05/06, *Percy Thomas Partnership International* (locations not specified); Ortolano, *Thatcher's Progress*, pp. 202–4; James and Tatton-Brown, *Hospitals*, p. 39.

42. RCAHMW, PTA 03/13, practice brochure, n.d. [c.1985], unpaginated; Barry Russell, 'CLASP Reappraisal', *Architects' Journal*, 16 May 1984, pp. 51–72; David Kimmins, 'For Richer Not Poorer', *Architects' Journal*, 27 February 1991, pp. 18–19; 'Four Standard Hospitals, Mascara, Algeria', *Archnet*, n.d., *https://www.archnet.org/sites/4385*, accessed 19 July 2022.

43. 'Pyramid Therapy', *Architect*, December 1976, pp. 31, 36–7; RCAHMW, PTA 03/13, practice brochure, n.d. [c.1985], unpaginated; 'The Week', *Architects'*

Journal, 1 September 1976, p. 385; 'Overseas', *Architectural Review*, January 1986, pp. 71–9 (75); Neil Embleton, video interview with the author, 9 March 2021.

44. RCAHMW, PTA 05/06, *Percy Thomas Partnership International: Architects & Planning Consultants*, n.d. [c.1974], unpaginated; RCAHMW, PTA 03/13, practice brochure, n.d. [c.1985], unpaginated; Cockle, interview, 2021.

45. Sarah G. Phillips and Jennifer S. Hunt, '"Without Sultan Qaboos, We Would Be Yemen": The Renaissance Narrative and the Political Settlement in Oman', *Journal of International Development*, 29/5 (2017), 645–60.

46. 'TV Interview for LWT Weekend World ("The Second Term")', 15 January 1984, Margaret Thatcher Archive, *www.margaretthatcher.org/document/105503* (accessed 20 July 2022); 'House of Commons PQs', 15 March 1984, Margaret Thatcher Archive, *www.margaretthatcher.org/document/105638* (accessed 20 July 2022); David Leigh, 'Return to the Spotlight for Sir Mark', *Guardian*, 12 April 2013; Mark Twain, 'The Trouble with Mark', *Daily Telegraph*, 5 October 2015.

47. '£48m Hospital in Oman', *Financial Times*, 7 February 1983, p. 7; RIBAL, Percy Thomas Partnership Biographical File, 'Military Hospital, Oman', *Percy Thomas Partnership: Review*, 1984, unpaginated; 'Percy Thomas Partnership: Architects', practice brochure, n.d. [c.1994], author's collection; Ian Pepperell, telephone interview with the author, 19 February 2021; Nightingale, interview, 2021; John Rudge, video interview with the author, 2 March 2021; Cockayne, interview, 2021.

48. RIBAL, Percy Thomas Partnership Biographical File, '500 Bed Hospital: Gubrah Oman', *Percy Thomas Partnership: Review*, 1984, unpaginated; RCAHMW, PTA 03/13, practice brochure, n.d. [c.1985], unpaginated.

49. Graham Ridout, 'Kind Hearts and Minarets', *Building*, 1 January 1988, pp. 30–4; 'A Royal Hospital: The Royal Hospital, Sultanate of Oman', *Concrete Quarterly*, March 1988, pp. 18–21; James and Noakes, *Hospital Architecture*, pp. 82–5; RCAHMW, PTA 03/13, practice brochure, n.d. [c.1985], unpaginated; RCAHMW, PTA 03/78, photographs; RIBAL, Percy Thomas Partnership Biographical File, '500 Bed Hospital: Gubrah Oman', *Percy Thomas Partnership: Review*, 1984, unpaginated and 'Royal Opening for Royal Hospital', *Percy Thomas Partnership: Review*, 1988, unpaginated; Mike Nightingale, 'Buildings with Information Technology 2: Hospitals', *Architects' Journal*, 20 June 1984, pp. 81–3; Pepperell, telephone interview, 19 February 2021; Nightingale, interview, 2021; Cockayne, interview, 2021; Mazuch, interview, 2021; Steve Crosland-Mills, telephone interview with the author, 1 December 2021.

50. 'A Cooperative Effort Meets a Very Tight Timescale: Sohar Hospital Submission, December 1984', *Percy Thomas Partnership: Review*, 1985, unpaginated, author's collection; Pepperell, interview with the author, Cardiff, 23 August 2022.

51. 'Malaysian Hospitals', *Financial Times*, 13 August 1990, p. 10; Percy Thomas Partnership, 'Percy Thomas Partnership: Architects', n.d. [c.1994], unpaginated, author's collection; Percy Thomas Partnership, 'Percy Thomas Architects and Planners', n.d. [c.2001], author's collection; Cockle, interview, 2021.

52. James Macneil, 'Hospital Transplant', *Building*, 22 July 1994, pp. 50–1.

53. Colin Brown, 'Malaysian Trade Ban: Hurd Says Deals and Aid Were Entangled', *Independent*, 26 February 1994, p. 2; Robert Ledger, 'The Road to Pergau Dam: Aid Policy, Ideology, and the Thatcher Government', *Diplomacy & Statecraft*, 30/1 (2019), 50–69; on earlier context, for example, N. J. White, 'The Survival, Revival and Decline of British Economic Influence in Malaysia, 1957–70', *Twentieth Century British History*, 14/3 (2003), 222–42; Frances E. Hutchinson, 'Malaysia's Independence Leaders and the Legacies of State Formation under British Rule', *Journal of the Royal Asiatic Society*, series 3, 25/1 (2015), 123–51.

54. Amy Balan, 'A Powerful Giant in the Making', *Business Times (Singapore)*, 14 May 1994, via Nexis; 'YTL to Export Malaysian Nucleus Hospital Design', *Business Times (Malaysia)*, 23 February 1995, p. 6.

55. See, for example, 'Giant Strides Still Leave a Long Way to Go', *Financial Times*, 21 June 1982, Property, p. xiv; 'North District Hospital', *Percy Thomas Partnership: Review*, n.d. [c.1994], unpaginated, author's collection; Doyle, *Percy Thomas Partnership*, pp. 20–5.

56. Eliza W. Y. Lee, 'The Politics of Welfare: Developmentalism in Hong Kong', in Huck-ju Kwon (ed.), *Transforming the Developmental Welfare State in East Asia* (Basingstoke: Palgrave Macmillan, 2005), pp. 118–39; Nathalie Roseau, 'The Shape of Things to Come: Hong Kong's Infrastructural City Fabric, 1989-2020', *Planning Perspectives*, 37/2 (2022), 369–99 (e.g., 374).

57. RCAHMW, PTA 05/06, practice brochure, 'Percy Thomas Partnership International: Architects & Planning Consultants', n.d. [c.1974], unpaginated; Peter Mulrenan, video interview with the author, 17 December 2021.

58. John Rawson, 'The Dragon Is Coming', *Architects' Journal*, 23 January 1991, pp. 30–9 (33).

59. 'Hong Kong Winner Mark Two', *Architects' Journal*, 6 July 1983, p. 25; RIBAL, Percy Thomas Partnership Biographical File, 'City Polytechnic of Hong Kong: Hong Kong', *Percy Thomas Partnership: Review*, 1984, unpaginated and F. S. J[ennett], 'Hong Kong University of Science and Technology Buildings', *Percy Thomas Partnership: Review*, 1988, unpaginated; 'Far East Farce', *Architects' Journal*, 6 January 1988, p. 12; 'Hong Kong Campus Double Honours', *Architects' Journal*, 4 April 1990, p. 12; Hattingh, interview, 2021.

60. 'Student Exchange: Hong Kong University of Science and Technology', *Building Journal Hong Kong China*, September 1991, pp. 58–68; Robin Forster, 'The Hong Kong University of Science & Technology', *Arup Journal*, Spring 1993, pp. 3–9; Charlie Q. L. Xue, *Hong Kong Architecture 1945-2015: From Colonial to Global* (Singapore: Springer, 2016), pp. 203–9, 219–22; Doyle, *Percy Thomas Partnership*, pp. 10–17, 38–45.

61. 'Student Exchange', p. 66.

62. 'Hong Kong Open Learning Institute', *Percy Thomas Partnership: Review*, n.d. [c.1994], unpaginated, author's collection; Doyle, *Percy Thomas Partnership*, pp. 24, 26-31; Angela Tam, 'Advanced Learning: The University of Hong Kong

Faculty of Medicine', *Building Journal Hong Kong China*, January 2002, pp. 28–35; Hattingh, interview, 2021.

63. 'Magnificent 7 Ride Into Town', *Architects' Journal*, 18 September 1991, p. 9; Ruth Owens, 'Cheltenham Goes for Excellence', *RIBA Journal*, December 1992, pp. 24–7; Colleen Hope and Claire Clench, video interview with the author, 10 February 2021; Elio Leo, telephone interviews with the author, 22 February and 4 March 2021; Arnot Hughes, interview with the author, Cardiff, 23 August 2022; Pepperell, email to the author, 6 September 2022.

64. David Verey and Alan Brooks, *Gloucestershire 2: The Vale and The Forest of Dean*, The Buildings of England (London: Yale University Press, 2009), p. 248; ADP, *New Media Facility, Park Campus, University of Gloucestershire: Design and Access Statement*, January 2011, Cheltenham Borough Council planning portal, *https://publicaccess.cheltenham.gov.uk/online-applications/files/10976C4BC89B3DBD18498C24265CF7AB/pdf/11_00022_FUL-DESIGN_AND_ACCESS_STATEMENT-373382.pdf*, accessed 23 August 2022.

65. Naomi Stungo, 'The Right Chemistry', *RIBA Journal*, April 2000, pp. 48–54; Deborah Singmaster, 'Chemistry Class', *Architects' Journal*, 22 June 2000, pp. 8–9; Harbinson, interview, 2021.

66. 'Charles Champions University Campaign', *Western Morning News*, 23 June 1998, p. 3; 'Battle On for a Proper University', *Western Morning News*, 24 June 1998, p. 10; 'Cornwall Still Needs to Make a Supreme Effort', *Western Morning News*, 1 July 1998, p. 10; Colin Gregory, 'Progress Report on Use of Objective One Cash', *Western Morning News*, 21 June 1999, p. 15; 'Cash Injection Helps Campus: Regional Development Agency Invests £1.5 Million in College', *Western Morning News*, 14 December 2000, p. 16; Clare Morgan, 'Cornwall Gets £19 Million for New University', *Western Morning News*, 7 May 2001, p. 1.

67. 'Site is Selected for Cornwall University', *Western Morning News*, 8 February 2000, p. 2; Zoë Blackler, 'PTP Rises to £40 Million Cornish Challenge', *Architects' Journal*, 2 May 2002, pp. 6–7; 'Projects Harmonise the Old and the New', *Western Morning News*, 13 March 2003, p. 12; Brian Cole, 'Combined Universities in Cornwall', *Concrete*, August 2004, pp. 42–3; 'Unique Design for Learning', *Western Morning News*, 5 October 2004, p. 36; 'Combined Universities of Cornwall, Tremough Campus', *Concrete*, December 2005, pp. 48–9; Jonathan Adams, video interview with the author, 12 February 2021.

68. Ian Gilmour, *Dancing with Dogma: Britain Under Thatcherism* (London: Simon & Schuster, 1992), p. 205.

69. Tower Hamlets Local History Library and Archives, London (THA), Tower Hamlets Borough Council (THBC) Education Sub-Committee, 23 February 1989, uncatalogued; THA, THBC Education Sub-Committee, for example, Chief Education Officer, 'Arrangements for the Transfer of ILEA Property and Property Services', 19 April 1989.

70. THA, THBC, Education Sub-Committee, Acting Chief Education Officer, 'Secondary School Building Programme', 6 September 1988 and Chief Education Officer (Bruce Glockling), 'Primary & Secondary Review of Accommodation Needs and Strategy', 18 July 1990, uncatalogued.

71. THA, THBC, Education Sub-Committee, Chief Education Officer (Bruce Glockling), 'Expenditure Capital Bid', 6 September 1989, uncatalogued.

72. Richard Weston, *Schools of Thought: Hampshire Architecture 1974–1991* (Winchester: Hampshire County Council, 1991).

73. THA, THBC, Education Committee, A. Douglas-Haydon, 'Whitechapel Secondary School: Selection of Consultants', 7 November 1990 and Chief Education Officer (Glockling), 'New Whitechapel Secondary School: Proposed Supplementary Consultancy Agreement', 13 February 1991, uncatalogued.

74. Dean Hawkes, 'Energetic Design: Netley Infants' School', *Architects' Journal*, 22 June 1988, pp. 31–46.

75. Ruth Owens, 'Sparkbrook Surprise: Nelson Mandela School', *Architects' Journal*, 4 April 1990, pp. 35–49; Brian Edwards, 'A Sense of Civic Pride and Responsibility', *Architects' Journal*, 20 October 1993, pp. 20–1.

76. Ruth Slavid and others, 'Benefits Beyond the Curriculum', *Architects' Journal*, 20 October 1993, pp. 37–47; Amanda Baillieu, 'Lessons of the Future', *The Observer*, 19 June 1994, via Nexis; Martin Spring, 'Building Revisited: Swanlea School, East London', *Building*, 14 May 1999, pp. 40–56; Hattingh, interview, 2021; Neil Embleton, interview, 2021.

77. Slavid and others, 'Benefits', pp. 38, 42; Bill Harrison, 'Fire Protection and Good Design', *Architects' Journal*, 20 October 1993, p. 32.

78. THA, THBC, Education Committee, Chief Education Officer (Bruce Glockling) and Bethnal Green Project Management (S. Pearce), 'New Whitechapel Secondary School', 6 March 1991; Jonathan Glancey, 'A Stylish Lesson - Under Our Noses', *Independent*, 3 November 1993, p. 22.

79. Jeremy Lowe and John Rosser, 'Building Study: Swansea Telephone Exchange Extension', *Architects' Journal*, 7 June 1972, pp. 1259–74 (1263).

80. 'Telephone Exchange', *Concrete Quarterly*, Autumn 1976, pp. 38–40.

81. 'In Passing', *Brick Bulletin*, September 1981, pp. 19–23.

82. Ivor Owen, 'New Severn Crossing May Be Privately Financed', *Financial Times*, 16 May 1989, p. 14; Michael Dynes, 'Cabinet Seeking More Private Cash for Roads', *The Times*, 2 November 1990, via Nexis.

83. Michael Prestage, 'Welsh MPs Snub Severn Bridge Ceremony', *Independent*, 15 September 1992, p. 6; Andrew Adonis, 'New Severn Bridge: For Whom the Toll Pays', *Financial Times*, 15 May 1996, p. 3; P. R. Head, P. Iley and E. T. Bradley, 'Second Severn Crossing: Initial Studies', *Proceedings of the Institution of Civil Engineers: Civil Engineering*, 120/6 (1997), 3–12 (10–11); J. N. Kitchener and D. H. Mizon, 'Second Severn Crossing: Pre-Construction Period and Design Development', *Proceedings of the Institution of Civil Engineers: Civil Engineering*, 120/6 (1997), 13–21 (13–15).

84. 'New Severn Crossing Study Urged', *Financial Times*, 19 November 1983, p. 3; Robin Reeves, 'Safety Problems of Severn Bridge Worry South Wales', *Financial Times*, 22 November 1983, p. 12; Robin Reeves, 'Severn Bridge Repairs

Demanded', *Financial Times*, 30 January 1984, p. 8; Max Wallis, 'How the Juggernauts Have Taken Their Toll: UK Road Transport Policy', *Financial Times*, 18 April 1984, p. 21; Robin Reeves, 'Taking on a Heavier Load', *Financial Times*, 13 July 1984, p. 7.

85. Head, Iley and Bradley, 'Second Severn Crossing'.

86. Kitchener and Mizon, 'Second Severn Crossing', p. 13.

87. On Dartford, see, for example, Marcus Binney, 'Spanners Still in the Works', *The Times*, 14 July 1993, via Nexis; Andrew Taylor, 'Private Finance Bridges the River Thames', *Financial Times*, 30 September 1986, p. 7.

88. Royal Fine Art Commission, *Bridge Design: Royal Fine Art Commission Seminar, 29 October 1992* (London: HMSO, 1993), pp. 18–20; Santhanam, interview, 2021 and email to the author, 14 September 2022; Paul Cross and Margo Cole, '1996 Concrete Society Awards', *Architects' Journal*, 12 September 1996, pp. 4–10 (10); D. H. Mizon and J. N. Kitchener, 'Second Severn Crossing: Viaduct Superstructure and Piers', *Proceedings of the Institution of Civil Engineers: Civil Engineering*, 120/6 (1997), 35–48; D. H. Mizon, N. Smith and A. J. Yeoward, 'Second Severn Crossing: Cable-Stayed Bridge', *Proceedings of the Institution of Civil Engineers: Civil Engineering*, 120/6 (1997), 49–63.

89. Kitchener and Mizon, 'Second Severn Crossing', p. 20.

90. 'Bristol: Second Severn Crossing Tolls', *Architects' Journal*, 12 September 1996, p. 34.

91. Matthew Carmona and Andrew Renninger, 'The Royal Fine Art Commission and 75 Years of English Design Review: The Final 15 Years, 1984–1999', *Planning Perspectives*, 32/4 (2017), 577–99.

92. 'Entries', *Architects' Journal*, 1 January 1997, pp. 30–50 (40, 46); 'A Design Using an Enclosed Space Frame' etc., *Architects' Journal*, 1 January 1997, p. 21.

93. David Walker, 'Nerves of Steel Pay Dividends', *The Times*, 29 January 1990, via Nexis.

94. See G. M. Clark and P. N. Curran, 'Bridging the Ironbridge Gorge: The Jackfield Bridge, Shropshire – Design and Construction', *Proceedings of the Institution of Civil Engineers: Structures and Building*, 122/1 (1997), 92–103; and J. Fisher and G. M. Clark, 'Bridging the Ironbridge Gorge: The Jackfield Bridge, Shropshire – Planning and Development', *Proceedings of the Institution of Civil Engineers: Structures and Building*, 122/1 (1997), 104–16.

95. 'Royal Crossing', *Architects' Journal*, 5 March 1998, p. 12; Peter Curran and Graham Tilly, 'Design and Monitoring of the Flintshire Bridge, UK', *Structural Engineering International*, 9/3 (1999), 225–8; Edward Hollinghurst, 'Flintshire Bridge/Pont Sir Y Fflint, Wales: Design Aesthetics and Innovation', *Transportation Research Record*, 1696/1 (2000), 25–30.

96. 'Project to Bring Cleaner Water', *South Wales Evening Post*, 14 October 1998, p. 7; 'Taking Cover', *New Civil Engineer*, 5 November 1998, via Nexis; 'Recognising Excellence: The Concrete Society Awards', *Architects' Journal*, 3 December 1998, pp. 4–11; Mary Rees, 'Banking on Bay Scheme', *South Wales Evening*

Post, 26 April 1999, p. 3; Susan Buchanan, 'All Cisterns Go (Officially)', *South Wales Evening Post*, 17 September 1999, p. 12; 'Landscape Design Enhances Water Improvement Scheme', *Percy Thomas Partnership: Review*, n.d. [c.1994], unpaginated, author's collection.

97. Leon Gooberman and Trevor Boyns, 'The Welsh Development Agency: Activities and Impact, 1976–2006', in Louise Miskell (ed.), *New Perspectives on Welsh Industrial History* (Cardiff: University of Wales Press, 2020), p. 207–32; Gooberman, *Depression to Devolution*, for example. pp. 95–100, 123–32, 143–4.

98. Dick Hensby, 'New Factory at Abercanaid', *Arup Journal*, September 1983, pp. 12–15; RCAHMW, PTA 03/13, Percy Thomas Partnership brochure, n.d. [c.1985], unpaginated.

99. Simon Phillip and Jackie Bow, 'Our Gain is Their Jobs Loss', *Merthyr Express*, 11 December 1986, p. 8; 'So What's Next at Pentrebach?', *Merthyr Express*, 11 December 1986, p. 9; 'View from the Boardroom: Merthyr Will Be Hoover's Window for the World', *Merthyr Express*, 11 December 1986, p. 8; 'Stressing Dragonparc's Importance', *Merthyr Express*, 4 May 1989, p. 24; Nick Renwick, telephone interview with the author, 8 October 2021.

100. Peter Spinks, 'Laura Ashley Goes Dutch', *Guardian*, 22 September 1984, via Nexis; Robin Reeves, 'Dutch May Win Laura Ashley's New Plant', *Financial Times*, 25 September 1984, p. 13; Robin Reeves, 'Laura Ashley Rejects Netherlands Project', *Financial Times*, 11 December 1984, p. 9; Anthony Moreton, 'Rushed Deal Blocks the Seduction of Laura', *Financial Times*, 12 June 1985, p. 28; NLWA, Development Board for Rural Wales Records, DB/CF/144/1, 'Mochdre Industrial Estate: Phase 5; Laura Ashley Project; File Note of Meeting Held on 3 October 1984 between DBRW and Percy Thomas Partnership'.

101. NLWA, Development Board for Rural Wales Records, DB/CF/144/1, Percy Thomas Partnership (I. D. Owen), 'Note on Meeting at Laura Ashley, Carno, 18 October 1984', and Percy Thomas Partnership, 'Notes on Meeting at Carno, 10 October 1984'.

102. 'New Factory for Laura Ashley at Newtown', *Percy Thomas Partnership: Review*, 1985, unpaginated, author's collection; NLWA, Development Board for Rural Wales Records, DB/CF/144/1, Percy Thomas Partnership, minutes of Project Team Meeting, 24 January 1985, Arnot M. Hughes (Percy Thomas Partnership) to R. Griffiths (Mid Wales Development Board), 11 February 1985 and 'Laura Ashley', publicity booklet, n.d. [c.1985]; photographs at GAC, D900/U/5.

103. 'Radiochemical Set to Expand', *Buckinghamshire Examiner*, 6 August 1976, p. 5; Sean L. Kitson, 'Amersham Radiochemistry to GE Healthcare', *Journal of Labelled Compounds and Radiopharmaceuticals*, 50/9–10 (2007), 737–45; Jon Agar, *Science Policy Under Thatcher* (London: UCL Press, 2019), pp. 171–6.

104. Key articles include Bob Maltz, 'Backbone of the Industry', *Building Design*, 3 March 1978, pp. 14–15; Stevan Brown, 'Radiochemical Centre, Cardiff', *RIBA Journal*, April 1979, pp. 157–9; Deyan Sudjic, 'What Makes an Award Winning Building?', *RIBA Journal*, August 1982, pp. 29–39; Brian Coles and Gerald Pickin, 'Amersham International Plc, Cardiff', *Arup Journal*, 18/3 (1983), 10–11; further sources include RIBAL, Percy Thomas Partnership Biographical File, 'Amersham

International Plc: Cardiff', *Percy Thomas Partnership: Review*, 1984, unpaginated; 'Amersham International Cardiff Laboratories', *Percy Thomas Partnership: Review*, 1985, unpaginated, author's collection; Doyle, *Percy Thomas Partnership*, pp. 66–7; Hope and Clench, interview, 2021; Ian Pepperell, telephone interview, 19 February 2021, interview with the author, Cardiff, 23 August 2022 and emails to the author of 21 April 2021 and 24 September 2022; Chris Coombs, video interview, 22 March 2021; John Garrard, video interview, 12 May 2021.

105. Ian Pepperell, email to the author, 21 April 2021.

106. Coombs, interview, 2021.

107. Adrian Cozmuta, 'Selling "The World's Favourite Airline": British Airways' Privatisation and the Motives Behind It', *Business History*, 66/1 (2024), 181–200.

108. Arthur Reed, 'Wales Wellspring', *Air Transport World*, July 1994, pp. 59–63.

109. Chris Jofeh, 'British Airways Avionics Facility', *Arup Journal*, 31/1 (1996), 28–31 (28); Anthony Moreton, 'BA Avionics Plant to Be Built in Wales Will Create 400 Jobs', *Financial Times*, 28 March 1992, p. 6.

110. 'British Airways Avionics Facility', *Percy Thomas Partnership: Review*, 1992, unpaginated, author's collection; 'From the Valleys to the Clouds', *Percy Thomas Partnership: Review*, n.d. [c.1994], unpaginated, author's collection; Martin Spring, 'BA Avionics: Jet Setter', *Building*, 28 January 1994, pp. 22–5; Thom Gorst, 'Maintaining Altitude: PTP in Llantrisant', *Architecture Today*, April 1994, pp. 20–5; Doyle, *Percy Thomas Partnership*, pp. 68–9; Pepperell, telephone interview with the author, 19 February 2021.

111. DTZ, *Evaluation of the Technium Programme – Stage 1: Scoping and Review* (Cardiff: Welsh Assembly Government, n.d. [c.2008]), *https://gov.wales/sites/default/files/statistics-and-research/2018-12/101119techniumstage1en.pdf* (accessed 5 October 2022), for example. pp. 7–10; James Abbey, Gareth Davies and Lynn Mainwaring, 'Vorsprung Durch Technium: Towards a System of Innovation in South-West Wales', *Regional Studies*, 42/2 (2008), 281–93; Mary Rees, '£3.2m Project to Boost Docks: New Technology Centre Will Bring Regeneration', *South Wales Evening Post*, 14 August 1999, p. 3; Mary Rees, '"Sexy" Centre Could Spark Jobs Boom', *South Wales Evening Post*, 15 October 1999, p. 11; 'The Technium Centre is a Flagship Soon to Lead a Fleet', *Western Mail*, 31 January 2001, p. 3.

112. 'Assembly Launches Technium Network with £150m Price-Tag', *Western Mail*, 5 November 2002, p. 16.

113. DTZ, *Technium Case Studies: Appendix 1 to Evaluation of the Technium Programme Stage 1, Final Report* (Cardiff: Welsh Assembly Government, n.d. [c.2008]), *https://gov.wales/sites/default/files/statistics-and-research/2018-12/101119techniumcasestudyen.pdf* (accessed 7 October 2022), pp. 17–22.

114. Pepperell, interview, Cardiff, 23 August 2022 and Adams, interview, 2021; DTZ, *Technium Case Studies*, p. 17.

115. Patrick Hannay, 'Working Differently', *Touchstone*, August 2004, pp. 9–12 (11–12); Kristina Smith, 'Houston, We Have a Problem', *Building*, 6 January 2004, *www.building.co.uk/houston-we-have-a-problem/3030972.article* (accessed

6 October 2022); 'Designed to Be a Real Winner', *Daily Post (North Wales)*, 9 November 2005, via Nexis; Andrew Davies, 'The Minister's Column: An Innovative Wales in A Rapidly Changing World', *Western Mail*, 5 March 2003, p. 15; David Jones, 'This Is Key to Digital Round-Up Success', *Daily Post (North Wales)*, 25 February 2005, p. 29; Rhiannon Pugh, Niall G. MacKenzie and Dylan Jones-Evans, 'From "Techniums" to "Emptiums": The Failure of a Flagship Innovation Policy in Wales', *Regional Studies*, 52/7 (2018), 1009–20.

116. 'Building Illustrated: Birch Vale Industrial Development', *Architects' Journal*, 21 May 1980, pp. 1001–11; also, Peter Buchanan, 'Civilising the Shed', *Architectural Review*, July 1981, pp. 16–22.

117. Frank Gardner, 'Porton Down: What's Inside the UK's Top Secret Laboratory?', BBC News, 13 June 2019, *www.bbc.co.uk/news/uk-48540653* (accessed 13 October 2022); Garrard, interview, 2021; Peter Q. Kendall, letter to author, 28 June 2021.

118. Ian Taylor, 'Yes, It Hurts; Yes, It Works', *Independent*, 3 February 1997, p. 20.

119. London Borough Council of Richmond upon Thames, 'Planning Application Number: 97/2314', 10 January 2019, *www2.richmond.gov.uk/lbrplanning/Planning_CASENO.aspx?strCASENO=97/2314&DocTypeID=41#docs* (accessed 14 October 2022); Santhanam, interview, 2021.

120. Mark Gaudet, 'The Design of Buildings for Very Low Levels of Vibration', *Noise & Vibration Worldwide*, 32/8 (2001), 12–17; Grant Prior, 'An Explosion in the Lab', *Construction News*, 18 May 2006, via Nexis.

121. John Leitch, 'Ignoring Adviser Cost Laing £41m', *Contract Journal*, 14 February 2001, p. 9; Terry Macalister, 'Laing Sells Ailing Business for £1', *Guardian*, 28 September 2001, p. 27; 'DTI Blamed for National Physical Lab Fiasco', *Building*, 12 May 2006, *www.building.co.uk/news/dti-blamed-for-national-physical-lab-fiasco/3067329.article* (accessed 14 October 2022).

122. David Rogers, 'PFI Contract Bursts Hole in Laing Profits', *Construction News*, 23 November 2000, via Nexis; National Audit Office, *The Termination of the PFI Contract for the National Physical Laboratory* (London: The Stationery Office, 2006).

123. National Audit Office, *Termination*, p. 36.

124. Julian Cockayne, 'Megastores in Europe', *Percy Thomas Partnership: Review*, 1992, unpaginated, author's collection; 'Focus on Multiple Refit', *Percy Thomas Partnership: Review*, n.d. [c.1994], unpaginated, author's collection; Richard Mazuch, video interview with the author, 15 March 2021.

125. Anthony Williams, 'Building Dossier: Savacentre, London Colney', *Building*, 22 June 1990, pp. 43–8; see also Jonathan Glancey, 'Design: Behind the Facade of the Retail Revolution', *Independent*, 22 April 1989, p. 37.

126. Sam Wetherell, 'Freedom Planned: Enterprise Zones and Urban Non-Planning in Post-War Britain', *Twentieth Century British History*, 27/2 (2016), 266–89; Otto Saumarez Smith, 'Action for Cities: The Thatcher Government and Inner-City

Policy', *Urban History*, 47/2 (2020), 274–91; Brenner, *New State Spaces*, for example, pp. 172–248.

127. Wetherell, 'Freedom Planned', p. 280.

128. Martin Spring, 'Design and Gild', *Building*, 22 November 1991, pp. 58–63.

129. Neil Graham, 'Point North: Offices for the New Millennium', *Percy Thomas Partnership: Review*, 1992, unpaginated, author's collection.

130. Tony Struthers, 'The Redevelopment of Salford Quays, Greater Manchester: Its Impact on Urban and Regional Development from 1983 to 2003', *DisP – The Planning Review*, 39/154 (2003), 11–18; Salford City Council, *Salford Quays Milestones: The Story of Salford Quays* (Salford: Salford City Council, 2005); Andreas Schulze Bäing and Cecilia Wong, 'The Impact of Brownfield Regeneration on Neighbourhood Dynamics: The Case of Salford Quays in England', *Town Planning Review*, 89/5 (2018), 513–34.

131. Deirdre Salmon and Jane Findlay, 'Salford: A Quay Success', *Percy Thomas Partnership: Review*, 1992, unpaginated, author's collection; Penny McGuire, 'PS: Glass Products', *Architectural Review*, April 1992, pp. 82–92 (82); Knape, interview, 2021; RCAHMW, PTA 03/25, 'The Anchorage, Salford Quays', n.d.

132. Untitled article, *Architects' Journal*, 23 March 1988, p. 13; McGuire, 'Glass Products', p. 84; Ian Pepperell, email to author, 21 April 2021; Hughes, interview, 2022; Philip Bintliff, video interview with the author, 20 October 2022.

133. Rosemary D. F. Bromley and Joan C. M. Rees, 'The First Five Years of the Swansea Enterprise Zone: An Assessment of Change', *Regional Studies*, 22/4 (1988), 263–75.

134. Gooberman, *Depression to Devolution*, 94; Geoffrey K. Fry, 'The Thatcher Government, The Financial Management Initiative, and the "New Civil Service"', *Public Administration*, 66/1 (2007), 1–20; Christine Cooper, Jonathan Tweedie and Max Baker, 'From "Business-Like" to Businesses: Agencification, Corporatization, and Civil Service Reform Under the Thatcher Administration', *Public Administration*, 100/2 (2022), 193–215.

135. Peter Collymore, 'DOE: Property Services Agency', *Architects' Journal*, 26 September 1973, pp. 719–37; RIBAL, Percy Thomas Partnership Biographical File, 'Business Statistics Office: Newport, Gwent', *Percy Thomas Partnership: Review*, 1984, unpaginated; RCAHMW, PTA 05/04, 'Percy Thomas Partnership. Architects & Planning Consultants' [n.d.], *c.*1975, unpaginated; Ian Pepperell, interview with the author, Cardiff, 23 August 2022.

136. 'Anthology of British Architecture', *Journal of the Royal Institute of British Architects*, March 1981, pp. 26–61 (56); Garrard, interview, 2021; Peter Mulrenan, interview, 2021; Hughes, interview, 2022.

137. RCAHMW, PTA 01/07, 'Photographs of Work by Percy Thomas', vol. 7; RCAHMW, PTA 05/04, 'Percy Thomas Partnership: Architects & Planning Consultants' [n.d., *c.*1975], unpaginated; RCAHMW, PTA 05/05, 'Percy Thomas Partnership: Architects & Planning Consultants' [n.d., *c.*1977], unpaginated.

138. John Welsh, 'Yesso', *Building Design*, 5 April 1991, pp. 18–19; RIBAL, Percy Thomas Partnership Biographical File, 'Operation & Development Centre for Esso: Leatherhead', *Percy Thomas Partnership: Review*, 1984, unpaginated; Ian Pepperell, telephone interview with the author, 19 February 2021; Santhanam, interview, 2021; Crosland-Mills, interview, 2021; Mulrenan, interview, 2021.

139. John Winter, 'Esso House: The Atrium as Generator', *Architecture Today*, October 1991, pp. 22–7; Penny McGuire, 'Products Survey: Glass Blocks', *Architectural Review*, July 1994, pp. 89–94 (9–1); Doyle, *Percy Thomas Partnership*, pp. 48–9.

140. RIBAL, Percy Thomas Partnership Biographical File, 'Amersham International Head Office: Little Chalfont, Bucks', *Percy Thomas Partnership: Review*, 1984, unpaginated; 'Designs Blend into the Landscape', *Financial Times*, 4 February 1986, section 'Financial Times Survey: UK Building Industry – Industry and Offices', p. vi; Ian Pepperell, email to author, 21 April 2021.

141. 'Abbey Wood: The Facts and Figures', *Abbey Wood Update*, n.d. [c.1996], unpaginated, author's collection, from Clifford Martin; James Macneil, 'Ship Shape and Bristol Fashion', *Building*, 9 February 1996, pp. 40–7 (40); Geoff King, 'MOD Transfers Jobs Out of Capital', *The Times*, 28 March 1990, via Nexis; Anthony Moreton, 'MOD Jobs Switch Will Be Reviewed', *Financial Times*, 21 October 1991, p. 10; Ross Tieman, 'Defence Contractors to Be Given Greater Freedom', *Times*, 6 April 1991, via Nexis.

142. Philip A. G. Sabin, 'British Defence Choices beyond "Options for Change"', *International Affairs*, 69/2 (1993), 267–87 (276).

143. Moray Stewart, 'Future Resource Management in Defence', *The RUSI Journal*, 138/2 (1993), 73–6; 'PE Collocation at Abbey Wood: Costs and Benefits', n.d. [c.1995], author's collection, from Clifford Martin; untitled document on MOD Procurement Executive Building, 1995, author's collection, from Clifford Martin.

144. Andy Cook, 'The Meaning of Life', *Building*, 21 November 1997, pp. 82–5.

145. Key sources are Macneil, 'Ship Shape'; Rab Bennetts, 'Purchasing Power: The MOD's Abbey Wood Campus', *Architecture Today*, June 1996, pp. 30–44; other sources include 'Ministry of Defence: New Headquarters', *Percy Thomas Partnership: Review*, n.d. [c.1994], unpaginated, author's collection; Martin Spring, 'Working Order', *Building*, 14 June 1996, pp. 50–5 (54); Percy Thomas Partnership and Hoare Lea and Partners, *MOD (PE) Collocation, Bristol: Office Environment*, n.d. [c.1995], author's collection, from Clifford Martin; MOD (PE) Collocation Team, 'Abbey Wood', 1996, author's collection, from Clifford Martin; John Gulvin, Jane Findlay and Ken Fieldhouse, 'Defence of the Landscape', *Landscape Design*, September 1997, pp. 45–52; John Rudge, video interview with the author, 2 March 2021; Jane Findlay and Sue Thomas, video interview, 17 March 2021; Harbinson, interview, 2021; Clifford Martin, interview with the author, Bristol, 16 April 2021.

146. Frank Duffy, 'SAS Co-Operation', *Architectural Review*, March 1989, pp. 42–51.

147. Macneil, 'Ship Shape'.

148. David Harvey, *The Condition of Postmodernity: An Enquiry into the Origins of Cultural Change* (Cambridge MA: Blackwell, 1990), p. 66; see also Florian Urban,

'Glasgow's Royal Concert Hall and the Invention of the Post-Modern City', *Journal of Architecture*, 23/5 (2018), 829-71.

149. Wolfson Centre for Archival Research, Library of Birmingham, Birmingham (WCARB), BCC 1/AG/37/1/25, Town Clerk to William Emerys-Williams, October 1959; Birmingham City Council, *Developing Birmingham, 1889 to 1989: 100 Years of City Planning* (Birmingham: Birmingham City Council, 1989), pp. 98-101.

150. WCARB, BCC 1/AG/37/1/37, John Madin Design Group, 'A Concert Hall for Birmingham', 1970.

151. Birmingham City Council, *Developing Birmingham*, p. 100; WCARB, BCC 1/AG/37/1/31, Civic Development Subcommittee, 26 April 1965.

152. Birmingham City Council, *Developing Birmingham*, pp. 115-16.

153. WCARB, BCC 1/AG/37/1/31, Civic Development Subcommittee, 26 April 1965, and BCC 1/AG/37/1/38, City Architect, Engineer, Surveyor and Planning Officer, 'Gas Street Basin', December 1971.

154. Patrick Loftman, *A Tale of Two Cities: Birmingham the Convention and Unequal City* (Birmingham: Faculty of the Built Environment, Birmingham Polytechnic, July 1990), p. 10.

155. Bernard Zissmann, video interview with the author, 14 December 2022; Timothy Ross Hall, 'Urban Regeneration and Cultural Geography: The International Convention Centre, Birmingham' (unpublished PhD thesis, University of Birmingham, 1994), pp. 10-16, 238, 260-6; Liam Kennedy, 'Introduction: The Creative Destruction of Birmingham', in Liam Kennedy (ed.), *Remaking Birmingham: The Visual Culture of Urban Regeneration* (London: Routledge, 2004), pp. 1-10 (2-4); Phil Hubbard, 'Urban Design and Local Economic Development: A Case Study in Birmingham', *Cities*, 12/4 (1995), 243-51; Christopher Upton, *The Past, Present & Future: A Commemorative Book for the Opening of the International Convention Centre, Birmingham 1991* (Birmingham: Birmingham City Council, 1991), p. 4; Roger Evans, 'Making Places: Centenary Square', *Architects' Journal*, 5 February 1992, pp. 43-5.

156. David Franks, *City of Birmingham: International Convention Centre Birmingham - Feasibility Study* (Birmingham: Birmingham City Council, September 1983), Birmingham City Library (BCL); WCARB, NEC and ICC Committee Minutes, Box 1, 'Possible International Convention Centre', paper of 17 March 1982 for General Purposes Committee; Hall, 'Urban Regeneration', pp. 208-13.

157. Mark Ellis, 'Approval for £91m Centre "A Milestone"', *Birmingham Post*, 2 November 1983, unpaginated cutting in Hall, 'Urban Regeneration'; Grimley, *Symphony Hall*, p. 44.

158. Terry Grimley, *Symphony Hall: A Dream Realised* (Birmingham: Boydell and Brewer, 2014), pp. 43-4; Paul Raymer, 'Showpiece City', *Evening Mail* (Birmingham), 28 March 1985, cutting in Hall, 'Urban Regeneration'; 'Birmingham Reveals its £106m Conference Centre', *Building*, 29 March 1985, p. 7; 'Slim Chance for £106m Centre', *Building*, 5 April 1985, p. 9; David Vickerman, 'Big Euro Boost for Brum', *Evening Mail* (Birmingham, 28 November

1985), cutting in Hall, 'Urban Regeneration'; Neal Morris, 'Second City's Latest First', *Architects' Journal*, 18 November 1987, p. 13.

159. RIBAL, Percy Thomas Partnership Biographical File, 'International Convention Centre, Birmingham', *Percy Thomas Partnership: Review*, 1984, unpaginated; Convention Centre Partnership, *Birmingham International Convention Centre: Design Report* (Birmingham, 1985), BCL; Zissman, interview, 2022.

160. Tony Collier, 'The International Convention Centre Birmingham', *Architecture Today*, April 1991, pp. 57-68 (58-9, 68); Russ Swan, 'Unconventional Arrangements', *Concrete Quarterly*, Summer 1991, pp. 10-17 (12-14); RIBAL, Percy Thomas Partnership - Biographical File, 'Fun and Games', *Percy Thomas Partnership: Review*, 1988, unpaginated; Ian Pepperell, telephone interview with the author, 19 February 2021, email to the author, 7 April 2022 and interview with the author, Cardiff, 23 August 2022; Rudge, interview, 2021.

161. Grimley, *Symphony Hall*, p. 48.

162. Grimley, *Symphony Hall*, p. 74; James Steele, *Theatre Builders* (London: Academy Editions, 1996), pp. 169-71.

163. F. G. E. Irwin, 'The International Convention Centre, Birmingham', *Proceedings of the Institution of Civil Engineers: Civil Engineering*, 92/1 (1992), 8-17; T. R. Dix and K. M. Jones, 'International Convention Centre, Birmingham: Building Services Engineering', *Proceedings of the Institution of Civil Engineers: Structures and Building*, 94/3 (1992), 263-73; R. D. Greenwood and R. Cowell, 'International Convention Centre, Birmingham: Structures and Railway Vibration Isolation', *Proceedings of the Institution of Civil Engineers: Structures and Building*, 94/3 (1992), 253-62; Grimley, *Symphony Hall*, pp. 14-18, 54-64, 77; Steele, *Theatre Builders*, pp. 28-31 and 192-3; Denise Chevin, 'Sound Structure', *Building*, 15 September 1989, pp. 76-7; Jeff Charles and William Allen, 'Symphonic Variations', *RIBA Journal*, November 1989, pp. 52-5; Graham Ridout, 'Don't Shake Rattle's Role', *Building*, 17 November 1989, pp. 71-6 (72-3); Francis Reid, 'Rattle and Brum', *Architects' Journal*, 1 May 1991, pp. 24-7.

164. Marcus Binney, 'British Architecture Now', *Architectural Design*, April 1989, pp. ii-xi (ix); Huw Heywood, video interview with the author, 15 December 2022; Martin Spring, 'Hall Assembly', *Building*, 22 February 1991, pp. 40-5 (44).

165. Collier, 'International Convention Centre'.

166. Morris, 'Second City's Latest First'; Hall, 'Urban Regeneration', p. 20.

167. John Slim, 'Visions of Our Future', *Evening Mail* (Birmingham), 29 January 1986, cutting in Hall, 'Urban Regeneration'.

168. Spring, 'Hall Assembly', p. 41; Hubbard, 'Urban Design', p. 250.

169. Convention Centre Partnership, *Birmingham International Convention Centre: Design Report*, p. 5; Terry Grimley, 'Second City Will Be Number One', *Birmingham Post*, 7 January 1989, in Hall, 'Urban Regeneration'.

170. Paul Cheeseright, 'Writing on the Wall for Artists', *Financial Times*, 28 December 1991, Arts section, p. xiv; Rudge, interview, 2021; Upton, *Past, Present & Future*, pp. 66, 94; 'This Is Our New Heart!', *Evening Mail* (Birmingham, 29 March

1990), in Hall, 'Urban Regeneration'; Reid, 'Rattle and Brum', p. 27; John Kirwan, 'Frontis: International Convention Centre, Birmingham', *RIBA Journal*, June 1991, pp. 6–10; Rudge, interview, 2021.

171. Tim Hall, 'Public Art, Civic Identity and the New Birmingham', in Kennedy (ed.), *Remaking Birmingham*, pp. 63–71.

172. Birmingham City Council, *Developing Birmingham*, pp. 144, 148; Convention Centre Partnership, *Birmingham International Convention Centre: Design Report*, p. 23; WCARB, NEC and ICC Committee Minutes, Box 1, 'Joint Report of Director of Development and City Engineer', July 1986 and 'Broad Street Redevelopment Area: Urban Design Master Plan', 10 September 1986; Upton, *Past, Present & Future*, p. 66.

173. Swan, 'Unconventional Arrangements', p. 10; Rudge, interview, 2021; Morris, 'Second City's Latest First'.

174. Hall, 'Public Art'.

175. 'Boston is Coming to Birmingham', *Architects' Journal*, 27 April 1988, p. 10; Joe Holyoak, 'Waterside City', *Architects' Journal*, 22 May 1991, pp. 24–7.

176. Evans, 'Making Places', p. 43.

177. John Punter, 'Design-Led Regeneration? Evaluating the Design Outcomes of Cardiff Bay and Their Implications for Future Regeneration and Design', *Journal of Urban Design*, 23/3 (2007), 375–405; Richard Cowell, 'Environmental Compensation and the Mediation of Environmental Change: Making Capital out of Cardiff Bay', *Journal of Environmental Planning and Management*, 43/5 (2000), 689-710; Sian Best, *A Whim Set in Concrete: The Campaign to Stop the Cardiff Bay Barrage* (Bridgend: Poetry Wales Press, 2004).

178. Robin Reeves, 'Opera Centre Proposed', *Financial Times*, 13 September 1986, p. 4; 'Noises Off', *Financial Times*, 2 January 1991, p. 12; Rupert Christiansen, 'The Land of Song Spends Too Long Sitting on the Mud', *Observer*, 20 October 1991, p. 55.

179. Pepperell, telephone interview with the author, 19 February 2021; 'Hadid Selects Opera Players', *Building*, 20 October 1995, p. 8; Nicholas Edwards (Lord Crickhowell), *Opera House Lottery: Zaha Hadid and the Cardiff Bay Project* (Cardiff: University of Wales Press, 1997); Deyan Sudjic (ed.), *An Opera House for Wales/Tŷ Opera i Gymru* (London: Wordsearch, 1994).

180. Deyan Sudjic, 'A Sad Song from Wales', *Guardian*, 11 January 1995, p. 20; David Gow, 'Rival Plan Threat to Opera House', *Guardian*, 27 February 1995, p. 6; Edwards, *Opera House Lottery*, pp. 130–2.

181. 'Percy Thomas Wins Cardiff', *Building*, 13 September 1996, p. 8.

182. David Fanning, 'Private Sector Snubs Wales Millennium Centre', *Architects' Journal*, 14 November 1996, p. 18; 'Astragal', *Architects' Journal*, 21 November 1996, p. 58.

183. Doyle, *Percy Thomas Partnership*, p. 71; Sudjic (ed.), *Opera House*, pp. 42–3; David Fanning, 'Welsh Lottery Hand-Out Deals Zaha Another Slap in the Face', *Architects' Journal*, 20 November 1997, p. 24.

184. Giles Barrie, 'RFAC Slams Cardiff's Hadid Successor', *Building*, 31 October 1997, p. 8.

185. Adams, interview, 2021.

186. James Fisher, 'PTP Redesigns Again', *Building Design*, 10 July 1998, p. 5; 'Images of Welshness Inspire PTP's Cheaper Wales Centre', *Architects' Journal*, 16 July 1998, p. 22; 'It's a Welsh Thing, You Wouldn't Understand', *Building Design*, 24 July 1998, p. 7; Paul Finch, 'Millennium Centre Optimism, Welsh Assembly Worries', *Architects' Journal*, 8 October 1998, pp. 20–2; David Taylor, 'Mine of Inspiration in PTP's Cardiff Plan', *Architects' Journal*, 26 November 1998, pp. 10–11.

187. Key accounts are 'Bay Watch', *Architectural Review*, April 2000, p. 101; Thomas Lane, 'Slated', *Building*, 14 May 2004, pp. 42–6; Austin Williams, 'Poetic Licence', *Architects' Journal*, 3 June 2004, pp. 30–7; Jonathan Glancey, 'Inside the Whale: Cardiff's £106m Millennium Centre Seeks to Celebrate and Amplify Welsh Culture', *Guardian*, 27 September 2004, p. 14; Harry Charrington, 'Rock of the Bay', *Building Design*, 26 November 2004, pp. 14–19; Chris Jofeh, 'Wales Millennium Centre: A New Stage for the Art of Engineers', *Proceedings of the Institution of Civil Engineers: Civil Engineering*, 158/1 (2005), 3–48; see also John Grindrod, *Iconicon: A Journey Around the Landmark Buildings of Contemporary Britain* (London: Faber & Faber, 2022), pp. 285–9.

188. Isabel Allen, 'Life After the Opera House: Did Zaha Do Cardiff a Favour?', *Architects' Journal*, 3 June 2004, p. 24.

189. Tom Bodden, 'How North Wales Slate Will Form Spectacular Facade of £104m Centre', *Daily Post* (North Wales), 12 November 2002, pp. 6–7; Amanda Birch, 'The New Rock Star', *Building Design*, 12 December 2003, pp. 14–15; Sue Corbett, 'Slate of the Art', *Country Life*, 6 August 2008, pp. 64–5.

190. Susan Buchanan, 'Centre Highlights Artists' Glass Craft', *South Wales Evening Post*, 2 November 1999, p. 9; Miriam Cadji, 'Let's Stick Together', *RIBA Journal*, April 2000, pp. 75–9.

191. Patrick Hannay, 'The Matter in Question', *Touchstone*, April 2005, pp. 1–4.

192. Adams, interview, 2021; Mario Basini, 'Stage for a Nation', *Western Mail*, 20 November 2004, p. 4.

193. Dave King, 'Cardiff Arts Centre Critics Attacked', *Building*, 11 September 1998, p. 14.

194. 'So Near So Spa', *Building Design*, 8 September 2000, p. 2; 'Costly Budget Halts Centre', *South Wales Evening Post*, 14 September 2000, p. 5; Matt Weaver, 'First Zaha, Now PTP Comes to Grief in Cardiff', *Building Design*, 6 October 2000, p. 2; Brian Walters, 'Soaring Costs Spark Fears of Welsh Dome', *South Wales Evening Post*, 16 October 2000, p. 10.

195. 'New Design - But Still a Glass Act', *South Wales Evening Post*, 19 December 2000, p. 5.

196. Brian Walters, 'Spread the Jam to Reduce Bitterness', *South Wales Evening Post*, 5 June 2000, p. 10; Karen Price and Toby Mason, 'Millennium Centre A Stage in Wales to Rival Best in the World', *Western Mail*, 23 January 2002, p. 1; Nick Speed and Toby Mason, 'Wales Office Defends Spending', *Western Mail*, 24 January 2002, p. 8.

197. Jim O'Rourke, 'Urdd Bears the Torch of Welsh Youth', *Western Mail*, 28 March 2001, p. 10.

198. Geraint Talfan Davies, 'Stage for a Nation with Message for the World', *Western Mail*, 29 March 2001, p. 14.

199. Melanie Delargy, 'Council Steps in to Save Wales Millennium Centre', *Building*, 6 October 2000, p. 14; 'Council Agrees to Donate £3m Bay Site for Millennium Centre', *South Wales Echo*, 14 December 2001, p. 3.

200. Patrick Hannay, 'Slate of the Art', *Architecture Today*, February 2005, pp. 46–58 (text by Jonathan Adams, 52–3).

201. Adams, interview, 2021.

202. 'Bryn's Historic Voyage', *Western Mail*, 22 January 2003, p. 11.

203. Terry Crockford, 'Gala Opening for Our New Welsh Arts Icon', *South Wales Evening Post*, 27 November 2004, p. 23.

204. Byhannah Jones, 'One Key to Bind Us Culturally to the World', *Western Mail*, 28 February 2004, p. 2.

205. Lauren Turner, 'Young Will Be Taking Centre Stage', *South Wales Echo*, 24 November 2004, p. 26.

7

Conclusion

To attempt to characterise ten decades of work by an architectural practice as wide-ranging as that of Ivor Jones and Percy Thomas, Percy Thomas and Ernest Prestwich, Sir Percy Thomas & Son and the Percy Thomas Partnership (PTP), is in many ways as impossible as summarising twentieth-century architecture itself. The practice did not constitute a school: its leaders rarely attempted to impose stylistic uniformity on their colleagues, and did not usually advocate any ideological position. That non-doctrinaire approach to architecture did define it from its more avant-garde, artistic or personality-driven contemporaries, and from the official architecture of government ministries and local authorities, by turns bureaucratic and experimental. Yet while the practice may have been undogmatic, it certainly maintained an ethical stance. Moreover, the practice was distinctive among those of similar scale and approach by its position in industrial and urban south Wales, not so much because that affected its architects' approaches (although certainly in some cases it did), but rather because of the nature of the work that it undertook as a consequence of this position. The practice's architecture demonstrates a particular situated Welsh experience of twentieth-century British history – and indeed the architecture created that experience for a great many people.

Despite being a private practice, the great majority of Percy Thomas's work was for one branch or another of the state, whether local councils, nationalised utilities, ministries or health authorities; and when not literally involved with the state, it was often dependent on its funding and influence, as in the case of universities, factories or the BBC. That reflected the broad rise in the state's power and scope in Britain throughout the twentieth century, and the buildings often embodied political and structural shifts in the values and nature of the state over that time. The practice's body of work also demonstrates the especially high degree of influence of the state in south Wales, designated a Development Area and maintaining a politics of government-motivated development long after that status was dissolved, even against the grain of prevailing politics. While the practice's work contributed to an ever-greater integration of Wales within Britain, it also led to a particularly Welsh (especially southern and metropolitan Welsh) consciousness of the nation's identity and potential as a dramatically, continuously modernising society, though one in which deep-rooted and romantic traditions could yet be articulated and reinvented within a modern framework. At the same time, the expertise that the practice acquired in the often large-scale and technically challenging kinds of architecture it undertook in Wales, and the manpower (and machine power) that it accrued for such work, led to similar projects elsewhere in Britain, and, indeed, on Britain's behalf overseas.

The experience of modernity evident in the practice's work shows that it was one of turbulence, as the small scale, intimate aspects of everyday life and work were obliterated by new large, fast, anonymous, mechanised forms, whether of steelworks, hospitals, universities or motorways, structures whose new scale and qualities the practice often sought to dramatise as well as humanise. And the scale of new infrastructure created in the mid-twentieth century fixed in place social, cultural, economic and environmental structures that could later be questioned or themselves become painfully redundant, most notably with the increasing dependence on fossil fuels on which so much twentieth-century development was predicated. The decisions to create these spaces came both from the heart of government and from local people, politicians, administrators and industrialists; while the architect served as one of many interfaces between the state and its citizens.

Throughout its existence the practice's architects adhered to Thomas's own maxim that the architect had to 'serve the community', not just the client, thereby seeking to share out the social benefits of modernity, a principle that seems to have pervaded the practice culture long after its founder's words had been forgotten. That principle manifested itself in very different architectural forms across the century, while sustaining certain consistent design approaches: a legibility of symbols and volumes to a popular, democratic understanding; an openness and generosity of public or corporate space; a centripetal tendency, where interiors press inwards towards socially unifying cores. Buildings formed the spaces where occupants understood themselves in relation to others as citizens in an organised society, differentiated by character and ordered into spatial and social relationships. In that sense, Percy Thomas's architecture framed the ordinary lives of much of the population: steelworkers, healthcare workers, office workers; townsfolk; tenants; patients; concert goers and churchgoers; shoppers; students; children; commuters, tourists and lorry drivers on the post-war road network. It might not be an exaggeration to say that most people living in Britain today have been in or on a Percy Thomas building at some point in their lives.

Besides that legacy of places and their influences, there was a further legacy that should be acknowledged in the architects and practices that began within Percy Thomas's offices. While many talented architects had such design freedom and opportunities for significant work that their entire careers were contained within the practice, subsuming their identities into it and gaining freedom from the administrative burdens of independent practice, others used it as a training ground before leaving. Wyndham Powell, for example, left in 1964, later joining Ivor Jones's former partner John Bishop, establishing the long-running Cardiff firm of Wyndham Powell Associates and Powell Dobson. Mike Nightingale left in the 1980s to establish his own rival healthcare practice, taking several colleagues with him. Philip Bintliff founded an innovative small practice at Hebden Bridge, joined by John Knape from the Manchester office. PTP's financial woes from the mid-1990s until its takeover by Capita in 2004 prompted a wave of departures, some unhappy with Capita's corporate culture. Ian Pepperell left in 1997, becoming a director at BDG McColl, and later a consultant architect alongside RHWL for the Megaron conference centre and concert hall in Athens, later rejoining under Capita. Two architects that he took with him from PTP to BDG McColl - Huw Lloyd Jones and Richard Roberts - founded the prolific Cardiff practice of Rio Architects. The Bristol office produced two successors, CODA Architects, founded by Ronnie Rennoldson, Trevor Martin and Chris Coombs, and ESHA Architects, founded by Peterjohn Smyth, Willie Harbinson and Neil Embleton to sustain their traditional approach. Jonathan Adams established his own practice, while maintaining a role in the Capita office. Meanwhile, Jane Findlay and Sue Radley turned PTP Landscape and Urban Design into Fira in Birmingham, becoming a nationally celebrated landscape and planning practice with much continuing work for hospitals as well as urban landscaping, including at Poundbury and Ebbw Vale.

Many architects stayed, however, and Capita inherited and continued PTP's projects, especially hospitals, until international consultancy company WSP acquired its architecture and engineering offices in 2022. Today, such large corporate practices work by subdivision into intimate teams with distinct characters, giving similar opportunities for architectural and social principles to endure. As in the past, however, it will be up to those with political and financial power to decide whether the built environment of the twenty-first century will also contribute to civic culture, shared identity and social participation and therefore whether it will benefit communities; and whether respectful, sustainable and equitable approaches will be taken in dealing with our difficult inheritance of twentieth-century modernity. ■

Select Bibliography

The bibliography includes only significant works of background theory and key published works with significant information on Sir Percy Thomas and his practice, not including smaller pieces such as architectural magazine articles. Edited books are given one entry as a book; individual chapters are referenced in the text.

Alban, J. R. (ed.), *The Guildhall, Swansea: Essays to the Fiftieth Anniversary of its Opening* (Swansea: Swansea City Council, 1984).

Associated Bridge Builders Ltd, *The Severn Bridge Superstructure* (Birmingham: The Kynoch Press, 1966).

Bell, George H. (ed.), *Hospital and Medical School Design: International Symposium, Dundee 1961*, 2 vols (Edinburgh: E. & S. Livingstone Ltd, 1962).

Bird, Eric L. (ed.), *Industrial Architecture* (London: RIBA, 1949).

Birmingham City Council, *Developing Birmingham, 1889 to 1989: 100 Years of City Planning* (Birmingham: Birmingham City Council, 1989).

Bluemel, Kristin (ed.), *Intermodernism: Literary Culture in Mid-Twentieth-Century Britain* (Edinburgh: Edinburgh University Press, 2009).

Brassley, Paul, Jeremy Burchardt and Karen Sayer (eds), *Transforming the Countryside: The Electrification of Rural Britain* (Abingdon: Routledge, 2017).

Brenner, Neil, *New State Spaces: Urban Governance and the Rescaling of Statehood* (Oxford: Oxford University Press, 2004).

Brocklehurst, Helen, and Robert Phillips (eds), *History, Nationhood and the Question of Britain* (Basingstoke: Palgrave Macmillan, 2004).

Bromley, Rosemary D. F., and Joan C. M. Rees, 'The First Five Years of the Swansea Enterprise Zone: An Assessment of Change', *Regional Studies*, 22/4 (1988), 263-75.

Bryder, Linda, 'The King Edward VII Welsh National Memorial Association and Its Policy Towards Tuberculosis, 1910-1948', *Welsh History Review*, 13/2 (1986), 194-216.

Carless, Tonia, 'Producing Space, the Confrontation Between Abstract Space and Everyday Life: "I Wunder If Heaven Got a Ghetto"', *ARQ*, 17/2 (2013), 139-47.

Carmona, Matthew, and Andrew Renninger, 'The Royal Fine Art Commission and 75 Years of English Design Review: The Final 15 Years, 1984-1999', *Planning Perspectives*, 32/4 (2017), 577-99.

Charles, Prince of Wales, *A Vision of Britain: A Personal View of Architecture* (London: Doubleday, 1989).

Cherry, Monica, *Building Wales* (Cardiff: Arts Council of Wales, 2005).

Chick, Martin, *Industrial Policy in Britain, 1945–1951: Economic Planning, Nationalisation and the Labour Governments* (Cambridge: Cambridge University Press, 1998).

Clark, G. M., and P. N. Curran, 'Bridging the Ironbridge Gorge: The Jackfield Bridge, Shropshire – Design and Construction', *Proceedings of the Institution of Civil Engineers: Structures and Building*, 122/1 (1997), 92–103.

Cohen, Jean-Louis, 'Scholarship or Politics? Architectural History and the Risks of Autonomy', *Journal of the Society of Architectural Historians*, 67/3 (2008), 325–29.

Cole, David (ed.), *The New Wales* (Cardiff: University of Wales Press, 1990).

Collyer, Mark, *Dorset County Hospital: 175 Years of Rural Healthcare, 1840–2015* (Dorchester: Dorset County NHS Foundation Trust, 2015).

Colvin, Brenda, *Land and Landscape: Evolution, Design and Control* (London: John Murray, 1970).

Cooper, Christine, Jonathan Tweedie, and Max Baker, 'From "Business-Like" to Businesses: Agencification, Corporatization, and Civil Service Reform Under the Thatcher Administration', *Public Administration*, 100/2 (2022), 193–215.

Cotton, A. Calveley, *Town Halls* (London: Architectural Press, 1936).

County Council of Essex, *A Design Guide for Residential Areas* (County Council of Essex, 1973).

Cowell, Richard, 'Environmental Compensation and the Mediation of Environmental Change: Making Capital out of Cardiff Bay', *Journal of Environmental Planning and Management*, 43/5 (2000), 689–710.

Crickhowell, Nicholas, *Opera House Lottery: Zaha Hadid and the Cardiff Bay Project* (Cardiff: University of Wales Press, 1997).

Crinson, Mark, 'The Uses of Nostalgia: Stirling and Gowan's Preston Housing', *Journal of the Society of Architectural Historians*, 65/2 (2006), 216–37.

Crinson, Mark, and Jules Lubbock, *Architecture: Art or Profession? Three Hundred Years of Architectural Education in Britain* (Manchester: Manchester University Press, 1994).

Cronin, James E., *The Politics of State Expansion: War, State and Society in Twentieth-Century Britain* (London: Routledge, 1991).

Crowe, Sylvia, *The Landscape of Power* (London: Architectural Press, 1958).

Crowe, Sylvia, *The Landscape of Roads* (London: Architectural Press, 1960).

Crowe, Sylvia, *Tomorrow's Landscape* (London: Architectural Press, 1956).

Cunningham, Colin, *Victorian and Edwardian Town Halls* (London: Routledge & Kegan Paul, 1981).

Cupers, Kenny, Helena Mattsson and Catharina Gabrielsson (eds), *Neoliberalism on the Ground: Architecture and Transformation from the 1960s to the Present* (Pittsburgh PA: University of Pittsburgh Press, 2020).

Curran, Peter, and Graham Tilly, 'Design and Monitoring of the Flintshire Bridge, UK', *Structural Engineering International*, 9/3 (1999), 225–8.

Cutler, Tony, 'Economic Liberal or Arch Planner? Enoch Powell and the Political Economy of the Hospital Plan', *Contemporary British History*, 25/4 (2011), 469–89.

Darling, Elizabeth, *Re-Forming Britain: Narratives of Modernity Before Reconstruction* (London: Routledge, 2007).

Davey, Elaine, 'A National Architect? The Percy Thomas Practice and Welsh National Identity' (unpublished PhD thesis, Cardiff University, 2013).

Davey, Elaine, and Huw Thomas, '"Chief Creator of Modern Wales": The Neglected Legacy of Percy Thomas', *North American Journal of Welsh Studies*, 9 (2014), 54–70.

Davies, John, *Broadcasting and the BBC in Wales* (Cardiff: University of Wales Press, 1994).

Davis, Ian, Paul Oliver and Ian Bentley, *Dunroamin: The Suburban Semi and its Enemies* (London: Barrie and Jenkins, 1981).

Day, Graham, *Making Sense of Wales: A Sociological Perspective* (Cardiff: University of Wales Press, 2002).

De Figueiredo, Peter, 'Symbols of Empire: The Buildings of the Liverpool Waterfront', *Architectural History*, 46 (2003), 229–54.

Denning, Roy (ed.), *The Story of St Donat's Castle and Atlantic College* (Cowbridge and Barry: D. Brown & Sons and Stewart Williams, 1983).

Doyle, Jo, *Percy Thomas Partnership HK: Selected and Current Works* (Victoria: The Images Publishing Group, 1998).

Drake, James, H. L. Yeadon and D. L. Evans, *Motorways* (London: Faber & Faber, 1969).

Edgerton, David, *The Rise and Fall of the British Nation: A Twentieth-Century History* (London: Penguin, 2019).

Elliot, Arthur, *History of British Nylon Spinners* (Abertillery: Old Bakehouse Publications, 2009).

English, Richard, and Graham Walker (eds), *Unionism in Modern Ireland: New Perspectives on Politics and Culture* (Basingstoke: Macmillan, 1996).

Erten, Erdem, 'Thomas Sharp's Collaboration with H. de C. Hastings: The Formulation of Townscape as Urban Design Pedagogy', *Planning Perspectives*, 24/1 (2009), 29–49.

Esher, Lionel, *A Broken Wave: The Rebuilding of England 1940–1980* (London: Allen Lane, 1981).

Evans, Christopher J. (ed.), *The Book of Cardiff: Presented to the Delegates at the Annual Conference of the National Association of Head Teachers* (London: Oxford University Press, 1937).

Evans, Dinah, *A New, Even Better, Abertawe: Rebuilding Swansea, 1941–1961* (Llandysul: West Glamorgan Archive Service, 2019).

Evans, Neil 'The Welsh Victorian City: The Middle Class and Civic and National Consciousness in Cardiff, 1850-1914', *Welsh History Review*, 12 (1984), 350–87.

Fair, Alistair, *Modern Playhouses: An Architectural History of Britain's New Theatres, 1945–1985* (Oxford: Oxford University Press, 2018).

Fair, Alistair, '"Modernization of Our Hospital System": The National Health Service, the Hospital Plan, and the "Harness" Programme, 1962-77', *Twentieth Century British History*, 29/4 (2018), 547-75.

Fairbrother, Nan, *New Lives, New Landscapes* (London: Architectural Press, 1970).

Fevre, Ralph, and Andrew Thompson (eds), *Nation, Identity and Social Theory: Perspectives from Wales* (Cardiff: University of Wales Press, 1999).

Fisher, J., and G. M. Clark, 'Bridging the Ironbridge Gorge: The Jackfield Bridge, Shropshire - Planning and Development', *Proceedings of the Institution of Civil Engineers: Structures and Building*, 122/1 (1997), 104-16.

Foster, Andy, *Birmingham*, Pevsner Architectural Guides (London: Yale University Press, 2005).

Foyle, Andrew, *Bristol* (London: Yale University Press, 2004).

Francis, Martin, and Ina Zweiniger-Bargielowska (eds), *The Conservatives and British Society, 1880–1990* (Cardiff: University of Wales Press, 1996).

Fraser, Murray, and Joe Kerr, *Architecture and the 'Special Relationship': The American Influence on Post-War British Architecture* (Abingdon: Routledge, 2007).

Fry, Geoffrey K., 'The Thatcher Government, The Financial Management Initiative, and the "New Civil Service"', *Public Administration*, 66/1 (2007), 1-20.

Garrett, A. A., *History of the Society of Incorporated Accountants, 1885–1957* (Oxford: University Press, 1961).

Gaudet, Mark, 'The Design of Buildings for Very Low Levels of Vibration', *Noise & Vibration Worldwide*, 32/8 (2001), 12-17.

Genders, Amy, 'An Invisible Nation? The BBC and English-Language Arts Television in Wales', *Journal of British Cinema and Television*, 16/4 (2019), 409–28.

Giddens, Anthony, *The Consequences of Modernity* (Cambridge: Polity Press, 1990).

Gilbert, David, David Matless and Brian Short (eds), *Geographies of British Modernity: Space and Society in the Twentieth Century* (Malden: Blackwell, 2003).

Gilmour, Ian, *Dancing with Dogma: Britain Under Thatcherism* (London: Simon & Schuster, 1992).

Gladstone, David (ed.), *Before Beveridge: Welfare Before the Welfare State* (London: Institute of Economic Affairs, 1999).

Gold, John R., and John Pendlebury, 'The "Spirit of Living Continuity"? Revisiting the Urban Vision, Methodologies and Influence of the Studies in Conservation', *Town Planning Review*, 90/1 (2019), 33–56.

Goldhagen, Sarah Williams, 'Something to Talk About: Modernism, Discourse, Style', *Journal of the Society of Architectural Historians*, 64/2 (2005), 144–67.

Gooberman, Leon, *From Depression to Devolution: Economy and Government in Wales, 1934–2006* (Cardiff: University of Wales Press, 2017).

Gooberman, Leon, 'Public Governance of Private Munitions Businesses in Regional Britain: The Case of Wales, 1938 to 1945', *Business History* (2021), 1–20.

Gould, Jeremy, *Plymouth: Vision of a Modern City* (Swindon: English Heritage, 2010).

Greenhalgh, James, *Reconstructing Modernity: Space, Power and Governance in Mid-Twentieth Century British Cities* (Manchester: Manchester University Press, 2017).

Griffiths, Delme, *50 Years of the National Health Service Estate in Wales* (Cardiff: Welsh Health Estates, 1998).

Grimley, Terry, *Symphony Hall: A Dream Realised* (Birmingham: Boydell and Brewer, 2014).

Grindrod, John, *Iconicon: A Journey Around the Landmark Buildings of Contemporary Britain* (London: Faber & Faber, 2022).

Gropius, Walter, *Scope of Total Architecture*, World Perspectives (London: George Allen & Unwin, 1956).

Gruffudd, Pyrs, '"A Crusade Against Consumption": Environment, Health and Social Reform in Wales, 1900–1939', *Journal of Historical Geography*, 21/1 (1995), 39–54.

Gutzke, David W., *Pubs and Progressives: Reinventing the Public House in England, 1896–1960* (DeKalb IL: Northern Illinois University Press, 2006).

Guy, John R., *'Y.D.H.': The Story of Yeovil District Hospital* (Yeovil, 1983).

Hall, Timothy Ross, 'Urban Regeneration and Cultural Geography: The International Convention Centre, Birmingham' (unpublished PhD thesis, University of Birmingham, 1994).

Hammond, Peter (ed.), *Towards a Church Architecture* (London: Architectural Press, 1962).

Hardy, Dennis, *Poundbury: The Town That Charles Built* (London: Town and Country Planning Association, 2006).

Harris, Bernard, *The Origins of the British Welfare State: Society, State and Social Welfare* (Basingstoke: Palgrave Macmillan, 2004).

Harrison, Ewan, '"Money Spinners": R. Seifert & Partners, Sir Frank Price and Public-Sector Speculative Development in the 1970s', *Architectural History*, 61 (2018), 259–80.

Harvey, Alexander, 'One Hundred Years of Technical Education in Cardiff', *Glamorgan Historian*, 9 (1973), 173–90.

Harvey, David, *The Condition of Postmodernity: An Enquiry into the Origins of Cultural Change* (Cambridge, Massachusetts: Blackwell, 1990).

Harwood, Elain, *Space, Hope and Brutalism: English Architecture 1945–1975* (London: Yale University Press, 2015).

Harwood, Elain, and Alan Powers (eds.), *Holy Houses: Places of Worship in Twentieth-Century Britain*, 'Twentieth Century Architecture' 15 (London: Twentieth Century Society, 2023).

Harwood, Elain, and Alan Powers (eds), *The Architecture of Public Service*, 'Twentieth Century Architecture' 13 (London: Twentieth Century Society, 2018).

Hasegawa, Junichi, *Replanning the Blitzed City Centre: A Comparative Study of Bristol, Coventry and Southampton* (Buckingham: Open University Press, 1992).

Head, P. R., P. Iley and E. T. Bradley, 'Second Severn Crossing: Initial Studies', *Proceedings of the Institution of Civil Engineers: Civil Engineering*, 120/6 (1997), 3–12.

Henry, Dorothy, and J. A. Jerome, *Modern British Bridges* (London: Applied Science Publishers Ltd, 1965).

Hill, Dennis, *Bristol Fire Brigade 1877–1974: An Illustrated History* (Bristol: Redcliffe Press, 1999).

Hilling, John B., *The Architecture of Wales: From the First to the Twenty-First Century* (Cardiff: University of Wales Press, 2018).

Hilling, John B., *The History and Architecture of Cardiff Civic Centre: Black Gold, White City* (Cardiff: University of Wales Press, 2016).

Hise, Greg, 'Architecture as State Building: A Challenge to the Field', *Journal of the Society of Architectural Historians*, 67/2 (2008), 173–7.

Holden, Roger N., *Stott and Sons: Architects of the Lancashire Cotton Mill* (Lancaster: Carnegie Publishing, 1998).

Holder, Julian and Elizabeth McKellar (eds), *Neo-Georgian Architecture 1880–1970: A Reappraisal* (Swindon: Historic England, 2016).

Holder, Julian, and Steven Parissien (eds), *The Architecture of British Transport in the Twentieth Century* (London: Yale University Press, 2004).

Hollinghurst, Edward, 'Flintshire Bridge/Pont Sir Y Fflint, Wales: Design Aesthetics and Innovation', *Transportation Research Record*, 1696/1 (2000), 25–30.

Hubbard, Phil, 'Urban Design and Local Economic Development: A Case Study in Birmingham', *Cities*, 12/4 (1995), 243–51.

Hughes, Jonathan, 'The "Matchbox on a Muffin": The Design of Hospitals in the Early NHS', *Medical History*, 44/1 (2000), 21–56.

Hulme, Tom, *After the Shock City: Urban Culture and the Making of Modern Citizenship* (Woodbridge: Royal Historical Society and The Boydell Press, 2019).

Humble, Nicola, *The Feminine Middlebrow Novel, 1920s to 1950s: Class, Domesticity, and Bohemianism* (Oxford: Oxford University Press, 2001).

Hutchinson, Frances E., 'Malaysia's Independence Leaders and the Legacies of State Formation under British Rule', *Journal of the Royal Asiatic Society*, third series, 25/1 (2015), 123–51.

James, Paul, and Tony Noakes, *Hospital Architecture* (Harlow: Longman, 1994).

James, W. Paul, and William Tatton-Brown, *Hospitals: Design and Development* (Architectural Press, 1986).

Jameson, Fredric, *The Cultural Turn: Selected Writings on the Postmodern, 1983–1998* (London: Verso, 1998).

Jofeh, Chris, 'Wales Millennium Centre: A New Stage for the Art of Engineers', *Proceedings of the Institution of Civil Engineers: Civil Engineering*, 158/1 (2005), 3–48.

Johnes, Martin, '"M4 to Wales – and Prosper!" A History of a Motorway', *Historical Research*, 87/237 (2014), 556–73.

Jones, Paul, 'Private Finance Initiative Hospital Architecture: Towards a Political Economy of the Royal Liverpool University Hospital', *Sociology of Health & Illness*, 40/2 (2018), 327–9.

Karol, Eitan, *Charles Holden, Architect* (Donington: Shaun Tyas, 2007).

Kearns, Robin A., and J. Ross Barnett, 'Consumerist Ideology and the Symbolic Landscapes of Private Medicine', *Health & Place*, 3/3 (1997), 171–80.

Kennedy, Liam (ed.), *Remaking Birmingham: The Visual Culture of Urban Regeneration* (London: Routledge, 2004).

Kitchener, J. N., and D. H. Mizon, 'Second Severn Crossing: Pre-Construction Period and Design Development', *Proceedings of the Institution of Civil Engineers: Civil Engineering*, 120/6 (1997), 13–21.

Kitson, Sean L., 'Amersham Radiochemistry to GE Healthcare', *Journal of Labelled Compounds and Radiopharmaceuticals*, 50/9–10 (2007), 737–45.

Krier, Léon, *Architecture: Choice or Fate* (Windsor: Andreas Papadakis, 1998).

Kuliç, Vladimir, Monica Penick and Timothy Parker (eds), *Sanctioning Modernism: Architecture and the Making of Postwar Identities* (Austin TX: University of Texas Press, 2015).

Kwon, Huck-ju (ed.), *Transforming the Developmental Welfare State in East Asia* (Basingstoke: Palgrave Macmillan, 2005).

Kynaston, David, *Modernity Britain, 1957–62* (London: Bloomsbury, 2015).

Ledger, Robert, 'The Road to Pergau Dam: Aid Policy, Ideology, and the Thatcher Government', *Diplomacy & Statecraft*, 30/1 (2019), 50–69.

Lefebvre, Henri, *State, Space, World: Selected Essays*, ed. by Neil Brenner and Stuart Elden (Minneapolis MN: University of Minnesota Press, 2009).

Lefebvre, Henri, *The Production of Space* (Oxford: Basil Blackwell, 1991)

Lei, Yanhui, 'Urban Village Extension: Design Principles of New Urbanism – The Case Studies of Poundbury and Upton' (unpublished PhD thesis, University of Nottingham, 2014).

Manley, Christine Hui Lan, *Frederick Gibberd* (Swindon: Historic England, 2017).

Marquand, David, *Decline of the Public: The Hollowing-Out of Citizenship* (Cambridge: Polity Press, 2004).

Marquand, H. A., *South Wales Needs a Plan* (London: George Allen & Unwin, 1936).

Marwick, Arthur, *The Deluge: British Society and the First World War* (London: Macmillan, 1973).

Mason, Rhiannon, 'Nation Building at the Museum of Welsh Life', *Museum and Society*, 3/1 (2005), 18–34.

Maudlin, Daniel, 'Constructing Identity and Tradition: Englishness, Politics and the Neo-Traditional House', *Journal of Architectural Education*, 63/1 (2009), 51–63.

McKibbin, Ross, *Classes and Cultures: England 1918–1951* (Oxford: Oxford University Press, 1998).

Medhurst, Jamie, '"Nation Shall Speak Peace Unto Nation"? The BBC and the Nations', *Critical Studies in Television: The International Journal of Television Studies*, 17/1 (2022), 8–23.

Merriman, Peter, and Rhys Jones, 'Nations, Materialities and Affects', *Progress in Human Geography*, 41/5 (2017), 600–17.

Milani, Tommaso, 'Retreat from the Global? European Unity and British Progressive Intellectuals, 1930–1945', *The International History Review*, 42/1 (2020), 99–116.

Millward, Robert, and John Singleton (eds), *The Political Economy of Nationalisation in Britain 1920–50* (Cambridge: Cambridge University Press, 1995).

Ministry of Housing and Local Government (ed.), *Design in Town and Village* (London: HMSO, 1953).

Ministry of Housing and Local Government, *Historic Towns: Preservation and Change* (London: HMSO, 1967).

Ministry of Transport, *The Appearance of Bridges* (London: HMSO, 1964).

Miskell, Louise, 'Doing It for Themselves: The Steel Company of Wales and the Study of American Industrial Productivity, 1945-1955', *Enterprise & Society*, 18/1 (2017), 184-213.

Miskell, Louise (ed.), *New Perspectives on Welsh Industrial History* (Cardiff: University of Wales Press, 2020).

Mizon, D. H., and J. N. Kitchener, 'Second Severn Crossing: Viaduct Superstructure and Piers', *Proceedings of the Institution of Civil Engineers: Civil Engineering*, 120/6 (1997), 35-48.

Mizon, D. H., N. Smith, and A. J. Yeoward, 'Second Severn Crossing: Cable-Stayed Bridge', *Proceedings of the Institution of Civil Engineers: Civil Engineering*, 120/6 (1997), 49-63.

Mold, Alex, 'Making the Patient-Consumer in Margaret Thatcher's Britain', *The Historical Journal*, 54/2 (2011), 509-28.

Morgan, Kenneth O., *Modern Wales: Politics, Places and People* (Cardiff: University of Wales Press, 1995).

Morgan, Kenneth O., *Rebirth of a Nation: Wales 1880-1980* (Oxford: Clarendon Press, 1981).

Morrison, Kathryn A., *English Shops and Shopping: An Architectural History* (London: Yale University Press, 2003).

Morrison, Kathryn A., and John Minnis, *Carscapes: The Motor Car, Architecture and Landscape in England* (London: Yale University Press, 2012).

Mumford, Eric, *The CIAM Discourse on Urbanism, 1928-1960* (Cambridge MA: MIT Press, 2000).

Navickas, Katrina, 'Conflicts of Power, Landscape and Amenity in Debates over the British Super Grid in the 1950s', *Rural History*, 30/1 (2019), 87-103.

Newman, John, *The Buildings of Wales: Glamorgan* (London: Yale University Press, 2004).

Nuffield Provincial Hospitals Trust, *Studies in the Function and Design of Hospitals: The Report of an Investigation Sponsored by the Nuffield Provincial Hospitals Trust and the University of Bristol* (London: Oxford University Press, 1960).

O'Hara, Glen, *From Dreams to Disillusionment: Economic and Social Planning in 1960s Britain* (Basingstoke: Palgrave Macmillan, 2007).

Ortolano, Guy, *Thatcher's Progress: From Social Democracy to Market Liberalism through an English New Town* (Cambridge: Cambridge University Press, 2019).

Peate, Iorwerth, *The Welsh House: A Study in Folk Culture* (Liverpool: Hugh Evans & Sons Ltd, 1944).

Peate, Iorwerth C., *Amgueddfeydd Gwerin/Folk Museums* (Cardiff: University of Wales Press, 1948).

Pendlebury, John, 'The Modern Historic City: Evolving Ideas in Mid-20th-Century Britain', *Journal of Urban Design*, 10/2 (2005), 253–73.

Pendlebury, John, 'The Urbanism of Thomas Sharp', *Planning Perspectives*, 24/1 (2009), 3–27.

Percival, Geoffrey, *The Government's Industrial Estates in Wales, 1936–1975* (Cardiff: Welsh Development Agency, 1978).

Perry, Victoria, *Built for a Better Future: The Brynmawr Rubber Factory* (Oxford: White Cockade Publishing, 1994).

Pevsner, Nikolaus, *The Englishness of English Art* (New York: Frederick A. Praeger, 1956).

Phillips, Sarah G., and Jennifer S. Hunt, '"Without Sultan Qaboos, We Would Be Yemen": The Renaissance Narrative and the Political Settlement in Oman', *Journal of International Development*, 29/5 (2017), 645–60.

Pimlott, Ben, *Harold Wilson* (London: William Collins, 2016).

Prasad, Sunand (ed.), *Changing Hospital Architecture* (London: RIBA Publishing, 2008).

Proctor, Robert, *Building the Modern Church: Roman Catholic Church Architecture in Britain, 1955 to 1975* (Farnham: Ashgate, 2014).

Proctor, Robert, 'Constructing the Retail Monument: The Parisian Department Store and Its Property, 1855–1914', *Urban History*, 33/3 (2006), 393–410.

Proctor, Robert, 'Modern Church Architect as Ritual Anthropologist: Architecture and Liturgy at Clifton Cathedral', *ARQ*, 15/4 (2011), 359–72.

Proctor, Robert, 'Social Structures: Gillespie, Kidd & Coia's Halls of Residence at the University of Hull', *Journal of the Society of Architectural Historians*, 67/1 (2008), 106–29.

Pugh, Martin, *State and Society: A Social and Political History of Britain, 1870–1997* (London: Arnold, 2003).

Pugh, Rhiannon, Niall G. MacKenzie and Dylan Jones-Evans, 'From "Techniums" to "Emptiums": The Failure of a Flagship Innovation Policy in Wales', *Regional Studies*, 52/7 (2018), 1009–20.

Punter, John, 'Design-Led Regeneration? Evaluating the Design Outcomes of Cardiff Bay and Their Implications for Future Regeneration and Design', *Journal of Urban Design*, 12/3 (2007), 375–405.

Reading, Billy, *Fire Stations* (Stroud: Amberley, 2017).

Rice, Charles, *Interior Urbanism: Architecture, John Portman and Downtown America* (London: Bloomsbury, 2016).

Roberts, Gilbert, and Oleg Alexander Kerensky, 'Auckland Harbour Bridge: Design', *Proceedings of the Institution of Civil Engineers*, 18/4 (1961), 423–58.

Robinson, Emily, Camilla Schofield, Florence Sutcliffe-Braithwaite and Natalie Thomlinson, 'Telling Stories about Post-War Britain: Popular Individualism and the "Crisis" of the 1970s', *Twentieth Century British History*, 28/2 (2017), 268–304.

Roseau, Nathalie, 'The Shape of Things to Come: Hong Kong's Infrastructural City Fabric, 1989–2020', *Planning Perspectives*, 37/2 (2022), 369–99.

Royal Fine Art Commission, *Bridge Design: Royal Fine Art Commission Seminar, 29 October 1992* (London: HMSO, 1993).

Ryan, Deborah Sugg, 'Living in a "Half-Baked Pageant"', *Home Cultures*, 8/3 (2011), 217–44.

Saler, Michael T., *The Avant-Garde in Interwar England: Medieval Modernism and the London Underground* (New York: Oxford University Press, 1999).

Saumarez Smith, Otto, 'Action for Cities: The Thatcher Government and Inner-City Policy', *Urban History*, 47/2 (2020), 274–91.

Saumarez Smith, Otto, *Boom Cities: Architect-Planners and the Politics of Radical Urban Renewal in 1960s Britain* (Oxford: Oxford University Press, 2019).

Scalzo, Julia, 'All a Matter of Taste: The Problem of Victorian and Edwardian Shop Fronts', *Journal of the Society of Architectural Historians*, 68/1 (2009), 52–73.

Schulze Bäing, Andreas, and Cecilia Wong, 'The Impact of Brownfield Regeneration on Neighbourhood Dynamics: The Case of Salford Quays in England', *Town Planning Review*, 89/5 (2018), 513–34.

Scott, Peter, and James T. Walker, 'The Comfortable, the Rich, and the Super-Rich: What Really Happened to Top British Incomes during the First Half of the Twentieth Century?', *The Journal of Economic History*, 80/1 (2020), 38–68.

Sharp, Thomas, *Town and Countryside* (Oxford: Oxford University Press, 1932).

Shasore, N. E., '"A Stammering Bundle of Welsh Idealism": Arthur Trystan Edwards and Principles of Civic Design in Interwar Britain', *Architectural History*, 61 (2018), 175–203.

Shasore, Neal, and Jessica Kelly (eds), *Reconstruction: Architecture, Society and the Aftermath of the First World War* (London: Bloomsbury, 2023).

Sherwood, Marika, 'Elder Dempster and West Africa, 1891–*c*.1940: The Genesis of Underdevelopment?', *The International Journal of African Historical Studies*, 30/2 (1997), 253–76.

Sorkin, Michael (ed.), *Variations on a Theme Park: The New American City and the End of Public Space* (New York: Hill and Wang, 1992).

Stamp, Gavin, 'Neo-Tudor and Its Enemies', *Architectural History*, 49 (2006), 1–33.

Starkie, David, *The Motorway Age: Road and Traffic Policies in Post-War Britain*, Urban and Regional Planning Series 28 (Oxford: Pergamon Press, 1982).

Steele, James, *Theatre Builders* (London: Academy Editions, 1996).

Stratton, Michael, *Ironbridge and the Electric Revolution: The History of Electricity Generation at Ironbridge A and B Power Stations* (London: John Murray, 1994).

Struthers, Tony, 'The Redevelopment of Salford Quays, Greater Manchester: Its Impact on Urban and Regional Development from 1983 to 2003', *DisP - The Planning Review*, 39/154 (2003), 11-18.

Sudjic, Deyan (ed.), *An Opera House for Wales/Tŷ Opera i Gymru* (London: Wordsearch, 1994).

Tanner, Duncan, Chris Williams, Wil Griffith and Andrew Edwards (eds), *Debating Nationhood and Governance in Britain, 1885–1945: Perspectives from the 'Four Nations'* (Manchester: Manchester University Press, 2006).

Thomas, Ian C., 'The Beginnings of an Economic Development Policy in Mid-Wales: The Mid-Wales Industrial Development Association, 1957–1974', *Welsh History Review*, 17/3 (1995), 411-51.

Thomas, Norman Lewis, *The Story of Swansea's Markets and Additional Historical Data Relating to the Town* (Swansea: The Guardian Press, 1966).

Thomas, Percy E. (ed.), *Modern Building Practice*, 4 vols (London: George Newnes Ltd, 1935).

Thomas, Percy Edward, *Pupil to President: Memoirs of an Architect* (Leigh-on-Sea: F. Lewis, 1963).

Thompson-Fawcett, Michelle, '"Urbanist" Lived Experience: Resident Observations on Life in Poundbury', *Urban Design International*, 8/1-2 (2003), 67-84.

Thornborow, P., *Sir Percy Thomas: A Bibliography and Partial Catalogue of Works* (Cardiff: UWIST Library, 1984).

Upton, Christopher, *The Past, Present & Future: A Commemorative Book for the Opening of the International Convention Centre, Birmingham 1991* (Birmingham: Birmingham City Council, 1991).

Urban, Florian, 'Glasgow's Royal Concert Hall and the Invention of the Post-Modern City', *Journal of Architecture*, 23/5 (2018), 829-71.

Verey, David, and Alan Brooks, *Gloucestershire 2: The Vale and The Forest of Dean*, The Buildings of England (London: Yale University Press, 2009).

Vinen, Richard, *Thatcher's Britain: The Politics and Social Upheaval of the 1980s* (London: Simon & Schuster, 2009).

Weeks, Ronald, 'The Design and Construction of the Cathedral Church of SS. Peter and Paul, Clifton', *Pax: The Review of the Benedictine Monks of Prinknash*, 63/2 (1973), 60-9.

Weight, Richard, and Abigail Beach (eds), *The Right to Belong: Citizenship and National Identity in Britain, 1930–1960* (London: I.B. Tauris, 1998).

Westwood, Sallie, John M. Williams and John Williams (eds), *Imagining Cities: Scripts, Signs, Memory* (Psychology Press, 1997).

Wetherell, Sam, *Foundations: How the Built Environment Made Twentieth-Century Britain* (Princeton NJ: Princeton University Press, 2020).

Wetherell, Sam, 'Freedom Planned: Enterprise Zones and Urban Non-Planning in Post-War Britain', *Twentieth Century British History*, 27/2 (2016), 266–89.

Wiliam, Eurwyn, 'Three Giants: Iorwerth Peate, Cyril Fox and Peter Smith, and the Welsh Contribution to Vernacular Architecture Studies', *Transactions: Ancient Monuments Society*, 61 (2017), 8–33.

Xue, Charlie Q. L., *Hong Kong Architecture 1945–2015: From Colonial to Global* (Singapore: Springer, 2016).

Index

*Note: illustrations are shown by the use of **bold** text. Notes are referenced by the suffix 'n'. Buildings are listed primarily under their locations.*

A

B

C

D

E

F

G

H

I

J

K

L

M

N

O

P

Q

R

S

T

U

V

W

Y

Z